STRATEGIC ASIA 2011–12

STRATEGIC ASIA 2011–12

ASIA RESPONDS TO ITS RISING POWERS

China and India

Edited by

Ashley J. Tellis, Travis Tanner, and Jessica Keough

With contributions from

M. Taylor Fravel, Michael J. Green, Chung Min Lee, Rory Medcalf, Harsh V. Pant, Kenneth B. Pyle, Teresita C. Schaffer, Ashley J. Tellis, Carlyle A. Thayer, Dmitri Trenin, and S. Enders Wimbush

 THE NATIONAL BUREAU *of* **ASIAN RESEARCH**
Seattle and Washington, D.C.

THE NATIONAL BUREAU *of* ASIAN RESEARCH

Published in the United States of America by
The National Bureau of Asian Research, Seattle, WA, and Washington, D.C.
www.nbr.org

This material is based upon work supported in part by the Department of Energy (National Nuclear Security Administration).

This report was prepared as an account of work sponsored by an agency of the United States Government. Neither the United States Government nor any agency thereof, nor any of their employees, makes any warranty, express or implied, or assumes any legal liability or responsibility for the accuracy, completeness, or usefulness of any information, apparatus, product, or process disclosed, or represents that its use would not infringe privately owned rights. Reference herein to any specific commercial product, process, or service by trade name, trademark, manufacturer, or otherwise does not constitute or imply its endorsement, recommendation, or favoring by the United States Government or any agency thereof. The views and opinions of authors expressed herein do not necessarily state or reflect those of the United States Government or any agency thereof.

NBR makes no warranties or representations regarding the accuracy of any map in this volume. Depicted boundaries are meant as guidelines only and do not represent the views of NBR or NBR's funders.

Design and publishing services by The National Bureau of Asian Research

Cover design by Stefanie Choi

Front cover photo: © Werner Van Steen / The Image Bank / Getty Images

Publisher's Cataloging-In-Publication Data
(Prepared by The Donohue Group, Inc.)

Asia responds to its rising powers : China and India / edited by Ashley J. Tellis, Travis Tanner, and Jessica Keough ; with contributions from M. Taylor Fravel ... [et al.].

    p. : ill., maps ; cm. -- (Strategic Asia 1933-6462 ; 2011-12)

    Based upon work supported in part by the Department of Energy (National Nuclear Security Administration).

    Includes bibliographical references and index.

    ISBN: 978-0-9818904-2-5

    1. Asia--Foreign relations--China. 2. Asia--Foreign relations--India. 3. China--Foreign relations--Asia. 4. India--Foreign relations--Asia. 5. China--Foreign economic relations. 6. India--Foreign economic relations. 7. Asia--Strategic aspects. I. Tellis, Ashley J. II. Tanner, Travis. III. Keough, Jessica. IV. Fravel, M. Taylor. V. National Bureau of Asian Research (U.S.) VI. Series: Strategic Asia ; 2011-12.

DS33.3 .A85 2011

320.95

Printed in Canada

The paper used in this publication meets the minimum requirement of the American National Standard for Information Sciences—Permanence of Paper for Printed Library Materials, ANSI Z39.48-1992.

Contents

Overview

> An overview of the themes and conclusions of the volume, examining the causes behind the rise of China and India, the implications for the U.S., and the responses of other Asian states.

Special Study

> An examination of how Asia's rise relates to classic questions about the integration of rising powers into the international system.

Country Studies

> An examination of how China views the rise of India and the implications of India's rise for China's core interests and strategic objectives.

India Next Door, China Over the Horizon:
Teresita C. Schaffer
An assessment of the responses of countries in South Asia to the
rise of India and China.

The Rise of China and India:
Carlyle A. Thayer
A comparative analysis of the impact of China's and India's rise on
Southeast Asian regional autonomy that considers implications
for the United States.

Indicators

Preface

Richard J. Ellings

Strategic Asia 2011–12: Asia Responds to Its Rising Powers—China and India is the eleventh volume from NBR's Strategic Asia Program. With or without America's economic travails, the rise of China and, secondarily, India is the salient factor driving strategic interests and policies in Asia and beyond. This year's volume seeks to provide policymakers and Asia specialists alike with the best research on an absolutely critical topic: how the Asia-Pacific nations are responding to the transformation in the global balance of power that is being led by these fast-rising giants.

The volume begins with two big-picture, insightful pieces: the overview chapter by Ashley J. Tellis, which provides a remarkable assessment of the volume's research findings and the issues before us, and the second chapter, "International Order and the Rise of Asia: History and Theory," a penetrating analysis by Kenneth B. Pyle of what the history of rising powers in the modern world and theories of international relations suggest about the possibilities and dangers ahead. Professor Pyle is concerned principally with China's rise and the wild card of nationalism. Subsequent chapters explore how China's and India's rise affects the important perceptions and interests of countries across Asia along geopolitical, economic, military, cultural, and historical dimensions. The chapters also examine the strategies that key Asian players are pursuing to protect their interests and the implications for U.S. interests and leadership in the Asia-Pacific.

The modern emergence of the world's two largest civilizations is producing a seismic shift in post–Cold War geopolitics, comparable in many ways to the emergence of the United States, Germany, Japan, and Russia in the late nineteenth and early twentieth centuries. China's and India's explosive economic growth has already given the two states more sway in regional politics and will reshape or undermine the management of global affairs as well. China's capacity to make an impact on global political norms is as yet unclear, but China has already set off debates in emerging markets about the role of government in guiding economic development.

Within Asia, China and India are both natural trade partners and competitors because of their comparable population and proximity sharing the Eurasian landmass and borders. Economic, technological, and military accomplishments have reduced the importance of the Himalayas that historically provided a strategic buffer between them.

In the past decade China and India have forged strong economic ties. Trade volume between the two countries rose from $1.2 billion in 1995 and $3 billion in 2000 to $51 billion in 2008 and an estimated $60 billion in 2010. Both countries are benefiting. Likewise, the two countries have shown a willingness to increase cooperation in the cultural, diplomatic, and security domains. Pervading their relations, however, is China's enormous economic lead. Though the economies of the two nations continue to be complementary in many ways, with China the dominant player in manufacturing and India stronger in software development, China is encroaching on India's comparative advantage even in the latter.

Geopolitical considerations, vastly different political systems, and historical wounds lie just beneath the surface of this new cooperation. Serious issues such as border disputes, Tibetans in exile, energy security, and relations with Pakistan continue to hamper bilateral relations and perpetuate mutual mistrust. Rivalry and competition are the overriding realities and will have significant long-term implications for the region, particularly given arms competition and the rapid changes to the regional balance of power.

Correspondingly, India has adopted a prudent dual strategy, reaching out to China to reap the benefits of trade and diplomatic engagement while hedging and balancing China by striking strategic partnerships with Japan and the United States, deepening ties with Western Europe and Southeast Asia, and keeping up ties with Russia.

It is in the context of these dynamics that the United States is responding to protect its interests, including international leadership. The opportunities and challenges posed by China versus India are distinct. The most obvious opportunities with regard to China lie in the economic realm. The United States and China have managed to forge extraordinarily complex economic ties over the past three decades, and on a mammoth scale. China's meteoric rise and openness put a damper on global inflation and gave many U.S. companies a huge new market, but the resulting imbalances made economic relations highly sensitive and volatile. China's industrial and trade policies have plagued trade relations and are now making them even more difficult.

China's new economic and military power has made the country a potential contributor ("responsible stakeholder," as Robert Zoellick put it) to solving international economic, political, and security issues, from financial problems to terrorism and nuclear proliferation, but cooperation, let alone leadership, has been mercurial at best. One could argue that in recent years the Chinese are actually contributing less to solving international problems, not more. Evidence is widespread that China is backing away from some of its economic reforms and stiffening its resistance to political reform. Industrial policy is tilting the playing field of the domestic market and hurting trade relations. China's international policies are frequently mercantilist.

At a broader level, very different political systems, competing national interests, and rising nationalism in China make for a tough slog ahead for those charged with managing U.S.-China relations. The issue of purposes adds to this difficulty. China's emerging, long-term strategic intentions seem to include pushing U.S. power out of the Western Pacific. Intentions are difficult to ascertain and may change, of course. In this regard, the underlying issue of the future of Chinese nationalism may be the biggest question of all, as Kenneth Pyle points out.

While many Indians' views of the United States remain colored by legacies from the 20th century, the realities of the 21st century compel far closer relations between the world's two largest democracies. The much vaunted sharing of democratic systems is helpful, but common interests in economic growth, moderate politics and stability in South and Central Asia, and balancing the rise of China would seem sufficient to boost economic and strategic collaboration. Policymakers in Washington must assume that India will be a critical player in the balance of power in Asia and therefore should become one of America's strongest partners in the region. Yet India is a complex partner in just about every policy realm, possessing much pride, powerful entrenched bureaucracies, and unpredictable, if exciting, democratic politics. Perseverance on both sides will be required to reap the potential benefits of economic and strategic cooperation.

All of this adds up to a new and highly complex international order in Asia, a skewed and dynamic multipolar structure in which U.S. influence and credibility are declining. Unchecked, this trend will cause the United States to face increasing—or suddenly bold—challenges to its military, economic, political, and cultural leadership. In particular, Washington will be constrained in the policy tools it can employ unilaterally, for example its military and diplomatic options over the fate of Taiwan, and will need to calculate economic considerations and new Chinese and Indian capabilities in adjusting its relations with allies, other nations, and international institutions such as the World Bank and IMF. America will still need to strengthen bilateral relationships throughout the region and to cooperate with China to respond effectively to a host of mutual concerns such as failing states, nuclear proliferation, international terrorism, energy and resource competition, transnational health threats, and open global trade.

The stakes could not be higher. China and India are the population epicenters of the human species. They are the major rising powers and thus the principal issues of international relations. History always contains surprises, of course, and internal or external shocks could alter the trajectory of the two giants. The tremendous lag in political development in China and the course of nationalism there, as noted above, are huge question marks for the world.

With all the changes and uncertainties ahead, the post–World War II leadership of the United States in Asia will require careful adaptations, in my view, but hardly abandonment. To the contrary, the changes and uncertainties ahead are a clarion call for a reinvigorated American presence in the region and a level of diplomatic and strategic attention that has not been needed since the Cold War or the debacle of the 1930s. Continuing development of appropriate relations with China is the first part of that presence and attention. The world needs the two greatest powers to do all they can to get along, including strengthening international institutions and the global economy. Still, human rights abuses, related manifestations of tyranny, and policies that threaten or damage U.S. interests have to be met with calibrated responses. The second part of that presence and attention is building on U.S. leadership as the offshore balancer and model for a democratic society based upon rule of law and commitment to political and economic freedom. In Asia, America's most visible leadership is its role as security "hub" and guarantor in Asia, a role that has fostered the most economically dynamic region in the world. Looking forward, the United States' military presence in Asia, coupled with its alliances with Japan, South Korea, the Philippines, Thailand, and Australia and varying partnerships— especially with India but also with Vietnam, Singapore, and others—forms a flexible, balancing framework that could sustain regional stability so long as America possesses the will and is perceived as credible. Bolstering its leadership are America's political and economic principles and institutions. Legitimacy is derived, in other words, from more than the sheer possession of guns and material wherewithal. This third part of the strategy is the most fragile and probably least effective, yet it is necessary; this is supporting in a strategic way the shallow, if earnest and busy, multilateral mechanisms that are a growing feature of the region. Suffice to say here that these mechanisms are in flux and by their varying memberships find more favor or less among the important powers. These venues will be useful to regional security and economic relations if they can represent arrays of viewpoints together with coalitions of sufficient power and will to back them up. The nations of the region benefit from demonstrations of effective cooperation. The fourth part of the strategy is rejuvenating the bases of American power, both the country's economy and military. American power must be sufficient for meeting the great and rising challenges in the Asia-Pacific.

On these four pillars U.S. policy must succeed. The rise of China and India and the uncertainties that surround any core-power transition in global affairs will necessitate an adept, stabilizing U.S. presence. The stakes and complexities have never been more profound.

Acknowledgments

On July 23, 2011, we lost our first and senior advisor to the Strategic Asia Program, General John Shalikashvili. A naturalized U.S. citizen, General "Shali" joined the army after college and rose from the lowest noncommissioned rank to the highest military position in the free world. He joined the NBR Board of Directors shortly after retiring as chairman of the Joint Chiefs of Staff in 1997. He championed the concept of Strategic Asia, helped obtain initial funding for the program, insisted on useful executive summaries of all *Strategic Asia* volumes, and reviewed the development of the Strategic Asia database. General Shali opened doors for us, accompanying then research director Aaron Friedberg and me on our first briefings to National Security Advisor Condoleezza Rice, and engaging in numerous briefings and meetings with senior officials across the national security community on behalf of the program. On a personal level, he was a great friend and a wonderful, fabulously charming human being. His passing is a huge loss to all of us. We look back at establishing the NBR chair in his name in 2006 even more enthusiastically than we did at the time.

As the *Strategic Asia* series moves forward into its eleventh year, we are reminded of our mission as an organization to put the most pertinent, timely analysis in the hands of policymakers, industry leaders, thought leaders, and educators of the next generation of Asia scholars. One nation in particular drew our attention this year when Japan experienced the devastating earthquake and subsequent tsunami on March 11, 2011. With more than 15,000 lives lost, many injured or missing, and enormous numbers of people displaced, the human suffering resulting from this catastrophic event cannot be overemphasized. For its part, NBR acted swiftly to report on the activities of Operation Tomodachi, a relief and rescue initiative in which the United States brought tremendous logistical support to bear and the two governments worked together to provide critical humanitarian relief. NBR provided up-to-date tracking of this joint response, along with expert interviews that explored implications for public health, economics, and political relationships as well as of the malfunctioning of Fukushima's nuclear reactors.

NBR senior vice president Karolos Karnikis and senior advisor Erick Thompson focused considerable effort this past year on developing a new and unique mapping feature in the Strategic Asia database that uses cutting-edge technology to display current and historical Asian military developments, including international military exercises. In addition to mapping features, we have updated the database to include data for 70 indicators across 37 countries from 1990 to 2009. Under Karolos' and Travis Tanner's guidance, interns Jacob Dowd, Jake Emerson, Kevin Shimota, and Nazariy Stetsyuk and Next Generation Fellow Ryan Zielonka worked extensively to make the newly revitalized Strategic Asia database a reality. Next Generation Fellows Lyle Morris and Anton Wishik were instrumental in the development of the mapping feature.

The production of this year's volume would not have been possible without the hard work and dedication of many individuals. The program's two senior advisors—General Shalikashvili and the founding research director Aaron Friedberg, professor of politics at Princeton University and former deputy national security advisor to the vice president—once again provided valuable guidance and support. Their experience serves as the foundation for many programs at NBR, including Strategic Asia.

Ashley Tellis served as Strategic Asia Program research director for his eighth consecutive year. As always, the architecture and quality of the authors of this volume are testaments to his extraordinary intellect and leadership. Travis Tanner, director of the Pyle Center for Northeast Asian Studies, continues to manage the Strategic Asia Program as part of his extensive portfolio at NBR. As program director, Travis contributed to every stage of the book and worked to build cohesiveness across the program's activities. Jessica Keough, publications director, has worked tirelessly over the past seven years to ensure successful publication of the research contained in each year's volume, this one being no exception.

Melissa Colonno, Strategic Asia program manager, provided essential logistical and production support for this year's publication. In April, Erin Fried joined the Strategic Asia team as program coordinator and, in addition to supporting the publication process, organized outreach and book launch events in Washington, D.C. Members of NBR's editorial team—Joshua Ziemkowski, NBR copy and style editor, Next Generation Fellow Jonathan Walton, and intern David Schlangen—were instrumental in the technical editing, layout, and proofreading processes. Much of the day-to-day work in the program has relied on NBR fellows and interns. Next Generation Fellows Ryan Zielonka, Lyle Morris, Jonathan Walton, and Anton Wishik provided extensive research assistance for the scholars and contributed in many valuable ways throughout the process.

Since the inception of Strategic Asia in 2000, Karolos Karnikis and vice president Michael Wills have worked in every capacity on the program and their persistence and innovation have contributed tremendously to sustaining the program's institutional support. This year Michael was especially instrumental to the internal review process for the drafts, along with senior associate Mahin Karim, and Karolos, as mentioned above, helped raise the database to a new level.

Our stellar group of authors did an excellent job in assessing the strategic implications of Asia's rising giants. This year, the authors brought unique regional and national perspectives to bear: special thanks to them for such diligent work in wrestling with the challenges implicit in the research design while meeting the volume's tight publication schedule. These authors join a community of nearly one hundred leading specialists who have written for the series. In addition, the anonymous reviewers, both scholars and government experts, deserve acknowledgement for their substantive evaluations of the draft chapters that were essential to developing the final product.

Finally, I would like to express my deep gratitude to the Strategic Asia Program's core sponsors—the National Nuclear Security Administration (NNSA) at the U.S. Department of Energy and the Lynde and Harry Bradley Foundation. NNSA was early to recognize and appreciate the vision of the Strategic Asia Program, supporting it since 2002 and becoming a partner and participant in our many activities and events. Likewise, the Bradley Foundation has generously supported the Strategic Asia Program since the beginning. It is indeed an honor to have colleagues at these organizations who share deeply NBR's commitment to truth and light and to strengthening and informing policy in the Asia-Pacific.

Richard J. Ellings
President
The National Bureau of Asian Research
August 2011

STRATEGIC ASIA 2011–12

OVERVIEW

EXECUTIVE SUMMARY

This chapter overviews the themes and conclusions of the volume, examining the causes behind the rise of China and India, the implications for the U.S., and the responses of other Asian states.

MAIN ARGUMENT:
China and India will likely sustain high levels of economic growth for some time due to favorable factor endowments, sensible national policies, and the benefits of late integration into the liberal international order maintained by U.S. power. Although the global dominance of Asia's rising giants is not inevitable, given that they both face significant domestic challenges, other Asian states are integrating economically with China especially, and at the same time are seeking ways to preserve their own security and autonomy against China's economic, political, and military ambitions. While India is far from becoming the central strategic focus of Asia, its internally powered rise foreshadows greater future possibilities and its democratic system makes it an attractive partner for other states seeking to counterbalance China's growing might.

POLICY IMPLICATIONS:

- Whereas the U.S. tolerated relative decline during the first wave of Asian ascendance due to alliances with Japan, Korea, Taiwan, and Singapore, the rise of China and India requires policymakers to grapple with managing the dilemma of sustaining economic interdependence that generates overall growth but produces new geopolitical rivals to U.S. primacy.

- The U.S. and India share a strategic affinity that neither can easily replicate with China. However, unlike the dependency developing between the U.S. and China, engagement with India has not yet produced a relationship deep enough that its failure would cost both sides dearly.

- The U.S. cannot presume that the extant international order will pacify a rising power such as China. Instead, the U.S. must seek to rebuild its strength and reinvigorate the Asian alliance system.

Overview

The United States and Asia's Rising Giants

Ashley J. Tellis

The rise of China and India exemplifies most dramatically Asia's resurgence in the global system. Although there has been a steady shift in the concentration of capabilities from West to East ever since the end of World War II, this transformation has gathered steam as the smaller early-industrializing nations of Asia—Japan, South Korea, Taiwan, and Singapore—have been joined by the large continental-sized states, China and India.

Both these giants have experienced dramatic levels of economic growth in recent decades. China's economic performance, for example, has been simply meteoric, exceeding even the impressive record set by the first generation of Asian tigers between 1960 and 1990. During the last 30 or so years, China has demonstrated average real growth in excess of 9% annually, with growth rates touching 13% and 14% in peak years. As a result, China's per capita income rose by more than 6% every year from 1978 to 2003—much faster than that of any other Asian country, significantly better than the 1.8% per year in Western Europe and the United States, and four times as fast as the world average. This feat has made the Chinese economy—when measured by purchasing power parity methods and other measures—the second largest in the world, with a GDP of roughly $10 trillion in 2010, and many scholars believe that China will likely overtake the United States in size of GDP at some point during the first half of this century.[1]

Ashley J. Tellis is Senior Associate at the Carnegie Endowment for International Peace and Research Director of the Strategic Asia Program at NBR. He can be reached at <atellis@carnegieendowment.org>.

[1] Ashley J. Tellis, "China's Grand Strategy: The Quest for Comprehensive National Power and Its Consequences," in *The Rise of China: Essays on the Future Competition*, ed. Gary Schmitt (New York: Encounter Books, 2009), 26; and Uri Dadush and William Shaw, *Juggernaut* (Washington, D.C.: Carnegie Endowment for International Peace, 2011), 3.

India's economic performance has not yet matched China's in either intensity or longevity. The country's economic reforms, which have produced its recent spurt in growth, began only in the early 1990s, a decade or more after China's. To date, these reforms have been neither comprehensive nor complete, and have been hampered by the contestation inherent in India's democratic politics, the complexity of its federal system, the lack of elite consensus on critical policy issues, and the persistence of important rent-seeking entities within the national polity. Yet, these disadvantages notwithstanding, the Indian economy has grown at about 7.5% during the first decade of this new century, thus eclipsing its own historic underperformance, enabling a doubling of per capita income about every decade, and placing the Indian economy, when measured by purchasing power parity methods, in fourth place globally with a GDP of approximately $4 trillion in 2010.[2] More interestingly, India's growth—unlike China's, which relies extensively on foreign capital and export markets—has derived largely from internal sources, leading many analysts to conclude that continuing economic reforms will enable the country not only to reach its targeted objective of sustained double-digit growth but to actually catch up with China in coming decades, since the trend growth rates between the two are comparable (see **Figure 1**).[3]

Even if these expectations are not borne out, the fact remains that China and India are likely to sustain their relatively high levels of GDP growth for some time to come. This continual accretion of economic power will likely position them among the top three economies internationally by the year 2050, if not earlier, thus conclusively confirming their status as global giants. This dramatic, and likely sustainable, increase in productive capabilities might at first sight appear surprising, given that most episodes of economic enlargement historically have been somewhat short-lived. Yet if the current predictions pertaining to China and India materialize, by 2050 their high economic growth rates will have continued more or less uninterrupted for a period of some 70 and 60 years, respectively—clearly an anomaly by historical standards.

---

[2] Montek S. Ahluwalia, "India's Economic Reforms: An Appraisal," Planning Commission, Government of India, August 26, 1999, http://planningcommission.nic.in/reports/articles/msalu/index.php?repts=ier.htm; and World Bank, "GDP, PPP (current international $)," World Development Indicators, August 7, 2011, http://data.worldbank.org/indicator/NY.GDP.MKTP.PP.CD.

[3] Rajiv Kumar and Pankaj Vashisht, "Crisis, Imbalances, and India," Asian Development Bank Institute (ADBI), Working Paper, no. 272, March 2011, 20, http://www.adbi.org/files/2011.03.29.wp272.crisis.imbalances.india.pdf.

FIGURE 1 Post-reform growth rates for China versus India

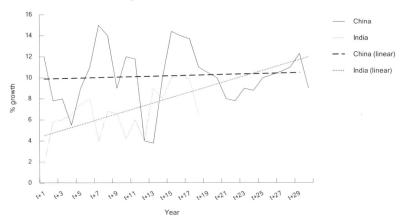

SOURCE: Rajiv Kumar and Pankaj Vashisht, "Crisis, Imbalances, and India," Asian Development Bank Institute (ADBI), Working Paper, no. 272, March 29, 2011, 20, http://www.adbi.org/files/2011.03.29.wp272.crisis.imbalances.india.pdf.

NOTE: t = 1978 for China and 1991–92 for India.

Why Have the Asian Giants Grown So Fast?

Several variables, interacting in various ways, have contributed to the growth experienced in China and, more recently, India. The first and perhaps most obvious, but often overlooked, driver has been systemic: the liberal economic order built and sustained by the hegemonic power of the United States. This order, with its cluster of stable trading rules, durable economic institutions, a reliable international reserve currency, and protected commons through which merchandise and invisibles can be exchanged globally, created the preconditions that allowed the Asian giants to maintain their growth in ways that were rare historically.[4] China has clearly been the most conspicuous beneficiary in this regard. The United States jump-started Chinese economic growth by supporting the country's membership in the World Trade Organization and offering Beijing continual access to the large U.S. market despite reservations about some of China's trade practices, the character of its regime, and its mercantilist attitudes. This U.S. backing for China's integration into the global economy enabled Beijing to successfully implement its trade-driven strategy of growth, which relies substantially on both external

---

[4] Michael Mastanduno, "System Maker and Privilege Taker: U.S. Power and the International Political Economy," *World Politics* 61, no. 1 (January 2009): 121–22, 124, 147–48.

markets and imported foreign capital for sustained expansion. Although one unintended, yet nevertheless problematic, consequence of this approach has been the creation of severe global imbalances—an outcome made possible by inadvertent but complicitous U.S. choices as well—Beijing's strategy has been wildly successful to date in that it has protected the opportunities for high rates of GDP growth.

Although India followed a different path compared to China, its dependence on the U.S. postwar international economic order has been no less significant. From access to international financial institutions, to the benefits of security for external trade, to the global market for services, not to mention the gains accruing from participating in the dollar-denominated international trading system, India has profited in different ways from the liberal international economic regime, which in effect created a favorable environment for the success of the country's reforms.[5] Although Indian economic growth has been driven largely by domestic consumption, this consumption has been financed by an increasing share of service exports and by a growing ratio of trade to GDP. Not surprisingly, then, Indian prime minister Manmohan Singh has become the biggest champion of both the rules-based liberal order and the United States, arguing on several occasions during the recent economic crisis that Washington must regain its strength in order to preserve the viability of the existing global system that has served the developing world, and especially India, all too well.

If American hegemony created the context for the rise of China and India, the fact that both countries started their most recent growth spurts from relatively low levels of development only helped further. That China and India were still largely underdeveloped when they began their reforms implies that their economies were located at levels below their potential production-possibility frontiers. In other words, both states had considerable resources that were not being productively employed, either for want of opportunities or because of the absence of appropriate catalyzing mechanisms. The advent of economic reforms in each country, centered on the revitalization of internal markets and the progressive rollback of state control, spurred the utilization of these hitherto unused resources to create new and higher levels of economic growth.[6] In India, economic reforms

---

[5] For different aspects of India's linkages with the larger liberal international order, see Sanjaya Baru, *Strategic Consequences of India's Economic Performance: Essays and Columns* (London: Routledge, 2007).

[6] For useful comparisons of China's and India's growth stories, see Nirupam Bajpai, Tianlun Jian, and Jeffrey D. Sachs, "Economic Reforms in China and India: Selected Issues in Industrial Policy," Harvard Institute for International Development, Development Discussion Paper, no. 580, April 1997; Pranab Bardhan, "Awakening Giants, Feet of Clay: A Comparative Assessment of the Rise of China and India," *Journal of South Asian Development* 1, no. 1 (2006): 1–17; and Lawrence R. Klein, "China and India: Two Asian Economic Giants, Two Different Systems," *Applied Econometrics and International Development* 4, no. 1 (2004): 7–19.

resulted in previously accumulated pools of capital—physical, financial, and human—being employed in more disciplined ways, subject to the laws and constraints of the market. The increasing returns produced as a result of more efficient investment not only reduced the allocative distortions throughout the economy but also generated enhanced opportunities in many arenas, thus stimulating even more investment in all areas of demonstrated profitability. Against the backdrop of dividends produced by previous state investments in building institutions, mobilizing savings, and creating human capital, the progressive alignment of market prices with relative scarcity thus paid off in increased growth rates resulting from productivity growth in the services sector and more effective accumulation in agriculture and industry.[7]

The Indian production-possibility frontier thus moved outward as a result of both productivity growth and the mobilization of fallow resources, thanks to the creation of new open markets in at least some segments of the economy. The Chinese growth story resembles the Indian experience in some ways, but with important differences. While China's growth rates have been more dramatic than India's, this expansion has occurred because of significant productivity gains, especially in industry, coupled with energetic resource mobilization. The latter phenomenon, however, may not always be necessarily virtuous if economic expansion ends up being fueled by what economists term "extensive" growth, where increased inputs account for growing marginal outputs. In the case of China, the propensity for extensive growth derives from a confluence of two factors: an authoritarian polity and the liberalization of commodity, but not always factor, prices. Since critical factors of production such as land and capital are still controlled by the state rather than the market, they have often been mobilized in accordance with political interests rather than allocative efficiency. Although marshaled ruthlessly when required, such resources have often been utilized wastefully and unproductively, leading to extensive environmental despoliation and inefficiency in many areas compared to India as well as China's other peers.[8] While the long-term sustainability of such practices is suspect, the important point is that China's high contemporary growth rates are engendered in part because its initially low levels of development permitted extensive growth strategies, which allowed for the absorption of the undeveloped resources that exist when any state subsists below its potential production-possibility frontier.

---

[7] For the best single-volume analysis of India's economic growth thus far, see Arvind Panagariya, *India: The Emerging Giant* (New York: Oxford University Press, 2008).

[8] See Prem Shankar Jha, *Crouching Dragon, Hidden Tiger: Can China and India Dominate the West?* (New York: Soft Skull Press, 2010).

If the existence of substantial latent resources waiting to be mobilized has proved a distinct benefit to China and India because they began their growth spurts from low levels of development, the fact that both countries have ascended later than the currently leading states has also proved advantageous. In a celebrated essay, "Economic Backwardness in Historical Perspective," published in 1962, Alexander Gerschenkron identified the dramatic advantages accruing to "late industrializers."[9] Noting that states developing later than the leaders of the pack gain because they do not have to, in effect, reinvent the wheel, Gerschenkron contended that late industrializers are likely to enjoy higher rates of growth and higher average degrees of capital intensity because they can emulate production techniques already in existence, exploit the externalities deriving from extant technologies and industrial processes, and avoid acquiring the outmoded capital stocks possessed by the early modernizing cohort.[10] Both China and India have profited handsomely from late development. As the example of wireless communications demonstrates, both countries have been able to unify their huge landmasses by employing such technologies far more easily in comparison to early industrializers who achieved the same gains but through the far more cumbersome route of physically laying copper wire across vast distances.

Because newer technologies are more capital intensive, however, the average capital intensity and levels of investment in late developers also tend to be higher compared to early starters, ultimately with positive impact on their growth rates. In this regard, China's and India's abilities to achieve high growth rates have been aided considerably by their abilities to absorb technology that, thanks to globalization, is now more accessible than ever before. This advantage has produced progressive increases in the total factor productivity of each country, which, although not matching that of the United States, still remains at decent levels compared to their peers in other developing countries. Increased productivity, in turn, has enabled both states to achieve increasing returns to scale in many sectors early in their development cycles and, by extension, has contributed to their historically atypical superior growth rates. These gains in productivity are often reflected in their appreciating exchange rates—greater productivity implies that their currencies become more valuable relative to other counterparts—which increase their purchasing

[9] Alexander Gerschenkron, "Economic Backwardness in Historical Perspective," in *Economic Backwardness in Historical Perspective: A Book of Essays* (New York: Praeger, 1962).

[10] C.P. Chandrasekhar, "Alexander Gerschenkron and Late Industrialization," in *The Pioneers of Development Economics: Great Economists on Development*, ed. Jomo Kwame Sundaram (London: Zed Books, 2005), 181–92.

power in international markets and make both countries more attractive trading partners.[11]

While China and India have thus been beneficiaries of favorable structural conditions, their high growth rates are also due to their own enlightened national choices. In both cases, credit must be given to their governments and elites who have sought to maintain the requisite institutional frameworks that have allowed their slowly liberalizing markets to work their magic.[12] On this score, China has perhaps done better than India by some measures. Beijing's capacity to exercise both self-control and social control—the former referring to the ability to set goals, the latter to the ability to attain goals—has been impressive, partly because of China's authoritarian system. In contrast, the fact that India has managed to do as well as it has economically, despite critical weaknesses in state infrastructural capacity, is also a marvel, but Indian growth could be at risk over the longer term if its polity fails to rectify current deficiencies in national performance. Although China's successes here thus far are striking, they are by no means impregnable. In fact, the record suggests that China has not yet done as well as it should in regard to either extraction or the regulation of social relations—despite the presence of authoritarian politics—and its command polity will be increasingly at odds with the market liberalism, however segmented, that has hitherto produced its most impressive successes. The long-term social foundations of growth in both China and India are thus more fragile than is sometimes recognized, and this reality has only been obscured by the impressive achievements of the last decades.[13]

Until the moment of reckoning, however, the evidence suggests that Chinese and Indian state and societal choices have had critically beneficial consequences for growth. Two good examples are China's decisions to create incentives for manufacturing and India's continued investments in sustaining service exports after this sector initially took off outside state attention. But the state-society decisions that produced increased national savings and investments are perhaps among the most important drivers of these countries' impressive growth rates. In contrast to the West, where

---

[11] Chinese productivity has been examined in Carsten A. Holz, "Measuring Chinese Productivity Growth, 1952–2005" (unpublished manuscript, 2006), http://www.oecd.org/dataoecd/46/45/37601286.pdf; and India's productivity growth is examined in Deb Kusum Das et al., "Total Factor Productivity Growth in India in the Reform Period: A Disaggregated Sectoral Analysis" (paper prepared for the first WORLD KLEMS conference at Harvard University, Cambridge, August 19–20, 2010), http://www.worldklems.net/conferences/worldklems2010_das_wadhwa.pdf.

[12] For an excellent comparative analysis of China and India by sector—and the role institutional choices have played—see Joseph C.H. Chai and Kartik C. Roy, *Economic Reform in China and India* (Northampton: Edward Elgar Publishing, 2006).

[13] The concepts of self-control and social control are discussed in Ashley J. Tellis et al., *Measuring National Power in the Post-Industrial Age* (Santa Monica: Rand Publishing, 2000), 108–21.

private savings have hovered around 20%–25% of GDP in the Euro area and have stayed well under 10% in the United States, as well as to Japan, which saves about 25%–30% of GDP, China's private savings rate has consistently exceeded 40% of its domestic product. When government savings are included, it exceeds 50% of GDP, and this average savings rate has only been rising over time.[14] India's savings rate, in contrast to China's, has been much lower—it now stands at some 35% of GDP—but it is higher than all the Organisation for Economic Co-operation and Development (OECD) countries. The significantly higher savings rates in China and India—partly a product of conscious government policies, partly a rational private response to the absence of public safety nets—have nonetheless contributed to sustaining relatively high rates of investment, which then find reflection in impressive national growth. It would therefore be ironic if the Chinese disinclination to consume, though currently contributing to high national rates of growth, were to undermine its past success by subverting successful global rebalancing, which is necessary if long-term Chinese growth is to be preserved on sustainable terms.

While the capital provided by high savings rates in China and India has been critical to fueling the impressive growth witnessed in both countries, this economic expansion could not have been maintained without consistent labor force growth. As neoclassical economics has long demonstrated, economic growth ultimately derives from the injection of technology, capital, and labor in varying proportions.[15] Although any one of these factors of production can be substituted, within limits, for deficits in another, it has long been a truism that labor force growth is critical for economic expansion because human beings are the ultimate producing and consuming engines that make an economy run. Both China and India have thus benefited greatly from having large populations that can be employed productively to create the largest possible pool of goods and services, whose trade yields the incomes that are saved and invested to further extend the cycle of growth.

---

[14] Guonan Ma and Wang Yi, "China's High Saving Rate: Myth and Reality," Bank for International Settlements (BIS), Working Paper, no. 312, June 2010, 7, http://www.bis.org/publ/work312. pdf; and John Ross, Dong Nan, and Li Hongke, "Savings in India, Germany, Japan, the U.S. and China," Key Trends in Globalisation, web log, January 9, 2010, http://ablog.typepad.com/ keytrendsinglobalisation/2010/01/saving-by-india-germany-japan-the-us-and-china-by-john-ross-dong-nan-and-li-hongke.html.

[15] For a useful overview, see F.H. Hahn, "Neoclassical Growth Theory," in *The New Palgrave Dictionary of Economics*, 2nd ed., ed. Steven N. Durlauf and Lawrence E. Blume (New York: Palgrave Macmillan, 2008). For a survey of neoclassical growth theories in comparison to their competitors, see Michael P. Todaro and Stephen C. Smith, *Economic Development*, 10th ed. (Harlow: Addison-Wesley, 2009), chap. 3.

When compared to the OECD countries, the expansion of the Chinese and Indian labor force has indeed been impressive—at least where raw numbers are concerned. But what has been even more significant are the choices each state made historically with regard to advancing its human capital. China's past investments in public health, educational attainment, and life expectancy have paid off handsomely in creating the labor pool that today sustains its economic expansion.[16] India, in contrast, has done less well on each of these three counts, except for its historic overinvestment in tertiary education, which has provided the means for sustaining a large middle class, stimulating an innovation economy, and supporting a services sector that underwrites the information technology industry worldwide.[17]

Yet in both countries different issues pertaining to labor cast a dark shadow on the prospects of future growth. China's "one child" policy, which for years was upheld as an example of how third world countries ought to control their populations, now threatens to short circuit the country's future economic growth because it has resulted in a smaller proportion of working-age individuals at precisely the time when the dependency ratio—the number of people of non-working age, both young and old, as a proportion of those of working age—is certain to almost double. This transformation makes it likely that China will grow old before it grows rich, at least in per capita terms. While high growth rates can undoubtedly be sustained in the interim by importing capital or increasing the rate of innovation, there is simply no way for China to sustain high growth rates over the secular period if its labor force contracts inexorably.

India, in contrast, has a favorable demographic profile: specifically, its dependency ratios are falling. By 2030, it is projected to have a dependency ratio of 0.4, meaning that there will be more bread winners than dependents in India's large but steadily stabilizing population. The benefits for savings, investment, and growth are obvious, but, in India's case, there is an unwelcome catch: much of its young population is uneducated, lacks access to adequate health care and nutrition, and suffers increasingly from dreadful sex-ratio imbalances due to pernicious social attitudes. The much-vaunted Indian "demographic dividend" that many analysts presume will sustain the country's long-term growth inexorably could thus prove to be more evanescent than usual if the Indian state fails to remedy its human capital deficiencies in a hurry. Although these challenges are well

---

[16] Thomas G. Rawski, "Human Resources and China's Long Economic Boom," *Asia Policy*, no. 12 (July 2011): 33–78.

[17] Devesh Kapur, "The Causes and Consequences of India's IT Boom," *India Review* 1, no. 2 (April 2002): 91–110.

recognized in India, its weaknesses in program implementation could come to haunt it in the years to come.[18]

How Does the Rise of the Asian Giants Impact the United States?

The foregoing discussion suggests that the impressive rise of China and India is likely to continue for a while longer because both countries have favorable factor endowments, are pursuing sensible national policies, and benefit greatly as late modernizers from the liberal international order maintained by U.S. power. Yet their global dominance cannot be treated as simply inevitable. Both nations are confronted by a variety of domestic challenges—social, economic, and political—that have yet to be satisfactorily managed, even as there are uncertainties about the durability of the supportive international order given the current infirmities of the United States.

This incertitude notwithstanding, the continuing growth of China and India will likely remain a fact of life in the policy-relevant future. It has already proved to be an enormously consequential development domestically, regionally, and globally. Domestically, the high growth rates enjoyed by China and India have resulted in moving millions of people out of poverty and toward the promise of a better life; growth has helped create an empowered middle class in both countries as well as a smaller class of wealthier citizens who offer the hope of helping to renegotiate state-society relations over time.[19] Regionally, the rise of China and India has created opportunities for deeper economic integration beyond their borders. This is already the case where China is concerned: all the peripheral countries, to a greater or lesser degree, are now economically intermeshed with China either as suppliers of raw materials, capital, or technology or as markets for Chinese exports. Regional integration in the case of India still remains a work in progress partly because of India's domestically driven growth strategy and partly because geography and poisonous South Asian geopolitics have prevented the regional states from benefiting as much as

---

[18] See the very sobering assessment of China and India in Nicholas N. Eberstadt, "Asia-Pacific Demographics in 2010–2040: Implications for Strategic Balance," in *Strategic Asia 2010–11: Asia's Rising Power and America's Continued Purpose*, ed. Ashley J. Tellis, Andrew Marble, and Travis Tanner (Seattle: National Bureau of Asian Research, 2010), 236–77.

[19] See Zhou Xiaohong and Qin Chen, "Globalization, Social Transformation, and the Construction of China's Middle Class," in *China's Emerging Middle Class: Beyond Economic Transformation*, ed. Cheng Li (Washington, D.C.: Brookings Institution, 2010), 98–100; and Leela Fernandes, *India's New Middle Class: Democratic Politics in an Era of Economic Reform* (Minneapolis: University of Minnesota Press, 2006), 215.

they could otherwise have from India's economic expansion.[20] Globally, the rise of China and India has moved the international production-possibility frontier further outward as a result of more effective specialization. China not only has become the newest workshop of the world and India the most economical provider of IT services, but the consumptive patterns now exhibited by their populations of over two billion progressively drive increases in global aggregate demand, thus making the two states the critical motors of global economic growth.[21]

All these realities imply that the rise of China and India represents largely good news for the United States (and the global system), at least from an economic perspective. The story at the level of international politics, however, is a little more complicated. And from this vantage point, the customary conflation of China and India as Asia's "emerging giants" breaks down because each nation encounters the United States (and the international system more generally) in dramatically different ways.

At the most fundamental level, China's larger size and substantially superior growth rates, which have persisted far longer than India's, place it on a path that could result one day in China overtaking the United States in gross economic strength, if no consequential internal or external disruptions occur in the interim. This possibility, portended by the current trend lines defining relative economic growth, suggests the prospect of a coming power transition wherein the existing hegemonic power, the United States, could be replaced by the rising alternative, China.[22] Because India's growth rates have been neither close to China's nor as prolonged—despite being high in absolute and historical terms—the probability of India surpassing the United States in economic power is insignificant by comparison. Hence, the attention garnered by Beijing as a likely competitor, and perhaps even a direct antagonist, to Washington in power-political terms does not quite carry over to India.

The fact that Beijing and New Delhi are locked into a complex rivalry of their own—a product of their extant territorial disputes, mutual efforts at encirclement and counter-encirclement, direct military competition, and competitive efforts at alliance making and breaking in regard to states along

---

[20] See Michael R. Chambers, "Rising China: The Search for Power and Plenty," in *Strategic Asia 2006–07: Trade, Interdependence, and Security*, ed. Ashley J. Tellis and Michael Wills (Seattle: National Bureau of Asian Research, 2006), 65–103; and Devesh Kapur and Kavita Iyengar, "The Limits of Integration in Improving South Asian Security," in ibid., 241–69.

[21] World Bank, "Global Economic Prospects: Maintaining Progress amid Turmoil," June 2011, http://siteresources.worldbank.org/INTGEP/Resources/335315-1307471336123/7983902-1307479336019/Full-Report.pdf.

[22] For an excellent examination of this prospect, see Ronald L. Tammen and Jacek Kugler, "Power Transition and China–U.S. Conflicts," *Chinese Journal of International Politics* 1, no. 1 (2006): 35–55.

their mutual peripheries—in circumstances where Beijing and Washington view each other warily because of the prospect of a power transition at the core of the global system increases the strategic affinity between the United States and India in a way that is hard to replicate in the case of China and the United States.[23] After all, as Kautilya elaborated as early as the fourth century BCE in Book VI of his treatise *Arthashastra*, "the enemy of my enemy must be my friend."

While the threat of a future power transition conditions American attitudes toward China today—attitudes that are likely to become more rivalrous and even hostile as Chinese power grows more comprehensively—India's potential to become a significant U.S. partner, either explicit or tacit, only increases. Given the proximity of the two Asian giants, China's rise could undermine India's security, autonomy, and standing, even before the United States is affected directly. Even if this were not the case, however, American attitudes toward China are characterized by growing discomfort because rising Chinese strength has spawned three distinct challenges for Washington that simply have no counterparts in its relationship with New Delhi.

First, China's rapid economic growth has produced painful economic challenges for the United States.[24] Although the U.S. economy undoubtedly benefits doubly—first, from low-cost Chinese products and, second, from Chinese capital exports—these gains have come at the cost of considerable deindustrialization at home and an acute dependence on capital from abroad. Although economists would lucidly explain these transformations in terms of both national policies and shifting global patterns of comparative advantage, the loss of U.S. manufacturing domestically and its accompanying risks to the American middle class have left the United States in a situation where China, for all the benefits produced by its growth, has become a significant threat to specific sections of the U.S. economy. While India too is sometimes seen to mount similar challenges in the service sector, the fact that its economic growth is internally driven, its exchange rates are set by the market, and its bilateral trade with the United States is quite modest—unlike China on all counts—makes New Delhi a relatively insignificant threat to American prosperity and growth.

Second, the economic challenge posed by China, which affects millions of Americans in their everyday lives, is increasingly complemented by a

---

[23] For more, and different, perspectives on the Sino-Indian relationship and its impact on the United States, see Francine R. Frankel and Harry Harding, ed., *The India-China Relationship: What the United States Needs to Know* (Washington, D.C.: Woodrow Wilson Center Press, 2004).

[24] Douglas Holtz-Eakin, "Economic Relationships between the United States and China," statement before the Committee on Ways and Means, U.S. House of Representatives, Congressional Budget Office (CBO), CBO Testimony, April 14, 2005, 11, http://www.cbo.gov/ftpdocs/62xx/doc6274/04-14-ChinaTestimony.pdf.

geopolitical challenge to the United States' status as a hegemonic power, potentially globally but most immediately in Asia.[25] For most of the postwar period, U.S. influence in Asia was uncontested, thanks to the United States' unrivalled economic strength, strong economic ties with key Asian states, and robust security umbrella manifested through the hub-and-spoke alliance system. Even at the high tide of Soviet supremacy, Moscow's coercive reach in Asia was much more modest than its capabilities in Europe. The recent rise of China threatens for the first time to undermine a core U.S. objective in Asia—namely, to prevent the domination of the continent by any indigenous power that might over time accumulate sufficient strength to control the region's resources and eventually threaten the United States' local allies or even U.S. security itself. The prospect that China might integrate the Indo-Pacific periphery through a network of trading relations that could become the foundation for an impermeable sphere of influence centered on Chinese economic, geopolitical, and cultural primacy in Asia is deeply threatening to U.S. interests at a time when many regional states find themselves increasingly pulled by China's growing power-political mass. India, in contrast, poses no comparable challenges to the United States in Asia and beyond—and, if anything, has been slow to parry China's rising influence along its periphery, despite repeated entreaties by the United States and other Asian nations to do so.

Third, the growing geopolitical challenge represented by China in Asia both to the United States and to its littoral friends and allies is increasingly substantiated by the military challenges deriving from the rapid modernization of the People's Liberation Army (PLA).[26] This modernization, when complete, will radically undermine a key precondition for strategic stability in Pacific Asia, namely, the U.S. ability to assist its allies unimpeded when they are threatened by external dangers. PLA investments to deny the United States easy access to the Asian periphery, though motivated initially by a desire to resolve the Taiwan imbroglio favorably in the face of possible U.S. interference, have evolved in the direction of maintaining a substantial maritime zone of influence some one thousand nautical miles from Chinese shores. The Chinese military capabilities now being developed for this purpose effectively challenge the traditional U.S. command of the maritime, cyber, and space commons, all of which are essential for the successful discharge of U.S. extended deterrence obligations in Asia. These capabilities

---

[25] Aaron Friedberg, "The Struggle for Mastery in Asia," in *South Asia in 2020: Future Strategic Balances and Alliances*, ed. Michael R. Chambers (Carlisle: Strategic Studies Institute, U.S. Army War College, 2002), 449–72.

[26] A useful overview of the Chinese military challenge can be found in Richard D. Fisher Jr., *China's Military Modernization: Building for Regional and Global Reach* (Westport: Praeger Security International, 2008).

also lay the foundation for challenging the security of the key regional states perceived to be Chinese rivals, while increasing the threats that China can mount against the U.S. homeland over time. On all these counts, India not only does not pose a similar challenge to the United States but is actually threatened directly by many of the capabilities now entering into service in the PLA. The incentives for closer U.S.-Indian cooperation in defense matters, then, only become more pressing.

These three reasons considered together provide the United States— though it welcomes the economic rise of both China and India—with sufficient justification to treat the former with a degree of caution that also warrants deepening ties with the latter by way of precaution. This dynamic is only reinforced by the character of the regime in each country. China's authoritarian dispensation, its long history of superordination in East Asia, and its troublesome streak of nationalism domestically make it highly suspect in the eyes of most U.S. policymakers and in important parts of the Indo-Pacific region. By contrast, India's democratic polity, with its liberal orientation and its culture of strategic restraint, makes New Delhi almost automatically a desirable partner for Washington as well as for many other Asian capitals. That India also happens to be a large, rapidly growing, militarily potent, continental entity capable of cooperating with other regional states (especially the democratic nations in Asia) to create the objective structural constraints that could discourage Beijing from abusing its growing strength—even as all Asian countries and the United States preserve strong economic ties with China—creates a virtuous combination where power and liberty combine to support a subtle U.S. strategic policy that enhances continental stability.

The necessity for such subtlety grows out of the structural predicament that defines the second wave of Asian success. During the Cold War, Asian success was manifest by the emergence of new industrializing states such as Japan, Korea, Taiwan, and Singapore. All these states grew as a result of their progressive integration into the U.S.-led liberal trading order. Their growth, though undoubtedly signaling the United States' relative decline, was in any event a desirable outcome because it implied an overall strengthening of the Western alliance in its struggle against the Communist coalition led by the Soviet Union. Because the Soviet Union and its allies were not part of the liberal economic order promoted by the United States, the economic regime fostered by Washington internationally did not undermine the political goal of containing the Warsaw Pact states. In fact, the tight economic interdependence among U.S. alliance partners, coupled with strong autarky across the competing geopolitical blocs, implied that the strategic containment of adversaries and the economic integration among allies dovetailed perfectly. In these circumstances, the United States could tolerate its own relative decline because such a deterioration occurred only vis-à-vis its friends, while the Western alliance as a whole became ever more powerful vis-à-vis its enemies.[27]

The second wave of Asian success, however, has generated contradictions in the traditional U.S. strategy of expanding the liberal economic order. Because the new rising powers, China and India, are ascending in part because they are embedded in the liberal international regime underwritten by the United States—even though they are not U.S. allies and could well become its geopolitical competitors over time—the second wave of Asian accomplishment has brought to the fore two critical dilemmas that brook no easy solutions. To begin with, the growing economic interdependence between the United States and the new Asian giants has indeed accelerated increases in growth and welfare across the international system, but at uneven rates among its key constituents. This dynamic, then, raises the prospect of the return of the "relative gains" dilemmas, which arise when states become sensitive to the fact that others, especially their competitors, might be growing at faster rates. When uneven growth occurs among allies—as was the case during the first wave of Asian success—the consequences are rarely deleterious because no member of the coalition expects that the faster-growing partners would utilize their increases in capability to challenge their allies. In current circumstances, however, this contingency becomes a realistic prospect because neither China nor India is a formal ally of the United States, and, hence, they are not bound to refrain from using their increased capabilities to undermine larger U.S. interests.

Given this possibility, it is not surprising that the rise of the new Asian giants, while obviously beneficial to the United States in many ways, is nonetheless raising old questions about whether the expanded liberal order is an unambiguous good if its net result is the creation of new economic rivals who could threaten the well-being of the United States. If Beijing and New Delhi were Washington's alliance partners, this problem might have been somewhat mitigated—though not necessarily, if the concerns about Japan's ascent during the 1980s are any indication. But this problem is certainly exacerbated by the possibility that at least one country, China—the faster-growing and the more capable of the two Asian giants, with an authoritarian regime to boot—appears poised to become a serious geostrategic competitor to the United States.

---

[27] For an elaboration of this argument, see Ashley J. Tellis, "Power Shift: How the West Can Adapt and Thrive in an Asian Century," German Marshall Fund of the United States, Asia Paper Series, January 2010, http://www.gmfus.org/galleries/ct_publication_attachments/AsiaPowerShiftGMFPaper.pdf.

This danger, in turn, raises more central questions: Is the current U.S. strategy of expanding the liberal international order actually breeding new rivals and producing new competitors and new threats to Washington's power and dominance? And if it is, is it worth the cost? A positive answer to the second question could be defended if, at the end of the day, the liberal international system would assuredly defang the harmful ambitions of all new rising powers. Liberal conceptions of international politics suggest that this outcome will in fact obtain and, hence, that even the reigning hegemon ought to view all emerging powers that are part of the open international order with equanimity.[28] U.S. policymakers, however, tasked with the responsibility of protecting U.S. power, interests, and standing in the global system, cannot presume that the extant international order will inevitably pacify a rising power such as China, which has its own history and traditions of primacy and now the power and ambitions to match them. Hence, they must grapple with that axial problem confronting statecraft in this new century: How does Washington manage the dilemma of sustaining the economic interdependence that generates overall growth but simultaneously produces new geopolitical rivals to American primacy?

Clearly, the answer cannot consist of jettisoning the liberal economic order and the global interdependence engendered as a result of 60 years of conscious U.S. policy. An alternative approach could of course be implemented but would involve a radical renovation of the current strategy and the existing global order—and its success would by no means be certain. Consequently, U.S. policy has settled for upholding the liberal economic order so that the country may continue to enjoy the welfare benefits of global interdependence, while at the same time seeking to protect the nation against its potential geopolitical downside. The twin pillars of this evolving insurance strategy consist of, first, rebuilding the sinews of U.S. strength, primarily economic but also military—a task that has not gotten off to a great start—and, second, reinvigorating the Asian alliance system surrounding China by deepening existing formal alliances and supplementing them with new partnerships involving key states, such as the other rising power, India—a project that has, at least in relative terms, been far more successful. Washington's effort to develop a new strategic partnership with New Delhi, first initiated by President George W. Bush and now continued by President Barack Obama, thus constitutes

---

[28] The most cogent defense of this proposition has been provided by G. John Ikenberry, "The Rise of China and the Future of the West: Can the Liberal System Survive?" *Foreign Affairs* 87, no. 1 (January/February 2008): 23–37; and G. John Ikenberry and Anne-Marie Slaughter, "Forging a World of Liberty Under Law: U.S. National Security in the 21st Century," Final Paper of the Princeton Project on National Security, Princeton Project Papers, Woodrow Wilson School of Public and International Affairs, September 27, 2006, 47–51, http://www.princeton.edu/~ppns/report/FinalReport.pdf.

a quintessentially realist solution to a predicament engendered by a long-standing liberal internationalist policy.[29]

While this solution is eminently sensible and constitutes one way out of a difficult conundrum, it is constantly challenged by the reality that the United States is locked into a relationship of tight interdependence with its potential chief rival, China, while enjoying weaker economic links with its potential key ally, India. Thus, although Beijing may threaten Washington's regional and global interests more than India ever might, the United States is compelled to be more cautious in how it responds to any challenges involving China because the pain associated with a devastating meltdown implicating Beijing is very high. All engagement with India, in contrast, while desirable and important, generally falls short of being compelling because neither Washington nor New Delhi has yet been able to deepen the relationship to a point where a failure of the partnership would end up costing both sides dearly.

The irony, therefore, is that despite fears and suspicions being greater in the U.S.-China relationship, this interaction has turned out to be the more important of the two dyads. Hence, the attention it incurs is stronger because both the benefits of success and the penalties of failure are relatively high. The U.S.-India relationship, by way of comparison, lacks such intensity and thus remains consigned primarily to the arena of the desirable—at least for now. As a result, this bilateral partnership risks forgoing the protection and the benefits that might otherwise arise from a tighter embrace. While the United States would undoubtedly value deeper cooperation—and, in fact, craves it—India's traditional yearning for strategic autonomy, the inability of its leaders and elites to carry a consensus in favor of a stronger affiliation, and the failure of its government to pursue consistent and coherent policies vis-à-vis Washington—the travails of a postcolonial democracy in a complex society—all end up exposing India to greater strategic risk in the face of rising Chinese power.

As the Sino-Indian War of 1962 ought to have demonstrated, the current Indian willingness to discount the benefits of tighter coordination with the United States, an arrangement that protects India in the face of its inability to successfully balance China through internal means alone, could end up leaving New Delhi in a situation where it lacks the resources within and without to cope with the worst depredations of Chinese power. To be sure, India is much stronger today than it was in 1962, and it will only get stronger over time. But the essence of its predicament is still the same— and shows no signs of easing—because power in the international system

---

[29] Ashley J. Tellis, "Indo-U.S. Relations Headed for a Grand Transformation?" *YaleGlobal*, July 14, 2005, http://yaleglobal.yale.edu/content/indo-us-relations-headed-grand-transformation.

is always relative and, for the moment at least, Chinese power appears to be outstripping India's across almost every dimension and in some cases by orders of magnitude.

The Indian calculus may over time, however, prove to be right. That is, New Delhi's quest to preserve its strategic autonomy and avoid unnecessary entanglements with the United States may turn out to be justified if, as many Indian analysts argue, Indian growth rates begin to approximate China's current pace at some point in the future (while China's own prospective growth rates begin to flag), and the Indian economy begins to rival China's in technological capacity, if not in size. If such an outcome obtains, India's desire to stay "nonaligned" in the interim will have paid off. But much can happen in this interim, and not all of it good for either India or the United States, while the interregnum itself could prove to be extended and long-drawn. In such circumstances, not only would India find itself potentially adrift, but the United States would also be hard-pressed to justify preferential involvement with India at a time when U.S. relations with China—however problematic they might be on many counts—are turning out to be deeper, more encompassing, and, at least where the production of wealth is concerned, more fruitful.

Echoing the U.S. Predicament:
Asia Responds to Its Rising Giants

If this volume demonstrates anything clearly, it is that the U.S. predicament detailed above in regard to China and India is replicated in the case of almost every Asian state, except Pakistan. Outside of Pakistan, every Asian state or region examined remains profoundly entwined with China economically. Each values the material benefits that commercial intercourse with China brings to it individually or to the larger environment; yet each is in different ways deeply concerned about Beijing's long-term objectives as China rises in power. Consequently, each entity seeks to protect its security and autonomy vis-à-vis Beijing, but without forsaking the material gains that come from tighter economic integration.

The range of choices in this context is complex. A state can choose to exploit the positive externalities flowing from the complicated U.S. deterrence-cum-engagement of China; or it can formally (or tacitly) ally with the United States even as it engages China. A state can become part of regional political groupings that provide it with a degree of geopolitical leverage vis-à-vis China, even as it deepens economic ties with Beijing, or it can entice India (in partnership with others such as the United States and Japan) to play the role of a latent balancer to China by engaging more vigorously in economic and political affairs outside the subcontinent proper. Or states can work toward creating pan-Asian institutions that integrate all the continent's great powers and the United States to permit continued economic integration while simultaneously "enmeshing" or "binding" growing Chinese power in order to prevent it from being used coercively in the wider region.

The chapters in this volume suggest that all the Asian states use one or more of these approaches in their efforts to manage China. In so doing, these states confirm that they are responding to the same structural problem facing the United States: how to profit from China's growth without allowing its rising power to be used to their disadvantage. The difficulty of managing this conundrum also validates another reality: that, at least for now, China, not India, remains the central strategic focus of Asia. This does not imply that India is unimportant—the continued desire for Asian engagement with India suggests that the regional states only expect it to grow further in wealth, power, and influence—only that today it is derivative of the challenge faced by all other Asian nations in regard to managing China.

For some time to come, China's enormous economic vitality and mass (which already exert a global impact in multiple issue areas ranging from energy to the environment), its dramatic growth rates (which signal even greater distention in size and power than witnessed already), its central location on the Asian continent (which affects all land, littoral, and maritime powers equally), its trade-centered economic strategy (which inevitably knits the destinies of others with its own), its huge foreign exchange reserves (which drive both its acquisitive and its capital-exporting ability), its pivotal position as the axis of Asian economic integration (which increasingly makes all the major states in the continent dependent on China for their well-being), and its rapidly modernizing strategic and military capabilities (which will be progressively capable of mounting major threats to both regional states and any offshore balancers) all combine to make China the power of consequence in Asia and globally outside of the United States. All others, including major entities such as Russia, Japan, and India, play largely ancillary roles.

This reality is unnerving from a regional perspective because although the rise of China (and, secondarily, India) represents the most graphic example of the power shift from West to East in recent decades, Asia's growing economic power has not translated into either strategic equilibrium or geopolitical integration. This should not be surprising because, for all its achievements, "Asia" still remains fundamentally an artifact of geographical imagination. Hence, the gains of growth, which have materialized thus far mainly in littoral Asia (and neither uniformly nor proportionately even there), not only have failed to produce any significant Asian unity but, more problematically, may have exacerbated the fissures arising from the differential distribution of economic success.

Kenneth Pyle's special study in this volume, "International Order and the Rise of Asia: History and Theory," which describes how contending theories of international relations prognosticate different futures for Asia, provides still other reasons for concern. Pyle reminds the reader that the last time Chinese power was ascendant in Asia, order was produced through a hierarchic system wherein

> the Chinese emperor…[was]…acknowledged not only as the preeminent temporal power but also as a power of cosmic significance who mediated between heaven and earth. In contrast to the Westphalian concept in Europe of a number of independent nations recognized as theoretically equal with their own independent legitimacy and sovereignty, the Sinocentric concept was one of countries in East Asia subsumed within the Chinese sphere of civilized society. Rulers of the various countries within this sphere were expected to present themselves to the Chinese emperor and be invested with his authority, to receive a seal symbolizing the authority granted, to date all memorials according to the Chinese calendar, and to make regular visits to the Chinese imperial court to reaffirm their subordination. In return these rulers could receive trade benefits, legitimacy, and sometimes security.

While such a hierarchic system did provide a particular form of international order, the historical record demonstrates that this order was neither uniformly peaceful nor uniformly beneficial for the peripheral states—and sometimes not particularly advantageous for China either.[30] In any event, this kind of order could be sustained only in the premodern era before the rise of nationalism and expanding economic growth created the capable, self-regarding states that now exist on China's periphery. Because these countries fear, however, that growing Chinese power might entice Beijing into attempting to replicate some version of the old Sinocentric system in time to come, many other scholars have speculated that the future of Asia—resembling Europe's past—might be characterized by persistent rivalries and jockeying for advantage as a rising China that seeks recognition of its ascendancy is challenged by other competitors seeking to protect their own security, autonomy, and privileges.[31] Whether this prognosis will come to pass cannot be determined right now, but Pyle's survey of Asia's history

---

[30] See the discussion in Michael D. Swaine and Ashley J. Tellis, *Interpreting China's Grand Strategy: Past, Present, and Future* (Santa Monica: RAND Corporation, 2000), 9–95.

[31] Aaron L. Friedberg, "Will Europe's Past Be Asia's Future?" *Survival* 42, no. 3 (Autumn 2000): 147–59; Aaron Friedberg, "The Future of U.S.-China Relations: Is Conflict Inevitable?" *International Security* 30, no. 2 (Fall 2005): 7–45; Robert Kagan, "Ambition and Anxiety: America's Competition with China," in Schmitt, *The Rise of China*, 1–24; and Swaine and Tellis, *Interpreting China's Grand Strategy*, 151–229.

in light of the competing intellectual traditions of international relations theory usefully sets the context within which all the other chapters of this book ought to be read.

In its totality, this volume of *Strategic Asia* explores in some detail how the key Asian states and specific subregions of Asia are responding to the rise of China and India across a range of issue areas that matter to their strategic interests. Toward that end, each country or regional chapter addresses how the rise of the two Asian giants affects the strategic interests of a given country or region in light of its own assessment about the future of U.S. power in Asia and globally. To tell this story at an appropriate level of detail, the individual studies examine the key forms of interaction between a state or region and China and India with regard to historical dealings, geopolitical and strategic relations, economic intercourse, cultural affinities or competition, military rivalries, and any other matters that may be pertinent.

The central objective in each case is to explicate how a particular state or region perceives the rise of China and India in the context of its current and prospective exchanges with each giant and against the backdrop of its relations with other key states. The chapters have also attempted to assess how the regional states are juggling considerations pertaining to the balance of power, economic interdependence, and other ideational and institutional factors in their approaches to China and India. When important internal differences about China or India can be identified in the country or region examined, they are flagged and evaluated to determine how these contending perspectives are adjudicated. In so doing, each chapter represents a balanced appraisal of the strategies that each of the relevant Asian powers (or regions) is pursuing toward China and India (and other states) in order to protect its core interests as well as the impact on the United States. A somewhat different approach is adopted by the two studies focusing on China and India themselves: here, the emphasis is on understanding how each Asian giant views the other's rise in the context of its own grand strategy, relations with the other Asian powers and with regional institutions (to the degree relevant), and ties with the United states.

M. Taylor Fravel's study of China's perceptions and relations with India is instructive for the complexity it conveys about contemporary Chinese foreign policy. Similar to the way it has handled relations with other major Asian states, Beijing has sought to minimize the chances of active conflict with India in order to avoid disrupting the peaceful regional environment necessary for its accumulation of comprehensive national power. Yet this effort at maintaining stability in the bilateral relationship with New Delhi has not come at the cost of Chinese compromise on the key irritants such as the status of the disputed territories, ongoing support for Pakistan, aid to the smaller South Asian states, modernization of military infrastructure in Tibet, and substantial ongoing nuclear targeting of India. Based on a broad survey of Chinese elite opinion, Fravel concludes that China views India's rise largely as a positive development because it conduces to a global multipolarity that helps limit the power of the United States while simultaneously offering opportunities for China to profit economically from expanded trade with the growing Indian economy.

Yet this optimistic conclusion is tinged by a significant degree of uncertainty for several reasons. First, Indian national security elites do not view China's perceptions of India in similarly benign terms, despite the growing trade between the two countries. Second, the evolving character of U.S.-Indian relations and India's relations with major Chinese rivals, such as Japan, may yet turn out to be constraining from Beijing's point of view (notwithstanding its current rhetoric on these issues, which has not been borne out in its diplomatic practice in any case). And, third, Chinese strategy toward India has always been far more subtle and hardnosed than its exoteric expressions—which generally convey a feigned indifference toward India coupled with the consistent denial that New Delhi is a potential rival—might suggest. Despite the danger that Sino-Indian competition might become malignantly antagonistic over time, Fravel's analysis provides a useful reminder that, at least for the moment, relations between the two remain a complex "mixed-sum" game.

Harsh Pant's chapter on Indian perceptions of China provides the counterpart to Fravel's analysis in this volume. In contrast to Fravel's depiction of China as at best welcoming of, and at worst ambivalent about, India's rise, Pant depicts Indian perceptions of China in more straightforward terms as a strategic challenge to be countered by a combination of external and internal balancing. This does not imply that Sino-Indian relations are plainly and simply confrontational. To the contrary, Pant describes the two sides' interactions as characterized by substantial convergence on issues of global order, including a desire for a multipolar international system, strategies on climate change that shift the burdens of combating the problem asymmetrically on to the developed world, trade regime innovations that promise disproportionately greater access for developing countries to developed countries' markets, and a robust global norm that upholds national sovereignty.

For all this convergence on world order issues, however, Pant sees New Delhi as viewing Beijing's intentions, strategies, and actions far more suspiciously in the one arena that actually matters for local stability: the bilateral relationship between the two states. Here, he describes a dangerous security dilemma developing because of the growing Indian conviction that the local military balances are tilting to its disadvantage, China's increasing penetration of India's previously secure oceanic frontier, and the emergence of new arenas of competition in the nuclear realm, in relations with near and extended neighbors, and even in regard to energy, trade, and investment. Pant's reading of these challenges suggests that a crucial driver of any prospective Sino-Indian competition will be India's fears of China. Being the weaker power in the dyad, India is likely to be far more concerned about China than is reciprocally true, but this inference must be excogitated carefully if the conventional mistake that India's lesser priority for China equates to Beijing's strategic neglect of New Delhi is to be avoided. Given the likely evolution of the Sino-Indian competition, Pant views the role of the United States as crucial, both as a protector of Indian security and as an Indian partner in preserving a favorable global balance of power.

Michael Green's chapter on Japan—the first of the country studies that examines how a major Asian power center relates to the rise of China and India—captures succinctly how Tokyo's response mimics in many ways the U.S. predicament vis-à-vis China. China's growth during the last few decades has provided Japan with numerous opportunities to expand bilateral trade and investment in the face of economic stagnation at home. The profitability of doing business in China, combined with the assumptions that Japan's technological superiority would permit it to maintain its economic lead indefinitely while being able to shape China's strategic direction, resulted in substantial Japanese investments in its larger neighbor. Yet growing Sino-Japanese trade and investment—China replaced the United States as Japan's biggest investment destination in 2007—has not mitigated the security competition between these two Asian contenders. In an echo of U.S.-China relations today, Green describes how "strategic rivalry now coexists with economic interdependence as the defining characteristic of Sino-Japanese relations."

This fraught situation has provoked a classic realist effort at external balancing. Although Indo-Japanese ties traditionally have been relatively thin, Japanese leaders have responded to China's growing assertiveness by revitalizing the alliance relationship with the United States and, more interestingly from the perspective of this volume, by attempting to renew ties with that other rising power, India. Green summarizes this shift by noting that "India offers Japan a security hedge against China (particularly given common Japanese and Indian interests in the maritime domain), an economic hedge against overdependence on the Chinese market, an alliance hedge against overdependence on the United States for security, and an ideational hedge with a fellow democratic state against the Beijing Consensus and criticism of Japan's past." While Japan, like the United States, thus seeks in India a fellow partner in preserving the continental balance of power, it too labors against the reality that its economic ties with China are, at least for now, far deeper than its economic ties with India. Thus, managing the new relationship with India, however promising, will prove to be as much a challenge for Japan as it is for the United States. As a solution to the larger problems of continental stability, Green observes that ties between New Delhi and Tokyo are still in a relatively nascent stage, but, more importantly, he concludes that preserving an appropriate Asian balance of power from Japan's perspective will require a thorough internal renewal just as much as effective external balancing.

Chung Min Lee's study of South Korea's response to the rise of China and India describes how a successful Asian middle power is attempting to navigate between complex gravitational forces represented by a deadly proximate threat, North Korea; three capable neighbors, China, Japan, and Russia (one clearly rising, the other currently stagnating, and the third potentially declining); a long-standing alliance with an external protector, the United States; and new rising, but more distant, powers such as India, Indonesia, and Vietnam, of which India could be the most important in both economic and strategic terms. In this complex environment, South Korea's search for security, prosperity, and autonomy takes it quickly to the United States as its most important security guarantor. But even as Seoul tries to renegotiate this long-standing alliance to accommodate its own maturation, there is little doubt that China looms large as the next most important regional actor both because of the opportunities Chinese growth offers South Korea in economic terms and because of Beijing's critical role in restraining North Korean adventurism—the one threat that could directly undermine Seoul's wealth and safety.

The significance of China to South Korea is only boosted by the large volume of bilateral trade—which shows no signs of slowing—even though, as Lee notes, "centuries of truncated autonomy shaped by Korea's place at the core of China's historical sphere of influence are never far from the surface." Preserving Korean independence in the face of deeply ingrained anxieties about China, while at the same time enjoying the benefits accruing from growing common interests, thus turns out to be a critical challenge. For the moment, however, this tension has been mitigated by the Korean conviction that China still does not have what it takes to become a genuine hegemonic power capable of denuding Seoul's sovereignty in any fundamental sense. Yet, to protect against just this contingency, South Korea has embarked on a policy of strategic diversification that, in Lee's telling, includes multiple components such as taking U.S.-Japan-South Korea trilateral security and defense coordination into new directions, exploring new political engagements throughout Pacific Asia, and even reaching as far south as India, despite the twin historical hurdles represented by "the tyranny of distance and mutual disinterest."

Consistent with this approach, Korean-Indian trade has increased significantly in recent years, though it still remains a small fraction of Sino-Korean trade. Although both New Delhi and Seoul share important interests—such as containing rising Chinese power, managing two linked but failing states with nuclear weapons on their peripheries, and ensuring maritime freedoms in the Indian and Pacific oceans—not to mention a "high degree of still largely untapped economic potential," Lee concludes that the bilateral relationship with India will, for understandable structural reasons, remain only "an important supplement to Seoul's foreign policy rather than a driving factor."

Rory Medcalf's chapter on the Australian response to the rise of China and India discusses similar themes and predicaments to those found in Lee's study of South Korea. Medcalf notes that the rise of China and India reflects a dramatic transformation of Australia's strategic landscape in that, for the first time in the postwar period, Canberra is confronted by a geographic milieu wherein its formal alliance partners, the United States and Japan, are no longer dominant in the way that they once were. Again, reflecting a theme that recurs throughout the volume, Australia finds itself in an increasingly close economic embrace of China—driven by Beijing's huge appetite for Australian raw materials and energy—but remains diffident about Beijing's strategic ambitions, China's potential for rivalry with the United States and India, and the prospect that Canberra might be confronted by unpalatable choices if it were forced to take sides in any future confrontation among these giants.

What complicates matters further—and in a different way from many other countries examined in this book—is that Australia's economic relations with India are also booming, even as its own trade with China continues to dominate. Medcalf notes that "India has become Australia's fourth-largest export market and one of its fastest-growing," thus making the search for an enhanced partnership with New Delhi a self-recommending proposition. But, as U.S. policymakers can readily attest, this quest can also be frustrating, despite the common values and interests otherwise shared with India. This challenge notwithstanding, Medcalf argues that Australia, just like the United States, will slowly, hesitatingly, yet inexorably, drift toward the following strategy to deal with the concurrent rise of China and India: Canberra will seek to protect the gains accruing from its strong economic partnership with Beijing and its growing ties with New Delhi, while simultaneously increasing its own military capabilities, energizing the security alliance with the United States, and deepening the strategic partnerships with its fellow Asian democracies—including India, especially in a trilateral context involving the United States—as the best insurance in case Chinese assertiveness were to become dangerous in the Indo-Pacific.

The Russian reaction to the emergence of China and India is fascinating because until not so long ago the former Soviet Union had an uncomfortably antagonistic relationship with Beijing and a close strategic partnership with New Delhi. As Dmitri Trenin's chapter details, Russia's relations with both countries are now in the midst of a profound transformation, embedded as they are in the as yet incomplete struggle between Russia's European and Asian identities, its important but fragile relationship with the United States, and its ongoing effort to integrate its far eastern provinces into the national mainstream. Against this backdrop, the recent rise of Chinese power has been nothing short of cataclysmic because it overturns the traditional power relationships existing between Moscow and Beijing for much of the modern era. While China's ascendency undoubtedly offers benefits to Russia—China remains a large market for Russian energy and raw materials; a significant, though less reliable, consumer of Russian arms; and a provider of space for Russian political maneuver because of Beijing's own rivalry with the United States—China also remains a serious long-term competitor that could end up coveting Russian territory, replacing Russia as a major arms exporter, and overwhelming it through sheer asymmetries in economic growth and technological modernization. For these reasons, Trenin concludes that "constructing an essential equilibrium in its relations with Beijing is Moscow's prime policy goal."

In contrast to the relationship with China, Russia's ties with India are comfortable enough to permit Moscow's "unreservedly welcoming India's rise." Thanks to strong past friendship and the benefits afforded by distance, Indo-Russian relations have been "not merely peaceful but virtually problem-free," as New Delhi is perceived by Moscow as a "friend for all times." But this favorable disposition is challenged, like many other bilateral partnerships with India, by "weak economic foundation[s] and [the] primitive infrastructure of Russo-Indian ties." The rise of the United States as India's newest strategic partner only complicates matters further, but the central challenge bedeviling Indo-Russian relations is their lack of depth. With the passing of the old, amicable intergovernmental ties, nothing has yet been found to replace them. Consequently, while India's growth does not threaten Russia in a way that China's could, New Delhi has yet to find new avenues through which it could aid Moscow as the latter redefines its own global role.

The three regional studies that conclude this volume capture the diversity of Asian responses to the rise of China and India, while still reflecting the theme running throughout the volume: the rise of the two Asian giants offers new economic opportunities for collective growth, but China's outward-looking economic strategy tends to have a more palpable impact on its neighbors, who, even while benefiting from its ascendancy, seek to diversify their engagement to include India as an additional source of growth, if not assurance. The three regions surveyed in this volume represent the spectrum of how this dynamic plays out: the Central Asian states remain increasingly integrated with China, much less so with India; the South Asian states are split down the middle, with Pakistan actively allying with China against India, while the smaller regional entities cautiously seek to benefit from India's rise; and the Southeast Asian region, though actively trading with China, looks just as insistently to India to play a complementary role that offsets Beijing's predominance.

S. Enders Wimbush's examination of Central Asia is grounded in the proposition that Central Asia, far from being a homogenous post-Soviet space, consists of multiple self-regarding entities that cooperate and compete among themselves in different ways. These states remain buffeted by many outsiders—not just China and India, but Russia, the United States, the Persian Gulf states, Turkey, and, to a lesser extent, Europe. Of these, China and Russia remain preeminent in influence, the former dominating their economic interests and the latter their politics. Wimbush sums up the situation elegantly by noting that most of the local powers

> see China as the emerging hegemon in the region. Russia, in contrast, remains a force to be mollified despite being eclipsed by China across most measures of power and influence. India remains in the distant background, a rumor of economic power and technological accomplishment. It is not in the same league as China or Russia, nor half so visible, but is potentially a future balancer of either or both.

Like in many other places, India remains in Central Asia largely as a potential force, while China is active in the here and now, dominating the region's energy resources and transportation infrastructure and shaping interstate relations through the Shanghai Cooperation Organisation. The Central Asian states have welcomed China's economic engagement and, though aware of the risks to their political interests, appear to have acquiesced to its regional predominance because of the benefits it brings and because both sides share common adversaries in the form of Islamist extremism. In this newest version of the Great Game, all the local states have actively sought India's interest and investment in the region, but lacking China's two great advantages—contiguous territory and deep pockets—New Delhi has ended up only a bit player in this critical quadrant of Asia despite enjoying old ties, cultural links, and personal relationships with key Central Asian leaders.

If Central Asia remains an arena where China continues to enjoy lopsided advantages over India, South Asia—New Delhi's own natural hinterland—displays a Janus-faced response to the growth of its largest constituent state. As Teresita Schaffer's chapter on the region conveys clearly, India's ascendency remains Pakistan's worst "strategic nightmare," thanks to the ongoing security competition between the two states, whereas the rise of China is viewed by Islamabad as "an opportunity to curb India's advancement and reduce dependence on the United States." In contrast to Pakistan, whose animosity toward India is unyielding, the other, smaller South Asian states have more relaxed attitudes toward India, though these stances have varied considerably depending on the political exigencies of the day.

In general, South Asia remains one of the most poorly integrated regions in the world for complex reasons having to do with geopolitics, national economic strategies, and historical legacies. The pressures for greater integration, however, are rising, but unlike China's trade-driven economic growth, which opens larger vistas for exchange across borders, India's domestic consumption-driven growth model has opened fewer opportunities. Increasingly, however, several smaller countries such as Afghanistan, Bangladesh, Nepal, and Sri Lanka see benefits to be gained from greater connectivity with India's growth, and all "accept India's primacy in their region," even if at times they do not welcome it. China's ascendency, in this context, lacks immediate impact. Although Beijing has become more active in South Asia in recent years—partly in response to the smaller states seeking increased autonomy vis-à-vis India—New Delhi's weight is sufficiently overwhelming that any overtures toward China can only occur with Indian acquiescence.

Of the three regions explored in the book, the last, Southeast Asia, is in many ways not only directly critical to U.S. economic and geopolitical interests but also most fascinating because it lies at the intersection of the old Sinic and Indian empires. The region also hosts the critical waterways through which raw materials, energy, and finished goods travel across the Indo-Pacific. Almost all the regional states today are deeply integrated into the East Asian economic system centered on China. As Carlyle Thayer's chapter describes in some detail, Southeast Asian states value the benefits that China's rise brings them in economic terms; yet because they are relatively small and weak compared to China, they are fearful of what growing Chinese power may mean for their security. In attempting to manage this challenge, these states have relied on a combination of instruments: the Association of Southeast Asian Nations (ASEAN) as a device for preserving their autonomy; larger pan-Asian institutions such as the ASEAN Regional Forum (ARF), Asia-Pacific Economic Cooperation (APEC), the ASEAN Free Trade Area (AFTA), and the East Asia Summit (EAS); the security guarantees and military presence of the United States; and, more recently, deepened engagement with extraregional powers such as Japan and India in an effort to simultaneously enmesh and balance rising Chinese power.

The Southeast Asian solution to the rise of China and India has thus centered on welcoming the ascendency of both powers, seeking to profit from greater economic integration with both, and soliciting their participation in larger regional institutions, while—with an anxious eye on China—encouraging "the United States to remain engaged in the region while viewing India as adding ballast—that is, geostrategic weight—to relations with China." By so doing, the Southeast Asian states seek to deter China from utilizing its growing strength for coercive purposes and, so long as Beijing refrains from behaving threateningly, hope to avoid being put in a position where they are "forced to choose between external powers." Unlike in the other two regions investigated in this volume, India's growing economic involvement in East Asia, its comparative advantages in sea power vis-à-vis China, its easy access to the region unconstrained by geography and aided by both geopolitics and history, and the assurance that derives from its increasingly closer relations with the United States make New Delhi a welcome and valued ally in the regional effort to develop a stable equilibrium vis-à-vis a rising China.

Conclusion

The current wave of globalization created and sustained by U.S. power in the postwar period has proved to be the most fecund of the three iterations witnessed thus far in the modern era. It has generated substantial increases in economic growth and human welfare, shifting in the process the center of gravity in the international system from West to East. The rise of China, followed by India, remains only the most recent manifestation of this fundamental power shift in global politics. Because the growth of these two new centers has had enormously beneficial effects for their own populations and for the international economy more generally, the United States has not merely supported China's and India's rise but welcomed it.

Yet there is no denying the fact that the deepening globalization that has nurtured the growing economic power of these two states has not eradicated the traditional security competition endemic to international politics but rather has transmogrified it in complex and challenging ways. Beijing's ascendency in particular—because China is the larger and the faster growing of the two Asian giants—has resurrected concerns throughout the Asian continent and in the United States about what China's rise implies for regional security. That China remains governed by an authoritarian regime, has a long history of superordination in East Asia, and nurtures a troublesome streak of nationalism domestically only accentuates these anxieties. While all Beijing's partners nonetheless seek to maximize the gains arising from China's growth and their own deep linkages with its expanding economy, they are looking simultaneously for alternative instruments that could limit their own vulnerability to the potential threats that could be posed by an ever stronger China.

Both the United States and India figure prominently in this connection—the former as the traditional hegemonic provider in Asia and globally, the latter as the new rising power that, although weaker than China today, not only possesses the potential of becoming a significant counterweight to Beijing in tandem with other important littoral states but also appears less threatening because of its democratic polity and its culture of strategic restraint. The United States and the other Asian powers, therefore, have sought to deepen their ties with New Delhi in recent years—all in the hope that creating sturdy links among the key nations on China's periphery will produce objective constraints that might limit Beijing's potential to abuse its growing power, even as all its partners continue to profit from its ongoing growth. Whether this solution is capable of generating simultaneously the requisite deterrence and reassurance that sustains stability in Asia remains to be seen. But until a better solution to the problems of preserving security under conditions of economic interdependence is devised, the regional interest in engaging India, while continuing to rely deeply on the United States, will persist.

STRATEGIC ASIA 2011–12

SPECIAL STUDY

EXECUTIVE SUMMARY

This chapter examines how Asia's rise relates to classic questions about the integration of rising powers into the international system.

MAIN ARGUMENT:
The shift of wealth and power from the North Atlantic to the Asia-Pacific, accompanied by the rise of new powers, is creating a crisis in international governance that will challenge the legitimacy of the U.S.-led order and compel the U.S. to find ways to accommodate this new distribution of power. While liberalism suggests that interdependence, international institutions, nuclear weapons, and new forms of security threats will impel nations to cooperate, realism holds that the new distribution of power will create the kind of tensions that have been historically resolved through war. Asia's first modern power, early twentieth-century Japan, provides an example of the failure to manage a new rising power. This and other precedents suggest that Europe's history of interstate conflict could be Asia's future. While theories based on history are often upended by surprise events, such theories can also sharpen the questions we ask about future changes and how we should prepare for and respond to them.

POLICY IMPLICATIONS:
- The key issue is whether the U.S. and other status quo states are willing to concede enough to satisfy rising powers without compromising their own values or appearing weak. If they are not, the rising powers will likely attempt to change the system.

- Asia is in an interregnum, lacking a structure for coping with its diverse peoples and tensions. Though Asian countries are seeking their own norms and will not be satisfied to have them imposed from outside, the number and diversity of actors will complicate creating new rules and institutions.

- All rising states in the modern era have been driven by nationalism, and China will prove no exception. It is unlikely that China will be smoothly integrated into the evolving U.S.-led international order.

International Order and the Rise of Asia: History and Theory

Kenneth B. Pyle

The great, still unresolved issue of our time is how to achieve a legitimate and lasting international order. In a world of sovereign states, how is order created and maintained? Why does it so often break down? Can order be maintained so as to manage changes in the distribution of power? Is war inherent to great-power transitions? And of most immediate concern today, how best can newly rising powers be accommodated into governance of international order? Such questions are complex and have long preoccupied historians and theorists of international relations, but there is greater urgency for answers today in light of the dramatic shifts in power that are underway and a past that demonstrates that redistribution of power often creates conflict. The problem is endlessly debated by theorists, but it is not an academic issue. Rather, it is one with which today's policymakers must constantly wrestle.

The world is experiencing a massive shift of wealth and power from the North Atlantic to the Asia-Pacific region, and this shift is accompanied not only by a redistribution of regional wealth and power but also by the rise of new powers with new ambitions. History has taught us to regard the rise of a new power with great caution. The rise of an entire region and its new powers demands all the more attention. Integrating this new regional power center and its rising states into the international system will require policies of unusual wisdom and whatever useful lessons scholars can offer.

Kenneth B. Pyle is the Henry M. Jackson Professor of History and Asian Studies at the University of Washington and Founding President of The National Bureau of Asian Research. He can be reached at <kbp@uw.edu>.

The rise of the West in modern times was stunning in its extent. The technological changes begun by the Industrial Revolution were of so great a magnitude that they gave Western peoples a military and economic advantage large enough to transform their relationship to other peoples of the world. Asia, which by virtue of its larger population had previously accounted for a far-larger portion of world manufacturing output than Europe, was now abruptly relegated to a position of backwardness. Owing to new economic forces and improvements in transport and communication, Asia was drawn increasingly into an integrated global economy centered on the North Atlantic. Industrial developments translated into greatly enhanced military power, and the West, which in 1800 had controlled 55% of the world's land surface, increased this figure to 67% in 1878 and 84% by 1914.[1]

As stunning as the speed and extent of the rise of the West was, the shift in wealth and power from West to East that began at the end of the twentieth century will be even faster.[2] The end of the Cold War opened a new era for Asia. After being dominated by the Eurocentric world throughout the modern era, Asia began to come into its own—increasingly subject to its own internally generated dynamics. A region that had been a colonial backwater when the Cold War began was the emerging new center of world power and influence. For the first time in modern history, Asian nations acquired the power to adopt active roles in the international system and shape the regional order. Also for the first time, two Asian nations in particular are rising in a fashion bound to have an impact on the issue of order. Asia's share of global output, which was 16% in 1950 and rose to 34% in 1998, is projected to reach 44% by 2030 and be larger than that of Europe and the United States combined.[3]

In the two centuries since the Industrial Revolution, with a huge preponderance in power over Asia and the rest of the world, the West had the capacity to construct the governance of the international system. In the twentieth century, it was principally the United States that used its power to shape the institutions of the system according to its own interests and values. The rapid growth of the wealth and economic power of China and the rest of Asia will challenge the legitimacy of the U.S.-led order and compel it to find ways to accommodate this new distribution of power. The international order faces an impending crisis of governance. Will the

---

[1] See D.K. Fieldhouse, *The Colonial Empires: A Comparative Survey from the Eighteenth Century* (London: Weidenfeld and Nicolson, 1966), 178.

[2] To view this shift from West to East on the broadest possible historical canvas, see Ian Morris, *Why the West Rules—For Now: The Patterns of History and What They Reveal about the Future* (New York: Farrar, Straus and Giroux, 2010).

[3] See Ashley J. Tellis, "Power Shift: How the West Can Adapt and Thrive in an Asian Century," German Marshall Fund of the United States, Asia Papers Series, January 22, 2010.

United States agree to relinquish its hegemonic authority and control to include a wider set of states in governing the international system? Will China, the most powerful of the newly emerging states, seek a fundamental revision of the international order to fit its own national aspirations and cultural norms?[4]

The prospect of such rapid power transition from one region of the world to another has brought an unprecedented awareness and examination of this process and the dynamics of international change. Never before, among theorists and statesmen or among commentators in the mass media, has there been such a degree of reflection on the implications of the rise of new powers. The newly rising powers themselves are extraordinarily self-conscious of the historical precedents. In 2003 and 2004, China's most senior leaders set aside time to receive lectures and together study the past history of the rise of great powers. Likewise, over a two-week period in 2006, China Central Television screened a twelve-part documentary entitled "The Rise of the Great Powers" during prime time. Scholars from abroad such as Yale historian Paul Kennedy appeared in the series, which examined the history of nine great powers—Portugal, Spain, the Netherlands, Great Britain, France, Germany, Japan, Russia, and the United States. The documentary gave particular attention to Japan, the first modern Asian power, and the lessons of its rise. The television series raised the question of whether war and destruction, which had hitherto been the result of the rise of a new power, would be the future for China. Past experience seemed to confirm such pessimism. In response to the worldwide attention to China's rise, Chinese leaders have been at pains to emphasize that theirs will be a "peaceful rise."

In the United States, the question of whether China's rise is bound to bring conflict was uppermost in the minds of policymakers and commentators when President Hu Jintao made his state visit to Washington in January 2011. In an address on the eve of Hu's visit, Secretary of State Hillary Clinton admitted that "history teaches that the rise of new powers often ushers in periods of conflict and uncertainty," but she dismissed such bleak theorizing. "In the 21st century, it does not make sense to apply zero-sum 19th century theories of how major powers interact." She offered a more sanguine view. Conditions in international relations have changed. In the context of a "new and more complicated landscape," U.S.-China relations

---

[4] For an excellent probing of the future of the economic dimensions of world governance posed by the emerging states, see Michael Spence, *The Next Convergence: The Future of Economic Growth in a Multispeed World* (New York: Farrar, Straus and Giroux, 2011).

cannot be fitted neatly into "black and white categories like friend or rival."[5] The zero-sum nineteenth-century theories to which Clinton referred are the theories of classical realism that came out of the experience of Europe and that have become the dominant tradition in international relations theory. Her reference to a "new and more complicated landscape" undoubtedly implies the newer tradition of liberal analysts who believe that conditions such as the growth of interdependence, international institutions, and lethal new weaponry have changed the dynamics of world politics and impelled nations to cooperate.

Realists would not disagree that the dynamics of international politics are different today from what they were in the nineteenth century, but would insist, nevertheless, that the continuities in international relations remain stubbornly persistent. As Aaron Friedberg observed in the last volume of *Strategic Asia*,

> Despite changes in technology, patterns of economic exchange, the role of nonstate actors, and the increasing prominence of international rules and institutions, the stability and character of relations in any system of states is still largely determined by the distribution of power among those states… "Hard power"—measured roughly by the size and sophistication of a nation's economic, scientific, and industrial base, and the quality and quantity of its armed forces—remains the essential currency of politics among nations.[6]

If the continuities in the "deep structure" of international order outweigh the changes in the 21st century, the rise of Asia and its powers raises the stark question that Friedberg posed in the title of a recent essay: "Will Europe's past be Asia's future?"[7]

Europe's Past and Realist Theory

Realist thought is commonly traced to the philosophic-historical reflections of Thucydides and to the more concrete prescriptions of Machiavelli, but it was especially during the centuries of conflict in the tightly woven European state system that modern realism was incubated.[8] Statesmen from Richelieu to Bismarck depended on the principles of

---

[5] Hillary Rodham Clinton, "Inaugural Richard C. Holbrooke Lecture on a Broad Vision of U.S.-China Relations in the 21st Century," U.S. Department of State, January 14, 2011, http://www.state.gov/secretary/rm/2011/01/154653.htm.

[6] Aaron L. Friedberg, "The Geopolitics of Strategic Asia, 2000–2020," in *Strategic Asia 2010–11: Asia's Rising Power and America's Continued Purpose*, ed. Ashley J. Tellis, Andrew Marble, and Travis Tanner (Seattle: National Bureau of Asian Research, 2010), 25.

[7] Aaron L. Friedberg, "Will Europe's Past Be Asia's Future?" *Survival* 42, no. 3 (Autumn 2000): 147–60.

[8] See Ashley J. Tellis, "Reconstructing Political Realism: The Long March to Scientific Theory," *Security Studies* 5, no. 2 (Winter 1995/96): 3–94.

realpolitik, *raison d'etat*, and balance of power to regulate relations among states. Order became dependent on assessing power relations and the opportunistic adjustment to changing circumstances. There were periods when equilibrium was achieved; for example, Voltaire observed in 1751 that Europe was "a sort of great republic divided into several states, some monarchical, the others mixed...but all in harmony with each other, all possessing the same religious foundation...all possessing the same principles of public and political law, unknown in other parts of the world." The European states were "above all...at one in the wise policy of maintaining among themselves as far as possible an equal balance of power."[9] During the decades after the Napoleonic Wars, the Concert of Europe succeeded in solidifying a balance by agreeing on principles designed to keep the peace. By the beginning of the nineteenth century, Great Britain's role as a balancer, pragmatically intervening on the continent when equilibrium was threatened, became a matter of conscious British strategy and contributed to the maintenance of order.

Nevertheless, as the historian Leopold von Ranke's famous 1833 essay on *die grossen Machte* (the great powers) stressed, interstate conflict and competition were persistent. States were committed to pursuing power at each other's expense, he wrote, and must give constant attention to the balance of power. The existence of the state depended on constant struggle: "The world has been parceled out. To be somebody you have to rise by your own efforts. You must achieve genuine independence. Your rights will not be voluntarily ceded to you. You must fight for them." Counseling the Prussian state, Ranke and his disciples urged *der Primat der Aussenpolitik* (the primacy of foreign policy): the dangers of war and defeat required that foreign policy take precedence. Domestic policy must be subordinated to the exigencies of foreign affairs and the state must organize itself internally so as to succeed externally. "The position of a state in the world," Ranke wrote, "depends upon the degree of independence it has attained. It is obliged, therefore, to organize all its internal resources for the purpose of self-preservation. This is the supreme law of the state."[10]

The unification of Germany and the aspiration of the newly formed state to enhance its military power and catch up with the early industrial nations brought new turmoil to the European state system. Bismarck worked a balance of power strategy with deftness during his tenure as the shaper of foreign policy. After aggressively pursuing German unification,

---

[9] F.H. Hinsley, *Power and the Pursuit of Peace: Theory and Practice in the History of Relations between States* (Cambridge: Cambridge University Press, 1963), 163.

[10] Theodore H. Von Laue, *Leopold Ranke: The Formative Years* (Princeton: Princeton University Press, 1950), 167.

he subsequently acted with notable restraint to tend the balance in the European state system, understanding the limits imposed by the wariness with which other states regarded Germany's growing power. His successors after 1890 lacked the same prudence.

By the end of the nineteenth century, great-power rivalries were playing out in a much wider arena. Far from Europe, they were contested in Asia and Africa over markets and territorial control. Inherent in the imperialist international system was the interrelationship of economics and security, of wealth and power. The advent of industrial civilization made the sustained economic growth that came from modern science and technology essential to the power of the state. According to Robert Gilpin, "economic wealth and military power became increasingly synonymous." As the relative importance of productive technology in the generation of wealth and power grew, "the position of the state in the world market (the so-called international division of labor) became a principal determinant, if not the determinant, of its status in the international system."[11]

As the Industrial Revolution made possible greater wealth and power, swift changes in the distribution of power resulted in new territorial ambitions, armament races, and unrestrained, all-encompassing contests for primacy. The political awakening of the masses and their mobilization as a matter of national strength provoked a nationalism that eroded any sense of shared values that remained from the Concert of Europe.

New powers Germany, Italy, Japan, and the United States emerged at the beginning of the twentieth century. The challenge of integrating these new rising powers and their conflicting ambitions into a stable order ultimately proved beyond the capacity of statesmen. On the eve of World War II, British scholar E.H. Carr, observing that "the science of international politics is in its infancy," questioned whether it was possible to achieve peaceful change in the face of such rapid shifts in the distribution of power.[12]

Realist Theory in the United States

It was in the United States after 1945, when scholars became preoccupied with American world power and the onset of the Cold War, that the academic field of international relations flowered. As Stanley Hoffman observed, the study of international relations theory became a

---

[11] Robert Gilpin, *War and Change in World Politics* (Cambridge: Cambridge University Press, 1981), 124, 134.

[12] E.H. Carr, *The Twenty Years' Crisis, 1919–1939* (London: MacMillan, 1962), 1.

quintessentially American social science. Born and raised in the United States, the discipline grew up in the shadow of the immense U.S. role in world affairs. But it drew early inspiration from Hans Morgenthau and other realist scholars who had immigrated from abroad:

> They often served as conceptualizers, and blended their analytic skills with the research talents of the "natives." Moreover, they brought with them a sense of history, an awareness of the diversity of social experiences, that could only stir comparative research and make something more universal of the frequently parochial American social science...In addition to Morgenthau, there was a galaxy of foreign-born scholars, all concerned with transcending empiricism: the wise and learned Arnold Wolfers, Klaus Knorr, Karl Deutsch, Ernest Haas, George Liska, and the young Kissinger and Brzezinski, to name only a few. They...wanted to find out the meaning and the causes of the catastrophe that had uprooted them, and perhaps the keys to a better world.[13]

In the time since the pioneers in this emerging field wrote in the early post–World War II era, a rich and burgeoning body of realist theory on the problem of international order—how it is devised and sustained, why it breaks down, and how it is re-established—has grown, replete with controversies and competing theories. Most notably, the realist school in the United States developed an approach to interstate relations that answered major questions of international order by treating its dynamics as operating like a system in which states pursue strategies of self-interest according to observable patterns.

How Is Order Created?

Drawing on the experience of the European state system, a systemic approach to international relations emerged out of the application of theories of economics to the framework of state action. In this view, nation-states that come into regular interaction constitute an international system. The interaction of states, seeking wealth and power in the struggle for survival, could be analyzed like the competitive behavior of firms rationally seeking out of self-interest to maximize profits by cost-benefit analysis. The interactions are generally anarchic—not in the sense that they are chaotic but rather in that there are no formal organs of government that are supreme. In the absence of a central authority to maintain order, states cannot be sure of other states' intentions. They have no choice, therefore, but to seek constantly to maximize their own power, even though these actions will increase the insecurity of other states and cause those states to take further steps to protect themselves. In this anarchic environment,

---

[13] Stanley Hoffman, "An American Social Science: International Relations," *Daedalus* 106, no. 3 (Summer 1977): 41–60.

the strongest nations will try to establish order by using their power to construct a framework of rules and practices that will secure their interests. In this way, a stable order may be attained. The unequal distribution of power among states results in a recognized hierarchy of prestige, which is an essential element in a stable order. Countries respect and are reluctant to challenge a nation known for its power. Prestige is akin to authority in domestic politics.

The dominant states, relying on their military, economic, and even cultural power and prestige, shape the system's fundamental rules, principles, and institutions. The values and interests of the dominant states establish the prevailing mores or ideology that gives the system its distinctive character and serves to legitimate the authority exercised by the dominant states. That is, once an order is established, ordinarily through the exercise of raw military power in war, the dominant powers underwrite their position through a legitimating ideology. The weaker states in the system are compelled to play by the rules of the game that are established by the dominant powers. The realist tradition holds that the international system shapes the pattern of behavior of an individual state. Structure influences behavior.

In his influential approach, known as structural realism, Kenneth Waltz sometimes sounded very much like Ranke. Waltz saw the international system as "a self-help system…in which those who do not help themselves, or who do so less effectively than others, will fail to prosper, will lay themselves open to dangers, will suffer."[14] Structural realism held that states act primarily out of the strategic needs of the international system rather than to further domestic ends; external pressures weigh more heavily than domestic politics in determining a state's international behavior. That is, "states conduct their foreign policy for 'strategic' reasons, as a consequence of international pulls and pushes, and not to further domestic ends."[15]

The realist claim that a nation's foreign policy is determined less by domestic politics and more by a state's position in the international system gives realism a predictive ability, but lays it open to the criticism that it is deterministic and underrates the role of domestic factors in the determination of a state's foreign policy. Realists such as Waltz strongly disagreed with their critics who held that the internal organization of states was the key to understanding their external behavior. Although he would not deny the influence of domestic politics, Waltz contended that in the

---

[14] Kenneth Waltz, *Theory of International Politics* (Reading: Addison-Wesley, 1979), 118.

[15] Fareed Zakaria, "Realism and Domestic Politics: A Review Essay," in *The Perils of Anarchy: Contemporary Realism and International Security*, ed. Michael E. Brown, Sean M. Lynn-Jones, and Steven E. Miller (Cambridge: MIT Press, 1995), 464.

formation of foreign policy "the pressures of [international] competition weigh more heavily than ideological preferences or internal pressures."[16]

Nevertheless, many theorists insist on retaining an important role for domestic politics as the source of foreign policy, observing that in different countries statesmen react differently to the same environment. No historian could discount the role of an occasional leader (a Bismarck, for example) in changing the direction of events. In other words, even where the influence of the external environment is the strongest, a considerable margin of choice remains. Therefore, after assessing the influence of international structure, one must turn to domestic politics—to the role of elites, their values and perceptions, their definition of national interest, their distinctive sense of national identity—or to the occasional decisive leader.

How Do Systems Change?

An international order is dynamic, and its power relationships change and shift over time. At momentous times in modern history, the structure of the international system undergoes profound changes as pressures build. The systemic approach explains such moments as resulting from shifts in the distribution of power among states. The relative strength of nations is subject to constant change, which has become more rapid since the rise of industrial civilization. The interplay between economics and strategic power became especially defining as industrialization became the foundation of military power. As Robert Gilpin put it, "a distinguishing feature of the modern world has been that superior economic competitiveness and superior military power have tended to accompany one another."[17] States keenly recognize the need to be both rich and strong, to enhance their wealth and power, and to use their productive economic resources as efficiently as possible. Nations, therefore, rise and decline, owing to their uneven rate of growth and to the technological and organizational breakthroughs that bring advantage to one state or another. Some states grow more rapidly than others. The strong states must constantly see to their sources of power lest they become wedded to the status quo and lose their vitality.

For an international system to be stable and enduring, the most powerful states must be satisfied with the existing territorial, political, and economic framework. They must be committed to upholding the status quo, and its governing institutions and norms, through their prestige and their willingness to use force to preserve the order. The legitimacy of the rules and institutions

---

[16] Kenneth Waltz, "Reflections on Theory of International Politics: A Response to My Critics," in *Neorealism and Its Critics*, ed. Robert O. Keohane (New York: Columbia University Press, 1986), 323.

[17] Gilpin, *War and Change*, 139.

must continue to be widely accepted. Legitimacy implies, as Kissinger observed with regard to the Concert of Europe, "the acceptance of the framework of the international order by all the major powers, at least to the extent that no state is so dissatisfied that, like Germany after the Treaty of Versailles, it expresses its dissatisfaction in a revolutionary foreign policy."[18]

What Is the Character of Rising Powers?

As the distribution of power changes among the major states, rising powers test the stability and equilibrium of a system.[19] As they become stronger and richer, they expect to exercise a greater influence, commensurate with their new capabilities. If this is denied to them, if they are not accommodated, they may turn revisionist. Rising powers may be tempted either by opportunities offered to them where obstacles are surmountable to expand their access to new territories, new sources of raw materials, and markets or by the lure of intangible gains in prestige, leadership, and security. Depending on many factors, including the degree of alienation, the nature of domestic politics, and the willingness and skill of the other powers to cope with dissatisfaction, a rising power may be prepared to seek the overthrow of the existing system.

As Gilpin observes, using terms of cost-benefit analysis, "the critical significance of the differential growth of power among states is that it alters the cost of changing the international system and therefore the incentives for changing the international system."[20] A rising power may seek to revise that order and may even come to believe that its interests lie in contesting and overthrowing the order along with its rules and institutions. If that state succeeds in challenging the old order, often through warfare that results in a new distribution of power among states, a fundamental change in the organization and governance of the international system occurs.

Nationalism as a characteristic of rising powers is a wild card that realists have generally not found ways to incorporate as a powerful motivating force. As economic growth brings newly awakened masses into politics, the role of nationalist emotion and its power to drive national behavior become powerful dynamics not readily captured by rational cost-benefit analysis. Bland references to problems of national identity and ideology do not reveal the explosive and volatile force of nationalist

---

[18] Henry A. Kissinger, *A World Restored: Metternich, Castlereagh, and the Problems of Peace, 1812–1822* (Boston: Houghton Mifflin, 1957), 1.

[19] For a thoughtful discussion of the future of China from the perspective of rising powers in history, see Michael D. Swaine and Ashley J. Tellis, *Interpreting China's Grand Strategy: Past, Present, and Future* (Santa Monica: RAND Corporation, 2000), 199–229.

[20] Gilpin, *War and Change*, 95.

emotion that historically is intrinsic to rising powers with past grievances and status ambitions.

Rising states tend to be driven by distinctive complexes of ideas, norms, and values. Their construction of national purpose and mission is a powerful determinant of their international behavior. In the words of Alexander Wendt, "anarchy is what states make of it."[21] Wendt is a leading scholar among the so-called constructivists, who have faulted realism for underplaying the role of ideas and culture in driving change in world politics.

Nationalism is a modern phenomenon constructed by leaders to provide a motivating identity for a people arriving in the international state system and pursuing rapid industrialization. It is an instrument to maintain social cohesion in the midst of the turmoil and tensions accompanying rapid catch-up industrialization. Nationalism is not simply a top-down phenomenon. The mobilization of nationalism is first a tool of leaders, but it easily slips beyond the control of state leadership. It has its most combustible moments when a people is in a rising, nation-building phase and is being drawn into heightened political consciousness. At this stage, nationalism inevitably spills over to have a strong influence on foreign policy. Historically, industrialization has often been accompanied by expansionist impulses. As Samuel Huntington observed, "The external expansion of the U.K. and France, Germany and Japan, the Soviet Union and the United States coincided with phases of intense industrialization and economic development."[22] This is the work of nationalism.

Is Peaceful Change Possible?

Great-power transitions historically have almost always been accompanied by conflict. When mismanaged, as they most often are, power transitions can have cataclysmic consequences. They typically have been accompanied, Gilpin argues, by warfare:

> In these situations, the disequilibrium in the system becomes increasingly acute as the declining power tries to maintain its position and the rising power attempts to revise the system in ways that will advance its interests. As a consequence of this persisting disequilibrium, the international system is beset by tensions, uncertainties, and crises…Throughout history the primary means of resolving the disequilibrium between the structure of the international system and the redistribution of power has been war, more particularly what we shall call a hegemonic war.[23]

---

[21] Alexander Wendt, "Anarchy Is What States Make of It: The Social Construction of Power Politics," *International Organization* 46, no. 2 (Spring 1992): 391–425.

[22] Samuel P. Huntington, "America's Changing Strategic Interests," *Survival* 33, no. 1 (January/February 1991): 12.

[23] Gilpin, *War and Change*, 197.

War need not be inevitable, however. British willingness to appease the United States at the beginning of the twentieth century is an exception that will be discussed below.

The challenge for statesmanship is how to avoid war and maintain peace in the midst of such fundamental shifts in relative power among nations. Often the primary issue is whether the status quo powers are willing to make concessions generous enough to satisfy the revisionist power without seeming to appease or confess weakness. The political historian David Calleo, reflecting on the onset of World War I, wrote that "geography and history conspired to make Germany's rise late, rapid, vulnerable, and aggressive. The rest of the world reacted by crushing the upstart...Perhaps the proper lesson is not so much the need for vigilance against aggressors, but the ruinous consequences of refusing reasonable accommodation to upstarts."[24] Status quo powers always find not only their interests but also their values endangered by compromise with the rising states. Statesmanship continues to be challenged to find peaceful means to adjust to the consequences of the uneven growth of power among states.

Evolution of the Modern System in East Asia

International relations theory has been built largely on the study of the West. As Gilpin observed pointedly,

> for a profession whose intellectual commitment is the understanding of the interactions of societies, international relations as a discipline is remarkably parochial and ethnocentric. It is essentially a study of the Western state system, and a sizable fraction of the existing literature is devoted to developments since the end of World War II....In large measure...this is because of the paucity of reliable secondary studies of non-Western systems.[25]

Since these words were written, the advance of studies of the non-Western world has begun to repair that shortcoming. Nevertheless, theorists have only made limited efforts to study the way Asian states have acted within the international state system since it was established nearly two centuries ago, when the arrival of the modern world created for the first time a single international system. The Industrial Revolution brought waves of technological advances in transportation and communication that made possible the first truly global international system into which Asia was integrated. During this time, the Sinocentric system was overwhelmed and

---

[24] David Calleo, *The German Problem Reconsidered: Germany and the World Order, 1870 to the Present* (Cambridge: Cambridge University Press, 1978), 6.

[25] Gilpin, *War and Change*, 5.

the West imposed order in the region until Asian states (beginning with Japan) began to rise and challenge the existing order.

Structural realism provides useful categories of analysis with which to trace the evolution of the international system and the successive efforts of the great powers to impose order in East Asia. **Table 1** summarizes the historical record of successive orders in modern Asia and shows their characteristics, their legitimating norms and values, and the dynamics associated with systemic transitions. The distribution of power has provided the effective basis upon which order has been created. The dominant power has set the rules by which nations have been influenced to act and has legitimated its position with an ideology that claims universality. In each case, the dominant powers have constructed a framework of rules, institutions, and practices to secure their interests. The rules of the system cover the conduct of diplomacy and political relations as well as economic and trade relations. Differential growth rates lead to the rise of new powers as challengers and to systemic change.

Destruction of the Sinocentric Order

The Sinocentric order that had governed relations among East Asian states for centuries centered on the theory of the universal preeminence of the Chinese emperor. In the Sinocentric order, the Chinese emperor had to be acknowledged not only as the preeminent temporal power but also as a power of cosmic significance who mediated between heaven and earth. In contrast to the Westphalian concept in Europe of a number of independent nations recognized as theoretically equal with their own independent legitimacy and sovereignty, the Sinocentric concept was one of countries in East Asia subsumed within the Chinese sphere of civilized society. Rulers of the various countries within this sphere were expected to present themselves to the Chinese emperor and be invested with his authority, to receive a seal symbolizing the authority granted, to date all memorials according to the Chinese calendar, and to make regular visits to the Chinese imperial court to reaffirm their subordination. In return these rulers could receive trade benefits, legitimacy, and sometimes security. When put to the test, this system could not cope with the raw military might that the powers of industrial civilization brought to bear.

The First New Order

The first new order in modern Asia, the imperialist system, was the longest lasting of the successive orders. Owing to the huge preponderance of power that the Industrial Revolution gave to the Western powers and

TABLE 1 East Asian orders

Types of structure	Sinocentric	Imperialism (1840–1918)	Washington system (1922–33)	East Asian Co-Prosperity Sphere (1938–45)	Cold War (1950–89)	Post–Cold War order (1989–)*
Character	• Hierarchical	• Informal control for commercial ends • Spheres of influence and colonies	• Multinational cooperation to ensure regional stability	• Japan-centered hierarchy, East Asian autarky	• Bipolar/hegemonic • Ideological and military stalemate • Asian growth under the U.S. umbrella	…
Dynamics of creation	• Premise of the supremacy of Chinese civilization	• Industrial Revolution in the West • The search for trade and materials	• Rise of Japanese power and the Anglo-American desire to contain it	• The Great Depression • Japanese military expansion • Japan's pursuit of regional hegemony	• Rise of Asian Communism • Chinese revolution • The Korean War	…
Dominant actors	• China	• Western powers • Japan	• United States • United Kingdom • Japan	• Japan	• U.S. and Soviet blocs	…
Legitimacy (claim to "universality")	• Ideology of Confucianism and beneficent rule	• The European "standard of civilization" and its formalization in international law	• Wilsonian ideals • Self-determination • Territorial integrity • Open Door policy • Collective security	• Pan-Asianism • anti–Western imperialism • anti-capitalism	• Democratic capitalism vs. Communism	…

Table 1 continued.

Types of structure	Sinocentric	Imperialism (1840–1918)	Washington system (1922–33)	East Asian Co-Prosperity Sphere (1938–45)	Cold War (1950–89)	Post–Cold War order (1989–)*
Rules, government	• System of tributary relations	• Unequal treaties • Cooperative imperialism (MFN)	• League of Nations • Washington treaties • Gold standard	• Proper place • Familial relationships • Division of labor	• Bilateral alliances • Collective security	...
Institutions	• Investiture of rulers of tributary states	• Treaty ports, tariff control, and extraterritoriality • Spheres of influence • Leaseholds	• League of Nations • Naval limitation treaties	• Military control • Great East Asia Conference	• GATT • IMF • World Bank • SEATO • ANZUS	...
Causes of decline	• The inability to cope with Western power	• World War I and the destruction of the old balance of power	• Lack of U.S. leadership • Japanese and Chinese nationalism • The Great Depression • Economic nationalism	• Defeat in war	• Decline of the Soviet Union • Sino-Soviet split • Relative decline of the United States in face of East Asian growth • The rise of economic nationalism	...

NOTE: Asterisk indicates that the post–Cold War era is in a kind of interregnum, lacking a fixed structure and a recognized legitimate order.

to the cooperative framework that they worked out among themselves, the system lasted nearly 80 years from the Treaty of Nanjing in 1842, which ended the Opium War, to the end of World War I. The institutions of this order, a subsystem of the Pax Britannica, were devised initially by the British to satisfy the demands of commercial opinion in the House of Commons. British merchants wanted unfettered access to trade in East Asia, not territorial control. Instead, the British brought to bear sufficient force to exercise "informal imperialism" through imposing treaties that assured "free trade." The imperial powers shaped a distinct body of rights and rules that reflected the values and interests of Western civilization. They called this system "international law" and considered it a code of conduct providing the basis for cooperation among modern states. By the middle of the nineteenth century, they had formulated a "standard of civilization" that must be met if non-European states were to be admitted to this society. A "civilized state" guaranteed the rights of private property and freedom of trade, travel, and religion through an effective system of law, courts, and political organization.

The imperialist system proved durable because the shared values and interests of the powers underwrote the multipolar system. The system took on a multilateral, cooperative, and collaborative character as a result of the most-favored-nation (MFN) clause inserted in treaties, which provided that rights and privileges granted to one power would be extended to the others. For a time at the end of the century, the system teetered on the edge of a scramble for separate spheres of influence, but cooperation was restored, and on the eve of World War I the imperialist order had achieved a kind of equilibrium with the various powers recognizing each other's interests through a series of treaties.

A Peaceful Great-Power Transition

For more than 60 years after the Napoleonic Wars, Britain "ruled the waves," maintaining its primacy in the world's first truly international system by virtue of naval supremacy. In East Asia the British dominated the cooperative system of imperialism until the end of the century. Britain's clear-cut worldwide naval supremacy began to slip, however, as the power of other navies grew. The rise of German naval power posed a growing threat in European waters, and in the western hemisphere the rising naval power of the United States jeopardized Britain's ability to be the unchallenged arbiter of its imperial possessions. In Asia the growing power of Japan eroded British domination of the system of informal imperialism.

As the realization of the relative decline of Britain's naval power sank in, British leaders quietly made momentous decisions that in effect ended their nation's "unique role as the independent, detached arbiter of world affairs."[26] Giving priority to maintaining dominance in European waters, they reduced their naval strength in North America and in East Asia, making diplomatic agreements that would permit the British a reduced presence. In 1901, Britain acquiesced in what it had long resisted: the U.S. ambition to build independently a trans-isthmian canal. The undeniable power of the U.S. Navy was an important part of this decision to appease the Americans. The Spanish-American War in 1898 demonstrated the U.S. military's increased power and gave the United States new possessions in the Caribbean and the Pacific. With the Panama Canal providing the U.S. Navy the ability to move at will between oceans, and with the acquisition of the Philippines and Guam and the annexation of Hawaii, the United States was becoming a power in the Asia-Pacific region.

Only months after this decision to appease the United States, Britain abandoned its "splendid isolation" and entered into an alliance with Japan in 1902. By this diplomatic arrangement, Britain was able to withdraw some of its naval strength on the China coast, balance the rise of Russian power in the region, and still ensure the security of its imperial possessions and trading privileges.

The decision to appease the United States in 1901 and to conclude the Anglo-Japanese alliance in 1902 represented one of the smoothest great-power transitions in modern history. At the time, however, it was a change within the imperialist system rather than a change of the system itself. Undoubtedly, Britain's decision to accommodate the United States was driven by shared values and cultural heritage as well as by the realist appraisal of the cost that a hard-line stance against American ambitions would entail. Within a generation, Britain became the second-ranked naval power, but by establishing a "permanent friendship" with the United States, it prolonged British influence and protected its vital interests. As for Asia, Britain's decision marked the rise of two new great imperial powers in the region, the United States and Japan, whose relations did not proceed as smoothly. Rather, their competition and confrontation ultimately led to the greatest conflict in the history of Asia.

---

[26] Aaron L. Friedberg, *The Weary Titan: Britain and the Experience of Relative Decline, 1895–1905* (Princeton: Princeton University Press, 1988), 152.

Asia's First Rising Power

The devolution of British power in East Asia and the defeat of Russia in 1905 left Japan and the United States facing each other as potential rivals in the region. In many ways, Japan's rise readily fits the classic pattern of realist theory. Whereas other Asian states took refuge in their traditional values and institutions in resisting the imperialist system, Japan's ruling elite, with realist predilections inbred by the longest experience of feudalism in world history, readily grasped the norms and practices that the imperialist system prescribed. With a remarkable pragmatism, Japan accommodated itself to the prevailing structure, adopted the institutions of the great powers, and accepted the principles of "civilization" at the same time that it built its military and industrial power by importing the science and technology of the West. By its pragmatic approach, Japan was readily socialized by the prevailing practices of the international system and emerged as an imperialist power itself. Structural realism could find no better example of its theoretical principles.

As a rising power, Japan became increasingly assertive, expansionist, and challenging to the stability of the international order. Following its success in the Russo-Japanese War, regional hegemony became the goal of an influential segment of the Japanese leadership. After annexing Korea in 1910, Japan occupied German colonial possessions in China and the Pacific when war broke out in Europe in 1914, imposed its "21 Demands" designed to dominate the fledgling Chinese republic in 1915, and dispatched an army force of 70,000 troops into the Russian Far East in 1918. Japan's unilateralism undermined the balance in the Asian system and provoked the animosity of the other powers.

The United States, itself a rising world power, set out not only to contain Japanese expansionism but to bring its own historically shaped values to bear on the workings of the international system. The Americans sought to transcend reliance on the balance of power with a new Wilsonian set of rules and practices to govern the regional system. Applied to Asia at the Washington Conference of 1921–22, the American agenda of liberal internationalism included the establishment of principles of self-determination, respect for territorial integrity, free trade, arms limitation, and collective security. A naval arms limitation agreement, a treaty to guarantee the territorial integrity of China, and a treaty to "consult" should there be any threats to peace in the Pacific constituted the new U.S. order that was to bring stability to the region. For the remainder of the 1920s, the Japanese, in the midst of opening to liberal democratic reforms at home, were willing to accommodate to this new order, seeing their interests as best ensured by cooperation with the established powers—or as one might say in recent parlance, by a "peaceful rise."

Trimming its sails to the demands of the Washington Conference system, however, engendered a deep division within Japan's elite military and political leadership between the accommodationists and the revisionists. The former believed Japanese interests were best served by accommodating to the Anglo-American order while the latter were enraged by the system's containment of Japanese ambitions and determined to challenge the established order. The role of nationalism in domestic politics became a key factor in tilting this debate among the elites. In Japan's modern history, the determination to recover from the humiliation that Western imperialism had brought to Japanese civilization and the drive to catch up with the advanced countries and restore pride in Japanese values were persistent motivations. Through generations of indoctrination, these themes were inculcated in the politically awakened masses. By the 1930s, nationalism had become an all-pervasive influence on decisionmaking.

A combination of the economic vulnerabilities of the United States and Britain, brought on by the Great Depression and the isolationist mood of the Americans, gave the revisionists their opportunity to test the viability of the Washington Conference system. Japan's seizure of Manchuria in 1931, in violation of treaties signed in Washington, revealed the weakness of the system, giving the emboldened revisionists the opportunity to gain power at home and push on to further continental expansion, as well as the determination to shape a new Japan-designed regional order.

In contrast to the transcendental, universal ideals that were written into the Washington system, Japan adopted its own values of respect for hierarchy and status as a basis for international order. It was this principle of observing a just ranking that the Anglo-American powers were accused of violating. On the day of the attack on Pearl Harbor, Japanese diplomats handed to Secretary of State Cordell Hull a memorandum breaking off negotiations and declaring that "it is the immutable policy of the Japanese Government to insure the stability of East Asia and to promote world peace and thereby to enable all nations to find each its proper place in the world."[27]

As the "leading race" of Asia, Japan would create a hierarchical order in which there would be a division of labor with the people of each nation in Asia performing economic functions for which its inherent capabilities prepared it. Nationalist writings often contained themes of pan-Asianism and the liberation of Asians from Western imperialism, and for a time these themes appealed to Asian nationalists seeking liberation from their colonial status.

---

[27] U.S. Department of State, *Papers Relating to the Foreign Relations of the United States: Japan, 1931–1941*, vol. 2 (Washington, D.C.: U.S. Government Printing Office, 1943), 786.

Mismanaging Asia's First Rising Power

U.S.-Japan relations provide a case study of how not to manage the rise of a new great power. American leaders made a series of missteps that helped to bring on a great hegemonic Japanese-U.S. conflict. First, the attempt to create a new regional system at the Washington Conference of 1921–22 was flawed in its conception. While asserting new legalistic principles to replace the balance of power, the U.S.-inspired regional order failed to provide an enforcement mechanism, instead relying on the sway of international opinion and moral suasion to maintain these principles. For an international system to be stable and enduring, the most powerful states must be committed to upholding the governing institutions and norms through their prestige and their willingness to use force to preserve the system. While declaring ratios of naval strength, the United States neglected to maintain these ratios, whereas Japan built up to and beyond the agreed levels. At the Washington Conference, the United States had signed the Nine Power Treaty, which committed the country to upholding the territorial integrity of China, but when the order faced its ultimate test in Japan's 1931 seizure of Manchuria, the United States chose to let the violation stand and for the remainder of the decade disengaged from Asia, creating a vacuum of power that Japan was ready to fill.

Second, the United States failed to engage a proud and sensitive nation—a nation that it had little interest or capability to understand or appreciate. The treatment of the immigration issue at Versailles and in the Immigration Act of 1924, which in effect singled out the Japanese for no further immigration to the United States, was a continuous source of antagonism that played into Japanese nationalist feeling. Rising states present a special challenge to a system. As one writer observes, "the status quo powers must exhibit empathy, fairness, and a genuine concern not to offend the prestige and national honor of the rising power."[28] This the Anglo-American powers had not done. They failed to reach out to, much less understand, this proud but highly vulnerable and insecure new power. The psychic wound inflicted by Western imperialism at the time Japan entered the modern international system was repeatedly reopened by experiences it had in this system.

Third, the United States was inconsistent and unpredictable in its policies toward Japanese expansionist ambitions. After first establishing a framework at the Washington Conference designed to contain these ambitions, the United States retreated into isolationism and protectionism

---

[28] Randall L. Schweller, "Managing the Rise of Great Powers: History and Theory," in *Engaging China: The Management of an Emerging Power*, ed. Alastair Iain Johnston and Robert Ross (New York: Routledge, 1999), 15.

and abandoned the liberal principles of the Western-imposed East Asian order. After Japan's success in seizing Manchuria and when it became clear that the Washington system could muster no credible opposition to Japan's flouting of the system's principles, revisionist sentiment gained ascendancy among Japan's leadership. Emboldened by its success, Japan openly defied the Washington accords and set out to establish a regional hegemony. Belatedly in the summer of 1941 the United States sought to reinstate the liberal principles upon which it originally created the order. Too late the Americans constructed a deterrent strategy, using Japan's trade and resource dependence to exercise leverage over its foreign policies. Lurching from prolonged neglect of Japanese expansion to imposing an embargo and requiring total Japanese capitulation—withdrawal from Southeast Asia and China—as the price for lifting it, the administration managed policy in such an inconsistent and clumsy fashion that it helped to bring on war. It failed to negotiate in a step-by-step process that might have averted conflict. U.S. policymakers did not see that they had presented Japan with "two equally repugnant alternatives," as Scott Sagan has aptly described the situation.[29] Japan was confronted not simply by the prospect of war with a country eight to ten times as powerful as itself but also with the prospect of accepting a settlement that would deny the very self-image that it had of itself as a great power, the prime goal it had pursued for a century. A reading of the records of the conferences of Japanese leaders in the autumn of 1941 makes it clear that the Japanese felt their sense of national identity endangered. It is probably true that "no nation will submit to a settlement…that totally denies its vision of itself."[30]

Finally, as a further mismanagement of its relations with Japan, when war did break out the United States framed war goals in absolute terms. Ruling out any confidential discussion with the enemy as a basis for ending the conflict, Roosevelt cast the war in moral terms as a crusade to rid the world once and for all of militarism. As such, there could be no room for compromise. Rather than fight the war to an armistice and a negotiated peace agreement as all other foreign wars in U.S. history have been waged, this would be fought to total victory. Rather than a war, as the Prussian strategist Carl von Clausewitz would have it, waged to achieve the concrete goals that diplomacy had failed to achieve, the Asia-Pacific War would be fought until the enemy agreed to surrender its sovereignty,

---

[29] Scott D. Sagan writes aptly that "if one examines the decisions made in Tokyo in 1941 more closely, one finds not a thoughtless rush to national suicide, but rather a prolonged, agonizing debate between two repugnant alternatives." See Scott D. Sagan, "The Origins of the Pacific War," in *The Origin and Prevention of Major Wars*, ed. Robert I. Rotberg and Theodore K. Rabb (Cambridge: Cambridge University Press, 1989), 324.

[30] Kissinger, *A World Restored*, 146.

accept permanent disarmament, and have its leaders tried as war criminals, its government re-engineered, and its society re-educated. Demanding unconditional surrender most likely lengthened the conflict, ignored the effect on the postwar balance of power, and contributed to the onset of the next cycle of great-power conflict. In sum, the U.S. management of its competition with Japan for leadership in Asia offers a textbook example of deeply flawed great-power leadership. Whether conflict with Japan of such total and traumatic character could have been avoided remains an issue for counterfactual history.

Is the Fundamental Nature of International Relations Changing?

The example of Japan as Asia's first rising modern power provides a great deal of confirmation of realist theory. The liberal internationalist order, as Wilson and his successors had administered it, was a failure. Liberals, however, are optimistic that there has been learning and progress in managing the problems of the changing distribution of power. Rather than sharing with realists the tragic view of competition for power as inevitable and a cyclical pattern of rise and fall, liberals believe that progress is possible. The failures of Wilson and the shortcomings of Franklin Roosevelt have provided lessons from which an enduring order can be devised.[31]

Liberal analysts believe that realism is growing less persuasive as a way of understanding the fundamental dynamics of international relations. Conditions in the world have changed or are changing in fundamental ways that improve the possibilities of peaceful change. Liberals place great hope in an evolving U.S.-led liberal international order left standing after the collapse of the Soviet system. They point to a number of factors that make war less likely, including the advent of nuclear weapons, the increasing number of democratic states, and the growth of economic interdependence as a result of globalization. But their greatest hope is placed in the development of international institutions. This evolving liberal order has "an unusual capacity to accommodate rising powers. Its sprawling landscape of rules, institutions, and networks provide newer entrants into the system with opportunities for status, authority and a share in the governance of

---

[31] G. John Ikenberry, "Liberal Internationalism 3.0: America and the Dilemmas of Liberal World Order," *Perspectives on Politics* 7, no. 1 (March 2009): 71–87.

the order."[32] This order, writes John Ikenberry, "is easy to join and hard to overturn."[33] The mechanism of hegemonic war as the means to achieve great-power transition is, liberal analysts conclude, no longer necessary.

Another new aspect of international relations that liberals see as significant is a change in the nature of what constitutes security. Rather than the military threats of the past, globalization has brought with it a host of new threats that confront not just the United States but other countries as well: global warming, health pandemics, dwindling energy sources, jihadist terrorism, and so forth. These common threats to the security of all states hold the potential to impel cooperation and encourage integration in a liberal order designed to confront these problems. "All the great powers," Ikenberry avers, "have alignments of interests that will continue to bring them together to negotiate and cooperate over the management of the system. All the great powers—old and rising—are status quo powers."[34]

Liberals see a reformed international order as requiring new or reorganized institutions that will have a more universal aspect in the sense that states are no longer dependent on a unipolar, hegemonic power. The impending crisis of international governance, however, will require the United States to cede a considerable amount of its hegemonic authority and control—much more than Britain did at the beginning of the twentieth century. In that case, Britain's accommodation of the United States was made easier because of shared values and because it prolonged British power and did not immediately change the international system. The impending crisis cannot be settled by simply adjusting voting rights in international organizations such as the Bretton Woods institutions, the International Monetary Fund and the World Bank. The new nature of security threats together with "the human rights revolution" will increasingly require a capacity for the international community to establish rules and institutions that will intrude on domestic politics and erode Westphalian sovereignty.[35] Some new form of constabulary security force that is not dependent on a single country or small group of nations will be required to ensure the legitimacy of the international order.

---

[32] G. John Ikenberry, *Liberal Leviathan: The Origins, Crisis, and Transformation of the American World Order* (Princeton: Princeton University Press, 2011), 345. See also G. John Ikenberry and Thomas Wright, "Rising Powers and Global Institutions," Century Foundation, February 6, 2008, http://www.centuryinstitute.org/list.asp?type=PB&pubid=635.

[33] Ikenberry, *Liberal Leviathan*, 9.

[34] Ibid., 341.

[35] Ikenberry, "Liberal Internationalism 3.0."

Will the Rise of Asia Be Different?

Asia in the post–Cold War era is still in a kind of interregnum (as Table 1 indicates). It lacks a fixed regional structure, a recognized legitimate order to cope with its diverse cultural and political systems, vast differences of wealth and population, competition for energy resources, arms races, border disputes, conflicting historical legacies, rampant nationalisms, and limited experience with multilateral organizations. The future of this rapidly rising region inevitably provokes immense controversy about its future. In addition to the liberal critique of realism's value in viewing the future course of international order, there is the contention of some theorists that because realism has been based on the experience in the West, it will not prove appropriate to forecasting the future of Asia. It was essays by Aaron Friedberg suggesting that Europe's experience held ominous implications for Asia's future that provoked their reaction. Writing in 1994, Friedberg observed that while post–Cold War Europe was finding solutions to its long-term problems with multipolarity, the complex multipolar structure of Asia was "ripe for rivalry." With a group of major powers, including China, Japan, Russia, India, and the United States, and a number of middle-ranking powers, Asia could experience the competitive struggles and rivalries that Europe underwent. He observed that "the half millennium during which Europe was the world's primary generator of war (as well as of wealth and knowledge) is coming to a close. But for better and for worse, Europe's past could be Asia's future."[36] Friedberg and other realists argued that Asia will be characterized by sizeable power asymmetries. Economies will grow at differing rates. Resources, military power, and productive efficiency will be distributed unevenly. Emerging multipolarity in Asia is likely to make the region prone to conflict. Balances of power may emerge, but this is an uncertain process. Coalitions can shift. Occasions for miscalculation can increase. Arms races, border disputes, historical animosities, and nationalisms are apparent. In fact, post–Cold War Asia exhibits much greater complexity than did the historical European state system.

Friedberg's assertion that Asia is likely to become the cockpit of great-power conflict, for all the reasons (and more) that Europe had been, provoked a variety of responses that viewed Asia's future as being determined by different fundamentals from Europe. The theoretical arguments for Asian exceptionalism take different forms. The most common of these is the assertion that Asia is both geographically and culturally distinct from Europe. In this view, the emphasis is on the great size and resources of

---

[36] Aaron L. Friedberg, "Ripe for Rivalry: Prospects for Peace in a Multipolar Asia," *International Security* 18, no. 3 (Winter 1993/94): 5–33. See also Friedberg, "Will Europe's Past Be Asia's Future?"

China as well as on the cultural values of hierarchy that predispose East Asian countries to bandwagon with China. In his influential work, *The Clash of Civilizations and the Remaking of World Order*, Samuel Huntington concluded that

> the choice for Asia is between power balanced at the price of conflict or peace secured at the price of hegemony. Western societies might go for conflict and balance. History, culture, and the realities of power strongly suggest that Asia will opt for peace and hegemony....China is resuming its place as regional hegemon, and the East is coming into its own.

In short, "Asia's past," as Huntington put it, "is Asia's future."[37]

Similarly, David Kang argued that realism "gets Asia wrong" by failing to understand the distinctive cultural mores of Asia. Discerning a trend of Asian countries to cast their lot with a rising China, he traced this to historic traditions of deference to Chinese hegemony. A strong China had been a source of order and as a consequence "East Asian regional relations have historically been hierarchic, more peaceful, and more stable than those in the West."[38]

Still, while one must acknowledge the undeniable differences of Asia's geography and history, these factors are not necessarily enough to dismiss the claims of realist theory. Bandwagoning may be seen as the realistic response to the distribution of power, and therefore, as Friedberg observed in the last volume of *Strategic Asia*, "there is no reason to believe that Asian decisionmakers are any less rational than their counterparts in other parts of the world. If balancing appears fruitless, and possibly dangerous, it should come as no surprise that many will opt for bandwagoning instead."[39]

The liberal optimism that international institutions can succeed in Asia is widely held, especially among Asian scholars. Amitav Acharya, for example, is critical of both the Huntington/Kang thesis and the pessimism of Friedberg: "Western realist pessimism need not be countered by Asian cultural historicism." Faulting Kang for excluding South Asia from his analysis and thus ignoring India's growing role in balancing China, he finds little evidence of genuine bandwagoning with China and argues that "Asia's future will not resemble its past." Acharya draws his optimism from a liberal

---

[37] Samuel P. Huntington, *The Clash of Civilizations and the Remaking of World Order* (New York: Simon Schuster, 1996), 238.

[38] David C. Kang, "Getting Asia Wrong: The Need for New Analytical Frameworks," *International Security* 27, no. 4 (Spring 2003): 66. See also David C. Kang, *China Rising: Peace, Power, and Order in East Asia* (New York: Columbia University Press, 2007); and David C. Kang, *East Asia before the West: Five Centuries of Trade and Tribute* (New York: Columbia University Press, 2010).

[39] Friedberg, "Geopolitics of Strategic Asia," 41.

confidence in "shared regional norms, rising economic interdependence, and growing institutional linkages."[40]

It is true that Asian countries are seeking their own norms and will not be satisfied to have them imposed from outside. Asian leaders since 1989 have with increasing frequency asserted alternative values, institutions, and rules of order. These assertions reject Western claims of universalism as dogmatic and legalistic, and against the "Washington Consensus" they advocate an Asian form of capitalism with a legitimate role for state-led economic growth and, in the cultural sphere, social goals beyond individualism. What this means, of course, is that Asian countries are seeking a greater say in determining the rules and institutions that govern international economic and political affairs.

What Is the Prognosis?

Popular assertions of Asia's distinctive values over those of the West by no means can give confidence to the hopeful expectation of regional cooperation and international harmony. On the contrary, they are more accurately seen as evidence of nationalism arising out of the decolonization struggles and the subsequent process of nation-building. When the Cold War began, most of these countries were newly liberated colonies or, as in the case of China, had newly escaped from imperialist domination. Only Japan had been an industrial nation and had experienced nationalist mobilization of its people. Decolonization, however, completed the modern state system in Asia. During the Cold War, the process of state-building— forming a central state structure, extracting resources, organizing a military, establishing mass education, undertaking rapid catch-up industrialization— inevitably promoted nationalism in Asian countries, but it was restrained and muted by the overlay of the ideological superpower conflicts between democratic capitalism and Communism. With the end of the Cold War, the age of full-blown nationalism arrived in Asia, and it has become the most powerful political emotion. The sheer number and diversity of Asian actors are likely to make agreeing on governing rules and institutions more difficult. The fact that these new actors are experiencing the rise of mass nationalism will further complicate matters.

No historian of the modern world can gainsay the disruptive potential of nationalism. All the rising powers in the last two centuries, especially Asia's first rising power, have been driven by some form of nationalism

---

[40] Amitav Acharya, "Will Asia's Past Be Its Future?" *International Security* 28, no. 3 (Winter 2003/04): 149–64.

that has spilled over into foreign policies pursuing power and advantage. This prospect now seems most germane to the future role of China. China is a "swing state" so far as the liberal expectation of achieving a reformed global order is concerned. The question is: "Will China seek to oppose and overturn the evolving Western-centered liberal international order, or will it integrate into and assert authority within that order?"[41] In the awe and excitement over China's rise, it is easy to overlook the staggering problems in its future. As Michael Spence points out, China is the first country to become a major power at a time when its per capita income is quite low.[42] It still faces the acute problems of nation-building, especially the challenge of incorporating the newly awakened masses into the political community. With the collapse of Marxian socialism, China's leaders face a challenge to their legitimacy at the very time that the social system itself is undergoing massive change, including urbanization that "involves more people leaving the land in a shorter period than at any previous time in human history."[43] Although Minxin Pei has argued that China may be in for a prolonged developmental autocracy, the day will arrive when economic growth slows, social problems become unmanageable, and the leadership will be tempted to turn to a more strident form of nationalism in order to save the regime.[44] Perceived policy failures of the regime might be blamed on foreign treachery or domestic rivals. Unity will be sought to meet the crisis of the state. Under such conditions, a smooth integration into the evolving liberal international order will be unlikely.

Conclusion

This very brief summary of theoretical debates about great-power transitions, especially the realist-liberal stand-off, cannot do justice to the complexities and nuances of the writings that produced them. Yet it is clear enough that inquiry into the rise of new powers is one of the most thoughtfully considered aspects of international relations theory; and in Asia, we confront the rise of the world's two new rising powers, China and India. Theoretical sophistication, however, has brought anything but consensus, and theory is often upended by surprise. The purpose of theory is to make the complexity of the past comprehensible and useful. The danger

---

[41] Ikenberry, *Liberal Leviathan*, 343.

[42] Spence, *The Next Convergence*, 48, 195–96.

[43] Kenneth Lieberthal, *Governing China: From Revolution through Reform* (New York: Norton, 1995), 315.

[44] Minxin Pei, *China's Trapped Transition: The Limits of Developmental Autocracy* (Cambridge: Harvard University Press, 2006).

in making theory is that it will oversimplify the past in order to anticipate the future.[45]

The historian John Lewis Gaddis, for one, has been highly critical of the scientific claims of international relations theory. He observes that

> the efforts theorists have made to create a "science" of politics that would forecast the future course of world events have produced strikingly unimpressive results: none of the...approaches to theory...that have evolved since 1945 came anywhere close to anticipating how the Cold War would end....If their forecasts failed so completely to anticipate so large an event as that conflict's termination, then one has to wonder about the theories upon which they were based.

Gaddis quoted approvingly the wry remark of the distinguished historian of the Soviet Union Robert Conquest, who when he was asked what lesson people might learn from the surprise ending of the Cold War replied: "If you are a student, switch from political science to history."[46] Nevertheless, whatever its limitations in anticipating the future, international relations theory at its best provides us with perspectives and conceptual tools to apply to our thinking about the complex reality of the new era in Asia. We can draw on what international relations theorists tell us about patterns of state behavior extending across time and space. Theory can sharpen the kinds of questions we should be asking about the objective conditions with which policymakers must deal.

---

[45] See the extended discussion of this danger in John Lewis Gaddis, *The Landscape of History: How Historians Map the Past* (New York: Oxford University Press, 2002), especially chap. 5.

[46] John Lewis Gaddis, "International Relations Theory and the End of the Cold War," *International Security* 17, no. 3 (Winter 1992/93): 5–58.

STRATEGIC ASIA 2011–12

COUNTRY STUDIES

EXECUTIVE SUMMARY

This chapter examines how China views the rise of India and the implications of India's rise for China's core interests and strategic objectives.

MAIN ARGUMENTS:

- Contrary to the conventional wisdom, China views India's rise as a positive development that promotes China's own core interests and strategic objectives more than it threatens or challenges them. Enhanced cooperation with a rising India allows Beijing to avoid a potentially costly confrontation that would harm the growth of both countries, block the formation of a close U.S.-India relationship, and reduce the overall influence of the U.S. over China.

- China's strategy toward a rising India combines engagement with deterrence. China pursues comprehensive political, economic, and international engagement with India to advance its broader strategic objectives. China also seeks to deter India from undermining Chinese interests by withholding cooperation or maintaining its policies on specific issues, such as its ties with Pakistan.

POLICY IMPLICATIONS:

- Heightened security competition between China and India in the next decade or two is unlikely because China does not view India as a major threat and because of the common interests that the two countries share.

- Because the gap in wealth between India and China continues to grow and because security competition between the two states will be limited, India will not serve as an effective counterweight for other states seeking to gain leverage over China.

- The stark difference in Chinese and Indian elite perceptions of each other may increase misperceptions and miscalculations, thus introducing greater uncertainty into the future of the relationship. China may underestimate Indian concerns, while India may exaggerate the threat posed by China.

China Views India's Rise: Deepening Cooperation, Managing Differences

M. Taylor Fravel

The relationship between the People's Republic of China (PRC) and India is poised to reshape Asia's geopolitical landscape. How these two rising powers manage relations with each other will have an impact not only on the level of stability in the region but also on the region's weight and influence in world politics. Nevertheless, key questions about how China views India's more recent emergence remain unanswered: How does China view India's rise? What are the implications of India's rise for Chinese strategic interests and objectives? Does China view India as a rival for power and influence, both within Asia and beyond?

Answers to these questions are important for several reasons. First, India will likely surpass Japan in the next decade to become the second-largest economy in Asia. China and India are both significant military powers, possessing small but growing arsenals of nuclear weapons and fielding two of the three largest militaries in the world. Power shifts are often dangerous moments in international politics, given that new interests create new insecurities. They could be especially dangerous in Asia because China and India share a history of armed conflict, including the 1962 border war, and may be predisposed to view the other's rise with suspicion and apprehension. Second, an assessment of Chinese views of India's rise is overdue. Much of the existing scholarship on Chinese perceptions of India either examines the period before the dramatic improvement in

M. Taylor Fravel is an Associate Professor of Political Science and member of the Security Studies Program at the Massachusetts Institute for Technology. He can be reached at <fravel@mit.edu>.

The author would like to thank Vipin Narang and Paul Staniland for helpful comments and Lyle Morris, Joshua Shifrinson, and Jonathan Walton for invaluable research assistance.

Chinese-Indian ties in the mid-2000s or relies only on English-language materials as sources of Chinese perceptions.[1]

On balance, China views India's rise as a positive development that promotes core Chinese interests and strategic objectives more than it threatens or challenges them. China believes that it shares many common interests with India as a large developing country seeking to rise amid continued U.S. unipolarity. Although Chinese elites see India as a competitor in certain areas and acknowledge the frictions created by long-standing contentious issues such as the border dispute, as well as new issues such as access to the Indian Ocean, they do not foresee a relationship dominated by competition or rivalry. Enhanced cooperation with India benefits China by preventing a potentially costly confrontation that would harm the growth of both countries, by blocking the formation of a close relationship between India and the United States, and by reducing U.S. influence over China through increasing the weight of the developing world on issues such as trade, climate change, military intervention, and the role of the United Nations.

China's current strategy toward India combines engagement and deterrence. Beijing pursues comprehensive engagement to reassure New Delhi about China's rise and realize economic and diplomatic cooperation that promotes China's own grand strategy. Nevertheless, Chinese engagement with India has limits because the PRC continues to pursue policies that India opposes, such as support for the government of Pakistan and its claims in the territorial dispute. Although most of these contentious issues preceded India's rise in the last decade, they allow China to hedge against future Indian power and deter New Delhi from challenging Beijing's interests. China desires an India strong enough to dilute U.S. power and help promote China's own strategic objectives, but not an India so strong that it would limit or check China's freedom of action or be able to harm Chinese core interests. Despite the element of hedging in this strategy, the benefits of cooperation with a rising India outweigh the need to balance against it. From Beijing's perspective, the challenge is to manage these contentious issues so that they do not prevent the deepening of the cooperation that China seeks.

---

[1] For earlier assessments, see John W. Garver, *Protracted Contest: Sino-Indian Rivalry in the Twentieth Century* (Seattle: University of Washington Press, 2001); John W. Garver, "Asymmetrical Indian and Chinese Threat Perceptions," *Journal of Strategic Studies* 25, no. 4 (2002): 109–34; Susan L. Shirk, "One-Sided Rivalry: China's Perceptions and Policies toward India," in *The India-China Relationship: What the United States Needs to Know*, ed. Francine Frankel and Harry Harding (New York: Columbia University Press, 2004), 75–100; and Waheguru Paul Singh Sidhu and Jing-dong Yuan, *China and India: Cooperation or Conflict?* (Boulder: Lynne Rienner, 2003). For studies that rely on English sources, see Manjeet S. Pardesi, "Understanding (Changing) Chinese Strategic Perceptions of India," *Strategic Analysis* 34, no. 4 (2010): 562–78; and Shaun Randol, "How to Approach the Elephant: Chinese Perceptions of India in the Twenty-first Century," *Asian Affairs* 34, no. 4 (2008): 211–28.

This analysis contains several implications for policy. Common interests that China and India share as rising developing states are likely to dampen the potential for security competition between them so long as these interests endure. Nevertheless, China's view of India's rise contrasts starkly with the more pessimistic views of China's rise in India that are documented in Harsh Pant's contribution to this volume and elsewhere.[2] This growing gap in perceptions not only may limit China's ability to deepen cooperation with India on economic and international issues but also introduces an element of uncertainty into the relationship that could increase misperceptions and miscalculations. Beijing may be more likely to underestimate Indian concerns about China, while New Delhi may be more likely to exaggerate the threat from China, which sees the United States and not India as its principal strategic competitor.

This chapter proceeds as follows. To set the context for Chinese views of India's rise, the first section reviews China's grand strategy. Next, the chapter examines Chinese views of India's rise, including views of the drivers of India's foreign policy and the implications of India's rise for China. The third section then reviews China's strategy toward a rising India, while the fourth section examines potential areas of conflict and obstacles to further cooperation. The final section discusses the policy implications of this analysis.

China's Grand Strategy: The Context for Assessing India's Rise

Beijing views India's rise, and the impact of this development on China, through the lens of its core interests and strategic objectives. In the last decade, and especially since 2008, Chinese leaders have been increasingly willing to articulate publicly the PRC's core interests. One authoritative description occurred during the July 2009 U.S.-China Security and Economic Dialogue when State Councilor Dai Bingguo, China's highest-ranking diplomat, identified three core interests.[3] The first is "maintaining China's basic system and national security." Although national security as a core interest is self-explanatory, the term basic system (*tizhi*) highlights continuing concerns of the Chinese Communist Party (CCP) about regime security and threats to its power. In a 2004 speech to the Central Military

---

[2] See also Francine Frankel, "The Breakout of China-India Strategic Rivalry in Asia and the Indian Ocean," *Journal of International Affairs* 63, no. 2 (2011): 1–17.

[3] "Shou lun Zhong-Mei jingji duihua: Chu shang yueqiu wai zhuyao wenti junyi tanji" [First Round of the China-U.S. Economic Dialogue: All Major Issues Discussed Except Landing on the Moon], *China News Net*, July 29, 2009, http://www.chinanews.com/gn/news/2009/07-29/1794984.shtml.

Commission, President Hu Jintao had described this interest in terms of upholding the absolute leadership of the CCP.[4] As demonstrated by the party's swift reaction to efforts by overseas activists to launch a "Jasmine revolution" (*molihua geming*) following the Arab Spring of 2011, China's leaders are hypersensitive to domestic challenges to their rule.

The second core interest outlined by Dai Bingguo is "national sovereignty and territorial integrity." This component emphasizes what Chinese leaders view as questions of internal sovereignty, especially in light of ethnic unrest in China's western frontier in 2008 and 2009. The two areas most frequently identified with this interest are Tibet and Taiwan. China's territorial disputes with others states, including its dispute with India on the border, have not yet been labeled specifically as core interests.[5]

China's third core interest, the "continued development of the economy and society," encompasses what will ensure both China's rise as a great power and regime security. Yet continued growth is far from assured. Reforms have upended Chinese society, sowing the seeds of discontent and unrest. Chinese leaders must manage rising urbanization, growing inequality within and among key provinces and cities, massive internal migration, growing unemployment, and local debt. The increase in the number of "mass incidents" from 8,700 in 1993 to potentially as high as 170,000 in 2009 underscores the leadership's concerns about future growth and, ultimately, continuing the country's remarkable ascent.[6]

China is pursuing and defending these core interests amid uncertainty. The biannual white papers on national defense offer an official assessment of China's security environment. According to the 2010 white paper, "the overall security environment for [China's development] remains favorable…[but] China is…confronted by more diverse and complex security challenges."[7] On the one hand, China views the Asian region as stable and the threat of major war as low, and states that multipolarization (*duojihua*) or the diffusion of U.S. power is progressing. On the other hand, the white papers note the continued competition among the great powers,

---

[4] General Political Department, *Shuli he luoshi kexue fazhanguan lilun xuexi duben* [A Reader for Establishing and Implementing the Theory of Scientific Development] (Beijing: Jiefangjun chubanshe [internal circulation], 2006), 77.

[5] Reports in April 2010 that the South China Sea had been described as a core interest were incorrect. See Michael D. Swaine, "China's Assertive Behavior—Part One: On 'Core Interests,'" *China Leadership Monitor*, no. 34 (Winter 2011).

[6] M. Taylor Fravel, "International Relations Theory and China's Rise: Assessing China's Potential for Territorial Expansion," *International Studies Review* 12, no. 4 (2010): 519.

[7] State Council Information Office, *China's National Defense in 2010* (Beijing: State Council Information Office, 2011).

especially in the military domain, and the potential for conflicts to erupt within and among states in the region.

The United States poses an acute dilemma for China. China's continued economic growth depends on access to the U.S. market and the free flow of trade, investment, and technology around the world that U.S. dominance has facilitated. Nevertheless, Beijing chafes at Washington's continued support for Taiwan, the U.S. military presence in East Asia, and what it sees as American unilateralism in international affairs. The 2010 white paper, for example, notes that the United States has sought to "occupy new strategic commanding heights in military affairs" and has been "reinforcing its regional military alliances, and increasing its involvement in regional security affairs."[8] More generally, many Chinese elites believe that the United States ultimately seeks to limit China's rise and pursue some form of regime change through democratization. Policy disputes over issues such as currency valuation and military transparency, for example, are often viewed as efforts by the United States to keep China weak.[9]

To defend and promote its interests amid an uncertain international environment and U.S. dominance, China's grand strategy emphasizes three objectives.[10] First, China seeks to maintain a "peaceful and stable external environment" to focus resources on economic development. Maintenance of such an environment requires deterring or preventing armed conflicts from occurring in the region, especially those that would involve China, as well as managing the potential for costly rivalries with other states. Second, Beijing seeks to reassure other states about how it will use its growing material capabilities to prevent them from balancing against China. As reflected in the discourse on "peaceful rise" and "peaceful development," China is well aware that its rise appears threatening to others. The PRC also seeks to avoid confrontational relationships with most states, especially those in East Asia, lest they seek to strengthen ties with the United States or increase costly security competition in the region. Third, China aims to maximize its autonomy in the international system to limit the constraints of unipolarity. Although all states desire autonomy and freedom of action, China feels unduly constrained by the United States and actively supports the rise of other powers, especially in the developing world.

---

[8] State Council Information Office, *China's National Defense in 2010*.

[9] Michael Chase, "Chinese Suspicion and U.S. Intentions," *Survival* 53, no. 3 (2011): 133–50.

[10] Avery Goldstein, *Rising to the Challenge: China's Grand Strategy and International Security* (Stanford: Stanford University Press, 2005); Evan S. Medeiros, *China's International Behavior: Activism, Opportunism, and Diversification* (Santa Monica: RAND, 2009); and Robert G. Sutter, *Chinese Foreign Relations: Power and Policy since the Cold War* (Lanhan: Rowman and Littlefield, 2008).

To achieve these objectives, China pursues an "omnidirectional diplomacy" (*quan fangwei waijiao*) combined with military modernization. Although this omnidirectional foreign policy was developed to help China emerge from diplomatic isolation after the 1989 Tiananmen Square massacre and the end of the Cold War, it has assumed new meaning in the past decade.[11] In 2004, the National People's Congress affirmed a new overall arrangement for diplomacy (*waijiao zongti bushi*) guided by the slogan that "great powers are the key, the periphery is the priority, developing countries are the foundation" (*daguo shi guanjian, zhoubian shi shouyao, fazhanzhong shi jichu*).[12] This slogan reflects China's effort to develop and deepen bilateral relations with all types of countries to advance its three strategic objectives.

China's omnidirectional diplomacy contains several elements. The first is political. With each country, China seeks to deepen interactions at the official level, including reciprocal visits by top leaders and dialogues on functional issues such as trade. As part of its political engagement, Beijing often pursues strategic partnerships to elevate ties with key countries by codifying shared principles, often regarding the management of common interests in the international system.[13] A second element of the PRC's omnidirectional diplomacy is the deepening of bilateral economic interactions. In addition to securing market access, free trade agreements are especially important as a tool for reassuring other states that China's rise will not come at the expense of their growth.[14] By deepening economic ties, China increases the costs for other states to take actions that might harm Chinese interests, such as supporting Taiwan. A third element is the active management of existing bilateral disputes to prevent open conflict or rivalry that would worsen the PRC's security environment, especially by encouraging other states to align with the United States. If disputes exist, China seeks either to resolve them or, if they cannot be resolved, to prevent them from hindering the development of political and economic cooperation.

In 2006, engagement with multilateral institutions was added as a fourth component of China's diplomatic strategy. Described as "multilateralism is the stage" (*duobian shi wutai*), this component highlighted the importance of deepening ties with, and at times even creating, multilateral institutions,

---

[11] Zhang Baijia, "Cong 'yi bian dao' dao 'quan fang wei': dui 50 nianlai Zhongguo waijiao geju yanjiu de sikao" [From 'Lean to One Side' to 'Omnidirection': Reflections on the Evolution of China's Foreign Policy Structure over the Past 50 Years], *Zhonggong dangshi yanjiu*, no. 1 (2000): 21–28.

[12] "Quanguo renda changweihui 2004 nian gongzuo yaodian" [Key Points for the Work of the NPC Standing Committee in 2004], *Zhongguo renda*, no. 7 (2004): 12.

[13] Medeiros, *China's International Behavior*, 82–88.

[14] Ibid., 61–69.

especially regional ones.[15] Participation in multilateral forums helps reassure other states because China embraces the principles and agendas of these organizations. Such participation also helps increase China's freedom of maneuver, given that the United States is often not a member or observer of these organizations, such as the Shanghai Cooperation Organisation (SCO) or the China-Africa Forum.

The modernization of the People's Liberation Army (PLA) complements omnidirectional diplomacy in China's grand strategy. In particular, China pursues a limited regional power-projection capability to cope with any armed conflicts that might occur on its periphery.[16] As scholars from the PLA's Academy of Military Science observe, because China's economy relies heavily on trade, "regional stability carries important significance for our economic development as well as resisting America's posture against us."[17] A strong military helps deter challenges to Chinese national security and sovereignty, especially regarding Taiwan, and enhances China's autonomy and protects its expanding international interests more generally.

Chinese Views of India's Rise

China views India's rise broadly through the lens of its grand strategy rather than narrowly through past interactions in the bilateral relationship. Contrary to the conventional wisdom, Chinese foreign and security policy elites hold positive views of India's rise, which is seen as benefiting China more than challenging it. India is described as a partner, albeit sometimes as a competitive one, but not as a major threat or rival. Cooperation with India is seen as advancing China's strategic objectives, including maintaining a peaceful environment for growth, reducing the constraints of unipolarity, and advancing the interests of developing countries.

These perceptions are detailed below, drawn from writings by prominent foreign and security policy elites in journals published by leading research institutes and universities over the past five years. These journals include *Contemporary International Relations* (published by China Institutes of Contemporary International Relations under the Ministry of State Security), *China International Studies* (China Institute for

---

[15] "'Zhongguo weixie' haishi 'Zhongguo jiyu': ruhe lijie zou heping fazhan dalu" [The 'China Threat' or 'China Opportunity': How to Understand Taking the Road of Peaceful Development], *Renmin Ribao*, September 29, 2006, 14.

[16] Zhang Quanqi, ed., *Jiang Zemin guofang he jundui jianshe sixiang yanjiu* [Research on Jiang Zemin's Thought on National Defense and Army Building] (Beijing: Guofang daxue chubanshe, 2003), 6.

[17] Shan Xiufa, ed., *Jiang Zemin guofang he jundui jianshe sixiang yanjiu* [Research on Jiang's Zemin's Thought on National Defense and Army Building] (Beijing: Junshi kexue chubanshe, 2004), 84.

International Studies under the Ministry of Foreign Affairs), *Foreign Affairs Review* (China Foreign Affairs University under the Ministry of Foreign Affairs), *South Asian Studies* (Institute of Asia-Pacific Studies under the Chinese Academy of Social Sciences), *South Asian Quarterly Studies* (South Asian Studies Institute at Sichuan University), and *Peace and Development* (a PLA-sponsored think tank), among others. Where possible, writings by analysts from the PLA are also examined.

These sources offer insight into Chinese perceptions of India's rise for several reasons. Most of the journals listed above are published by government-sponsored research organizations that play a role in China's foreign policymaking process as sources of information and analysis for China's top leaders. The authors whose views are examined include prominent analysts such as Ma Jiali from the China Institutes of Contemporary International Relations as well as retired ambassadors to India such as Cheng Ruisheng. These individuals are not currently government officials, however, nor do they speak and publish on behalf of the Chinese government.

The positive assessment of India's rise detailed below should not be confused with a positive or benign view of India overall. Instead, past sources of conflict in the relationship continue to color Chinese views of Indian intentions. The most important issues are the territorial dispute and India's support for the Dalai Lama, which China views as a government-in-exile challenging its core interest of national sovereignty. Nevertheless, as described below, Beijing views India's rise more as an opportunity than a challenge or threat because it helps further China's grand strategic objectives.

Goals and Drivers of India's Rise

Chinese views of India's rise start with the acknowledgment that India is indeed a rising power. Nearly all the sources examined for this chapter share this conclusion. A pair of scholars stated in 2010, for example, that "India's rise has already become an incontrovertible fact."[18] As former ambassador Cheng Ruisheng elaborates, "with the fast development of India's economy and considerable strengthening of its military power, India's international status has been further raised."[19]

In the eyes of Chinese foreign policy and security elites, India views economic growth as the basis for its rise and has reconfigured its foreign policy around this goal. As Ma Jiali describes, India "has made creating

---

[18] Zhang Li, "Yindu zhanlue jueqi yu Zhong-Yin guanxi: wenti, qushi yu yingdui" [India's Strategic Rise and Chinese-Indian Relations: Issues, Trends, and Responses], *Nanya yanjiu likan*, no. 1 (2010): 3.

[19] Cheng Ruisheng, "Yindu de waijiao zhanlue quxiang" [Trends in India's Diplomatic Strategy], *Guoji wenti yanjiu*, no. 2 (2008): 48.

a positive environment for economic revitalization a key point of its diplomacy."[20] Perhaps reflecting China's own experience, Chinese experts see India as pursuing a similar omnidirectional foreign policy. According to Cheng Ruisheng, "only by implementing an omnidirectional diplomatic strategy can India gain advantages from various sides."[21] Chinese analysts note India's emphasis on improving ties with all major powers (*daguo*)— Japan, the European Union (EU), and especially the United States—while maintaining its traditionally close relationship with Russia.[22] Chinese analysts also view New Delhi's willingness to improve ties with China as part of this broader framework. As a result of this approach, one analyst concludes that "India has good relations with almost every world power."[23] Other elements of India's foreign policy include deepening ties in adjacent regions, especially in East Asia through its "look east" policy but also in Central Asia, and playing a more active role in international institutions.[24]

Only in South Asia itself do Chinese experts conclude that India's foreign policy has been less successful.[25] India's rise is seen as sharpening the country's long-standing rivalry with Pakistan and the dispute over Kashmir. In addition, Chinese experts observe that it has created tensions with smaller neighbors such as Bangladesh, Nepal, and Sri Lanka, who fear growing Indian power.[26] As one analyst writes, "India's relations with its neighboring countries in South Asia is the weak link of its diplomacy."[27] Some Chinese experts conclude that such poor diplomatic ties in South Asia may limit New Delhi's ability to exercise influence in other regions. One researcher, for example, states that India's troubled relations in South Asia are "still a major constraining factor blocking India's emergence from South Asia toward becoming a major world power."[28]

In addition to diplomacy, Chinese experts note the role of military modernization in enhancing India's international status as a great power.

---

[20] Ma Jiali, "Yindu jueqi de taishi" [The Situation of India's Rise], *Xiandai guoji guanxi*, no. 6 (2006): 53.

[21] Cheng, "Yindu de waijiao zhanlue quxiang," 54.

[22] Hu Zhiyong, "Lengzhan hou Yindu duiwai guanxi tiaozheng, fazhan ji yingxiang" [The Adjustment, Development, and Influence of India's Foreign Relations after the Cold War], *Nanya yanjiu likan*, no. 2 (2010): 14–20; and Ma Jiali, "Yindu daguo waijiao de xin taishi" [The New Situation in India's Great Power Diplomacy], *Heping yu fazhan*, no. 1 (2008): 55–66.

[23] Shi Hongyuan, "Ruanshili yu Yindu de jueqi" [Soft Power and the Rise of India], *Guoji wenti yanjiu*, no. 3 (2009): 32.

[24] Hu, "Lengzhan hou Yindu duiwai guanxi tiaozheng, fazhan ji yingxiang."

[25] Shi, "Ruanshili yu Yindu de jueqi," 36.

[26] Zhang, "Yindu zhanlue jueqi yu Zhong-Yin guanxi."

[27] Zheng Ruixiang, "Touxi Yindu jueqi wenti" [Analysis of India's Rise], *Guoji wenti yanjiu*, no. 1 (2006): 41.

[28] Ibid.

The key turning point was the 1998 nuclear tests, which one analyst describes "as a shortcut for reaching such status."[29] More generally, Chinese analysts note the conventional capabilities of India's armed forces.[30] Ma Jiali, for example, writes that "India has all along sought to become a military power and nuclear power…to shape its image as a big power in conformity with its rise."[31] Enhanced military power is also seen as helping India maintain superiority over Pakistan, increase its influence with other major powers, consolidate its "superpower position" in South Asia and the Indian Ocean, and make progress toward becoming a permanent member of the UN Security Council.[32]

Chinese assessments of India's military capabilities, however, are mixed. As demonstrated in **Figure 1**, India's armed forces receive far less coverage in the *Jiefangjun Bao*, the official PLA newspaper, than the U.S., Japanese, or Russian militaries. Nevertheless, a detailed study of Chinese writings on India's military modernization shows that Chinese strategists and technical experts have been devoting more attention to Indian capabilities since 2005.[33] These writings emphasize the development of India's air, strategic, and especially naval forces. Chinese technical experts analyzing India's military modernization view the Indian Navy as having the greatest potential to surpass that of China.[34] At the same time, Chinese elites note many challenges that India faces in modernizing its force, especially its reliance on imported military equipment and associated spare parts.[35]

Chinese experts disagree about the ultimate goal of India's rise. Some claim that India seeks regional hegemony in South Asia and dominance of the Indian Ocean.[36] Others downplay India's aspirations for hegemony but recognize that India seeks to be a regional power that can also play a global

---

[29] Zheng, "Touxi Yindu jueqi wenti," 39.

[30] See, for example, the annual assessments of the Indian military in *Waiguo junshi xueshu*, a monthly journal published by the PLA's Academy of Military Science.

[31] Ma, "Yindu jueqi de taishi," 52.

[32] Ibid.

[33] Lora Saalman, "Between 'China Threat Theory' and 'Chindia': Chinese Responses to India's Military Modernization," *Chinese Journal of International Politics* 4, no. 1 (2011): 87–114.

[34] Ibid., 99.

[35] Zhang Fuyuan and Liu Zhanling, "Yindu wuqi zhuangbei jianshe fazhan de zhuyao jingyan ji qishi" [The Main Experience and Implications of India's Armaments Construction and Development], *Guofang keji*, no. 5 (2008).

[36] Hu Wei, "Cong diyuan zhengzhi jiaodu kan Yindu de daguo zhanlue he yingxiang" [Viewing India's Great Power Strategy and Influence from a Geopolitical Perspective], *Heping yu fazhan*, no. 5 (2010): 64–67; and Zhang, "Yindu zhanlue jueqi yu Zhong-Yin guanxi," 7.

FIGURE 1   Number of articles on selected militaries in the *Jiefangjun Bao*, 1990–2010

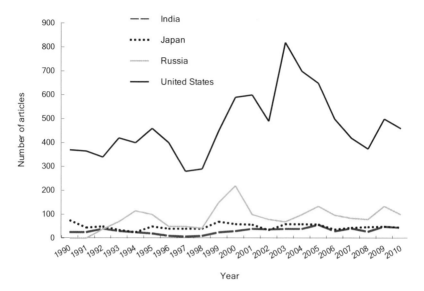

SOURCE: *Jiefangjun Bao* database.

role.[37] Either way, Chinese experts believe that India faces many challenges in furthering its own rise. The first is the continued high rates of poverty and illiteracy as "serious weaknesses [that] are obvious."[38] A second perceived obstacle to future growth is India's fragmented political system. According to one scholar, India's democracy is characterized by "infighting among the political parties, political instability, and government inefficiency."[39] Ongoing internal ethnic and religious strife is seen as a third problem that Indian leaders must address to further their country's rise, with the caste system described as "hindering social progress."[40] A fourth set of challenges that Chinese experts note compromises economic obstacles to future growth.[41]

---

[37] Song Dexing and Shi Yinhong, "Shijie zhengzhi zhong Yindu heping jueqi xianshi yu qianjing" [Prospects and Realities of India's Peaceful Rise within Global Politics], *Nanya yanjiu*, no. 1 (2010): 15–24.

[38] Ibid., 21.

[39] Ma, "Yindu jueqi de taishi," 54.

[40] Ibid.; and Zheng, "Touxi Yindu jueqi wenti," 40.

[41] Shi Yinhong and Song Dexing, "Yindu heping jueqi wenti ji Zhong-Mei-Yin sanjiao guanxi" [The Question of India's Peaceful Rise and Chinese-American-Indian Trilateral Relations], *Guoji zhanwang*, no. 3 (2009): 12–16.

The development of infrastructure is "lagging behind" the requirements for further growth, which limits India's ability to develop its manufacturing sectors and attract foreign investment.[42] Lack of capital and a low savings rate (compared to China's) are other constraints, as is corruption.[43] Finally, the dispute with Pakistan over Kashmir and the threat of terrorist attacks require that India invest heavily in its armed forces and focus on managing these immediate problems.[44] As a result, although India's rise is viewed as "inevitable," Chinese experts also believe that it will "be a long process and India is now at the initial phase of its emergence."[45]

The Implications of India's Rise for China

In the sources consulted for this chapter, India is generally not viewed as a posing a significant threat to China's strategic objectives. Although Chinese elites certainly recognize a competitive dimension in the bilateral relationship, India is almost always described as a partner or "friendly competitor"[46] rather than as an adversary or rival.

Several themes about the implications of India's rise for China emerge from the writings of Chinese experts. First, they view India as occupying a central and perhaps unique position in China's omnidirectional diplomacy. With its vast population and possession of nuclear weapons, India is a major power with which China must maintain stable relations. Adjacent to Tibet and Xinjiang, India is also a neighboring state that can have an impact on China's immediate periphery as well as on the stability of China's restive western frontier. As an emerging country, India is a key state in the developing world. It is also active in multilateral forums. As a result, two scholars conclude that "a rising India is the most important country that China will face."[47]

Second, India's rise benefits China because it helps dilute U.S. power and lessen the constraints of unipolarity. According to Chinese experts, India's rise helps further China's effort to maximize its autonomy in a U.S.-dominated international order, an objective that is often described in official texts as promoting the "democratization of international relations" and

---

[42] Ma, "Yindu jueqi de taishi"; and Zheng, "Touxi Yindu jueqi wenti," 40.

[43] Shi, "Ruanshili yu Yindu de jueqi"; and Zheng, "Touxi Yindu jueqi wenti," 40.

[44] Ma, "Yindu jueqi de taishi," 55.

[45] Zheng, "Touxi Yindu jueqi wenti," 41.

[46] Zhang Guihong, "Zhong-Yin guanxi de quedingxing he buquedingxing" [Certainty and Uncertainty in Chinese-Indian Relations], *Nanya yanjiu*, no. 1 (2010): 38.

[47] Lou Chunhao and Zhang Mingming, "Nanya de zhanlue zhongyaoxing yu Zhongguo de nanya zhanlue" [The Strategic Importance of South Asia and China's South Asian Strategy], *Xiandai guoji guanxi*, no. 2 (2010): 43.

"multipolarization." The rise of India furthers both goals by constituting a new power center that will reduce U.S. influence. As one researcher states, India's rise, along with the rise of China, is a significant event "resulting in a change in the world balance of power."[48] As another analyst writes more bluntly, the rise of India and other countries will "contribute to balancing and restricting the tendency toward [American] unilateralism."[49] Ma Jiali concurs, noting that China and India "are in favor of a multipolar world and against unipolar hegemony."[50]

Third, India's rise helps advance common interests that the two states share as large, developing countries in what China views as a Western-dominated world. According to Chinese experts, these interests include support for the norms of national sovereignty and noninterference in states' internal affairs, the central role of the UN in international politics, and the settlement of international disputes through peaceful means as well as opposition to military interventions that lack a mandate from the UN.[51] As Ma Jiali writes, "China and India share much in common in the process of building this new post–Cold War world order."[52] In addition, both countries are seen as sharing similar positions on issues facing developing countries, such as climate change and trade negotiations in the WTO. According to former ambassador Zhou Gang, "the stronger China and India become, the bigger say they will have in multilateral institutions such as the United Nations and the World Trade Organization and the better they could safeguard the rights and interests of the developing countries."[53]

Fourth, India's rise benefits China by facilitating China's own economic growth and Asian regionalism more generally. Enhanced economic ties between the two countries, as major economies in different regions of the world, are seen as fostering Asian integration, which will help further China's development.[54] Deepened economic ties are also seen as helping each reduce its dependence on developed countries, as China and India can

---

[48] Zheng, "Touxi Yindu jueqi wenti," 41.

[49] Lan Jianxue, "Zhong-Yin dui waijiao zhanlue yitong yu shuangbian guanxi" [Similarities and Differences in Chinese and Indian Diplomatic Strategies and Their Bilateral Relationship], *Waijiao pinglun*, no. 3 (2008): 40.

[50] Ma Jiali, "Zhong-Yin guanxi de fazhan qianjing" [Prospects for the Development of Chinese-Indian Relations]," *Heping yu fazhan*, no. 2 (2007).

[51] Ibid.; Zhang, "Zhong-Yin guanxi de quedingxing he buquedingxing," 37–38; and Zhou Gang, "Zhong-Yin jianjiao 60 nian liangguo guanxi de huigu yu zhanwang" [Reflections and Prospects of 60 Years of Chinese-Indian Relations], *Dangdai shijie*, no. 7 (2010): 30–34.

[52] Ma, "Zhong-Yin guanxi de fazhan qianjing."

[53] Zhou, "Zhong-Yin jianjiao 60 nian liangguo guanxi de huigu yu zhanwang."

[54] Cheng Ruisheng, "Lun Zhong-Yin zhanlue hezuo huoban guanxi" [On the China-India Strategic and Cooperative Partnership Relationship], *Guoji wenti yanjiu*, no. 1 (2007): 15.

learn from each other in areas where they lack experience.[55] According to one expert, for example, China can gain expertise from India in areas such as genetic engineering and software, while India can gain expertise in areas such as blast furnaces and hydropower.[56]

What explains this largely positive view about the implications of India's rise for China? First, China engages India from a favorable position in multiple dimensions. Although India is a rising power, the gap in material capabilities between the two is large and in China's favor.[57] Using current exchange rates, China's GDP in 2010 was more than three times as large as India's at $5.88 trillion and $1.73 trillion, respectively.[58] Moreover, as shown in **Figure 2**, the gap in wealth between the two states continues to widen, from $1 trillion in 2003 to more than $4 trillion in 2010. When viewed in a bilateral context, India is actually not a rising power in material terms compared to China. A similar story exists in the area of defense spending, where China's estimated military expenditure in 2010 of $119 billion was more than three times as large as India's.[59] Diplomatically, China arguably enjoys more robust political and economic relations with its neighbors in East Asia than India maintains with its neighbors in South Asia. Even in their territorial dispute, China already controls the disputed territory that it values most, except for Tawang, and enjoys a relatively favorable geographic position for defending the territory under its control.[60]

Second, Chinese experts judge that India, like China, needs a peaceful and stable security environment for its continued development. Because of this focus on growth, they see India as inward-looking and thus as having strong incentives to avoid a confrontational relationship with China that would harm India's own growth prospects. As one scholar writes, for example, "both China and India face the task of developing the economy and raising people's living standard, thus both must have a peaceful and stable international environment and a good-neighborly and friendly peripheral environment."[61]

Third, Chinese experts view the common interests that the two countries share as powerful and enduring. According to one analyst,

[55] Ma, "Zhong-Yin guanxi de fazhan qianjing."

[56] Ibid.

[57] Zhang, "Zhong-Yin guanxi de quedingxing he buquedingxing," 38–39.

[58] World Bank, World Development Indicators, 2010, http://databank.worldbank.org/ddp/home.do.

[59] Stockholm International Peace Research Institute (SIPRI), SIPRI Military Expenditure Database, 2010, http://www.sipri.org/databases/milex.

[60] For a recent review of the territorial dispute, see M. Taylor Fravel, *Strong Borders, Secure Nation: Cooperation and Conflict in China's Territorial Disputes* (Princeton: Princeton University Press, 2008).

[61] Lan, "Zhong-Yin dui waijiao zhanlue yitong yu shuangbian guanxi," 39.

FIGURE 2   Chinese and Indian GDPs, 1990–2010

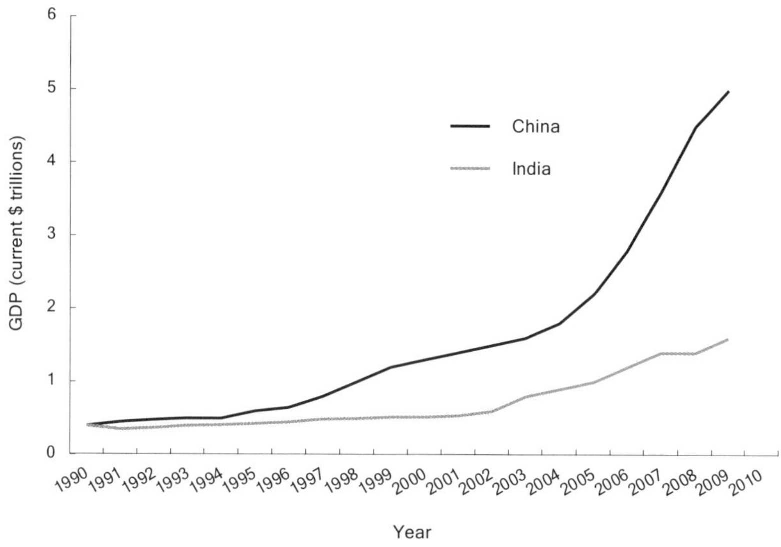

SOURCE: World Bank, World Development Indicators, 2011.

"mutual strategic interests exist between the two countries, and both do not want bilateral relations leading to confrontation or conflict." As a result, Chinese-Indian relations "will last for a long period, and the two countries [will] have common views and common interests and worries instead of tactical, short-term, or expedient ones."[62]

Yet despite the prevailing optimism, Chinese experts express two types of concerns about India's rise. The first set of concerns revolves around existing contentious bilateral issues that either have attracted more prominence or continue to exert a negative effect on the relationship. These include the long-standing territorial dispute and India's support for the Dalai Lama, as well as Indian suspicions of China's future intentions, which are seen as a legacy of India's defeat in the 1962 border war. The second set of concerns identifies new potential conflicts of interest that might emerge during the course of India's rise. First, China's vulnerability to a blockade of sea lanes through the Indian Ocean, including the Strait of Malacca, may create a new security dilemma. Beijing's efforts to secure alternative routes through Pakistan and Burma will be seen as threatening

---

[62] Lan, "Zhong-Yin dui waijiao zhanlue yitong yu shuangbian guanxi," 39.

to India, while Indian naval modernization will be seen as threatening to China.[63] A second concern is that tensions will grow in South Asia itself as China seeks to strengthen ties with India's neighbors. According to one researcher, "China will not accept India's policy of seeking hegemony over the South Asian subcontinent and the Indian Ocean."[64] Third, one Chinese scholar fears the onset of "a new round of the Great Game" in Central Asia.[65] Although China and India share interests in combating terrorism and developing energy resources, India is seen as seeking basing rights and security cooperation with states in the region at China's expense. A fourth issue that alarms several scholars is the future of India's look east policy of expanding and deepening ties with states in East Asia, which many see as partly directed against China.[66] Fifth, Indian suspicions about China may further increase the attractiveness of closer U.S.-India ties. One analyst, for example, notes that tension in China's relations with either the United States or India will create incentives for cooperation among the two at China's expense.[67] Last, the debate over UN reform and India's desire to become a permanent member of the UN Security Council have also strained relations between the two states.[68] China's approach to some of these problems is discussed at the end of this chapter.

Yet, although suspicions about India remain and Chinese analysts and elites expect new sources of friction to arise, they do not foresee a fundamental change in the Chinese-Indian relationship. As noted by Zhou Gang, because China and India do not have "fundamental conflicts of interest," they "pose no threat to each other [and] are neither competitors nor enemies." Although competition exists, it "is not [competition] for survival, but positive and normal [competition]."[69] In the words of one analyst, "there is cooperation and competition in the Chinese-Indian relationship. But cooperation is the main aspect of the relationship of the two countries."[70]

---

[63] Zhang, "Zhong-Yin guanxi de quedingxing he buquedingxing."

[64] Zhang, "Yindu zhanlue jueqi yu Zhong-Yin guanxi," 6.

[65] Ibid., 8.

[66] Wang Chuanjian, "Yindu de Nanzhongguohai zhengce: Yitu yu yingxiang" [India's South China Sea Policy: Intentions and Influence], *Waijiao pinglun*, no. 3 (2010): 107–22.

[67] Zhang, "Zhong-Yin guanxi de quedingxing he buquedingxing," 41.

[68] Ibid., 42.

[69] Zhou, "Zhong-Yin jianjiao 60 nian liangguo guanxi de huigu yu zhanwang," 33.

[70] Zheng, "Touxi Yindu jueqi wenti," 42.

China's Strategy toward a Rising India

China's strategy toward a rising India combines comprehensive engagement with limited deterrence. The main thrust of this strategy is to deepen political, economic, and international engagement with India in order to advance China's broader strategic objectives. China has also sought to prevent existing contentious issues from hindering the deepening of Chinese-Indian relations. At the same time, it seeks to preserve the ability to deter India from harming other Chinese interests, especially relating to sovereignty, by maintaining policies and positions that India opposes, such as support for Pakistan. Despite the element of hedging in this strategy, engagement rather than deterrence dominates China's approach.

Comprehensive Engagement

China pursues comprehensive engagement with India to reassure New Delhi about its rise and realize economic and diplomatic cooperation that promotes its own strategic objectives. This engagement occurs across the political, economic, and international dimensions of the Chinese-Indian relationship.

Political engagement. The foundation of China's approach to India has been to deepen the political relationship with New Delhi. Political engagement consists of creating a web of high-level visits, dialogues, and mechanisms that institutionalize the bilateral relationship to reassure India and achieve the economic and international cooperation that supports China's grand strategy. Such engagement also buffers the political relationship from existing and future sources of tension by increasing the costs for both sides of a return to a more confrontational relationship.

Although China and India began to deepen their relationship in the mid-1990s, progress stalled after India's nuclear tests in 1998. India had invoked a threat from China to justify the tests, and China reacted sharply. Following visits by Indian president K.R. Narayanan in May 2000 and Chinese premier Zhu Rongji in January 2002, progress toward deepening political ties resumed when Prime Minister Atal Bihari Vajpayee visited China in June 2003. During his visit, India and China signed the Declaration on Principles for Relations and Comprehensive Cooperation, which contained a framework for developing the relationship. In this declaration, China and India agreed that "the common interests of the two sides outweigh their differences. The two countries are not a threat to each other."[71] During Premier Wen Jiabao's visit to India in April 2005, China and India agreed to establish a Strategic and Cooperative Partnership for Peace and Prosperity.[72] The two sides also reached an agreement on guiding principles for developing a framework to resolve their territorial dispute.[73] The effort to deepen political ties reached its zenith during President Hu's visit to India in November 2006, the first such visit by China's top leader in ten years. The lengthy joint statement from his meeting with Prime Minister Manmohan Singh contained a "ten-pronged strategy" to develop the relationship.[74] In January 2008, Singh's visit to China produced a statement entitled "A Shared Vision for the 21st Century of the Republic of India and the People's Republic of China," which detailed the common interests behind the strategic partnership.[75] During Wen's second visit to India in December 2010, the two countries reaffirmed their common interests and agreed to hold regular high-level exchanges between top leaders. Earlier in 2010, China and India had agreed to establish a hotline between the offices of each country's prime minister.[76]

In addition to high-level visits, Beijing and New Delhi have increased the scope of their functional interactions at the ministerial and working levels. To enhance diplomatic cooperation and coordination, the two sides have established various mechanisms and dialogues. In 2008, for example, a hotline between the two foreign ministries was connected, and as noted above, in December 2010, China and India agreed to hold annual meetings of foreign ministers along with regular high-level visits of top leaders. They now hold a strategic dialogue (which has met four times) and maintain dialogue mechanisms on counterterrorism, policy planning, and security.

A similar mix of dialogues and mechanisms exists to address economic issues. At the ministerial level, the ministers of commerce lead a joint economic group, which has met eight times since 1988. During the

---

[71] "Declaration on Principles for Relations and Comprehensive Cooperation between the People's Republic of China and the Republic of India," Beijing, June 23, 2003, available from the Ministry of Foreign Affairs of the People's Republic of China, http://www.fmprc.gov.cn/eng/wjdt/2649/t22852.htm.

[72] "Joint Statement of the People's Republic of China and the Republic of India," Xinhua, April 12, 2005, http://news.xinhuanet.com/english/2005-04/12/content_2819789.htm.

[73] "Agreement between the Government of the Republic of India and the Government of the People's Republic of China on the Political Parameters and Guiding Principles for the Settlement of the India-China Boundary Question," New Delhi, April 11, 2005, available from India's Ministry of External Affairs, http://www.mea.gov.in/mystart.php?id=53059329.

[74] "China-India Joint Declaration," New Delhi, November 21, 2006, available at http://in.chineseembassy.org/eng/sgxw/2006en/t282045.htm.

[75] "A Shared Vision for the 21st Century of the People's Republic of China and the Republic of India," Beijing, January 14, 2008, available from http://in.chineseembassy.org/eng/zgbd/t399545.htm.

[76] Qin Jize and Cheng Guangjin, "Hotline to Connect China, India Leaders," China Daily, April 8, 2010.

mid-2000s, a joint study group was formed to examine ways to increase trade, which resulted in the creation of a joint task force to study the possibility of a free trade agreement. In December 2010, China and India agreed to establish a strategic economic dialogue, which will hold its first meeting in 2011.[77] Furthermore, since 2006 the two countries have held an annual ministerial-level dialogue on finance and have established working groups on trade, agriculture, and energy.

In the area of defense cooperation, ties have deepened substantially. During Wen's 2005 visit to India, the two countries agreed to additional confidence-building measures along their disputed boundary.[78] In addition, between 2003 and 2008, China and India held four joint military exercises, while in 2007 they initiated an annual defense dialogue that has now met three times. High-level exchanges of senior officers have also occurred, including PLA Navy (PLAN) Commander Wu Shengli's visit to India and India Air Force Marshall F.H. Major's visit to China, both in 2008. Professional military education institutes likewise hold regular exchanges of officers, and two ships from the Indian Navy participated in the April 2009 International Fleet Review in Qingdao held to commemorate the 60th anniversary of the founding of the PLAN. Although military exchanges were suspended in 2010 over the issue of stapled visas, they resumed in 2011, and new military exercises have been scheduled.

Economic engagement. The most noteworthy result of the renewed political interaction between China and India in the past decade has been the explosion of trade between the two countries. Since 2000, the volume of trade has increased twenty-fold, from $2.9 billion in 2000 to $61.7 billion in 2010. China is now India's top trade partner, while India has become one of China's top-ten trade partners. Moreover, the increase in trade between China and India has surpassed the expectations set by their leaders. In 2006, for example, China and India pledged to raise the volume of trade to $40 billion by 2010, a target that was ultimately exceeded by 50%.

To date, bilateral trade has largely leveraged each side's comparative advantages. China has been exporting manufactured products, especially electronics, while India has been exporting raw materials, including iron ore and cotton. Overall, however, China has benefited more from the economic relationship: it not only exports higher-value products but also runs a substantial surplus with India, as shown in **Figure 3**.

---

[77] Qin Jize and Ai Yang, "China, India Look to Energy Cooperation," *China Daily*, April 14, 2011.

[78] "Protocol between the Government of the Republic of India and the Government of the People's Republic of China on Modalities for the Implementation of Confidence Building Measures in the Military Field along the Line of Actual Control in the India-China Border Areas," New Delhi, April 11, 2005, available from India's Ministry of External Affairs, http://meaindia.nic.in/mystart.php?id=55039330.

FIGURE 3   China's trade with India, 2000–2010

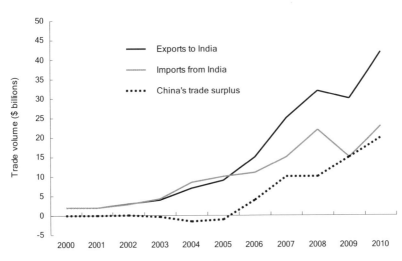

SOURCE: International Monetary Fund, Direction of Trade Statistics, 2011.

Boosting the economic relationship was the focus of Wen's visit to India in 2010. The Chinese delegation consisted of around four hundred people, and agreements worth more than $16 billion were signed. In addition, as mentioned above, both sides agreed to establish a strategic economic dialogue to address the trade-related and other economic issues in the relationship that had developed since 2008. These include India's growing deficit with China and the unprecedented number of antidumping suits that New Delhi has filed with the WTO, as well as energy cooperation and macroeconomic policy.[79]

International engagement. One driver of China's engagement with India is gaining diplomatic support to advance China's strategic objective of reducing the influence of the United States. As a result, in addition to deepening their bilateral relationship through high-level visits and dialogues, China and India have increased their interaction and cooperation on a range of international issues where the two share common interests as developing countries.

---

[79] Mehul Srivastava, "India-China Trade Tensions Rise," *Bloomberg Businessweek*, February 11, 2009.

First, China and India are now either members of or have observer status in various regional multilateral organizations. Importantly, the United States is often not a participant in these groups. These organizations include the SCO and the South Asian Association for Regional Cooperation (SAARC), where India and China, respectively, are observers in institutions where the other state plays a leading role. Both countries were founding members of the East Asia Summit, which first met in 2005 (despite China's initial objection to India's inclusion), and now participate in the Asia-Europe Meeting, which is convened biannually by the European Commission. Participation in these forums as well as other international meetings creates additional opportunities for top leaders and diplomats to exchange views and coordinate positions outside of high-level visits.

Second, apart from their activities in international institutions, India and China have established *ad hoc* multilateral mechanisms to coordinate policy among developing countries. Since 2002, foreign ministers from India, Russia, and China have held meetings as part of a trilateral grouping that Russia promoted in the late 1990s, and coordination among the three countries accelerated after top leaders met on the sidelines of the group of eight (G-8) in 2006. One purpose of this trilateral is to balance U.S. power through increased diplomatic coordination. A 2007 joint statement, for example, noted the importance of "building [a] multi-polar world order that would be based on principles of equality of nations...respect for sovereignty and territorial integrity of countries, international law and mutual respect."[80] More specific common interests articulated in 2010 include the "indispensable role" of the UN in international affairs, support for a UN convention on terrorism, the role of the SCO in Afghanistan, Iran's right to use nuclear energy for "peaceful purposes," maintaining peace on the Korean Peninsula through dialogue, and Russia's core interests in the Caucasus region—all issues that reflect concerns about U.S. power.

In addition to this trilateral grouping, India, China, and Russia are key actors in an evolving dialogue among the so-called BRICS countries, which also include Brazil and (since 2011) South Africa. BRICS foreign ministers have been meeting annually since 2006. In 2009, the dialogue expanded to include an annual summit of heads of state, and China hosted the 2011 summit in Sanya, Hainan. Although the BRICS dialogue embraces many of the same political interests as the trilateral with Russia, it emphasizes economic issues. According to the declaration issued at Sanya, these include support for the G-20 "playing a bigger role in global economic governance,"

---

[80] "Joint Communiqué on the Results of the Trilateral Meeting of the Foreign Minister of India, Russia and China," New Delhi, February 14, 2007, available from http://in.china-embassy.org/eng/zygxc/wx/t773893.htm.

reform of the IMF, and reform of the international monetary system, among other issues.

Finally, India and China play a leading role in the BASIC group, which also includes South Africa and Brazil. This group was formed in November 2009 to coordinate policy among the four large developing economies on the eve of the Copenhagen Summit on climate change and resist pressure from developed countries.[81] At the summit, this group played a central role in negotiating with the United States to reach the Copenhagen Accord.[82] Since then, the group has met six times as global talks on climate change have continued.

Hedging and the Limits of Engagement

Despite the emphasis on comprehensive engagement, China's engagement of India has not extended to contentious bilateral issues and other Chinese policies that India opposes. By limiting its cooperation with India in certain areas, China seeks to maintain the ability to deter India from harming Chinese interests and objectives in the future. Comprehensive engagement also bolsters China's ability to deter India by highlighting the costs to New Delhi of a more confrontational relationship with Beijing. The diplomatic and political elements of China's hedge against India are discussed below.

First, despite its deepening relationship with India, China maintains its "all-weather" relationship with Pakistan. Although China sought to distance itself from Pakistani policies during the 1999 Kargil War and no longer links support for Pakistan with its relationship with India, Beijing continues to provide substantial, even if not unconditional, support for Islamabad and maintains a close relationship with Pakistan's armed forces. Following India's civil nuclear agreement with the United States in 2005, for example, China agreed to provide Pakistan with two additional nuclear reactors for its facility at Chashma, a move that allowed China to signal its displeasure with the U.S.-Indian pact and show support for its ally. More recently, in May 2011, China agreed to provide Pakistan with 50 JF-17 fighter jets.[83]

Second, China is actively developing ties with India's immediate neighbors in South Asia. Although the "string of pearls" was never a Chinese naval strategy, it does capture China's efforts to improve ties with India's

---

[81] Saibal Dasgupta, "Copenhagen Conference: India, China Plan Joint Exit," *Times of India*, November 28, 2009.

[82] Charles Babington and Jennifer Loven, "Obama Raced Clock, Chaos, Comedy for Climate Deal," Associated Press, December 19, 2009.

[83] Jane Perlez, "China Gives Pakistan 50 Fighter Jets," *New York Times*, May 19, 2011, A8.

neighbors, especially in order to develop alternative energy transportation routes through Pakistan and Burma. India's poor ties with many of these states created an opportunity that China has exploited deftly. Despite India's concerns about encirclement, Chinese diplomacy with South Asian states has continued even as Beijing has deepened ties with New Delhi. Partly for historical reasons, China maintains closer ties than India does with Pakistan and Burma, while it has improved ties with Bangladesh, Sri Lanka, and Nepal.

Third, China has confronted India on specific issues. As mentioned above, China opposed India's civil nuclear deal with the United States, which it viewed as potentially strengthening India's nuclear forces. In 2008, China nearly blocked the exception to full-scope safeguards granted to India by the Nuclear Suppliers Group. The group's rules require consensus, but Chinese representatives walked out of the negotiations on the evening of September 5. Beijing ultimately supported the final waiver on the morning of September 6 after it became clear that no other country would block it and in the wake of intensive U.S. and Indian diplomacy.[84] Likewise, China continues to withhold support for India's bid to become a permanent member of the UN Security Council, likely fearing that India could use the council's veto power against China.

Fourth and finally, China has maintained a firm position on the border dispute. In 2003 and 2005, progress in the dispute helped to further the development of political relations with India. During Vajpayee's visit to China in 2003, China and India agreed to upgrade long negotiations over their disputed border from the working group level to talks between high-level special representatives appointed by each side. During Wen's 2005 visit to India, the two countries signed an agreement on guiding principles for a framework to resolve the dispute and a protocol for further implementing confidence-building measures along the border.[85] Various joint statements and declarations issued as recently as 2008 called for an "early settlement" of the dispute.

Nevertheless, since 2005 further progress has failed to materialize. Moreover, China has hardened its public stance. In November 2006, for example, the Chinese ambassador to India, Sun Yuxi, stated in an interview on Indian television that China's claim in the eastern sector included not just Tawang but also the Indian state of Arunachal Pradesh.[86] Although China has claimed these areas since the 1950s, such a public statement by

---

[84] Author's interview with a former official at the U.S. Department of State, April 2011.

[85] "Protocol between India and China on Confidence Building Measures."

[86] Surya Gangadharan, "Arunachal Is Chinese Land: Envoy," *CNN-IBN*, November 20, 2006, http://ibnlive.in.com/news/arunachal-is-chinese-territory-envoy-minces-no-words/26108-3.html.

a Chinese ambassador had a chilling effect. China's position appeared to harden substantially in 2009. In March, China attempted to block a $2.9 billion loan to India from the Asian Development Bank because it included $60 million for a flood relief project in Arunachal Pradesh. In May, China began to issue hand-written visas that were stapled and not stamped into passports to Indians from Kashmir, apparently to indicate that it viewed the territory as under dispute, after India objected to Chinese infrastructure projects in Pakistan-occupied Kashmir.[87] In October and November, China publicly objected to visits to Arunachal Pradesh by Singh and the Dalai Lama. Throughout this period, reports in the Indian press of Chinese incursions across the Line of Actual Control (LAC) increased, though Indian officials repeatedly denied these reports.

Several factors may play a role in explaining China's assertiveness in the territorial dispute in 2009. First, because of the history of the boundary dispute and India's support for the Dalai Lama, China views any potential threat from India through the lens of political stability in Tibet. As two scholars note, South Asian states such as India are "directly related to the stability and development of China's western frontier."[88] Unrest throughout Tibetan areas in spring 2008 likely increased Chinese concerns over its vulnerability in Tibet to external pressure, prompting a toughening of China's position. China may also have been seeking to create leverage in case the next Dalai Lama is reincarnated in Indian-controlled territory. Part of China's claim in the eastern sector includes the village of Tawang, which is close to the site of the reincarnation of the sixth Dalai Lama in 1683. A reincarnation of the Dalai Lama outside China would be seen as a significant challenge to China's efforts to weaken the Tibetan government-in-exile. China's public emphasis on its claims to Arunachal Pradesh in recent years is consistent with such concerns. Second, China may have toughened its position on the border to signal its displeasure with the completion of the U.S.-Indian nuclear deal and with India's improved ties with the United States more generally. By raising the border issue, China may have sought to convey to India the potential costs of closer ties with the United States in order to deter such a development. Third, Beijing may have been trying to signal concern about India's bolstering of its military forces in Arunachal Pradesh, which is adjacent to Tibet, so soon after the widespread unrest in 2008. In 2009, India announced that it would create two new mountain infantry divisions in

---

[87] Altaf Hussain, "Row over China Kashmir Visa Move," *BBC News*, October 1, 2009, http://news.bbc.co.uk/2/hi/south_asia/8285106.stml; and "India Objects to Chinese Activities in PoK," *Times of India*, October 14, 2009.

[88] Lou and Zhang, "Nanya de zhanlue zhongyao xing yu Zhongguo de nanya zhanlue," 43.

the state totaling 70,000 troops and deploy squadrons of newly purchased advanced Su-30 multi-role fighter jets to airfields that would allow them to conduct operations over Chinese territory.

The Military Dimension

Despite India's military modernization, its impact on China's own military strategy and force structure remains limited. China seeks to deter what it views as potential Indian aggression on its land border but does not currently stress military means over other ways of hedging against India discussed above.

India has played a role in China's military planning since the 1962 Sino-Indian War. In the grammar of China's military strategy, however, India and China's southwest are a "secondary strategic direction" (*ciyao zhanlue fangxiang*) for the PLA and not a top priority.[89] Instead, since the mid-1990s and especially after 1999, Taiwan and China's east coast have been the "main strategic direction," or principal focus, of Chinese military strategy and force modernization, in which the United States is viewed as China's likely opponent.

In addition, China's military planning concerning India emphasizes the potential for conflict along the disputed border, not access to the Indian Ocean. When the PLA published its first set of campaign outlines for joint operations in 1999, it included "a border area counterattack campaign" (*bianjing diqu fanji zhanyi*), which is the generic name for a scenario involving an armed conflict with India.[90] The campaign describes how the PLA will use offensive operations to expel "an opponent" who attacks China along its frontier in areas under Chinese control.[91] In the early 2000s, this campaign garnered additional attention as tensions mounted between China and Taiwan. PLA planners feared that India might seek to open a second front for China if a crisis occurred across the Taiwan Strait and began to refer to such a contingency as a "chain reaction counterattack" (*liansuo fangying fanji*).[92]

---

[89] Chen Ligong, ed., *"Liansuo fanying" beijing xia gaohan shandi bianjing fangyu zuozhan yanjiu* [Research on High and Cold Mountainous Area Border Defense Operations under the Background of a 'Chain Reaction'] (Beijing: Jiefangjun chubanshe, 2005).

[90] M. Taylor Fravel, "Securing Borders: China's Doctrine and Force Structure for Frontier Defense," *Journal of Strategic Studies* 30, nos. 4–5 (2007): 705–37.

[91] To be clear, the campaign is premised on using offensive operations in a defense scenario. It does not outline how China might take by force territory currently held by India.

[92] Chen, *"Liansuo fanying" beijing xia gaohan shandi bianjing fangyu zuozhan yanjiu.*

Consistent with the secondary importance of a potential conflict with India, PLA force levels in China's southwest have remained relatively constant over the past decade. Few of the PLA's main force combat units are based in Tibet near the border with India (only two mountain infantry brigades and one mechanized infantry brigade of about 10,000–15,000 troops in total), and the number has not increased appreciably due to the harsh environment of the Tibetan plateau. Instead, the 13th and 14th Group Armies from the Chengdu Military Region are based far from the border with India in Sichuan and Kunming provinces.[93] Likewise, contrary to reports in the Indian media, China has no ballistic missile launch brigades in Tibet and no short-range ballistic missiles with nuclear warheads.[94] China also has no deployed tactical nuclear weapons in Tibet or elsewhere.[95] China has been upgrading roads and other infrastructure along its border with India as part of a decade-long effort to improve infrastructure all along China's land borders. Such infrastructure, including the new rail link between Qinghai and Tibet, would facilitate the deployment of troops to the border if a conflict were to occur. Nevertheless, even after New Delhi announced that it would create two new mountain divisions to be based in Arunachal Pradesh and deployed advanced Su-30 multi-role long-range fighter aircraft to bases as close as eight miles from China, Beijing has maintained existing force levels along the border.

In the naval arena, China is not pursuing a string of pearls strategy of military bases designed to project power in the Indian Ocean and challenge Indian naval power. This term was coined in a report by the defense contractor Booz Allen Hamilton to ascribe strategic intent to Chinese-funded infrastructure projects in South Asian countries.[96] Nevertheless, it is misleading in several ways. First, the activities discussed in the report were limited to investments in various civilian port and road projects. Although these projects might boost bilateral ties with specific countries and enable access for China's navy in the future, none of them entailed the construction of naval bases for either China or the recipient of Chinese aid.[97] Second, due to their proximity to India, these ports, especially in Bangladesh and Sri Lanka, would be vulnerable to Indian

---

[93] *Directory of People's Republic of China Military Personalities* (Aiea: Serold Hawaii, 2010), 222–25.

[94] The launch brigades closest to India are located in Qinghai, Gansu, and Yunnan. See ibid., 80–91.

[95] The most authoritative sources on China's armed forces all note that China lacks deployed tactical nuclear weapons. See various editions of the *Bulletin of the Atomic Scientists* and *The Military Balance* and the reports on Chinese military power from the U.S. Department of Defense.

[96] "China Builds Up Strategic Sea Lanes," *Washington Times*, January 17, 2005.

[97] In May 2011, Islamabad invited China to build a naval base for Pakistan.

strikes if a conflict occurred.[98] Third, consistent with China's east coast being the PLA's primary strategic direction, the PLAN remains focused on developing what the U.S. Department of Defense refers to as anti-access capabilities to deal with the threat to China posed by U.S. naval forces. Despite the current counterpiracy patrols in the Gulf of Aden, the PLAN continues to stress operations in what it calls the "near seas" (*jinhai*), such as the Yellow, East, and South China seas, where China has maritime disputes, and has not yet adopted a "far seas" (*yuanhai*) strategy for conducting combat operations against other navies in distant waters such as the Indian Ocean. Chinese analysts do acknowledge the vulnerability of China's sea lanes in the Indian Ocean to a blockade, should a conflict erupt over Taiwan. However, their concerns have not yet translated into new forces, permanent overseas military bases, serial production of large replenishment ships to sustain substantial forces at sea, or robust antisubmarine warfare capabilities to protect Chinese naval and commercial vessels.

The Future of the Relationship

China faces a dilemma in sustaining cooperation with a rising India. On the one hand, it seeks to continue cooperation with New Delhi that promotes its own grand strategy. On the other hand, India may threaten some of China's core interests and strategic objectives, and the ways in which China hedges against India may also limit its ability to deepen cooperation further. Several issues related to China's interests and objectives that could become points of increased friction in Chinese-Indian ties over the coming years are discussed below

Indian-U.S. Alignment

Chinese experts acknowledge that a dramatic improvement has occurred in India's relationship with the United States over the past decade. A close U.S.-Indian security relationship could challenge China's strategic interests by imposing new constraints on China's freedom of maneuver. Yet most do not believe that such a relationship will materialize. Almost all observers conclude that the United States has courted India to

---

[98] Daniel J. Kostecka, "Hambantota, Chittagong, and the Maldives: Unlikely Pearls for the Chinese Navy," Jamestown Foundation, China Brief, November 19, 2010.

counter China,[99] but few assert that India and the United States will be able to form a close security partnership or alliance that would pose a real challenge to China. As one former ambassador concludes, "the possibility of India's forming an anti-China alliance with the United States and Japan is very small."[100]

Chinese experts highlight several reasons why such an alignment will not likely occur. The first is India's own tradition of strategic independence and identity as a great power. Because of these considerations, Chinese experts conclude that India does not want to be a "little companion" or "small partner" of the United States.[101] The conditions that the United States has attached to security cooperation with India, such as restrictions on arms sales, are frequently cited as an example of such a hierarchical relationship. A second reason is that Chinese experts believe that differences between the United States and India on key issues such as Iran, reform of the UN, India's support for multipolarization, and India's desire for hegemony in the Indian Ocean will prevent closer cooperation between Washington and New Delhi. A third reason is that political parties and interest groups within India are likely to oppose closer security cooperation with the United States against China, in particular the Communist parties that opposed the civil nuclear deal. The potential damage to India's long-standing security relationship with Russia is a fourth factor that may prevent closer U.S.-Indian security cooperation, as India would risk harming relations with its principal supplier of military equipment and spare parts. A final reason for Chinese analysts' skepticism of closer U.S.-India alignment is that, through an alliance with the United States, India would risk all that it has gained through improved ties with China in the past decade. Specifically, the confrontation with China that such an alignment might entail would destroy India's "peaceful environment."[102] According to Chinese experts, this would occur not only because of increased tensions in Chinese-Indian relations but also because China maintains good ties with India's neighbors

---

[99] Cheng, "Yindu de waijiao zhanlue quxiang"; Hu, "Cong diyuan zhengzhi jiaodu kan Yindu de daguo zhanlue he yinxiang"; Ma, "Yindu daguo waijiao de taishi"; and Zhao Qinhai, "Mei-Yin junshi hezuo jiqi zhiyue yinsu" [Military Cooperation between the U.S. and India and Its Restricting Factors], *Guoji wenti yanjiu*, no. 5 (2008): 22–27.

[100] Cheng, "Yindu de waijiao zhanlue quxiang," 50.

[101] Zhao, "Mei-Yin junshi hezuo jiqi zhiyue yinsu," 25; and Lan, "Zhong-Yin dui waijiao zhanlue yitong yu shuangbian guanxi," 38.

[102] Cheng, "Lun Zhong-Yin zhanlue hezuo huoban guanxi"; Cheng Ruisheng, "Guanyu Zhong-Yin-Mei sanbian guanxi de yixie sikao" [Reflections on Trilateral Relations between China, India, and the United States], *Nanya yanjiu likan*, no. 3 (2008): 3–4; and Cheng, "Yindu de waijiao zhanlue quxiang," 50.

and could use those ties, especially with Pakistan, to harm Indian interests in such a confrontation.[103]

Access to the Indian Ocean

The Indian Ocean poses an increasing challenge for China. As roughly 85% of China's oil imports currently pass through this large body of water en route from Africa and the Persian Gulf to China, Beijing is acutely aware of its vulnerability to the disruption of shipping in this area. As the dominant regional power with a capable and modernizing navy, India poses a potential threat that China must address.

Chinese writings on the security of sea lanes in the Indian Ocean all begin with the premise that India seeks maritime hegemony in these waters. In particular, Chinese experts view India's maritime strategy as pursuing a sea-control capability that would extend from the Arabian Sea to the South China Sea and include the ability to block key chokepoints such as the Strait of Malacca. In the event of a conflict, one analyst concludes that a blockade "would exert very negative influence on Chinese shipping and maritime security."[104] In peacetime, Chinese experts see India's naval aspirations as seeking to prevent Chinese vessels from entering the Indian Ocean and to limit China's ability to develop ties with the littoral states. The key challenge for China is to maintain access to the Indian Ocean, both in peacetime and in wartime, though most experts see this as a long-term challenge and not a short-term threat. Many analysts also note the nontraditional challenges that China might face in these waters, including terrorism and piracy.

Chinese experts suggest a range of options for reducing the PRC's vulnerability in the Indian Ocean and ensuring its ability to access these waters. Although almost all experts call for the development of a blue water navy, their specific suggestions start with the premise that for several decades China will lack the ability to project naval power that could challenge India's navy and emphasize instead political and diplomatic approaches that will limit India's ability to achieve or exercise sea control at China's expense.[105] One scholar describes this approach as "entering

---

[103] This section draws on Cheng, "Guanyu Zhong-Yin-Mei sanbian guanxi de yixie sikao," 3–4; Cheng, "Yindu de waijiao zhanlue quxiang," 50; Hu, "Cong diyuan zhengzhi jiaodu kan Yindu de daguo zhanlue he yingxiang," 67; and Zhao, "Mei-Yin junshi hezuo jiqi zhiyue yinsu," 25–26.

[104] Li Bin, "Yindu de haishang zhanlue yongdao sixiang yu zhengce" [The Ideas and Policies of India's Maritime Strategic Passageways], *Nanya yanjiu*, no. 2 (2006), 20.

[105] Shi Chunlin, "Yindu Yang hangxian anquan yu Zhongguo de zhanlue duice" [Transportation Security in the Indian Ocean and China's Strategic Countermeasures], *Nanya yanjiu likan*, no. 3 (2010): 7; and Wang Lirong, "Yindu Yang yu Zhongguo haishang tongdao anquan zhanlue" [The Indian Ocean and China's Strategy for Sea Lane Security], *Nanya yanjiu*, no. 3 (2009): 54.

the Indian Ocean indirectly."[106] Such an indirect approach stresses the importance of improving ties with the littoral states, especially Pakistan and Burma, who can provide alternative overland transportation routes into China. It also calls for increasing naval cooperation with India on matters relating to the Indian Ocean, as well as with other coastal states, especially Bangladesh and Sri Lanka. To check or limit India's ability to prevent China from accessing these waters, some experts call for developing multilateral initiatives and working within the UN to address sea lane security so as to constrain India's influence and give China a greater role in the region.[107]

Reducing India's Suspicions and Increasing Mutual Trust

A key challenge to Chinese-Indian relations that all experts note is the lack of mutual strategic trust between China and India. The lack of trust arises from many sources, especially the legacy of India's defeat in the 1962 war and the lack of a breakthrough in the long-standing territorial dispute. Other sources of mistrust include Beijing's diplomatic relationships with India's neighbors, especially Pakistan, which validate the argument that China seeks to encircle India; the increasing gap in the economies of the two countries; limited people-to-people contacts and exchanges; and India's fears about growing Chinese ties with its South Asian neighbors.[108]

This lack of trust is not a new problem. Ma Jiali noted in 2007 that "mutual strategic confidence is lacking between the two countries. India is still suspicious about China."[109] Nevertheless, many articles published in 2010 acknowledge that Indian suspicions of China have increased and should be addressed. Retired ambassador Cheng Ruisheng, for example, explains that the "inadequacy of mutual trust between the two countries remains a quite outstanding problem with certain negative impact on their

---

[106] Liu Xinhua, "Lun Zhong-Yin guanxi zhong de Yindu Yang wenti" [On the Indian Ocean in Chinese-Indian Relations], *Taipingyang xuebao*, no. 1 (2010): 45–58.

[107] Li, "Yindu de haishang zhanlue yongdao sixiang yu zhengce"; Liu, "Lun Zhong-Yin guanxi zhong de Yindu Yang wenti," 40–50; Ma Jiali, "Yindu de haiyangguan jiyi haiyang zhanlue" [India's Maritime Concept and Ocean Strategy], *Yafei zongheng*, no. 2 (2009): 47; Shi, "Yindu Yang hangxian anquan yu Zhongguo de zhanlue duice," 5–6; and Wang, "Yindu Yang yu Zhongguo haishang tongdao anquan zhanlue," 52–53.

[108] Cheng Ruisheng, "Zhong-Yin jianjiao 60 nian jingyan yu qishi" [Experience and Inspiration in 60 Years of Establishing Chinese-Indian Relations], *Dongnanya nanya yanjiu*, no. 3 (2010): 21–22; Lan Jianxue, "Zhong-Yin guanxi zhili maixiang xintaijie" [China-India Relations Strive to Move to a New Level], *Shijie zhishi*, no. 9 (2010): 26; Ma Jiali, "Zhong-Yin guanxi de huigui yu zhanwang" [Relations and Prospects for Chinese-Indian Relations], *Heping yu fazhan*, no. 4 (2010): 9–10; Yang Zhizhen, "Yindu zhizao Zhong-Yin guanxi bu hexie yuanyin tanxi" [Exploration of the Causes of Discord in Chinese-Indian Relations Created by India], *Nanya yanjiu*, no. 3 (2010): 37–38; and Zhang, "Zhong-Yin guanxi de qedingxing he buqudingxing," 40–41.

[109] Ma, "Zhong-Yin guanxi de fazhan qianjing," 26.

relations."[110] Many Chinese experts note how in India's democratic system interest groups (including the military) and the media have helped shape and, in Chinese eyes, encourage concerns about China.[111]

Chinese experts have offered a variety of suggestions for reducing India's suspicion and enhancing trust. All agree that the territorial dispute must be resolved for a real breakthrough to occur in the relationship. Many advocate maintaining dialogue through increased high-level meetings, while also seeking to deepen people-to-people interactions.[112] Others, including Cheng Ruisheng, suggest that China and India should "take more active steps to support each other on major issues involving core interests of the other side."[113] Cheng cites India's efforts in 2008 to ensure the smooth passage of the Olympic torch and China's "flexibility" in the Nuclear Suppliers Group. He also recommends increasing transparency "on important questions to either side" by offering "more information to each other."[114] Echoing this view, another scholar suggests that the two sides discuss in more detail their strategies in South Asia and that China's strategy in the region should "actively regard relations with India."[115] Other recommendations include strengthening the strategic dialogue to improve China's and India's understanding of each other's intentions and holding a trilateral dialogue with Pakistan.[116]

Addressing the Territorial Dispute

China's India experts all agree that the territorial dispute poses the most significant obstacle to the further improvement of relations. For many, the dispute is the main reason for the lack of strategic trust discussed above. As Ma Jiali describes, "the twists and turns and ups and downs in Chinese-Indian relations have a geopolitical element, but in the final analysis they come down to the border issue."[117] According to another analyst, "the unsettled boundary dispute seriously damages the political

---

[110] Cheng, "Zhong-Yin jianjiao 60 nian jingyan yu qishi," 22.

[111] Ma Jiali, "Yindu zai jiannan zhong wenjian jueqi" [India's Steady Rise amidst Difficulties], *Dongnanya nanya yanjiu*, no. 1 (2010): 17–22; and Yang, "Yindu zhizao Zhong-Yin guanxi bu hexie yuanyin tanxi."

[112] Cheng, "Zhong-Yin jianjiao 60 nian jingyan yu qishi," 22.

[113] Ibid.

[114] This suggests that current dialogues and mechanisms are not being fully utilized.

[115] Zhang, "Yindu zhanlue jueqi yu Zhong-Yin guanxi," 8.

[116] Cheng, "Zhong-Yin jianjiao 60 nian jingyan yu qishi"; and Zhang, "Yindu zhanlue jueqi yu Zhong-Yin guanxi," 9.

[117] Ma, "Zhong-Yin guanxi de huigui yu zhanwang," 9–10.

mutual trust between China and India and impedes the development of bilateral relations."[118]

These analysts disagree, however, about the prospects for settling the dispute. According to Cheng Ruisheng, who argued in 2010 that "conditions are already ripe for a final settlement," the improvement in Chinese-Indian relations since 2005 forms the basis for a resolution.[119] He asserts that a final settlement would help maintain the peaceful environment "that serves the supreme national interests of both countries," that the 2005 guiding principles agreement provides a foundation for this settlement, and that, due to the past negotiating record, each side is well aware of the other's positions.[120] In contrast to Cheng's optimism, other experts note the obstacles that must be overcome to reach a settlement and believe that conditions are "not yet ripe."[121] Importantly, they acknowledge the role of public opinion in both countries in preventing a final agreement. As one analyst writes, "the boundary issue…has become a thorn that provokes the nerves of the people."[122] According to former ambassador Zhou Gang, because of the dispute's size, background, and "involvement of the feelings of the people from the two countries, this question is quite difficult to resolve."[123] Another analyst expresses pessimism about a peaceful settlement and fears that India might become more assertive in the dispute as it grows stronger.[124]

Consistent with the goal of improving Chinese-Indian relations, many analysts since 2010 have softened their tone and called for a final settlement. In contrast to the early and middle 2000s, Chinese experts have stopped referring to the sensitive area of Tawang in Arunachal Pradesh and the importance of its return to China. Many note the need to address the impact of the 1962 war and address the "excessive expectations" on both sides toward the dispute.[125] Others stress that "mutual understanding and mutual accommodation (*huliang hurang*) should be the only way for solving

---

[118] Lou Chunhao, "Zhong-Yin bianjing zhengyi qu: Yindu 'qianghua zhanling' buzai li" [Disputed Area on the Chinese-Indian Border: India's "Strengthened Occupation" Is Unreasonable], *Shijie zhishi*, no. 7 (2010): 24.

[119] Cheng, "Zhong-Yin jianjiao 60 nian jingyan yu qishi," 22.

[120] Ibid.

[121] Zhang, "Zhong-Yin guanxi de quedingxing he buquedingxing," 40.

[122] Lan, "Zhong-Yin guanxi zhili maixiang xintaijie," 26.

[123] Zhou Gang, "Setting the Border: Patience, Determination and Confidence Are Called to Solve the Sino-India Boundary Question," *Beijing Review*, December 9, 2010, 13.

[124] Zhang, "Yindu zhanlue jueqi yu Zhong-Yin guanxi," 5.

[125] Zhang, "Zhong-Yin guanxi de quedingxing he buquedingxing," 40.

the border dispute."[126] Chinese experts (as well as the government) have used similar slogans in the past, but their use in discussions of the dispute's negative impact on the bilateral relationship suggests growing support for a more moderate position and a final compromise agreement. As Cheng Ruisheng notes in a recent article on improving strategic trust, "it is not practical *for either side* to demand unilateral concessions from the other" (emphasis added).[127]

Conclusion

Although suspicions toward India remain, China views India's rise as a positive development that will support Chinese interests more than it will undermine them. Beijing pursues comprehensive engagement with India to realize cooperation on economic and international issues and promote China's own strategic objectives of maintaining a stable external environment for development, preventing the formation of a balancing coalition, and reducing the constraints of unipolarity. At the same time, China hedges against India's ability to obstruct Chinese interests by withholding cooperation or maintaining its policies on specific issues.

On balance, China's positive view of India's rise suggests that intense security competition between the two countries in the next decade is unlikely. Common interests as developing countries pursuing rapid growth in a unipolar international system create strong incentives for continued cooperation and the management of differences. Given the growing disparity in the size of the two economies, India will only serve as a limited counterweight to China in Asia.

Chinese views of India's rise contrast starkly with Indian views of China's rise. Most Chinese elites see India as neither a major threat to China nor a geopolitical rival but instead as a developing nation with which China shares many common interests. The relationship thus can still be described as what Susan Shirk termed in 2004 a "one-sided rivalry."[128] This gap in perceptions can largely be explained by the underlying asymmetry in material capabilities.[129] Put simply, China can threaten India more than India can threaten China, which limits India's ability to influence Chinese behavior. China may underestimate Indian

[126] Ma, "Zhong-Yin guanxi de huigui yu zhanwang," 9.

[127] Cheng, "Zhong-Yin jianjiao 60 nian jingyan yu qishi," 22.

[128] Shirk, "One-Sided Rivalry."

[129] For an excellent study of the effects of asymmetry on international relations, see Brantly Womack, *China and Vietnam: The Politics of Asymmetry* (New York: Cambridge University Press, 2006).

concerns about China's rise, while India may overestimate the threat from China, which views the United States as its principal strategic competitor. Such gaps in perceptions can prove dangerous by increasing uncertainty and the potential for miscalculation.

For now, China's positive assessment of India's rise appears unlikely to change. Nevertheless, several factors might cause a shift in Chinese views. Amid renewed concerns about stability in ethnic Tibetan areas of China as well as about the reincarnation of the Dalai Lama, Beijing may view India's continued deployments and upgrading of forces on the border as seeking to profit from China's worries about internal instability and gain leverage over China by challenging what Beijing has declared as its core interest. In addition, how India responds to the reincarnation of the Dalai Lama, especially if it occurs on Indian territory, will likely exert a powerful effect on Chinese views of India's rise. Finally, if China's and India's economic and international interests as developing countries eventually diverge, then the strategic rationale for cooperation will weaken. Nevertheless, as long as the United States remains China's principal strategic competitor, Beijing will likely view India's rise through the lens of a grand strategy that seeks to ensure China's rise amid U.S. unipolarity and thus will maintain the positive assessment of India described above.

EXECUTIVE SUMMARY

This chapter discusses the changing trajectory of Indian policy toward China and explores how India is responding to China's rise across a range of issue areas central to its strategic calculus.

MAIN ARGUMENT:
Despite the rhetoric of cooperation, distrust of China is growing in India at an alarming rate. The two sides seem locked in a classic security dilemma in which any action taken by one state is interpreted by the other as a threat to its interests. In India a consensus is evolving that China's rise is problematic for Indian global and regional interests. There is also a growing perception that, among the major powers, China is the only one that does not accept India as a rising player that should be accommodated into the global political order.

POLICY IMPLICATIONS:
- Indian policy toward China is becoming tougher as New Delhi embarks on a more forceful policy of internal and external balancing in an attempt to protect the country's core interests. New Delhi will be hard-pressed to balance its desire to deter China with its interest in avoiding an escalation of tensions.

- India will view the U.S. as a critical balancer in the India-U.S.-China triangular relationship and will look to Washington for support as both Sino-Indian and Sino-U.S. competition enter into sharper relief in the coming years. India's burgeoning relationship with the U.S. gives New Delhi crucial strategic room to maneuver vis-à-vis China.

- The U.S. faces the prospect of an emerging power transition in Asia, and a robust partnership with India will be a valuable asset in stabilizing the region's strategic landscape.

India Comes to Terms with a Rising China

Harsh V. Pant

In recent years, the world has grappled with the challenges posed by China's rapid rise, and India is no exception. The peculiar nature of Sino-Indian ties has been underscored by a sudden downturn in bilateral relations. The relationship has become so ruptured that some Indian strategists have even contemplated a "year of the Chinese attack on India," suggesting that China would attack India by 2012 to divert attention from its growing domestic troubles.[1] The Indian media, rather than interrogating these claims, further sensationalized this issue, which was then picked up by the official Chinese media.[2] Adding their own spin, voices in the Chinese media started suggesting that, while a Chinese attack on India is highly unlikely, a conflict between the two neighbors could occur in one scenario: India's adoption of an aggressive policy toward its border dispute with China, thereby forcing China to take military action.[3] The Chinese media

Harsh V. Pant is a Reader in International Relations in the Defence Studies Department at King's College London. He can be reached at <harsh.pant@kcl.ac.uk>.

This chapter draws on several previously published works by the author. See Harsh V. Pant, "China's Rise, India's Challenge," International Security and Relations Network, ISN Insights, October 27, 2010; Harsh V. Pant, "India's China Policy: Importance of a Strategic Framework," *Security Research Review* 1, no. 3 (2005); Harsh V. Pant, "India in the Indian Ocean: Growing Mismatch Between Ambitions and Capabilities," *Pacific Affairs* 82, no. 2 (Summer 2009): 279–97; and Harsh V. Pant, "Focus on China, Not India-Pakistan Rivalry," Rediff, April 29, 2010.

[1] "Nervous China May Attack India by 2012: Defence Expert," *Indian Express*, July 12, 2009.

[2] See, for example, "China Could Attack India by 2012, Claims Analyst," Press Trust of India, July 12, 2009.

[3] Li Hongmei, "Veiled Threat or Good Neighbor?" *People's Daily Online*, June 19, 2009, http://english.peopledaily.com.cn/90002/96417/6682302.html.

went on to speculate that the "China will attack India" line might actually be a pretext for India to deploy more troops to the border areas.[4]

As China and India have risen in the global interstate hierarchy, their bilateral relationship has become uneasy as they attempt to come to terms with each other's rise. The distrust between the two is actually growing at an alarming rate, notwithstanding the rhetoric of official pronouncements. Growing economic cooperation and bilateral political and socio-cultural exchanges have done little to assuage each country's concerns about the other's intentions.[5]

This chapter discusses the contemporary state of Sino-Indian relations with a focus on the changing trajectory of Indian policy toward the rise of China and how India is responding to this rise across a range of issue areas central to its strategic calculus. The first three sections explore the key forms of interaction between China and India and identify areas of global convergence and bilateral divergence. The chapter then examines the changing Indian policy trajectory toward China as New Delhi begins to more forcefully pursue a policy of internal and external balancing in order to protect core national interests. Finally, the chapter delineates the impact on the United States of India's attitudes and behavior toward China.

Historical and Diplomatic Interactions

Sino-Indian Historical Ties

As two ancient civilizations, India and China have had cultural and trade ties since at least the first century. The famous Silk Road allowed for economic ties to develop between the two neighbors, with the transmission of Buddhism from India to China giving a further cultural dimension to the relationship. Political ties between China and India, however, remained underdeveloped. During the colonial period, British trade and diplomacy linked India to China in both positive and nefarious ways as India became the jumping off place for the British exploitation of China, mostly by the East India Company. This history has continued to influence Chinese thinking about India and the perception that India still serves as the "cat's-paw" for the West.

In the early Cold War period, independent India's first prime minister, Jawaharlal Nehru, saw an anti-imperialist friendship between the two

---

[4] Li, "Veiled Threat or Good Neighbor?"

[5] For further discussion, see Harsh V. Pant, "China's Rise, India's Challenge," International Security and Relations Network, ISN Insights, October 27, 2010, http://www.isn.ethz.ch/isn/Current-Affairs/ISN-Insights/Detail?lng=en&id=123018&contextid735=123007.

largest states of Asia as imperative to avoid interference by the two external superpowers.[6] Solidarity with China was integral to Nehru's vision of Asian leadership. After the People's Republic of China (PRC) was founded in 1949 and India established diplomatic ties with it in 1950, India not only advocated for PRC membership in the United Nations but also opposed attempts to condemn the PRC for its actions in Korea. Yet the issue of Tibet soon emerged as a major point of contention between China and India. New Delhi sought to allay Beijing's suspicions about Indian designs on Tibet by supporting the Seventeen-Point Agreement between Tibetan delegates and China in 1951, which recognized PRC sovereignty over Tibet and guaranteed the existing socio-political arrangements. India and China signed the famed Panchsheel Agreement in 1954 that underlined the five principles of peaceful coexistence as the basis of their bilateral relationship.[7] These principles included mutual respect for each other's territorial integrity and sovereignty, mutual nonaggression, noninterference in each other's internal affairs, equality and mutual benefit, and peaceful coexistence. This was the heyday of Sino-Indian ties, with the phrase *Hindi-Chini bhai-bhai* (Indians and Chinese are brothers) being a favorite slogan for the seeming camaraderie between the two states.

But that camaraderie did not last long. Soon the border dispute between China and India escalated, leading to the 1962 Sino-Indian War.[8] Though short, the war would have a long-lasting impact on Sino-Indian ties. It demolished Nehru's claims of Asian solidarity, and the defeat by China psychologically scarred Indian military and political elites. The war also led China to develop close ties with India's neighboring adversary, Pakistan, resulting in what is now widely considered an "all-weather" friendship. China supported Pakistan in its 1965 and 1971 wars with India and helped Islamabad in the development of its nuclear weapons arsenal. Meanwhile, India accelerated its own nuclear weapons program following China's testing of nuclear weapons in 1964.

The border issue continues to be a major obstacle in Sino-Indian ties, with minor skirmishes at the border occurring since 1962. As China and the United States grew closer after their rapprochement in 1972, India gravitated toward the Soviet Union to balance the Sino-U.S.-Pakistan axis.

---

[6] For a detailed discussion of early Sino-Indian ties, see John Rowland, *A History of Sino-Indian Relations: Hostile Co-Existence* (Princeton: D. Van Nostrand Company, 1967).

[7] "India and the People's Republic of China: Agreement (with Exchange of Notes) on Trade and Intercourse between Tibet Region of China and India" (Beijing, April 29, 1954), recorded in United Nations, *Treaty Series* 299 (1958), 57.

[8] For a detailed account, see Steven A. Hoffmann, *India and the China Crisis* (Berkeley: University of California Press, 1990). For an earlier account that is quite critical of Nehru and his "forward policy," see Neville Maxwell, *India's China War* (London: Jonathan Cape, 1970).

In 1988, then Indian prime minister Rajiv Gandhi turned a new leaf in Sino-Indian ties when he went to Beijing and signed an agreement aimed at achieving a "fair and reasonable settlement while seeking a mutually acceptable solution to the border dispute."[9] The visit saw a joint working group (JWG) set up to explore the boundary issue and examine possible solutions to the problem.

However, bilateral relations between India and the PRC reached their nadir in the immediate aftermath of India's nuclear tests in May 1998. Just before the tests, the Indian defense minister had identified China as his country's top security threat.[10] Afterward, Indian prime minister Atal Bihari Vajpayee wrote to U.S. president Bill Clinton, justifying the tests as a response to the threat posed by China.[11] Not surprisingly, China reacted strongly, and diplomatic relations between the two countries plummeted to an all-time low.

The Diplomacy of Declarations

After more than a decade, relations between the two countries, at least superficially, seem to be on a much firmer footing, as both governments have tried to reduce the prospect for rivalry and expand areas of cooperation. A visit to China by the Indian external affairs minister in 1999 marked the resumption of high-level discussions, as the two sides declared that they were not threats to each other and began a bilateral security dialogue that helped them express and share their concerns with each other. Both China and India continue to emphasize that neither side should let differences impede the growth of functional cooperation. They also decided to expedite the process of demarcating the Line of Actual Control (LAC), and the JWG has been meeting regularly to resolve the boundary question. As a first step in this direction, the two countries exchanged border maps on the least-controversial middle sector of the LAC. More recently, in 2005 both sides established the Political Parameters and Guiding Principles for the Settlement of the India-China Boundary Question Agreement, broad principles to govern any dispute settlement. China has expressed its desire to seek a fair resolution to the

---

[9] "Sino-Indian Joint Press Communiqué," Ministry of Foreign Affairs of the People's Republic of China (PRC), December 23, 1988, http://www.fmprc.gov.cn/eng/wjdt/2649/t15800.htm.

[10] "China Is Threat No.1, Says Fernandes," *Hindustan Times*, May 3, 1998.

[11] "Nuclear Anxiety; Indian's Letter to Clinton on the Nuclear Testing," *New York Times*, May 13, 1998, http://www.nytimes.com/1998/05/13/world/nuclear-anxiety-indian-s-letter-to-clinton-on-the-nuclear-testing.html.

vexed boundary issue on the basis of "mutual accommodation, respect for history, and accommodation of reality."[12]

Vajpayee visited China in June 2003, the first such visit by an Indian premier in a decade. The joint declaration signed during this visit expressed the view that China was not a threat to India.[13] The two states appointed special representatives to impart momentum to the border negotiations, which have lasted now for more than twenty years, with the prime minister's principal secretary becoming India's political negotiator and replacing the JWG. India and China also decided to hold their first joint naval and air exercises. More significantly, India acknowledged China's sovereignty over Tibet and pledged not to allow "anti-China" political activities in India. For its part, China seems to have finally acknowledged India's 1975 incorporation of the former monarchy of Sikkim by first agreeing to open a trading post along the border with the former kingdom and by later rectifying official maps to include Sikkim as part of India.[14] After being closed for 60 years, the Nathu La pass, a traditional trading post between Tibet and Sikkim, was reopened in 2006. The two states have also set up institutionalized defense consultation mechanisms to reduce suspicion and identify areas of cooperation on security issues. Since then, high-level political interactions have continued unabated.

Soon after assuming office in 2004, the Manmohan Singh government made clear that it supported closer ties with China and would continue to work toward improving bilateral relations. When Singh visited China in 2008, the two states signed the "shared vision for the 21st century" declaration "to promote the building of a harmonious world of durable peace and common prosperity through developing the Strategic and Cooperative Partnership for Peace and Prosperity between the two countries,"[15] while also reiterating support for the 2005 boundary settlement agreement. The two sides have decided to elevate the boundary negotiations to the level of a strategic dialogue, with plans for a hotline between the Indian prime minister and the Chinese premier as a means to remove misunderstanding

---

[12] Anil K. Joseph, "Wen to Seek Resolution of Border Dispute," *Indian Express*, March 15, 2005.

[13] "Declaration on Principles for Relations and Comprehensive Cooperation between the People's Republic of China and the Republic of India," Ministry of Foreign Affairs of the PRC, June 23, 2003, http://www.fmprc.gov.cn/eng/wjdt/2649/t22852.htm.

[14] Amit Baruah, "China Keeps Its Word on Sikkim," *Hindu*, May 7, 2004. This discussion of recent Sino-Indian diplomacy draws from Harsh V. Pant, "India's China Policy: Importance of a Strategic Framework," *Security Research Review* 1, no. 3 (2005), http://www.bharat-rakshak.com/SRR/2005/03/30-indias-china-policy-importance-of-a-strategic-framework.html.

[15] "A Shared Vision for the 21st Century of the People's Republic of China and the Republic of India," Ministry of Foreign Affairs of the PRC, January 14, 2008, http://www.fmprc.gov.cn/eng/wjdt/2649/t399545.htm.

and reduce tensions. Their public vision suggests that this relationship will have "a positive influence on the future of the international system."[16]

The Global Convergence

At the international systemic level, India and China have found a convergence of interests by working together on climate change and global trade negotiations and demanding a restructuring of global financial institutions in view of the world economy's shifting center of gravity.[17] They share similar concerns about the international dominance of the United States, the threat of terrorism from religious fundamentalist and ethnic movements, and the need to accord primacy to economic development. India and China have also expressed concern about the United States' use of military power around the world and were publicly opposed to the war in Iraq. Such views are merely a continuation of both states' desire to contest U.S. *hyperpuissance* (hyperpower) since the end of the Cold War.

China and India, much like other major powers in the international system, favor a multipolar world order where the United States remains constrained by the other poles in the system. China and India zealously guard their national sovereignty and have been wary of U.S. attempts to interfere in what they see as the domestic affairs of other states, such as Serbia, Kosovo, and Iraq. Both countries took strong exception to the U.S. air strikes on Iraq in 1998, the U.S.-led air campaign against Yugoslavia in 1999, the U.S. campaign against Saddam Hussein in 2003, and more recently Western intervention in Libya. They argue that these actions violate sovereignty and undermine the authority of the UN system. China and India thus share an interest in resisting interventionist foreign policy doctrines emanating from the West, particularly from the United States, and display conservative attitudes on the prerogatives of sovereignty.

China and India have likewise coordinated efforts on issues as wide-ranging as climate change, trade negotiations, energy security, and the global financial crisis. Both nations favor more democratic international economic regimes. Some argue that the forces of globalization have led to a certain convergence of Sino-Indian interests in the economic realm, as the two nations become even more deeply engaged in the international

---

[16] "A Shared Vision for the 21st Century." The declaration included a statement of particular interest to India: "The Indian side reiterates its aspirations for permanent membership of the UN Security Council. The Chinese side attaches great importance to India's position as a major developing country in international affairs. The Chinese side understands and supports India's aspirations to play a greater role in the United Nations, including in the Security Council."

[17] The following discussion of convergent interests is drawn from Pant, "India's China Policy."

economy and more integrated into global financial networks.[18] China and India have strongly resisted efforts by the United States and other developed nations to link trade to labor and environmental standards—a policy that would put them at a huge disadvantage vis-à-vis the developed world, thereby hampering their drive toward economic development, which is the highest priority for both countries. Both have committed to crafting joint positions in the World Trade Organization (WTO) and global trade negotiations in the hope that this might increase their leverage over developed states. Beijing and New Delhi would like to see further liberalization of agricultural trade in developed countries, a tightening of the rules on anti-dumping measures, and the exclusion of non–trade related issues such as labor and the environment from the WTO. Both states have also fought carbon emission caps proposed by the industrialized world and have resisted Western pressure to open their agricultural markets.

In addition, China and India have strengthened their bilateral relationship in areas as distinct as cultural and educational exchanges, military exchanges, and science and technology cooperation. Military cooperation, something unthinkable a few years back, now takes place at some levels through joint exercises. Economic relations have been burgeoning as well, with China now India's largest trading partner. It was former Chinese premier Zhu Rongji who suggested that the combination of Chinese hardware and Indian software would be irresistible to the global market. Bilateral trade has recorded rapid growth, rising from a volume of $265 million in 1991 to $41.85 billion in 2008–9, or 8.56% of India's overall trade, exceeding $60 billion by the end of 2010.[19] The two nations are also evaluating the possibility of signing a comprehensive economic cooperation agreement and a free trade agreement (FTA), which would build on strong complementarities between the two economies.

Both China and India are feeling the pressure of diminishing oil discoveries and flat-line oil production at a time when the expansion of their economies is rapidly increasing the domestic demand for energy. Many have argued that cooperation on energy issues is the only way forward if both states want to gain economies of scale and negotiation muscle. In many ways, China and India face similar constraints in achieving energy security, and a coordinated approach would benefit them both, given that competition only drives up the costs of acquisition and diminishes future

[18] James Clad, "Convergent Chinese and Indian Perspectives on the Global Order," in *The India-China Relationship: What the United States Needs to Know*, ed. Francine R. Frankel and Harry Harding (New York: Columbia University Press, 2004), 267–93.

[19] For 2008–9, this level increases to $45.95 billion, an 11.24% share of India's trade, if Hong Kong is included in trade figures with China. "India, China Did $60-bn Trade in 2010," *Hindustan Times*, January 27, 2011.

returns. There has been a recognition of this at the highest levels of both governments. New Delhi and Beijing have signed a range of memoranda on energy cooperation in a variety of areas, including upstream exploration and production, the refining and marketing of petroleum products and petrochemicals, the construction of national and transnational pipelines, R&D, and the promotion of environmentally friendly fuels.[20]

Growing Bilateral Divergence

Despite the expansive agenda that China and India have identified for cooperation at the global level, bilateral tensions have been rising. China decided in 2009 to take the territorial dispute to the Asian Development Bank, where it blocked India's application for a loan that included money for development projects in the state of Arunachal Pradesh, which China continues to claim as part of its territory.[21] China's efforts to block the U.S.-India civilian nuclear energy cooperation pact in the Nuclear Suppliers Group (NSG) and its obstructionist stance on bringing to justice the masterminds of the November 2008 terrorist attacks in Mumbai seem to have further confirmed Indian suspicions about China's lack of sensitivity to India's security interests and failure to recognize India as a global power. This perception was only reinforced by China's suggestion to the U.S. Pacific Fleet commander in 2009 that the Indian Ocean be recognized as part of a Chinese sphere of influence.[22]

This deterioration in bilateral ties is happening at a time when China's economic and military rise is changing the strategic landscape around India. China's economic transformation has facilitated the country's emergence as a major military power. As a consequence, the PRC has begun to more actively flex its military strength, with People's Liberation Army Navy (PLAN) vessels combating piracy in the Gulf of Aden and Beijing considering deploying combat troops for UN peacekeeping efforts. This sustained military build-up will continue over the next few years, posing a challenge to Indian military planners as the Indian military modernization program struggles to catch up.

---

[20] Siddhartha Varadarajan, "India, China Primed for Energy Cooperation," *Hindu*, January 13, 2006.

[21] "China Blocked India's ADB Plan over Arunachal, Confirms Krishna," *Indian Express*, July 10, 2009.

[22] Yuriko Koike, "The Struggle for Mastery of the Pacific," Project Syndicate, May 12, 2010, http://www.project-syndicate.org/commentary/koike5/English. This section draws from Pant, "China's Rise, India's Challenge."

Power Projection and Military Development

China's enhanced military prowess is leading to a more forceful assertion of its interests, more often than not adversely affecting Indian interests. As its dependence on imported oil increases, the PRC will extend its capabilities to project military power in order to defend the sea lanes transporting oil from the Persian Gulf to China. This will require access to strategically placed advanced naval bases as well as forces that can gain naval and air superiority.[23] Given that almost 80% of China's oil imports pass through the Strait of Malacca, the PRC is reluctant to rely on U.S. naval power in the region for unhindered access to energy.

However, China is acquiring naval bases along the crucial chokepoints in the Indian Ocean not only to serve its economic interests but also to enhance its strategic presence.[24] There is evidence to suggest that China is comprehensively building up its maritime power in all dimensions.[25] The PLAN's growing reliance on bases across the region is a response to the logistical constraints that it faces due to the distance of the Indian Ocean waters from its own area of operation. Yet China is consolidating power over the South China Sea and the Indian Ocean with an eye toward India, something that comes out in a secret memorandum issued by the director of the General Logistics Department of the PLA: "We can no longer accept the Indian Ocean as only an ocean of the Indians…We are taking armed conflicts in the region into account."[26]

China has deployed Jin-class submarines at a base near Sanya on the southern tip of Hainan Island in the South China Sea, sounding alarms in India because the base is merely 1,200 nautical miles from the Malacca Strait.[27] Sanya is China's closest access point to the Indian Ocean and has an underground facility that can hide the movement of submarines. The concentration of strategic naval forces at Sanya will further propel China toward a consolidation of its control over the surrounding Indian Ocean region. The presence of access tunnels at the mouth of the deepwater base is particularly troubling for India because they will allow China to interdict shipping at three crucial chokepoints in the Indian Ocean. Although the

---

[23] See Rick Reece, "On the Myth of Chinese Power Projection Capabilities," *Breakthroughs* 8, no. 1 (Spring 1998), http://www.comw.org/cmp/fulltext/reecechina.pdf.

[24] Parts of this discussion of the China-India naval rivalry are drawn from Harsh V. Pant, "India in the Indian Ocean: Growing Mismatch between Ambitions and Capabilities," *Pacific Affairs* 82, no. 2 (Summer 2009): 279–97.

[25] Thomas Kane, *Chinese Grand Strategy and Maritime Power* (London: Frank Cass, 2002), 139.

[26] Youssef Bodansky, "The PRC Surge for the Strait of Malacca and Spratly Confronts India and the U.S.," International Strategic Studies Association, Defense and Foreign Affairs Strategic Policy, September 30, 1995, 6–13.

[27] Manu Pubby, "China's New N-Submarine Base Sets Off Alarm Bells," *Indian Express*, May 3, 2008.

choice of Hainan is less than ideal for China, no better alternatives exist. Other places are hemmed in by islands, and the navy will want open surrounding waters so that, among other things, no one can track its submarines. Thus, for the time being, Sanya is China's chief maritime nuclear base.

As the ability of the PLAN to project power in the Indian Ocean region grows, India is likely to feel even more vulnerable, despite enjoying distinct geographical advantages in the area. China's presence in and around Indian waters is troubling because it restricts India's freedom to maneuver in the region. Of particular note is what has been termed China's "string of pearls" strategy, which has significantly expanded the PRC's strategic depth in India's backyard.[28] This strategy of acquiring bases and solidifying diplomatic ties along Chinese sea lanes includes the Gwadar port in Pakistan, naval outposts in Burma, electronic intelligence-gathering facilities on islands in the Bay of Bengal, funding for the construction of a canal across the Kra Isthmus in Thailand, a military agreement with Cambodia, and the build-up of forces in the South China Sea.[29] Some of these claims have been exaggerated, as was the case with the Chinese naval presence in Burma. The Indian government had to concede in 2005 that reports of China turning the Coco Islands into a naval base were incorrect and that there were indeed no PRC naval bases in Burma.[30] Yet the Chinese presence in the Indian Ocean is gradually becoming more pronounced than before. China may not have a naval base in Burma, but it is helping upgrade infrastructure in the Coco Islands and may be providing some limited technical assistance to Burma. China is also courting other states in South Asia by building container ports in Bangladesh at Chittagong and in Sri Lanka at Hambantota. It is possible that the construction of these ports and facilities around India's periphery can be justified on purely economic and commercial grounds, but insofar as India is concerned, this is a policy of containment.

China's involvement in the construction of the deep-sea port of Gwadar has attracted a lot of attention due to its strategic location about 70 kilometers from the Iranian border and 400 kilometers east of the Strait

---

[28] The term "string of pearls" was first used in a report titled "Energy Futures in Asia" that was commissioned by the U.S. Department of Defense's Office of Net Assessment from defense contractor Booz Allen Hamilton. For details, see David Walgreen, "China in the Indian Ocean Region: Lessons in PRC Grand Strategy," *Comparative Strategy* 25, no. 2 (January 2006): 55–73.

[29] For a detailed explication of the security ramifications of China's string of pearls strategy, see Gurpreet Khurana, "China's 'String of Pearls' in the Indian Ocean and Its Security Implications," *Strategic Analysis* 32, no. 1 (January 2008): 1–22.

[30] For a nuanced analysis of the Burma issue, see Andrew Selth, "Chinese Military Bases in Burma: The Explosion of a Myth," Griffith Asia Institute, Regional Outlook Paper, no. 10, 2007, http://www.griffith.edu.au/__data/assets/pdf_file/0018/18225/regional-outlook-andrew-selth.pdf.

of Hormuz, a major oil supply route. Some have suggested that the port will provide China with a "listening post" from where it can "monitor U.S. naval activity in the Persian Gulf, Indian activity in the Arabian Sea, and future U.S.-Indian maritime cooperation in the Indian Ocean."[31] Though Pakistan's naval capabilities do not pose any challenge to India on their own, the combination of Chinese and Pakistani naval forces could indeed be formidable for India to counter. While India still possesses significant geographical advantages in the Indian Ocean and China will face difficulties in exerting an equal level of influence, China's naval prowess is raising vexing issues regarding the role of Indian naval power in the region.

To address these issues, Indian military planners are shifting their focus from Pakistan to China in future strategic planning. In May 2009, India's highest decisionmaking body on national security, the Cabinet Committee on Security, decided to initiate a comprehensive plan to bolster the country's military assets in order to counter China's rising military power.[32] Between 2010 and 2016, India is expected to spend $112 billion on capital defense acquisitions in what is being described as "one of the largest procurement cycles in the world."[33] The Indian Army is raising two new specialized infantry mountain divisions (35,000 soldiers) and an artillery brigade for Arunachal Pradesh, all aimed at redressing the imbalance on the Sino-Indian border. It is also revising its conventional war-fighting doctrine with the objective of deterring rather than dissuading China, though what this means in operational terms remains far from clear. As Dan Blumenthal has observed, the Indian military is "currently refining a 'two-front war' doctrine to fend off Pakistan and China simultaneously." India is giving equal attention to both fronts—China in the northeast and Pakistan in the northwest—and if attacked by either country will "use its new integrated battle groups to deal quick decisive blows against both."[34]

The augmentation of China's capabilities in the Indian Ocean has thus alarmed New Delhi and galvanized it into taking ameliorative measures. Underscoring this discomfort with China's so-called string of pearls strategy, the Indian naval chief has argued that "each pearl in the string is a link in a chain of the Chinese maritime presence" and has expressed concern that naval forces operating out of ports established by China could

[31] Ziad Haider, "Oil Fuels Beijing's New Power Game," *YaleGlobal*, March 11, 2005, http://yaleglobal. yale.edu/content/oil-fuels-beijings-new-power-game.

[32] Nitin Gokhale, "India Readies for China Fight," *Diplomat*, July 6, 2010, http://the-diplomat. com/2010/07/06/india-readies-for-china-fight.

[33] "Opportunities in the Indian Defence Sector: An Overview," KPMG, May 1, 2010, http://www. kpmg.com/IN/en/IssuesAndInsights/ThoughtLeadership/Opportunities_in_the_Indian_ Defence_Sector.pdf

[34] Dan Blumenthal, "India Prepares for a Two-Front War," *Wall Street Journal*, March 1, 2010.

"take control over the world energy jugular."[35] India views Chinese naval strategy as expansionist and intent on encircling India strategically. The Indian external affairs minister, for example, told the Indian Parliament in 2010 that New Delhi "has come to realize that China has been showing more than the normal interest in the Indian Ocean affairs" and that the Indian government is "closely monitoring the Chinese intentions."[36] The current Indian naval strategy is being driven by the idea "that the vast Indian Ocean is its *mare nostrum*…that the entire triangle of the Indian Ocean is their nation's rightful and exclusive sphere of interest."[37] Just as the PLAN seems to be concentrating on anti-access warfare to prevent the U.S. Navy from entering into a cross-strait conflict, the Indian Navy is working toward acquiring the ability to deny China access in the Indian Ocean.[38] While the Indian maritime doctrine of 2004 underlined China's efforts to strategically encircle India, the maritime strategy released three years later emphasized attempts by the PLAN to emerge as a blue water force through its ambitious modernization program, "along with attempts to gain a strategic toe-hold in the Indian Ocean Rim."[39]

The Indian Navy is aiming for a total fleet of 140–45 vessels over the next decade, built around two carrier battle groups: the *Admiral Gorshkov*, which will not be handed over from Russia to India until 2013, and the indigenous *Vikrant*, which is likely to be completed by 2015. India's ambition to equip its navy with two or more aircraft carriers over the next decade, as well as its decision to launch its first indigenous nuclear submarine in 2009, is seen as crucial for power projection and to achieve a semblance of strategic autonomy. India's emerging capability to put a carrier task force in the South China Sea and the Persian Gulf has given a boost to the navy's blue water aspirations. New Delhi hopes to induct a third aircraft carrier by 2017, ensuring that it has two operational carriers at any given point. China's deployment of Jin-class submarines at Hainan has also forced India to speed up its indigenous nuclear submarine project, which has been underway for more than a decade now, with the Indian Navy rather ambitiously aiming at the induction of five indigenous ATV (advanced technology vehicle)

---

[35] Quoted in Gavin Rabinowitz, "India, China Jostle for Influence in Indian Ocean," Associated Press, June 7, 2008.

[36] "China's 'Intentions' Being Closely Monitored: India," Press Trust of India, August 31, 2010.

[37] Eric Margolis, "India Rules the Waves," *Proceedings of the U.S. Naval Institute* 131, no. 3 (March 2005): 70.

[38] Sam J. Tangredi, "The Future of Maritime Power," in *The Politics of Maritime Power: A Survey*, ed. Andrew T.H. Tan (London: Routledge, 2007), 143–44.

[39] "Freedom to Use the Seas: India's Maritime Military Strategy," Integrated Headquarters Ministry of Defence (Navy), May 2007, 41, http://indiannavy.nic.in/maritime_strat.pdf.

nuclear submarines. Indian strategists consider a submarine-based nuclear arsenal to be critical for retaining a second-strike capability.

India is using this naval force to advance its diplomatic initiatives overseas and, in particular, to shape the strategic environment in and around the Indian Ocean. Given the convergence of Indian and U.S. interests in this region, New Delhi is trying to use the present upswing in U.S.-India ties to create a more favorable strategic environment for itself despite its historical sensitivities to the presence of U.S. forces in the Indian Ocean. The U.S. and Indian navies have stepped up joint exercises, and the United States has sold to India the amphibious transport dock USS *Trenton* (renamed INS *Jalashwa*), the first of its class to be inducted into the Indian Navy and a milestone in bilateral ties. India has also indicated that it would be willing to join the U.S.-proposed thousand-ship navy effort to combat illegal activities on the high seas, given the informal nature of the arrangement.

India's decision to establish its Far Eastern Command in the Andaman and Nicobar Islands in the Bay of Bengal is aimed at countering China's growing presence by complicating access to the region through the Strait of Malacca, the main bottleneck for oil transit to China. India has also launched Project Seabird, consisting of its third operational naval base in Karwar on the western seaboard, an air force station, a naval armament depot, and missile silos, in order to secure the nation's maritime routes in the Arabian Sea. In addition, New Delhi is set to establish a monitoring station in Madagascar, its first in another country, which is deemed vital to guard against the terrorist threat emanating from East Africa as well as useful to monitor China's plan in the region. The government is also considering developing a monitoring facility at an atoll near Mauritius and has strengthened naval contacts with Mozambique and Seychelles. India responded to Hu's offer of military assistance to Seychelles by donating one of its own patrol aircraft to the Seychelles Navy. Likewise, India's support for the construction of Chahbahar port in Iran, as well as for the road connecting it to Afghanistan, is an answer to the Chinese-funded Gwadar port in Pakistan. India's air base in Kazakhstan and space-monitoring post in Mongolia are also geared primarily toward China.

The Nuclear Issue

China remains the only major power that refuses to discuss nuclear issues with New Delhi for fear that this might imply de facto recognition of India's status as a nuclear power. It continues to insist on the sanctity of UN Resolution 1172, which calls for India and Pakistan to give up their nuclear weapons programs and join the Nuclear Non-Proliferation Treaty (NPT) as non–nuclear weapon states.[40] For the same reason, China refuses to discuss nuclear confidence-building and risk-reduction measures with India. It is interesting that a large section of China's political and military elite views India's nuclear tests in 1998 not as an attempt by India to address national security concerns but rather as an attempt by the United States to contain China by "allowing" India to go nuclear.[41]

The U.S.-India civilian nuclear energy cooperation pact came as a shock to Beijing, which made every possible effort to scuttle the deal until the last minute. In response, China reiterated its request that India sign the NPT as well as declared that it would sell new nuclear reactors to Pakistan. This was a less than subtle message to Washington that Beijing also retains the right to back its favorites. Beijing viewed the nuclear deal through the lens of the global balance of power and was perturbed by the U.S. desire to build India as a balancer in the region. In particular, China opposed India's exemption from the NSG guidelines, even threatening in 2008 to walk out of the NSG proceedings in Vienna in an attempt to derail negotiations at the eleventh hour. Only when the other states were persuaded by the United States to support the deal and China realized it would be the last state standing did it back down.

China's actions have signaled to India that, as New Delhi tries to increase its global power by crafting a strategic partnership with Washington, China will try to contain India by supporting its neighboring adversaries. As stated above, to counter the U.S.-India nuclear pact, China has decided to allow its state entities to supply two new nuclear reactors to Pakistan. Authorities have confirmed that the state-owned China National Nuclear Cooperation has signed an agreement with Pakistan for two additional reactors at the Chashma site, Chashma III and Chashma IV. This action clearly violates the NSG guidelines that forbid nuclear transfers to non-signatories to the NPT and countries that do not adhere to international nuclear safeguards. Yet China has suggested that "there are compelling political reasons concerning the stability of South Asia to justify the exports," echoing Pakistan's oft-repeated complaint that the U.S.-India nuclear pact has upset regional stability by assisting India's strategic program.[42] Unlike the much-debated U.S.-India nuclear deal, however, the Sino-Pakistani agreement is mired

[40] "China Against India, Pakistan Joining Nuclear Club," Press Trust of India, June 29, 2004.

[41] Andrew Scobell, *China and Strategic Culture* (Carlisle: Strategic Studies Institute, 2002), 19, http://www.strategicstudiesinstitute.army.mil/pubs/download.cfm?q=60.

[42] Mark Hibbs, "Pakistan Deal Signals China's Growing Nuclear Assertiveness," Carnegie Endowment for International Peace, Nuclear Energy Brief, April 27, 2010, http://www.carnegieendowment.org/2010/04/27/pakistan-deal-signals-china-s-growing-nuclear-assertiveness/4su.

in secrecy, with Beijing even ready to short-circuit the NSG process.[43] Disregarding Indian and global concerns, China has contended that the sale of two new reactors is "grandfathered" from before it joined the NSG in 2004 and, therefore, an exemption from the NSG is not required. As the *Financial Times* observes, the decision to supply reactors to Pakistan "reflects China's growing diplomatic confidence" and "underscores its view of Pakistan as a prized South Asian strategic power."[44]

China's role in the development of Pakistan's nuclear infrastructure has been well documented. Despite denials from Beijing, even A.Q. Khan, the father of Pakistan's nuclear weapons program, has acknowledged the crucial role China played by presenting Islamabad with 50 kilograms of weapon-grade enriched uranium, nuclear weapons drawings, and uranium hexafluoride for centrifuges. This is perhaps the only case where a nuclear weapon state has shared weapon-grade fissile material and designs with a non–nuclear weapon state.[45]

Among the five nuclear powers, China is making the most dramatic advances in its nuclear force with the introduction and deployment of new-generation land-based ballistic missiles and nuclear submarines. China's decision to upgrade its missile facilities near Tibet in 2007 has brought targets in northern India within range of Chinese forces. China is also developing a new, longer-range submarine-launched ballistic missile that will allow its submarines to strike targets throughout India from the secure confines of the South China Sea.

Moreover, while both India and China have a "no-first-use" nuclear policy, China's doctrine is not applicable to India because New Delhi is not a party to the NPT. China's nuclear arsenal is estimated to include about five hundred warheads, with two hundred strategic warheads and around three hundred tactical warheads. The latter are deployed at about twenty locations in China, including Tibet, and are well-integrated at the operational level. By contrast, India's no-first-use pledge and minimum-deterrence posture have precluded tactical nuclear weapons, leading to a serious operational shortcoming as well as depriving India of an appropriate level of deterrence against China.[46] Influential voices in India, including former external affairs minister Jaswant Singh and former army chief Deepak Kapoor, have

---

[43] Ashley J. Tellis, "The China-Pakistan Nuclear 'Deal': Separating Fact from Fiction," Carnegie Endowment for International Peace, Policy Outlook, July 16, 2010, http://www.carnegieendowment. org/files/china_pak_nuke1.pdf.

[44] Geoff Dyer, Farhan Bokhari, and James Lamont, "China to Build Reactors in Pakistan," *Financial Times*, April 28, 2010.

[45] See Harsh V. Pant, "Dragons and Paper Tigers," *Times of India*, May 24, 2010.

[46] See Harsh V. Pant, "India's Nuclear Doctrine and Command Structure: Implications for India and the World," *Comparative Strategy* 24, no. 3 (2005): 277–93.

suggested that India must revise its no-first-use policy in light of China's rising military prowess and nuclear assistance to Pakistan.[47] The government has rejected any such suggestions, but the debate has only just begun.

The Indian Army is in the process of incorporating into its forces the Agni-III, an intermediate-range missile capable of reaching all China's major cities, and has tested its 5,000-kilometer-range Agni-IV ballistic missile to bolster its deterrence posture against China. India has also deployed a squadron of its most advanced multi-role fighter aircraft, the Su-30MKI, to a base just 150 kilometers from the disputed Sino-Indian border.[48] New Delhi is considering missile defense systems, including the U.S. Patriot-3 and Israel's Iron Dome and David's Sling, in response to the Chinese military's plan to place Dongfeng-21 medium-range ballistic missiles on the Tibetan plateau.[49] India's indigenous ballistic missile defense (BMD) program has been accelerated and is now considered ready for integration into the nation's air defense assets. The Defence Research and Development Organisation (DRDO) has suggested that by 2011–12 the system would include Phase-I missiles, capable of neutralizing missiles at the 2,000-kilometer range. With an eye on China, Phase II will be aimed at thwarting threats from missiles up to 5,000 kilometers.[50] After China demonstrated its test-firing capability in space, India has suggested that it remains open to extending the BMD program to that arena, although its official policy remains one of staunch opposition to any attempt to place weapons in space.

Border Tensions

China has vigorously asserted its old claims along the border with India and has combined this with aggressive patrolling, which New Delhi views as a violation of the 1993 agreement on the LAC. Even as India considers the Sikkim border issue settled, repeated Chinese incursions in the "finger area" in northern Sikkim in the past few years are aimed at opening a fresh front against India. Concerns are growing about covert intrusions into Indian territory to strengthen Chinese claims over the disputed border areas. PLA forces are also regularly intruding into Bhutanese territory at the junction

---

[47] "May Have to Revisit Nuclear No-First Use Policy: Army Chief," *Times of India*, September 6, 2009; and "Jaswant: Is Indian Policy Drafted in Washington?" *Hindu*, March 16, 2011.

[48] Tim Sullivan and Michael Mazza, "The Next Nuclear Arms Race," *Wall Street Journal*, September 27, 2010.

[49] Dai Bing, "India and China's Great Game in Full Swing," China.org.cn, October 22, 2010.

[50] See Siddharth Srivastava, "India Hones Its Missile Shield," *Asia Times*, April 16, 2011.

where the three countries meet and destroying Indian Army posts.[51] These incursions are strategically directed at the Siliguri corridor that connects India with its northeast states.

China's rapid expansion and modernization of transport infrastructure across the border is also forcing India to respond, though India is already decades behind. The PRC's plans to modernize transportation across the Himalayas had been evident for decades. The railway link between Beijing and Lhasa further tightened China's grip on Tibet and helped the government to rapidly deploy troops in the region when riots broke out in 2008. China's ambition is to extend this rail line to Yatung, just a few miles from Sikkim's Nathu La, and subsequently to Nyingchi, north of Arunachal Pradesh, at the tri-border junction with Myanmar. China's plans for the development of its border areas contrast vividly with India's tentative stance on infrastructure development.

China's transformation of transport infrastructure in the provinces that border South Asia (Yunnan, Tibet, and Xinjiang), as well as its decision to build road and rail networks across the borders of these areas, is rapidly altering the geopolitical realities for India, which is struggling to cope with the decay of its border infrastructure.[52] Myanmar has also agreed to allow China to build a highway linking Kunming in its southeast with Chittagong in Bangladesh. The highway will provide China with direct access to the Bay of Bengal and "run very close to the northeastern Indian states of Tripura and Mizoram."[53]

According to an estimate by the Indian government's China Study Group, China now possesses the ability to move more than ten thousand troops to the Indian border in 20–25 days, compared to three to six months a decade ago, a consequence of efficient border management.[54] By engaging in repeated, though controlled, provocations, the Chinese military is carefully probing how far it can push India. This new military restiveness on the Sino-Indian border does not bode well for India, for the military balance on the long and contested border is rapidly changing in Beijing's favor. As a consequence, Tibet has become a militarized zone.

India, in response, has started building several tactically important roads along the border in the eastern and western sectors and upgrading airstrips to give itself the ability to deploy a large number of troops in

---

[51] Nirmalya Banerjee and Amalendu Kundu, "Chinese Troops Destroy Indian Posts, Bunker," *Times of India*, December 1, 2007.

[52] See C. Raja Mohan, "Drawn In at the Borders," *South Asia Monitor*, September 18, 2010, http://www.southasiamonitor.org/index.php?option=com_content&view=article&id=882&catid=54&Itemid=102.

[53] Ajay Banerjee, "Dragon Closing In on India?" *Tribune* (Chandigarh), October 2, 2010.

[54] Pranab Dhal Samanta, "The Dragon Has Now Got Wings," *Indian Express*, January 5, 2008.

forward areas at short notice. New Delhi has put 23 border roads on the fast track for construction and intends to commission a further 116 roads, totaling 3,765 kilometers.[55] At the same time, India is strengthening its military preparedness along the border with China by raising two new divisions consisting of about twenty-thousand troops.

Influence in South Asia and Beyond

For a long time, the dominant narrative in South Asia has been how the India-Pakistan rivalry has hampered economic growth and regional stability. That narrative is now rapidly losing its salience due to China's growing dominance of the South Asian landscape.[56] While China's rising profile in South Asia is not news, what is astonishing is the diminishing role of India and the speed with which New Delhi is ceding strategic space to Beijing on the subcontinent. Even as China is becoming the largest trade partner of most states in South Asia, including India, New Delhi's strategic hold on South Asia is weakening. China even entered the South Asian Association for Regional Cooperation (SAARC) as an observer in 2005, supported by most member states. Despite misgivings, India could do little to prevent this and had to acquiesce. Now, much to India's consternation, Pakistan, Bangladesh, and Nepal are supporting China's full membership in SAARC.

Pakistan's all-weather friendship with China is well-known, but the reach of China in other South Asian states has been extraordinary.[57] Bangladesh and Sri Lanka view India as more interested in creating barriers against their exports than in spurring regional economic integration. India's protectionist tendencies have allowed China to don the mantle of the region's economic leader. Instead of India emerging as facilitator of socio-economic development in Sri Lanka, Nepal, and Bhutan, it is China's development assistance that is having a larger impact.

To New Delhi, China's strategy toward South Asia seems premised on encircling India and confining it within the geographical coordinates of the region. The strategy of using proxies started with Pakistan and has gradually evolved to include other states in the region, such as Bangladesh, Sri Lanka, and Nepal. The PRC is entering markets in South Asia more aggressively through trade and investment, as well as improving linkages with South Asian states through treaties and bilateral cooperation. Following this up

---

[55] Manu Pubby, "Govt: China Linking Highways, Military Units with Border," *Indian Express*, March 25, 2011.

[56] This draws from Harsh V. Pant, "Focus on China, Not India-Pakistan Rivalry," *Rediff*, April 29, 2010, http://news.rediff.com/column/2010/apr/29/focus-on-china-not-india-pakistan-rivalry.htm.

[57] On China's growing role in South Asia, see Harsh V. Pant, *China's Rising Global Profile: The Great Power Tradition* (Portland: Sussex Academic Press, 2011), 29–50.

by building a network of roads and ports in India's neighborhood and deepening military engagements with states on India's periphery, China has firmly entrenched itself in New Delhi's backyard.

China's quiet assertion of influence has allowed smaller South Asian countries to play China against India.[58] Forced to exist between their two giant neighbors, the smaller states have responded with a careful balancing act, using the China card to balance against India's predominance. Pakistan, as discussed above, has always been a crucial foreign policy asset for China, but with India's rise and U.S.-India rapprochement, its role in China's grand strategy is bound to grow even further. Recent revelations about China shifting away from a three-decade-old cautious approach on Jammu and Kashmir, increasing its military presence in Pakistan, planning new infrastructure to link Xinjiang and Gwadar, issuing stapled visas to residents of Jammu and Kashmir, and supplying nuclear reactors to Pakistan all confirm a new intensity behind China's old strategy of using Pakistan to secure its interests in the region. China has gone even further than Pakistan in defining the Kashmir issue. While Pakistan insists that Kashmir is a disputed territory, recent Chinese actions have made it clear that Beijing believes that Pakistan-occupied Kashmir (PoK) is Pakistani territory and that India's Kashmir state is the only disputed part of the province.[59] Pakistan seems to have ceded responsibility for the Gilgit-Baltistan area of PoK to China, as is underscored by the reported presence of 7,000–10,000 PLA troops.[60] The real concern for India, however, is the number of projects that China has undertaken in these areas, and that footprint is likely to grow much larger.[61]

India's structural dominance in South Asia makes it a natural target of resentment among smaller states in the region and creates the unusual situation where the core regional power is seen as a security threat to its neighbors. Moreover, as the two regional giants compete with each other in South Asia, their focus remains on their relative gains vis-à-vis each other rather than on the absolute gains that cooperation can bestow. For example, competition is increasing between China and India for influence in Burma. The Andaman Sea is viewed as a crucial energy lifeline for China, while India needs Burma to meet its energy requirements. India has pledged to

---

[58] On the growing Sino-Indian rivalry in South Asia and beyond, see Harsh V. Pant, *The China Syndrome: Grappling with an Uneasy Relationship* (New Delhi: HarperCollins, 2010).

[59] C. Raja Mohan, "A New Challenge," *Indian Express*, August 31, 2010.

[60] Selig S. Harrison, "China's Direct Hold on Pakistan's Northern Borderlands," *International Herald Tribune*, August 26, 2010.

[61] Pranab Dhal Samanta, "More than Troops, Chinese Projects in PoK Worry India," *Indian Express*, September 5, 2010.

rebuild Burma's western Sittwe port and is one of the main suppliers of military hardware to the ruling junta. China's growing penetration of Burma is one of the main reasons New Delhi is reluctant to cease economic and military engagement with the Burmese junta, despite attracting widespread criticism from both outside and within India.

In response, India has moved to build strategic partnerships with many states that share its apprehensions about China, including the United States, Russia, Japan, Vietnam, Indonesia, and South Korea. It has been suggested that to more effectively counter a Chinese presence in the Indian Ocean and protect trade routes, India will need to seek access to Vietnamese, Taiwanese, and Japanese ports for the forward deployment of its naval assets. India is already emerging as an exclusive "defense service provider" for smaller states with growing economies that seek to strengthen their military capabilities, such as Vietnam, Indonesia, Malaysia, Singapore, Qatar, and Oman. This strategy has helped provide India with access to ports along the Arabian coast, Indian Ocean, and South China Sea. India is seen as a balancer in the Asia-Pacific, where U.S. influence has waned as China's has risen. Ties with Japan have also assumed a new dynamic, with some even mooting a "concert of democracies" proposal involving the democratic Asia-Pacific states working toward the common goal of a stable region. While such a proposal has little chance of evolving into anything concrete in the near term, especially given China's sensitivity, India's decision to develop natural gas with Japan in the Andaman Sea—as well as to participate in military exercises involving the United States, Japan, and Australia— underscores its emerging priorities.[62]

Regarding the latter point, India has been conducting naval exercises with the United States and Japan for the last few years and has been vigorously seeking military allies in the Asia-Pacific. In addition, the Indian Navy has been regularly visiting friendly states in the Pacific, such as Australia, Indonesia, Singapore, and Vietnam, in an attempt to build military-to-military relationships with key regional states. India also has been providing military assistance to Vietnam over the last decade with the aim of denying China control of the South China Sea. Both New Delhi and Hanoi view Beijing with wariness because of their historical territorial grievances with China.[63]

If India is indeed a swing state, then fear of China is making it swing considerably toward the United States. In this, it was helped by the George W. Bush administration, which redefined the parameters of U.S.-India bilateral

---

[62] For further discussion, see Pant, "India in the Indian Ocean," 281.

[63] Nitin Gokhale, "India's Quiet Counter-China Strategy," *Diplomat*, March 16, 2011, http://the-diplomat.com/2011/03/16/india%e2%80%99s-quiet-counter-china-strategy-2/.

engagement. In a *Foreign Affairs* article, Condoleezza Rice foreshadowed India's prominence in the Bush administration's global strategic calculus even before the 2000 presidential elections. Rice argued that "there is a strong tendency conceptually [in the United States] to connect India with Pakistan and to think only of Kashmir or the nuclear competition between the two states."[64] She made it clear that India has the potential to become a great power and that U.S. foreign policy should take that into account. Consequently, the Bush administration, from the very beginning, refused to look at India through the prism of nonproliferation and instead viewed it as a natural and strategic ally.[65] The administration went further in its new India policy, declaring that its goal was "to help India become a major world power in the 21st century."[66]

The initial step toward that goal was removing the age-old distrust between the two states over the nuclear issue. Both Washington and New Delhi realized nuclear cooperation could lay the groundwork for a healthy strategic partnership.[67] While relations were already on an upward trajectory, with the two countries' interests converging on a range of issues, the existing nonproliferation regime denied civilian nuclear technology to India and had larger implications across the entire high-tech spectrum. The landmark 2005 pact between the two nations on civilian nuclear energy cooperation helped overcome these barriers in the bilateral relationship.

In addition to the fact that the United States is India's largest trading and investment partner,[68] bilateral cooperation on strategic issues has also been growing. India's recent rise has been described by President Barack Obama as being in the best interests of both states as well as the world. Obama's declaration that that the United States would back India's bid for a permanent seat on an expanded UN Security Council was a major policy shift that India had long been clamoring for and Washington had been reluctant to offer. By suggesting that he looks "forward to a reformed UN Security Council that includes India as a permanent member," Obama warmed the hearts of Indian policymakers who have long viewed U.S.

---

[64] Condoleezza Rice, "Promoting the National Interest," *Foreign Affairs* 79, no. 1 (January/February 2000): 56.

[65] Robert D. Blackwill, "The Quality and Durability of U.S.-India Relationship" (speech by the U.S. ambassador to India, India Chamber of Commerce, Calcutta, November 27, 2002).

[66] See "Background Briefing by Administration Officials on U.S.–South Asia Relations," U.S. Department of State, March 25, 2005, http://2001-2009.state.gov/r/pa/prs/ps/2005/43853.htm.

[67] For a discussion of the changing trajectory of India-U.S. ties in recent years, see Harsh V. Pant, *Contemporary Debates in Indian Foreign and Security Policy* (New York: Palgrave Macmillan, 2008), 15–22.

[68] The details can be found in "India-U.S. Bilateral Relations," Indian Ministry of External Affairs, 2–3, http://www.mea.gov.in/mystart.php?id=50044540.

support as a litmus test.[69] This was probably the strongest endorsement Washington has given to any state for permanent Security Council membership. The Obama administration has also encouraged India to play a bigger role not only in South Asia but also in East Asia, where India has been trying to raise its profile.

New Delhi's "look east" policy, which began in large part as an attempt to integrate India's newly liberalizing economy with those of the Asian tigers, has now evolved "into a more robust military-to-military partnership with important nations in the region."[70] India is providing Vietnam with the support to enhance and upgrade the capabilities of its three services, especially its navy. India is also training Malaysia's Su-30 pilots, while the Singaporean army conducts training in India using cantonments and firing ranges.[71] Indian warships now regularly visit countries around the region from Australia to Singapore and Indonesia. In Northeast Asia, economic ties between India and South Korea have been diversifying across various sectors, but defense cooperation between the two states has also gathered momentum. In 2005, India and South Korea signed a memorandum of understanding (MOU) on cooperation in defense, industry, and logistics, followed in 2006 by another on cooperation between their coast guards. Given that South Korea is one of the world's leaders in naval shipbuilding technology, India would like to tap into Korean naval capabilities to augment its own. As a result, naval cooperation is increasingly a key feature of bilateral defense cooperation, with the two navies cooperating in antipiracy operations in the Indian Ocean and the Gulf of Aden. Both states also share a strong interest in protecting the sea lines of communication in the Indian Ocean region.[72]

India is also expanding its defense ties with Japan. Both Japan and India rely on the sea lines of communication for energy security and economic growth. They thus have a shared interest in guaranteeing the free transit of energy and trade between the Suez Canal and the Western Pacific. With this in mind, they are developing maritime capabilities to cooperate with each other and with other regional powers. Their navies are now exercising together regularly, and interactions between the two coast guards are increasing with a view to combat piracy and terrorism and to cooperate on disaster relief operations. Japan feels that the Indian Navy is the only

---

[69] Emily Wax and Rama Lakshmi, "Obama Supports Adding India as a Permanent Member of UN Security Council," *Washington Post*, November 8, 2010.

[70] Nitin Gokhale, "How India Is Undoing China's String of Pearls," Rediff, October 7, 2010, http://news.rediff.com/column/2010/oct/07/column-how-india-is-undoing-chinas-string-of-pearls.htm.

[71] Banerjee, "Dragon Closing In on India?"

[72] See Harsh V. Pant. "Rise of China Prods India–South Korea Ties," *Japan Times*, September 7, 2010.

one in the region that can be trusted to secure the sea lanes in the Indian Ocean that are vital for Japan's energy security. It is also important for India to join hands with the much larger Japanese Maritime Self-Defense Force, Asia's most powerful navy, to make sure that no adversarial power controls regional waterways.

India's attempts to raise its profile in East and Southeast Asia are geared toward not only preventing the region from emerging as China's exclusive sphere of influence but also countering China's stranglehold over South Asia. Whether India will succeed in this endeavor is still too early to determine.

Economic Troubles

The limits of Sino-Indian economic cooperation are becoming increasingly evident. Though India has achieved remarkable growth rates in the last few years, enjoying an average annual rate of 6% real income growth over the last two decades of the twentieth century, it still lags far behind China and will need many more years to match China's impressive economic performance. China has outperformed India in terms of levels of growth; the education, health, and living standards of its population; and the integration of its economy with the global economy. In sectors where India and China compete for export markets, such as textiles, China is far ahead, even as Sino-Indian competition for third markets is bound to further intensify. China's annual trade with India is only a fraction of Chinese trade with Europe, Japan, and the United States. Indian exports to China are primarily dominated by raw materials and iron ore. The challenge confronting New Delhi is thus to match the level of Chinese exports to India and diversify the country's export basket.[73] A rising trade deficit in China's favor is problematic for India, as is the Indian failure to use its core competencies to enter the Chinese market.

As the two states compete across the globe for export markets, energy assets, and investment projects, some amount of competition is inevitable. This economic rivalry is likely to intensify as both states intrude on each other's strengths, with China shifting its economy toward services and high-tech industries and India trying to rapidly expand its manufacturing base. India remains concerned about the Chinese imports flooding its domestic markets and has accused Chinese companies of swamping its markets with low-quality products. It even banned, albeit briefly, Chinese-made toys in early 2009 for safety reasons and is the largest initiator of anti-dumping

[73] Amit Mitra, "An Unequal Relationship," *Times of India*, January 12, 2008.

investigations against China under the WTO.[74] In the words of the Indian commerce secretary, "Cooperation hasn't really worked."[75]

India remains reluctant to open domestic industries that have not faced foreign competition and is ambivalent about allowing Chinese firms a level playing field. The Indian security establishment continues to view Chinese firms with suspicion as potential security hazards, given that the PLA holds a stake in a number of these companies. China has complained that its investments are subjected to rigorous security reviews and that work visas for its executives are not swiftly processed. Beijing has been vocal about its concerns vis-à-vis the investment climate in India, though most of the FDI proposals from Chinese companies have managed to receive clearance from the Indian government in recent years.[76] There has been talk of a Sino-Indian FTA for some time now, but it is not readily evident that this would be a good idea. Given China's manipulation of its currency exchange rate, some in India consider the FTA a "yuan trap."[77]

Recent Indian initiatives notwithstanding, China's diplomacy in the energy realm has also left India far behind. Despite all the talk of Sino-Indian cooperation on energy security, the two sides are actually competing aggressively as their energy demands surge. While there have been attempts at cooperation, engendering a lot of enthusiasm in some quarters, these constitute a small part of a much broader China-India energy relationship that remains largely competitive, if not conflictual. Chinese and Indian interests are colliding in almost every part of the world. While the two states may opt for more joint bids on foreign energy projects to avoid cutthroat competition, a lasting cooperative arrangement is highly unlikely. China is already far ahead of India in overseas development, and while it may try to assuage some Indian concerns by partnering with New Delhi on a few projects, the PRC is unlikely to gain much from the collaboration. India must cooperate with China, rather than the other way around, because it is difficult for New Delhi to outbid Beijing for assets given the latter's presence in the global oil market. But the Indian government's energy strategy is still often ambiguous and hampered by bureaucratic problems, diminishing the prospects for Sino-Indian energy cooperation in the near future.

Yet India is more assertive than it was before in trying to compete with China in far-flung areas of the world, not only for resources but also for

---

[74] Peter Wonacott, "Downturn Heightens China-India Tension on Trade," *Wall Street Journal*, March 20, 2009.

[75] Ibid.

[76] Shishir Gupta, "Contrary to What Left Says, 87% of FDI Proposals from Chinese Firms Cleared," *Indian Express*, November 13, 2006.

[77] Swaminathan S. Anklesaria Aiyar, "Free Trade Area or Yuan Trap?" *Times of India*, November 26, 2006.

influence. In response to the China-Africa Cooperation Forum of 2006, India hosted the India-Africa Forum Summit in 2008, where it declared its intention to grant African states radically improved terms of trade, making clear that it intends to compete strongly with China for influence over the continent.[78] To counter China's deepening engagement with the Gulf states, India is also reaching out to the Gulf Cooperation Council (GCC) for structured exchanges on bilateral and collective security issues.[79]

India's Balancing Act

The development of Indian policy toward China is evolving as India starts to pursue a policy of internal and external balancing more forcefully in an attempt to protect its core interests. The government is trying to fashion an effective response to the rise of China at a time of great regional and global turbulence. Though it is not entirely clear if there is a larger strategic framework shaping India's China policy, India's approach toward China is indeed undergoing a transformation, the full consequences of which will only be visible a few years down the line.

While there has always been and continues to be a range of opinions in India on how best to deal with China, a consensus seems to be evolving among the highest echelons of military planners and policymakers.[80] For a long time now, Indian defense officials have been warning their government in rather blunt terms about the growing disparity between the two Asian powers. The naval chief had warned that India neither has "the capability nor the intention to match China force for force" in military terms, while the former air chief had suggested that China poses more of a threat to India than does Pakistan. But the political leadership in India continued to act on the assumption that Beijing is not a short-term threat to India but rather needs to be watched over the long term. However, that assessment seems to be undergoing a change. After trying to ignore significant differences with China, Indian decisionmakers are finally acknowledging that the relationship between the countries is becoming increasingly contentious. Prime Minister Singh has suggested that "China would like to have a foothold in South Asia and we have to reflect on this reality…It's

---

[78] Rhys Blakely, "India Takes on China over Africa's Riches," *Times* (London), April 9, 2008.

[79] On India's growing profile in the Arab world, see Harsh V. Pant, "India's Relations with Iran: Much Ado about Nothing," *Washington Quarterly* 34, no. 1 (January 2011): 61–74.

[80] For a good typology of India's China debate, see Mohan Malik, "Eyeing the Dragon: India's China Debate," Asia-Pacific Center for Security Studies, Special Assessment, December 2003, http://www.apcss.org/Publications/SAS/ChinaDebate/ChinaDebate_Malik.pdf.

important to be prepared."[81] The Indian defense minister has argued that China's increasing assertiveness is a "serious threat."[82] And a former national security advisor and special envoy to China, M.K. Narayanan, has openly accused Chinese hackers of attacking his website as well as those of other government departments.[83]

An elite consensus is evolving in India that China's rise is posing problems for the country. "We are friends, not rivals," said the Chinese premier in India.[84] But a growing number of Indians now see China as a competitor, if not a rival. A 2010 Pew poll suggested that only 34% of Indians held a favorable view of China, with four in ten viewing their neighbor as a "very serious threat."[85] More damaging is the perception gaining ground in India that China is the only major power that does not accept India as a rising global player that must be accommodated. The discord between the two countries thus remains entrenched, and their increasing economic strength and geopolitical standing have only underlined their rapidly growing ambitions. Though it is not entirely clear if China has well-defined policy objectives vis-à-vis India, Beijing's means, both economic and military, to pursue its goals are greater than at any time in the recent past. In response, a process of military consolidation and build-up of key external partnerships is underway in India.

India was previously not very important in China's foreign policy calculus. Instead, there was a perception that the country could be easily pushed around without incurring any costs, a perception that India's own actions helped reinforce. With a new robustness in its dealings with Beijing, however, New Delhi is signaling that there are limits to what is negotiable. In particular, it has adopted a harder line on Tibet by making it clear to Beijing that it expects China to reciprocate on Jammu and Kashmir just as India has respected Chinese sensitivities on Tibet and Taiwan. Overriding Chinese objections, for example, the Indian government went ahead and allowed one of its central universities, the Indira Gandhi National Open University, to confer an honorary doctorate on the Dalai Lama.[86] This is the same government that just a few years back sent a note to all its ministers

---

[81] "PM Warns on China's South Asia Foothold," *Indian Express*, September 7, 2010.

[82] Rajat Pandit, "Assertive China a Worry, Says Antony," *Times of India*, September 14, 2010.

[83] "Chinese Hacked PMO Computers, Says Narayanan," *Indian Express*, January 19, 2010.

[84] Jim Yardley, "In India, Chinese Leader Pushes Trade," *New York Times*, December 16, 2010.

[85] The details of this poll are available at "Key Indicators Database: Opinion of China, Percent Responding Favorable, All Years Measured," Pew Global Attitudes Project, http://pewglobal.org/database/?indicator=24&survey=12&response=Favorable&mode=table.

[86] Anubhuti Vishnoi, "MEA Gives Nod to IGNOU for Doctorate to Dalai Lama," *Indian Express*, April 24, 2011.

advising them against attending a function organized by the Gandhi Peace Foundation to honor the Dalai Lama so as to not offend China.[87]

Ignoring pressures from Beijing, India also decided to take part in the Nobel Peace Prize ceremony for Chinese dissident Liu Xiaobo in Oslo in November 2010. Beijing asked several countries, including India, to boycott the ceremony or face its displeasure, describing the prize as open support for criminal activities in China. India was among the 44 states that decided to participate, even as states such as Pakistan, Russia, Saudi Arabia, Iran, and Iraq were among the nations that did not attend. There were suggestions that the Chinese premier might cancel his India trip in response, but nothing of the kind happened. Likewise, after Beijing began issuing stapled visas to the residents of Jammu and Kashmir and then denied a visa to the head of the Indian Army's Northern Command, New Delhi reacted forcefully and hinted that it was ready to review its long-standing Tibet and Taiwan policies. India also declined to endorse the "one China" policy during Wen's visit to India, a departure from past statements.[88] These developments are further evidence that India is reassessing its policy toward China, as the latter's faster-than-expected rise has challenged the fundamentals of New Delhi's traditional approach to Beijing.

Conclusion

With Sino-Indian friction growing and the potential for conflict remaining high, the challenge to India is formidable. India is increasingly bracketed with China as a rising or emerging power—or even a global superpower—though it has yet to achieve the economic and political profile that China enjoys regionally and globally. India's main security concern today is not the increasingly decrepit state of Pakistan but rather an ever more assertive China, whose ambitions are likely to reshape the contours of the regional and global balances of power, with deleterious consequences for Indian interests.

India's ties with China are thus gradually becoming competitive, with a sentiment gaining ground among Indian policy elites that China is not sensitive to India's core security interests and does not acknowledge its status as a global player. India is rather belatedly gearing up to respond to China's rise with a mix of internal consolidation and external partnerships. The most important element in this matrix is India's emerging strategic

---

[87] "Pleasing Beijing, Govt Tells Its Ministers Don't Attend Dalai Lama Honour Function," *Indian Express*, November 4, 2007.

[88] Pramit Pal Chaudhuri, "China's Flip-Flop on Kashmir," *Hindustan Times*, April 15, 2011.

partnership with the United States. New Delhi has looked to Washington for support as both Sino-Indian and Sino-U.S. competition has come into sharper relief in recent years. As Sino-Indian ties pass through a phase of turmoil, Washington will need to play the critical role of a balancer with even greater finesse than before. The United States has a key stake in the trajectory of Sino-Indian ties in view of the changing balance of power in Asia and China's growing assertiveness. As a new balance of power takes shape, India will be an indispensable element in that architecture, even as the United States remains a key player in managing the Sino-Indian dynamic. New Delhi will not be part of an explicit alliance framework with the United States against China but instead will look to the United States to manage the power transition in Asia and its attendant consequences.

The dichotomy between China and India's global convergence and their growing bilateral divergence has allowed India to collude with China as a power bloc against Western positions at the global level, even as at the bilateral level New Delhi is not averse to leveraging its relationship with Washington in order to constrain China. India's burgeoning relationship with the United States gives New Delhi some crucial strategic room to maneuver. China's rapid global ascent will bring the United States and India even closer, but India's traditional desire to retain strategic autonomy will preclude the emergence of any formal structure defining this bilateral relationship. India is beginning to receive attention from Washington as a rising power on a par with China. This process should continue, with U.S. policymakers viewing Asia as a single region whose future will to a large extent be shaped by the trajectory of Sino-Indian ties. The United States faces the prospect of an emerging power transition in Asia, and a robust partnership with India will go a long way in stabilizing the strategic landscape of the region. This is especially true at a time when China's faster-than-expected rise is generating widespread apprehension.

Although it is clearly in the interest of both China and India to stabilize their relationship by seeking out convergent issue areas, a troubled history, coupled with the structural uncertainties engendered by their simultaneous rise, is propelling the two Asian giants on a trajectory that they might find difficult to navigate in the coming years. Pursuing mutually desirable interests does not inevitably produce satisfactory solutions to strategic problems. Sino-Indian ties have entered turbulent times, and they are likely to remain there for the foreseeable future.

EXECUTIVE SUMMARY

This chapter examines Japan's relations with and strategies toward China and India.

MAIN ARGUMENT:
Though Japan is declining in relative power, its strategic response to the rise of China and India will have a significant impact on the balance of power in Asia. After years of distant relations, Japan is increasingly turning to India as a counterweight to China, encouraging Indian participation in the East Asia Summit and moving forward on security and nuclear cooperation talks. Japanese corporations are also shifting future investment plans from China to India (and other developing Asian economies) to hedge against growing political and economic risk in China. The Japan-India relationship is still hampered by New Delhi's lingering Nehruvian socialism and nonalignment ideology and Japan's own anti-nuclear allergies and political malaise, but the trend of closer alignment will continue to increase the strategic equilibrium in Asia as China rises.

POLICY IMPLICATIONS:
- External balancing strategies are insufficient to prevent further waning of Japan's influence in Asia; economic reform and revitalization, defense spending increases, and more credible political leadership are also needed.

- Japan must work on establishing stable political linkages and crisis management channels with Beijing.

- The U.S. should encourage closer Japan-India alignment by realizing calls for an official trilateral strategic dialogue and enhancing trilateral military exercises, while reiterating U.S. interests in improved relations among all the region's powers, including China.

- The tragic earthquake, tsunami, and nuclear disasters of March 2011 will put downward pressure on Japan's economic and political performance in the near term but could be positively transformative in the medium to long term.

Japan, India, and the Strategic Triangle with China

Michael J. Green

Though Japan is declining in relative power, its strategic response to the rise of China and India will nevertheless have a significant impact on the overall military, political, economic, and ideational balance of power in Asia. Realist theory teaches that status quo powers such as Japan will respond to rising powers either by bandwagoning with them or by attempting to maintain the existing strategic equilibrium through internal or external balancing. Thus far, the dynamics of Japan-China relations have not suggested bandwagoning behavior, despite growing economic interdependence between the two nations. On the other hand, Japan has exhibited only limited internal balancing behavior. Postwar restrictions on the Self-Defense Forces are steadily fading and public attitudes about national security are dramatically different than in the past, but Japan's defense budget remains flat at less than 1% of GDP, economic restructuring has at least temporarily stalled, and Japan's unpopular political parties are failing to produce leaders capable of sustaining a mandate for change and revitalization. As a result, the most pronounced strategic behavior from Japan in response to the rise of Chinese power has been external balancing.

While the focus of Japanese external balancing strategy remains the U.S.-Japan alliance, India and other Asian middle powers have soared in importance to Japan. India offers Japan a security hedge against China (particularly given common Japanese and Indian interests in the maritime

Michael J. Green is Associate Professor at the Edmund A. Walsh School of Foreign Service at Georgetown University and Japan Chair and Senior Adviser at the Center for Strategic and International Studies (CSIS). He can be reached at <mgreen@csis.org>.

The author would like to thank research assistants R. Max Helzberg, Manuel Manriquez, and Nanase Matsushita for their contributions to the research for this chapter and Nick Szechenyi, senior fellow at CSIS, for his comments.

domain), an economic hedge against overdependence on the Chinese market, an alliance hedge against overdependence on the United States for security, and an ideational hedge with a fellow democratic state against the Beijing Consensus and criticism of Japan's past. However, with the strategic convergence between Tokyo and New Delhi still at a nascent stage, these propositions have yet to be fully tested. Will India be the new frontier for expanded Japanese defense cooperation, the focus of a new growth model based on infrastructure exports, and a pillar in a new partnership of democratic maritime states? Or will the promising Indo-Japanese relationship founder on traditional Japanese anti-nuclear sentiments, the risk aversion of corporate Japan, and the undertow of India's own residual ideologies of Nehruvian socialism and nonalignment?

For now, there appears to be a broad political consensus in Tokyo about the strategic importance of India and the threat from China. The Democratic Party of Japan (DPJ) came to power in 2009 promising to reverse the policies of the previous Liberal Democratic Party (LDP) by distancing Japan from the United States and placing new demands on India in terms of nuclear nonproliferation. However, the structural realities of international relations in Northeast Asia have shifted the DPJ back onto the same general foreign policy ground as the LDP. Indeed, since normalization of relations with the People's Republic of China (PRC) in 1972, the relationship between the two countries has never been worse, while relations with India have never been better. The tragic earthquake, tsunami, and nuclear disasters of March 11, 2011, will put further downward pressure on Japanese economic and political performance in the near term, although recovery is certain and a more dynamic and motivated political leadership may emerge from the crisis. There is no evidence, however, that the events of March 11 have changed the basic dynamics of Japan's relations with China and India.

This chapter dissects this new Japan-China-India strategic triangle. The first section provides historical background on Japanese strategic views of both China and India. This is followed by sections assessing (1) the recent intensification of Japan's rivalry with China and alignment with India, (2) the influence of increased economic dependence on China and attempted economic diversification toward India, and (3) the ideational drivers behind Japan's strategic responses to both nations. The chapter concludes with an assessment of the impact of March 11 on Japanese statecraft and a brief consideration of future scenarios for Japan's strategic responses to the growth of Chinese and Indian power.

Historical Context

For the first two millennia of its history, Japan's strategic worldview was shaped by the Sinocentric system in Asia. When China was weak, Japan expanded. When China was strong, Japan was restrained. After the imposition of Western imperialism on Asia and the end of Japan's so-called closed state period (*sakoku jidai*) in the nineteenth century, Japanese statecraft added a new card to its deck—alignment with the world's hegemonic power, first with Britain, then with Germany (with brief and tragic consequences), and finally with the United States. This strategy enhanced Japanese power against other states in the system, while giving Japan maximum latitude to develop its own foreign and economic policies within Asia.

It was precisely this latitude that the architect of Japan's postwar foreign policy strategy, Shigeru Yoshida, sought vis-à-vis Communist China after World War II. Under the Yoshida Doctrine, Japan would align with the United States and oppose Communism in principle but would avoid becoming entrapped in any U.S. conflict with Beijing. Prime Minister Yoshida, who had served in China as a diplomat before the war, believed that China would eventually split from the Soviet Union and reach an entente with Japan based on commercial ties. Japanese political elites were divided on the question of China, with "mainstream" politicians in the LDP following Yoshida's line and "anti-mainstream" politicians (including the fathers and grandfathers of Prime Ministers Junichiro Koizumi and Shinzo Abe) arguing for closer ties with Taiwan, revision of the pacifist Article Nine of Japan's Constitution, and more explicit security ties with the West. Yoshida's view prevailed, however, as successive Japanese governments used Article Nine to construct policy and legislative obstacles to military cooperation with the United States in Asia. Meanwhile, Japanese firms began trading with the PRC through the 1963 Liao-Takasaki agreement, pushing the envelope of commercial relations with the mainland even before official ties were established immediately after President Richard Nixon opened U.S. relations with China in 1972 (the United States would take another seven years to normalize relations with Beijing). Japan continued hewing closer to the PRC than the United States did over the next two decades, expanding investment in China after the appreciation of the yen in the 1985 Plaza Accord and then serving as a bridge between Beijing and Washington in the aftermath of the Tiananmen Square incident on June 4, 1989. By the early 1990s, Japan was China's largest trading partner and China was second only to the United States in terms of Japan's trade. Japanese strategic writers began to anticipate a more balanced U.S.-Japan-China triangle after the Cold War—one that would reduce dependence on the United States for security and put Japan in a leading position in Asia based on the country's inherent economic power.[1]

However, these strategic assumptions, and Yoshida's own framework for China, suffered from a flawed assumption: that economic interdependence would position Japan as the leader of Asia's "flying geese," with China content to be the junior partner. By the mid-1990s it had become increasingly apparent that closer economic relations would not necessarily allow Japan to shape Chinese power. The tipping point came in 1995–96 when China tested nuclear weapons at its Lop Nor site over Japanese objections and then bracketed Taiwan with missiles to punish Taiwan president Lee Teng Hui for moving toward independence from the mainland. Japanese threats to cut yen loans to China in response were met with Chinese insistence that these were reparations for the war and not normal loans at all.[2] Japanese public opinion toward China began to steadily deteriorate, anti-Yoshida views gained more currency (particularly in the context of slower economic growth), and in April 1996 Prime Minister Ryutaro Hashimoto issued a joint security declaration with President Bill Clinton reaffirming the centrality of the U.S.-Japan alliance and pledging to revise bilateral defense planning guidelines to meet new "situations that may emerge in the area surrounding Japan"—an ambiguous formulation, but one that clearly included scenarios with China that directly threatened Japan's defense.[3]

Both Beijing and Tokyo nonetheless worked to make 1998 a "Year of Friendship" commemorating the 1978 Sino-Japanese Peace and Friendship Treaty, but Chinese president Jiang Zemin's criticism of the Japanese emperor on historical issues during a state banquet in October of that year returned relations to a downward spiral. Hu Jintao's succession to the leadership in 2003 did little to reverse this negative trend. In 2004, China organized international opposition to Japan's bid for a permanent UN Security Council seat, while the People's Liberation Army (PLA) continued deployment of over one hundred medium-range ballistic missiles targeting Japan and increased naval and air

---

[1] For details, see Michael J. Green, *Japan's Reluctant Realism: Foreign Policy in an Era of Uncertain Power* (New York: Macmillan, 2001).

[2] For details on the deteriorating Japan-China relationship in this period, see ibid.; and Benjamin Self, "China and Japan: A Facade of Friendship," *Washington Quarterly* 26, no. 1 (Winter 2002–03), 77–88.

[3] "Japan-U.S. Joint Declaration on Security: Alliance for the 21st Century," Ministry of Foreign Affairs of Japan, April 17, 1996, http://www.mofa.go.jp/region/n-america/us/security/security.html.

operations in and around Japanese-claimed territorial waters.[4] For the first time in history, Japan and China were powerful at the same time, and neither was yielding ground. In spite of the fact that since 2007 China has replaced the United States as the top destination for Japanese overseas FDI, strategic rivalry now coexists with economic interdependence as the defining characteristic of Sino-Japanese relations.[5]

India's impact on Japanese strategic thinking has historically been far more limited. Although Buddhism originated in India, it traveled to Japan through the filters of China and Korea in the ninth century. European colonization of the Indian subcontinent fueled Western imperialism in East Asia, particularly with the Opium Wars, but even this had only an indirect impact strategically on Japan. By the late nineteenth and early twentieth centuries, India began to enter Japanese strategic consciousness in terms of pan-Asianism, but Japan's alliance with Britain until 1922 kept the subcontinent off limits for Japanese foreign policy. This changed soon after with the ideology of the Greater East Asia Co-prosperity Sphere and the narrative that Japan was fighting America, Britain, China, and the Dutch ("ABCD") to liberate Asia from Western imperialism. This narrative continued to be important for the right-wing, anti-Yoshida conservatives in postwar Japan, and to this day the museum at the Yasukuni War Shrine in Tokyo features a prominent paean to Indian judge Radhabinod Pal, who refused to find Japan guilty of aggressive war during the Tokyo War Crimes Tribunal, stating "I would hold that each and everyone of the accused must be found not guilty of each and every one of the charges in the indictment and should be acquitted of all those charges."[6]

As Japan-China relations deteriorated in the 1990s, it was primarily these conservative Japanese politicians on the right who found common cause with conservative, anti-Chinese Indian political figures such as Samata Party defense minister George Fernandes. However, these were

---

[4] Specific military and diplomatic threats also grew over the next decade. Japan's defense white papers steadily elevated warnings about China's military build-up, noting in 2007 that China holds a "significant number" of intermediate-range and medium-range ballistic missiles (IRBM and MRBM) that could target Japan, including the DF-3 and DF-21, in addition to having programs to develop cruise missiles, new submarines, and a rapidly increasing inventory of fourth-generation jet fighters including the J-10, Su-27, and Su-20. A Chinese submarine circumnavigated Japan in 2004 and then entered Japanese territorial waters in 2005, and three Chinese destroyers aimed their deck guns at Japanese P-3C patrol planes that were sent to monitor their activities around the disputed Senkaku/Diaoyutai Islands in 2005.

[5] "Wagakuni seizogyo kigyo no kaigai jigyo tenkai ni kansuru chosa hokoku" [Survey Report on Overseas Business Operations by Japanese Manufacturing Companies], Japan Bank for International Cooperation (JBIC), November 2006, http://www.jbic.go.jp/ja/about/press/2006/1122-01/houkokusyo.pdf.

[6] Norimitsu Onishi, "Decades after War Trials, Japan Still Honors a Dissenting Judge," New York Times, August 31, 2007, http://www.nytimes.com/2007/08/31/world/asia/31memo.html.

narrow strands upon which to build a strategic relationship. Even after Japan began revitalizing the alliance with the United States in the mid-1990s, the prospect of strategic alignment with India was distant for Tokyo, made even more so after India's nuclear tests in May 1998. India's strategic irrelevance to Japan as a counterweight to China in this period was evident in Tokyo's response to these tests. Japan not only joined the United States and the West in imposing economic sanctions against India but also proposed leading an international convention on the Kashmir problem, naively pouring salt in an Indian wound, which would not be soon forgotten. Economic ties remained negligible, meanwhile, with India not even ranking among Japan's top ten trading partners. As Satu Limaye wrote on the India-Japan relationship at the time, the two nations were as different as "sushi and samosa."[7]

Prime Minister Yoshiro Mori, a conservative political figure heavily influenced by foreign policy intellectuals on the right, began testing domestic Japanese support for closer relations with India when he overruled his political advisors and traveled to New Delhi in August 2000. The massive Mori, a former rugby player, trudged to the Taj Mahal in the searing heat of India's summer. Seven months later, he was out of office, plagued by Japan's economic lethargy, corruption scandals, and a curmudgeonly relationship with the press; however, he had recognized the centrality of the U.S.-Japan alliance in managing Chinese power and saw opportunities to enhance Japan's external balancing through closer relations with India. His successor, the maverick Koizumi, came into power with relatively few stated ideas about India, but he shared with Mori a background in the largest anti-mainstream faction of the LDP as well as a commitment to both a strengthened U.S.-Japan alliance and a more robust Japanese role on the global stage.

At first, India played a less central role in Koizumi's foreign policy. In January 2002, Koizumi proposed a major new initiative for the establishment of an East Asian economic community in which "the countries of ASEAN [the Association of Southeast Asian Nations], Japan, China, the Republic of Korea, Australia and New Zealand will be core members."[8] India was not included. As the idea of an East Asia Summit (EAS) began taking more concrete form throughout the region in late 2004, however, it became apparent that China intended to take a leading role in shaping the rules and agenda. Working through proxy states in

---

[7] Satu P. Limaye, "Sushi and Samosas: Indo-Japanese Relations after the Cold War," in *India Looks East: An Emerging Power and Its Asia Pacific Neighbors*, ed. Sandy Gordon and Stephen Herrington (Canberra: Strategic and Defence Studies Center of Australian National University, 1995), 183.

[8] "Speech by Prime Minister of Japan Junichiro Koizumi, 'Japan and ASEAN in East Asia: A Sincere and Open Partnership,' Singapore, January 14, 2002," Prime Minister of Japan and His Cabinet website, http://www.kantei.go.jp/foreign/koizumispeech/2002/01/14speech_e.html.

ASEAN, Beijing tabled a proposal that after the first EAS summit in Kuala Lumpur the second meeting should be held in Beijing and not controlled by ASEAN. In response, Japan, Singapore, and Indonesia, among other states, offered a counterproposal that would expand EAS membership to include Australia, New Zealand, and India.[9] The implicit message from Singapore and other states to Tokyo was that Japan's foreign policy weight alone was no longer enough to counterbalance China's growing influence. Koizumi's government concurred.

The Koizumi cabinet was also forced to weigh Japan's anti-nuclear sentiment against strategic imperatives vis-à-vis India when President George W. Bush and Prime Minister Manmohan Singh issued a joint statement in July 2005 agreeing to initiate negotiations on a peaceful nuclear cooperation agreement that would not require the government of India to join the Nuclear Non-Proliferation Treaty (NPT).[10] For the Japanese public, the NPT is a sacrosanct pillar of the nation's postwar anti-nuclear policy. Without Japan, however, the Bush administration would not have been able to implement the proposed agreement with New Delhi. Not only was Japan's vote critical to winning international support for nuclear-related exports to India in the Nuclear Suppliers Group (NSG), Toshiba Corporation's 2006 acquisition of Westinghouse and Hitachi's tie-up with General Electric on nuclear power meant that U.S. firms would not be able to invest in India without Japanese government approval for Toshiba and Hitachi to also participate. The 2005 U.S.-India agreement was opposed by the left-of-center newspaper *Asahi Shimbun*; the Non-proliferation, Science and Nuclear Energy Division within the Japanese Foreign Ministry; and the mayors of Hiroshima and Nagasaki.[11] However, Koizumi had long before committed to reinforcing the U.S.-led strategic equilibrium in Asia, and the U.S.-India deal was viewed in these terms by the more powerful North American Affairs and Foreign Policy Bureaus of the Foreign Ministry. The Ministry of Economy, Trade and Industry (METI) and Japan's nuclear power–related industries also saw obvious commercial benefits, particularly

---

[9] "Nicchuu shudouken arasoi Higashi Ajia Samitto" [Japan-China Struggle over Hegemony in East Asian Summit], *Asahi Shimbun*, December 4, 2005.

[10] "Joint Statement between President George W. Bush and Prime Minister Manmohan Singh," White House, Press Release, July 18, 2005, http://georgewbush-whitehouse.archives.gov/news/releases/2005/07/20050718-6.html.

[11] "Beiingenshiryokukyoutei hankou ni hantai seimei kaku hasanhe fuan hibakushyadantai nado" [Voices against India-U.S. Nuclear Agreement], *Asahi Shimbun*, August 22, 2008; and "Tai Indo kakuyushyutsu kaikin ni kougi, hibakushyara rokujyuunin suwarikomi" [Against India Nuclear Exportation, Atom Bomb Victims Stage Sit-in], *Asahi Shimbun*, September 9, 2008.

after nuclear power plant construction had slowed in Japan.[12] In August 2008, Japan confirmed that it would support the United States' position on India in the NSG, and it eventually voted for ending the ban on exports to India on September 6, 2008.

Cooperation on the EAS and Japanese support for peaceful nuclear cooperation with India opened the floodgates for further strategic and economic agreements with New Delhi. Koizumi's successor, Shinzo Abe—a critic of the Tokyo War Crimes Tribunal, an admirer of Judge Pal, and a vocal promoter of more ambitious Japanese foreign policy strategies— warmly embraced relations with India. In his enthusiasm for an alignment of maritime democracies to counterbalance China's growing power, Abe publicly called for a quadrilateral summit of Japan, the United States, Australia, and India.[13] Though cautious bureaucracies within all four countries chafed at the idea, it was not as far a leap as opponents claimed, given that the four nations had already joined naval forces to form a rapid-response Tsunami Core Group to provide humanitarian relief after the massive Asian tsunami in December 2004.[14] In the end, foreign affairs officials from the four countries met once in 2007 to discuss the "quad" idea, and then quietly let it die, fearing that the reaction from China would not be worth the effort. However, Abe's push for closer strategic ties with India did pave the way for agreement on a bilateral Japan-India Joint Declaration on Security Cooperation on the occasion of Prime Minister Singh's October 2008 visit to Tokyo. The agreement, only the second of its kind after a comparable bilateral joint statement with Australia the previous year, launched regular Japan-India strategic consultations, military-to-military staff talks, and joint exercises, including Japanese participation in the annual U.S.-India Malabar naval exercise in April 2009, which took place off the coast of Okinawa.[15]

Economic cooperation between Japan and India also exploded over the same period, though from a low base. In 2008, India surpassed China as a recipient of bilateral official development assistance (ODA) from Japan, as illustrated in **Table 1**, and became the second-largest recipient of Japanese

[12] "Overview of Post-Meeting Press Conference Given by METI Vice Minister Mochizuki," Japanese Ministry of Economy, Trade and Industry (METI), September 8, 2008, http://www.meti.go.jp/ speeches/data_ej/ej080908j.html.

[13] Shinzo Abe, *Utsukushii Kuni E* [Towards a Beautiful Country] (Tokyo: Kodansha, 2007).

[14] Amit Bruah, "Tsunami Core Group to be Disbanded," *Hindu*, January 5, 2005, http://www.hindu. com/2005/01/06/stories/2005010605590300.htm.

[15] "Annual Report 2009–2010," Indian Ministry of Defence, http://mod.nic.in/reports/AR-eng-2010.pdf.

TABLE 1   Japanese official development assistance

Year	Japanese ODA to China ($m)	Japanese ODA to India ($m)
1998	1,158.16	504.95
1999	1,225.97	634.02
2000	769.19	368.16
2001	686.13	528.87
2002	828.71	493.64
2003	759.72	325.79
2004	964.69	-82.05
2005	1,064.27	71.46
2006	561.08	29.53
2007	435.66	99.98
2008	278.25	599.81

SOURCE: "Kunibetsu enjyo jisseki 1991 nen kara 1998 nen no jisseki" [Aid Records by Country between 1991 and 1998], Ministry of Foreign Affairs of Japan, 1999, http://www.mofa.go.jp/mofaj/gaiko/oda/shiryo/jisseki/kuni/j_99/frame3.htm; "2005 nendo seifu kaihatsu enjyo (ODA) kunibetsu databook" [Japan's ODA Data by Country 2005], Ministry of Foreign Affairs of Japan, 2005, http://www.mofa.go.jp/mofaj/gaiko/oda/shiryo/kuni/05_databook/index.html; and "2010 nendo seifu kaihatsu enjyo (ODA) kunibetsu databook" [Japan's ODA Data by Country 2010), Ministry of Foreign Affairs of Japan, 2010, http://www.mofa.go.jp/mofaj/gaiko/oda/shiryo/kuni/10_databook/index.html.

NOTE: Values calculated on a net disbursement basis.

ODA (excluding debt relief), while China was the fourth largest.[16] The bulk of concessional yen loans focused on infrastructure investment in the Delhi-Mumbai industrial corridor (DMIC) with the aim of attracting further private-sector investment from Japan. Encouraged by government policy and apprehensive about overexposure to an increasingly assertive and economically nationalistic China, Japanese corporations began to embrace a new "China plus one" strategy to diversify risk across Asia, with India as the primary focus (followed by Vietnam and Indonesia).[17] Backed by surging ODA support for Indian infrastructure development, Japanese FDI into India

[16] Ministry of Foreign Affairs of Japan, "Japan's Official Development Assistance White Paper 2009: Japan's International Cooperation" (Tokyo, March 2010), 136, http://www.mofa.go.jp/policy/oda/white/2009/pdfs/part3-2.pdf.

[17] Kato Osamu, "Nikkeikigyou no Ajia senryoku Chuugoku kyoten tsugi no toushi ni katsuyou" [Japanese Companies' Asia Strategy: China Position, Apply to Next Investment], *Tokyo Yomiuri Shimbun*, November 15, 2007.

increased eighteen-fold between 2005 and 2008 to a total of 543 billion yen, before slowing again with the international financial crisis.

Foreign Minister Taro Aso trumpeted this burgeoning strategic relationship with India as a centerpiece of his "Arc of Freedom and Prosperity"—a broad vision for strengthening ties around China's periphery that he announced in November 2006 while foreign minister and continued to implement when he became prime minister in September 2008.[18] On July 2–5, 2009, Indian foreign minister S.M. Krishna visited Tokyo for the third strategic dialogue since the signing of the bilateral security agreement the year before to consolidate progress and plan further cooperation for the years ahead. When describing the visit, the Japanese Foreign Ministry oozed optimism about the future of bilateral relations. Six weeks later, regime change came to Japan.

The Strategic Triangle under the DPJ: A Return to the New Normal?

On August 30, 2009, the DPJ crushed the ruling LDP at the polls, complementing a July 2007 victory in the Upper House of the Diet by also taking control of the lower chamber and with it the government. Japan's first real electoral change of government in over five decades (the LDP lost power in 1993 after defections but did not lose an election) provides the closest thing possible to a controlled test of the domestic political determinants of Japanese foreign policy toward China and India. The DPJ campaigned on a policy promise to bring India back into the NPT, a nod to the anti-nuclear left of the party and an implicit critique of the LDP's alignment with the United States' India strategy and the peaceful nuclear cooperation agreement.[19] On China, the DPJ manifesto offered few specifics but did promise to establish an "East Asian community," which Prime Minister Yukio Hatoyama emphasized in both editorial pieces and a meeting with Chinese president Hu Jintao in September 2009 would serve to counterbalance Japan's dependence on the United States (neither the

---

[18] "Speech by Mr. Taro Aso, Minister for Foreign Affairs, on the Occasion of the Japan Institute of International Affairs Seminar, 'Arc of Freedom and Prosperity: Japan's Expanding Diplomatic Horizons,'" Ministry of Foreign Affairs of Japan, November 30, 2006, http://www.mofa.go.jp/announce/fm/aso/speech0611.html.

[19] "Minshuto seiken seisaku manifesto" [DPJ Regime Change Manifesto], Democratic Party of Japan (DPJ), July 27, 2009, http://www.dpj.or.jp/special/manifesto2009/pdf/manifesto_2009.pdf; and "Statement Following the Approval of a Nuclear Power Agreement Proposed by the U.S. which Exempts India from Certain Export Restrictions," DPJ, September 11, 2008, http://www.dpj.or.jp/english/news/080918/04.html.

idea of an East Asian community nor the stated intent was new).[20] Within months of taking power, DPJ secretary general and political strongman Ichiro Ozawa led a delegation of 600 followers, including 146 Diet members, to Beijing where every one of them posed for an individual handshake and photograph with Hu.[21] The new DPJ government also permanently pulled the Maritime Self-Defense Forces from coalition operations in the Indian Ocean under Operation Enduring Freedom (the DPJ had already blocked continuation of the deployment in 2007), commenced an investigation of alleged "secret nuclear deals" with the United States during the Cold War, and announced plans to renegotiate the 2006 U.S.-Japan agreement on realigning U.S. military forces on Okinawa.[22]

At first blush, the DPJ appeared intent on dramatically realigning Japanese foreign policy, principally vis-à-vis the United States but with profound implications for policy toward both China and India. On deeper examination, however, it quickly became evident that the parameters for change in Japanese foreign policy were far more limited. First, the DPJ was a polyglot of a party, consisting of former socialists on the left (primarily tied to public-sector unions), former democratic socialists in the center (tied to the private-sector unions), and policy wonks from the Matsushita Seikeijuku (Matsushita Institute of Government and Management), who tended to be right of center. In 2005, for example, then DPJ leader and Matsushita Seikeijuku graduate Seiji Maehara gave a speech at the Center for Strategic and International Studies (CSIS) in Washington, D.C., pointing to the threat posed by China and the importance of the U.S.-Japan alliance, which is close to the antithesis of the initial Hatoyama vision.[23] Public support for major changes in foreign policy also appeared to be minimal. Government polls taken shortly before the 2009 Lower House race, for example, showed that 66.6% of respondents did not feel close to China and

---

[20] Yukio Hatoyama, "A New Path for Japan," *New York Times*, August 26, 2009, http://www.nytimes.com/2009/08/27/opinion/27iht-edhatoyama.html; "Nityuu Shuno kaidan (gaiyo)" [Japan-China Summit Meeting (Summary)], Ministry of Foreign Affairs of Japan, September 22, 2009, http://www.mofa.go.jp/mofaj/area/china/visit/0909_sk.html; "Policy Speech by Prime Minister Yukio Hatoyama at the 173rd Session of the Diet," Prime Minister of Japan and his Cabinet website, October 26, 2009, http://www.kantei.go.jp/foreign/hatoyama/statement/200910/26syosin_e.html; and Shingo Ito, "Japanese PM Proposes East Asian Community to China," Agence France Presse, September 22, 2009.

[21] "Ruling Parties of China, Japan Agree on Seeking Stronger Overall Relationship," Xinhua, December 10, 2009, http://news.xinhuanet.com/english/2009-12/10/content_12626887.htm.

[22] Yuka Hayashi, "Japan Probes 1960s Nuclear Agreements with U.S.," *Wall Street Journal*, October 23, 2009, http://online.wsj.com/article/SB125623748164901865.html; and Helene Cooper and Martin Fackler, "U.S. Says Okinawa Up for Discussion, Obama Agrees to Reopen Talks on Military Base as He Starts Tour of Asia," *International Herald Tribune*, November 14, 2009.

[23] Seiji Maehara, "The National Image and Foreign Policy Vision Aimed for by the DPJ" (speech at CSIS, Washington, D.C., December 8, 2005), http://www.dpj.or.jp/english/news/051215/01.html.

71.9% rejected the idea of an alliance with Beijing. In the same poll, 73% of respondents said that they felt close to the United States, and 76.4% said that the U.S.-Japan alliance is useful for Japan.[24] Moreover, in exit polls from the election, only 3% of voters said they cast their ballot based on foreign or defense policy considerations.[25]

What did the Japanese people really vote for? According to exit polls, the overwhelming majority of the public wanted an end to LDP rule and the emergence of a more competitive and accountable two-party system.[26] While in opposition, the DPJ had assembled a foreign policy platform based on the general promise of a more "equal alliance" with the United States and on opportunistic opposition to specific government policies that could be tied to the unpopular Iraq War. This ambiguity held together the disparate components of the DPJ and allowed an anti-government narrative to accompany the party's winning theme of ending five decades of LDP dominance. But in reality, the DPJ never developed a coherent foreign or defense policy vision, as quickly became apparent.

Prime Minister Hatoyama backtracked on most of the DPJ's foreign policy pledges pertaining to the United States before plummeting public support rates forced him to resign on June 2, 2010. With India, however, he proved an enthusiastic partner from the beginning, traveling to New Delhi for a summit with Prime Minister Singh on December 29, 2009, at which the two leaders issued a joint statement on the "New Stage of Japan-India Strategic and Global Partnership." The partnership document included an action plan for implementing the October 2008 joint declaration between Aso and Singh and established subcabinet-level "two plus two" foreign and defense ministerial meetings modeled on the Security Consultative Committee of the U.S.-Japan Security Treaty.[27] Hatoyama's early continuity with LDP policy toward India reflected both the geostrategic logic and momentum already behind the relationship and the new prime minister's

---

[24] Polls cited in Michael J. Green, "The Democratic Party of Japan and the Future of the U.S.-Japan Alliance," *Journal of Japanese Studies* 37, no. 1 (Winter 2011): 102.

[25] "Sankei FNN yoron chosa: Omona shitsumon to kaitou" [Sankei-FNN Opinion Poll: Major Questions Answered], *Sankei News*, July 17, 2009.

[26] Polls taken after the election consistently demonstrated the public's desire to punish the LDP and create a more accountable and competitive two-party system after years of one-party rule, political corruption, and stagnant economic performance. DPJ policies were only a secondary consideration at best. See, for example, "*Asahi Shimbun* yoron chosa" [*Asahi Shimbun* Opinion Poll], *Asahi Shimbun*, September 2, 2009; Jiminto saisei kaigi [LDP Revival Committee], "Jiminto saisei e no teigen" [Suggestions to Revive the LDP], LDP, September 21, 2009, 3; "Sankei FNN yoron chosa: Hatoyama jiki shushou ni kitai" [Public Opinion Poll Shows People Have Hope for New Prime Minister Hatoyama], *Sankei Shimbun*, September 7, 2009; and "Sankei FNN yoron chosa: Omona shitsumon to kaitou."

[27] "Joint Declaration on Security Cooperation between Japan and India," Ministry of Foreign Affairs of Japan, October 22, 2008, http://www.mofa.go.jp/region/asia-paci/india/pmv0810/joint_d.html.

own desire to demonstrate closer relations with Asia where possible. (Hatoyama also made significant early rhetorical overtures to Korea, particularly on the vexing history issue.)

Perhaps even more striking in terms of early DPJ policy shifts was the decision to seek a 123 agreement with New Delhi to allow peaceful nuclear collaboration. While these negotiations were the logical next step after Japanese support for the U.S.-India position in the NSG, anti-nuclear sentiment within the DPJ might have presented a far greater obstacle than was actually the case. The new DPJ foreign minister Katsuya Okada, for example, had close ties to nuclear disarmament scholars and NGOs and had pledged to press the United States to adopt a "no first use" policy and other measures dear to the anti-nuclear supporters of his party.[28] His position shifted once in office, however. He wrote Secretary of State Hillary Clinton in December 2009, for example, urging her to work for both complete nuclear disarmament and reinforcement of the U.S. extended deterrent as the Obama administration undertook the Nuclear Posture Review.[29] Then, as the DPJ struggled to put together a credible economic growth strategy, the party leadership began focusing on infrastructure exports—including nuclear power—as a key pillar. METI officials won support early on from their minister, but within the Foreign Ministry a battle again brewed between the newly empowered Disarmament, Non-proliferation and Science Department and the traditional security-oriented parts of the ministry in advance of the first round of Japan-India nuclear cooperation negotiations on June 28, 2010.[30] This time, to the surprise of the disarmament community, Okada sided with the energy and national security realists in industry, METI, and the Foreign Ministry, and Hatoyama's replacement, Naoto Kan, agreed with Singh in Tokyo in October 2010 to "accelerate" nuclear talks. The bilateral India-Japan talks have since bogged down somewhat on Tokyo's insistence that the agreement would be reversible if India were to conduct a nuclear test, but New Delhi has clarified that it will give only the assurances it gave Washington on the same subject and no more. Participants in the talks from both sides have reported to this author that they think the gap will be bridged. The critical point, however,

---

[28] Katsuya Okada (remarks made at "Atarashii jidai no Nichibei kankei" [Japan-U.S. Relationship in a New Era], Kyoto, October 18, 2009).

[29] "Press Conference by Minister for Foreign Affairs Katsuya Okada," Ministry of Foreign Affairs of Japan, January 22, 2010, http://www.mofa.go.jp/announce/fm_press/2010/1/0122_01.html.

[30] "Negotiations on a Japan-India Agreement for Cooperation in the Peaceful Uses of Nuclear Energy," Ministry of Foreign Affairs of Japan, June 25, 2010, http://www.mofa.go.jp/announce/event/2010/6/0625_01.html.

is that the new DPJ government chose economic growth and geostrategic priorities over anti-nuclear idealism—just as the LDP had.[31]

While Japan-India relations reverted to their original trajectory quietly over the first year of the DPJ's rule, the relationship between Japan and China crashed with a fury that shook the DPJ establishment to its foundation. As noted earlier, views toward China within the DPJ began as diverse as those within the LDP. For Okada (foreign minister), Seiji Maehara (land, infrastructure, transport and tourism minister, who controlled Japan's Coast Guard), and Toshimi Kitazawa (defense minister), the intelligence briefings on PLA activities would have evaporated any early complacency about an easier relationship with Beijing. Japanese analysts took particular note of Hu's announcement in 2007 of a new maritime strategy that would expand from offshore defense to blue water defense.[32] In accordance with the new strategy, the PLA Navy (PLAN) executed unprecedented joint naval-air exercises in international waters south of Okinawa in March and April 2010.[33] Then, in June five ships from China's North Sea Fleet conducted exercises near Okinotorishima Island, far off the Pacific Ocean side of the Japanese archipelago. Tokyo claims Okinotorishima as an island in order to extend the Japanese exclusive economic zone (EEZ) eastward into the Pacific. Beijing has no claim, but adamantly maintains that Okinotorishima is a rock and thus Japan's EEZ should be limited to the island of Honshu. From the Japanese perspective, China's doctrine, diplomacy, and operations suggested a strategy of encircling the Japanese archipelago from the East China Sea around to the "second island chain" that connects the Bonin Islands and Guam—essentially strangling Japan and threatening access even to the Pacific side of the Japanese home islands.[34]

The generally menacing tone of Chinese claims to Okinotorishima and PLA operations in the second island chain became acute on September 7, 2010, when a Chinese fishing boat operating near the Senkaku Islands rammed a Japanese Coast Guard cutter. The Chinese captain, Zhan Qixiong, was detained and charged the next day on suspicion of "obstructing the public duties" of coast guard patrol boats in Japanese territorial waters. The Chinese Ministry of Foreign Affairs responded by declaring the detention and arrest "illegal and invalid" and postponing negotiations with Japan over possible joint development of gas fields around the islands, in addition to canceling

---

[31] Jonathan Soble, "Japan's Nuclear Industry Turns Focus Abroad," *Financial Times*, April 10, 2010.

[32] National Institute for Defense Studies (Japan), *East Asian Strategic Review 2010* (Tokyo: Japan Times, 2010), 126, http://www.iadb.org/intal/intalcdi/PE/2010/06045.pdf.

[33] Carlyle A. Thayer, "The United States and Chinese Assertiveness in the South China Sea," *Security Challenges* 6, no. 2 (Winter 2010): 71.

[34] National Institute for Defense Studies, *East Asian Strategic Review 2010*, 126.

the planned visit of Li Jianguo, vice chair of the Standing Committee of the National People's Congress, to the Japanese Diet.[35] At this point, Beijing's response appeared to be the usual tit-for-tat diplomatic retaliation Tokyo had anticipated, and Prime Minister Kan told the press on September 17 that "Japan and China basically continue to have friendly ties."[36]

However, after a Summary Court in Ishigaki, Okinawa Prefecture, approved a ten-day extension of Zhan's detention to allow for further questioning on September 19, the Chinese response suddenly became much fiercer. From Beijing's perspective, the court ruling represented a Japanese attempt to treat the Senkaku Island issue as an internal legal problem rather than a diplomatic issue—precisely what Maehara and others in the Kan government intended given that Japan already has administrative control over the islands. That day, China's Ministry of Foreign Affairs announced that Japan had "seriously damaged Sino-Japan bilateral relations" and cut off all exchanges with the central and local governments in Japan, warning that unless the captain was immediately released, "China will take strong countermeasures and Japan will bear all the consequences."[37]

On September 21, Japanese traders reported to the government that shipments of rare earth metals from China to Japan had been completely suspended. These shipments included alloys from dysprosium, neodymium, and samarium used for specialized magnets; materials used in lasers; lanthanum oxide used in advanced optical glass; and cerium oxide used in personal computers and hard drive manufacturing.[38] Japan was dependent on Chinese mining for over 90% of these specialized materials, and the boycott had the potential to stop Japanese manufacturing in numerous sectors within a matter of months. Meanwhile, the trial in Okinawa was expected to last three months. After four Japanese nationals working for the Fujita Corporation were arrested at a military base near the city of Shijiazhuang for allegedly videotaping a military installation, Kan and his chief cabinet secretary, Yoshito Sengoku, appeared to lose their nerve. The Prosecutor's Office in Naha, Okinawa, announced it would return Zhan

---

[35] "Statement by the Ministry of Foreign Affairs of the People's Republic of China," Ministry of Foreign Affairs of the People's Republic of China, September 25, 2010, http://www.fmprc.gov.cn/eng/zxxx/t755932.htm.

[36] See "Press Conference by Prime Minister Naoto Kan," Prime Minister of Japan and His Cabinet website, September 17, 2010, http://www.kantei.go.jp/foreign/kan/statement/201009/17kaiken_e.html.

[37] Martin Fackler and Ian Johnson, "Arrest in Disputed Seas Riles China and Japan," *New York Times*, September 19, 2010, http://www.nytimes.com/2010/09/20/world/asia/20chinajapan.html.

[38] See "Cooperation of Rare Resources User Countries," METI, Non-paper, October 2010.

after "careful consideration of future Japan-China relations."[39] Beijing's response was to humiliate Kan by demanding that "Japan must apologize to and compensate China for the incident," a demand Japan's Ministry of Foreign Affairs rejected as "groundless" and "totally unacceptable."[40]

With the arrival of Captain Zhan to a hero's welcome in China on September 25 and the subsequent release of the businessmen accused of espionage by China on September 30, the stand-off between Tokyo and Beijing appeared over. Seeking to turn a corner, Sengoku told reporters on September 27 that "from now on, I believe Japan will begin a process of enriching its mutually beneficial and strategic relationship with China," and over the ensuing months Beijing did gradually resume official dialogues with Tokyo.[41] However, the repercussions of the September 2010 diplomatic collision ran deep.

First, the encounter shattered the Japanese press's and public's already low confidence in China's future reliability. A typical example was *Yomiuri Shimbun*'s poll in October 2010 in which 84% of respondents said they "did not trust" China.[42] Newspaper editorials in Japan were close to unanimous in condemning Beijing's heavy-handed response to the confrontation, particularly the boycott on rare earth metals and the arrest of the Japanese businessmen. A December *Asahi Shimbun* poll found that 51% of respondents thought Japan should seek to deepen ties with China, 68% said that U.S.-Japan relations were more important than Japan-China relations, and only 15% of Japanese put China-Japan ties as most important.[43] In *Yomiuri*'s October poll, 71% said that Japan should deepen alliance ties with the United States after the crisis with China.[44]

The second repercussion of the Senkaku confrontation was accelerated external balancing. An influential group of 43 DPJ Diet members issued a public "Opinion Paper to the Kan Administration" on September 27 criticizing the release of the captain and urging a new China policy based on increased defense capabilities, alliance with the United States, and the establishment of a new "maritime order" in the Western Pacific. The paper

---

[39] Alex Martin and Kanako Takahara, "Friction Cited in Move to Free Chinese Skipper," *Japan Times*, September 25, 2010, http://search.japantimes.co.jp/cgi-bin/nn20100925a1.html.

[40] Martin Fackler, "Japan Rejects Apologizing to China," *New York Times*, September 25, 2010, http://www.nytimes.com/2010/09/26/world/asia/26japan.html.

[41] "Tensions with China Show No Signs of Easing," *Japan Times*, September 28, 2010, http://search.japantimes.co.jp/cgi-bin/nn20100928a1.html.

[42] "*Yomiuri Shimbun* October 2010 Telephone Public Opinion Poll," Maureen and Mike Mansfield Foundation, conducted October 1–3, 2010, http://www.mansfieldfdn.org/polls/2010/poll-10-31.htm.

[43] "December 2010 *Asahi Shimbun* Interview Survey," Maureen and Mike Mansfield Foundation, conducted December 4-5, 2010, http://www.mansfieldfdn.org/polls/2010/poll-10-34.htm.

[44] "*Yomiuri Shimbun* October 2010 Telephone Public Opinion Poll."

also urged new outreach to Russia and Central and South Asia, citing Japanese statements that one must "make friends with afar to fight your neighbors close at home."[45] Throughout the crisis, Foreign Minister Maehara sought to demonstrate the closest possible coordination with Washington. In his bilateral meeting with Secretary of State Clinton on October 27, the two addressed China's rare earth metals embargo, and Clinton noted that the United States and Japan should diversify suppliers. Maehara, Clinton, and Korean foreign minister Kim Sung Hwan also held a trilateral meeting on December 6, 2010, in Washington that focused on the North Korean threat but complemented Tokyo's external balancing strategy toward China. This external balancing strategy was highlighted in the Japanese government's National Defense Program Guidelines, released on December 17, which primarily emphasized a new doctrine of "dynamic defense" to defend Japanese islands and sea lanes but also highlighted the need for greater cooperation with other maritime states in Asia.[46] Meanwhile, METI fanned out in search of alternatives to China for rare earth metals and pursued new agreements with several countries, including Uzbekistan, South Africa, Mongolia, Vietnam, Australia, and India, throughout the rest of 2010.[47]

The third repercussion of the Senkaku collision concerned Japan's economic assistance strategies. Already reeling from the symbolism of China surpassing it to become the economy with the world's second-largest nominal GDP, Japan had announced in early March 2011 that it would conduct an official review of ODA policy, including aid to China, and in the wake of March 11 the ruling DPJ proposed to slash the ODA budget

---

[45] Shuji Kira et al., "Opinion Paper to the Kan Administration: Proudly Fly the Flag of National Interest, and Steer towards Strategic Diplomacy," September 27, 2010, http://www.nagashima21. net/download/20100927_Opinion_Paper.pdf.

[46] In the new National Defense Program Guidelines, security cooperation with South Korea, Australia, the ASEAN countries, and India is introduced as a complement to the U.S.-Japan alliance, under the rubric of "multilayered security cooperation with the international community." See Japanese Ministry of Defense, "National Defense Program Guidelines for JFY 2011 and Beyond," provisional translation, December 17, 2010, http://www.mod.go.jp/e/d_act/d_policy/pdf/guidelinesFY2011.pdf.

[47] "Reaasu kakuho he, kanminittai de shigen gaiko: Mongoru, Minami A, Burajiru nado he chotatsusaki kakudai" [Toward Securing Rare Earths, Resource Diplomacy by the Government and the People: Expanding Procurement Efforts toward Mongolia, South Africa, Brazil and So On], *Nikkei Shimbun*, October 2, 2010; "Signing of a Memorandum between Japan and the Republic of Uzbekistan," Ministry of Economy, Trade and Industry, February 7, 2011, http://www.meti.go.jp/ english/press/2011/0207_01.html; "Joint Statement: Vision for Japan-India Strategic and Global Partnership in the Next Decade," Ministry of Foreign Affairs of Japan, October 25, 2010, http:// www.mofa.go.jp/region/asia-paci/india/pm1010/joint_st.html; "Visit to Australia by Mr. Seiji Maehara, Minister for Foreign Affairs of Japan (Overview)," Ministry of Foreign Affairs of Japan, November 23, 2010, http://www.mofa.go.jp/region/asia-paci/australia/visit101123.html; "Japan-Mongolia Summit Meeting," Ministry of Foreign Affairs of Japan, November 19, 2010, http://www. mofa.go.jp/announce/announce/2010/11/1119_03.html; and "Japan-Vietnam Joint Statement on the Strategic Partnership for Peace and Prosperity in Asia," Ministry of Foreign Affairs of Japan, October 31, 2010, http://www.mofa.go.jp/region/asia-paci/vietnam/joint1010.html.

by 20%.[48] Not long before this, foreign minister Seiji Maehara, who has since resigned, had stated in testimony to the Diet on March 4 that it was inconceivable for Japan to increase aid to China.

Fourth and finally, the Senkaku fight with China dealt a major blow to public support for the Kan government. On October 5, 2010, in the wake of the stand-off, a *Yomiuri Shimbun* poll found that 72% of the public disagreed with the decision to release Zhan and for the first time over 50% also disapproved of the Kan government's performance.[49] After Japanese Coast Guard sources leaked damning video footage on November 7 showing the Chinese fishing vessel clearly and deliberately colliding with the Japanese vessel, *Asahi Shimbun* polling found that 79% of the public was critical of the Kan administration for not releasing the footage earlier to demonstrate China's culpability.[50] On November 26 the Upper House of the Japanese Diet passed a nonbinding no-confidence resolution against Kan, largely over the Senkaku issue. Kan survived, but his support slipped below 20%. Though other factors weighed down Kan, including corruption charges against Ozawa, the lesson to the Japanese political leadership was unmistakable: the public and the opposition will punish officials for being weak toward China.

In the end, the Senkaku stand-off was a modest diplomatic victory for Japan in Asia. The dispute coincided with assertive Chinese behavior elsewhere and thus evinced sympathy for Japan in Korea, India, and Southeast Asia and enhanced external balancing strategies. Yet the outcome was also a political defeat for Kan and a dangerous failure of nerve and deterrence in the face of Chinese escalation, the consequences of which are yet to be seen.

The Reverse Image: Economic Relations

The Senkaku stand-off highlighted for Japanese government and industry experts the need to reduce economic and resource dependence on China. In 2010, surveys of Japanese business executives conducted by the Japan Bank for International Cooperation (JBIC) showed that India had surpassed China as "the most promising country for investment in the long term [next 10 years]." India remained second after China on the list

[48] Kyung Lah, "Japan to Review Aid for Booming China," *CNN*, March 4, 2011, http://edition. cnn.com/2011/BUSINESS/03/04/japan.china.aid/index.html; and "DPJ to Redirect Overseas Aid to Rebuilding Efforts," *Asahi Shimbun*, April 8, 2011, http://www.asahi.com/english/ TKY201104070138.html.

[49] "*Yomiuri Shimbun* October 2010 Telephone Public Opinion Poll."

[50] "*Asahi Shimbun* November 2010 Emergency Public Opinion Poll," Maureen and Mike Mansfield Foundation, conducted November 13–14, 2010, http://www.mansfieldfdn.org/polls/2010/poll-10-32.htm.

of most "promising countries" over the medium term (next three years), which suggested a major shift in strategic intent rather than in specific investment planning. Indeed, the top reason given for investing in India was rather nonspecific: 89% of respondents cited "future growth potential of local market."[51] In relative terms, however, trade relations between Japan and India have actually declined since the 2008–9 financial crisis. Japan's share of total Indian trade decreased from 2.8% to 2.2% between 2005 and 2010, with Japanese imports from India decreasing from $3.20 billion in 2005 to $3.16 billion in 2009 and exports from Japan to India increasing from $3.53 billion to $5.37 billion.[52]

Meanwhile, Japan's economic interaction with China has grown, in contrast to their deteriorating security relationship and the relative softening of Japan's economic interaction with India. Overall Japan's trade with China increased 71.7% between 2005 and 2010 and ended up over twenty times as large as overall trade with India in 2010 (see **Figure 1**).[53]

China's huge cash holdings have further reshaped Japanese dependence on Beijing over this same period. Even as the two governments and publics squared off over the Senkaku issue, Chinese government-wealth investors were increasing their stake in Japanese financial firms. Using generic-sounding investment companies with names like "SSBT OD05 Omnibus Account Treaty Clients," Chinese sovereign wealth funds had poured more than $19.4 billion into leading Japanese firms such as Mitsubishi UFJ and Canon by early 2011.[54]

Japan's hedging strategy reflects risk management in government and industry planning as well as Japan's deteriorating strategic situation with respect to China. Still, it should be noted that the huge disparity in Japan-China and Japan-India trade relations does not translate into direct one-for-one political influence for Beijing. Japanese investment in and exports to China are intermediate steps in production networks that are ultimately aimed at North America and Europe. Japan still sits at a much higher point than China on the production value chain, particularly in terms of high

---

[51] "Survey Report on Overseas Business Operations by Japanese Manufacturing Companies," Japan Bank for International Cooperation (JBIC), December 2010, http://www.jbic.go.jp/en/about/press/2010/1203-01/eibunn.pdf.

[52] Japan Ministry of Internal Affairs and Communications, Statistics Bureau, http://www.stat.go.jp/english/data/index.htm; and "Japan," Export Import Data Bank, Department of Commerce of India, http://commerce.nic.in/eidb/default.asp.

[53] "EIU Country Data Japan," Economist Intelligence Unit, https://eiu.bvdep.com/version-2011510/cgi/template.dll?product=101.

[54] Atsuko Fukase, "China's Stealth Entry to Japan: Government-Backed Entities Ramp Up Stakes in Firms; Decoding SSBT OD05," *Wall Street Journal*, February 25, 2001, C-1.

FIGURE 1   Japan's total volume of trade with China and India

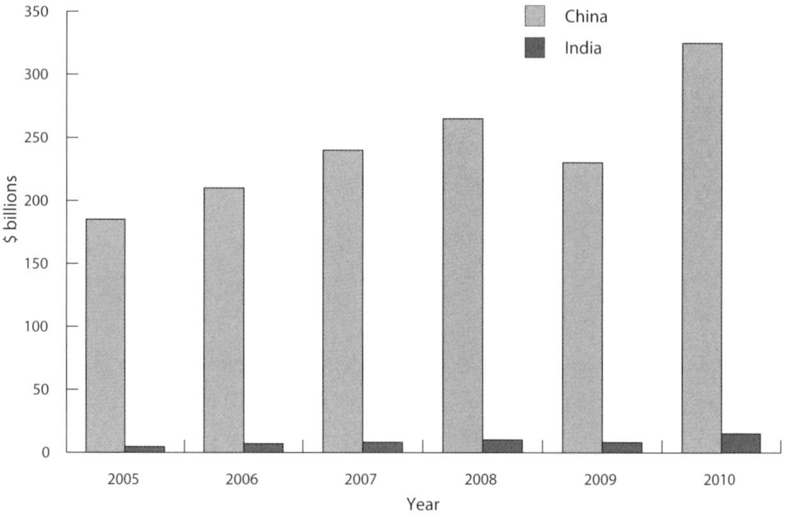

SOURCE: International Monetary Fund, *Direction of Trade Statistics Yearbook, 2011* (Washington, D.C.: IMF Statistics Department, 2011), 290–93.

technology. Japan also remains the top Asian nation in terms of Nobel Prizes won in the sciences and in citations in technical and scientific journals.

Japan's investment in India, by contrast, is aimed at the Indian market. The imbalance also reflects historical factors, such as India's belated economic opening and the impact of Japanese nuclear sanctions against India. The relatively flat trajectory of Japan-India economic relations over the past few years could change, however. Indeed, that is the expectation expressed by Japanese executives in the 2010 JBIC survey. It is with that exact hope in mind that Japan signed an economic partnership agreement (EPA) with India in February 2011 that will remove tariffs on 94% of bilateral trade in terms of value within ten years, potentially doubling bilateral trade by 2014.[55] Japan is negotiating similar EPAs elsewhere in Asia and is actively exploring participation in the Trans-Pacific Partnership (TPP). There is no plan for a direct bilateral EPA or FTA with China, though Japan, China, and

[55] "Press Conference by the Deputy Press Secretary," Ministry of Foreign Affairs of Japan, February 17, 2011, http://www.mofa.go.jp/announce/press/2011/2/0217_01.html.

Korea agreed to explore the feasibility of negotiating a trilateral EPA at their summit meeting in June 2011.[56]

The Ideational Factor

Over the past few decades, social scientists have increasingly focused on identity formation and norms in the dynamics of international relations. For the most part, this "constructivist" approach has emphasized the ways in which such ideational factors work against realist expectations that material factors and the distribution of power are the major variables shaping states' behavior in the international system.[57] Japan proved an early laboratory for constructivists to argue that material factors often take second place to identity and norms, particularly given Japan's self-restrained defense policies and postwar "culture of anti-militarism."[58] Until recently, scholars were particularly taken with the hypothesis that Japan would lead East Asian integration after the war based on a set of normative values that were different from those of the West. This was a theme that resonated for many intellectuals in Japan at the end of the Cold War, including former vice finance minister Eisuke Sakakibara, who argued that Japan had developed an economic model that "surpassed capitalism" and who tried to establish an Asian monetary fund (AMF) in the midst of the 1997–98 Asian financial crisis that would serve as a counterbalance to the U.S.-dominated International Monetary Fund and the so-called Washington Consensus. Japanese government advisory commissions echoed this theme as did leading economic analysts such as Hirohiko Okumura and Kiyohiko Fukushima at the Nomura Research Institute. The Finance Ministry also fought back against the Washington Consensus, not only with the AMF but in a major study at the World Bank on the roots of the "Asian economic miracles."[59]

The recalibration of Japanese relations with India and China over the past decade casts this constructivist hypothesis in a new light, suggesting

---

[56] See the "Summit Declaration" for the 4th Japan-China-ROK Trilateral Summit, available from the Ministry of Foreign Affairs of Japan website, May 22, 2011, http://www.mofa.go.jp/region/asia-paci/jck/summit1105/declaration.html.

[57] For more on the impact of identity and strategic culture on the behavior of states, see Alistair Iain Johnston, "Thinking about Strategic Culture," *International Security* 19, no. 4 (1995): 32–64; and Rawi Abdelai, Yoshiko M. Herrera, Alistair Ian Johnston, and Rose McDermott, "Identity as a Variable," *Perspectives on Politics* 44, no. 4 (2006): 696. On constructivism generally, see Alexander Wendt, *Social Theory of International Politics* (Cambridge: Cambridge University Press, 1999).

[58] See, for example, Thomas Berger, "From Sword to Chrysanthemum: Japan's Culture of Anti-militarism," *International Security* 17, no. 4. (1993): 119–50; and Peter Katzenstein and Nobuo Okawara, "Japan's National Security," *International Security* 17, no. 4, (1993): 84–118.

[59] Eisuke Sakakibara, *Shihonshugi wo Koeta Nippon* [Japan Beyond Capitalism] (Tokyo: Toyo Keizai Shinposha, 1990). For details on the AMF, see Green, *Japan's Reluctant Realism*, 229–67.

that formation of national identity actually has quite a bit to do with the distribution of power in the international system. When the United States was pressing Japan to embrace the free market–based Washington Consensus on economic development promoted by the IMF and the World Bank in the early post–Cold War years, the major ideational threat to Japan's economic development model and leadership legitimacy in Asia appeared to be the unipolar United States. By the end of the 1990s, Japanese financial strategists realized several things: first, that Japan would risk enormous moral hazard by trying to create regional financial institutions independent of the IMF, and, second, that Japan's economic model contained serious structural flaws. Meanwhile, Japanese industry and METI came to recognize that the greatest external challenge Japan faced in terms of norms and rules was China's capricious investment environment. Increasingly, Japanese interest in Asian "rule-making" focused on this China problem, as the JBIC found in its surveys of Japanese investment views of China.[60]

When Koizumi came into office, he also extended the normative message in his foreign policy to include democratic values. Most striking was his speech to the 50th anniversary of the Bandung Asia-Africa summit on April 22, 2005, in which he argued, "we should all play an active role in preventing disorderly trade in weapons, as well as in disseminating universal values such as the rule of law, freedom and democracy."[61] Subsequent strategy documents from the Ministry of Foreign Affairs on regional architecture emphasized Japan's role in advancing universal democratic norms in the process of regional integration—a "principled multilateralism" that would narrow the differences among Asia's diverse political systems by strengthening democracy, the rule of law, and good governance—in contrast to China's emphasis on maintaining the supposed Asian principle of "noninterference in internal affairs."[62] As the Sino-Japanese ideational (or ideological) clash spread across Asian regional forums, Foreign Minister Taro Aso chose to make democratic norms the centerpiece of his 2007 concept of an "Arc of Freedom and Prosperity" stretching from NATO to

---

[60] "Wagakuni seizogyo kigyo."

[61] "Speech by H.E. Mr. Junichiro Koizumi, Prime Minister of Japan," Prime Minister of Japan and His Cabinet website, April 22, 2005, http://www.kantei.go.jp/foreign/koizumispeech/2005/04/22speech_e.html.

[62] Takio Yamada, "Toward a Principled Integration of East Asia: Concept for an East Asian Community," *Gaiko Forum* 5, no. 3 (2005).

Japan around China's periphery.[63] Prime Minister Abe also highlighted the ideational linkages Japan could build with NATO, Australia, and of course India. A clause in the Japan-India Joint Declaration from August 22, 2007, noted that

> Japan and India share universal values of democracy, open society, human rights, rule of law and market economy and share common interest in promoting peace, stability and prosperity in Asia and the world. Based on this recognition, the two leaders reaffirmed that the Japan-India partnership is a bilateral relationship with the largest potential for growth.[64]

To be sure, conservatives in Japan were framing national identity and values in a way that would marginalize those on the left who had traditionally opposed closer linkages with the West or were against China. When the DPJ came to power in September 2009, Prime Minister Hatoyama made Eisuke Sakakibara and other advocates of "Asianism" from the 1990s his key advisors. The DPJ's initial joint statement with its coalition partners, the Social Democrats and the Japan Peoples Party, emphasized their resistance to Koizumi's "neocon" policies.[65] But the DPJ also had strong ties to Japan's small civil society and thus a historic commitment to human rights. Hatoyama, for example, is chairman of the Diet members' league to support Burmese dissident leader Aung San Suu Kyi, and Foreign Minister Okada emphasized human rights issues prominently in his meetings with his Chinese and Burmese counterparts. After the confrontations with China and North Korea in 2010 and 2011, the DPJ government also began emphasizing the democratic bonds with the United States, Korea, and India in joint statements and declaratory policy, beginning with Hatoyama's joint statement with Singh in December 2009 and including the

---

[63] See, for example, "Policy Speech by Minister for Foreign Affairs Taro Aso to the 166th Session of the Diet," Ministry of Foreign Affairs of Japan, January 26, 2007, http://www.mofa.go.jp/announce/fm/aso/speech0701.html;"On the Arc of Freedom and Prosperity: An Address by H.E. Taro Aso, Minister of Foreign Affairs on the Occasion of the Founding of the Japan Forum for International Relations, Inc.," Ministry of Foreign Affairs of Japan, March 12, 2007, http://www.mofa.go.jp/policy/pillar/address0703.html; and "Jiyu to hanei no ko" [The Arc of Freedom and Prosperity], special issue, *Gaiko Forum* 225 (2007). Fact sheets prepared for the Arc of Freedom and Prosperity speeches by the Foreign Ministry emphasized that the theme is not imposed by the United States, but is the result of "100 years of accumulated wisdom that comes from having the longest tradition of democracy and being the first country to modernize in Asia."

[64] "Joint Statement by Japan and the Republic of India on the Enhancement of Cooperation on Environmental Protection and Energy Security," Ministry of Foreign Affairs of Japan, August 22, 2007, http://www.mofa.go.jp/region/asia-paci/pmv0708/joint-3.html; and "Joint Statement on the Roadmap for New Dimensions to the Strategic and Global Partnership between Japan and India," Ministry of Foreign Affairs of Japan, August 22, 2007, http://www.mofa.go.jp/region/asia-paci/pmv0708/joint-2.html.

[65] "Santo renritsu seiken goisho" [Three-Party Coalition Government Agreement], DPJ, September 9, 2009, http://www.dpj.or.jp/news/files/20090909goui.pdf.

U.S.-Japan-ROK foreign ministers' trilateral statement on December 6, 2010.[66] Outside advisory groups to the Japanese government without a particular ideological stripe have also begun emphasizing the centrality of universal norms to Japan's role in East Asian "community building."[67]

The ideational dimension of external balancing is now almost as pronounced as it was under the LDP, though with many of the same limitations. India has embraced the democratic bond with Japan, but the two countries still differ sharply on whether the principle of noninterference in internal affairs should guide an Asian order, as was revealed in a 2009 survey of elite strategic thinkers in nine Asian countries conducted by CSIS.[68] The Indian government also takes a far more cynical and realpolitik approach to the Burma problem than Japan does; or, rather, one might say that it takes an "even more" cynical approach than Japan, considering that Japan supported UN Security Council actions on Burma while serving as a nonpermanent member and refrains from providing yen loans to the country. Finally, while the ideational glue between Japan and India represents a deliberate response to the challenge from China for Asian leadership, there are questions in Japan about whether India can in fact be a partner for rule-making in organizations such as the World Trade Organization or in global climate negotiations, as well as about whether India's unruly domestic politics can actually compete with China in the long run.[69] The general principle of a democratic bond is obvious, in other words, but Japanese cooperation with India on specific issues related to human rights, rule of law, and democracy support remains a work in progress.

The Impact of March 11

When a 9.0-magnitude earthquake and 23-meter tsunami smashed the Tohoku region of Japan's Honshu Island on March 11, 2011, history suggested that the Japanese economy would be back on track in a matter of months as it was after similarly massive earthquakes in 1923 and 1995. However, this time recovery was weighed down by three additional burdens. First, Japan's 200% debt-to-GDP ratio raised concerns about whether

---

[66] "Trilateral Statement Japan, the Republic of Korea, and the United States," U.S. Department of State, December 6, 2010, http://www.state.gov/r/pa/prs/ps/2010/12/152431.htm.

[67] "Policy Report: The State of the Concept of an East Asian Community and Japan's Strategic Response Thereto (Summary)," Council on East Asian Community, August 2005, 7, http://www.ceac.jp/e/pdf/policy_report_e.pdf.

[68] See also C. Raja Mohan, "Balancing Interests and Values: India's Struggle with Democracy Promotion," *Washington Quarterly* 30, no. 3 (Summer 2007): 99–115.

[69] See, for example, Takehiko Horimoto, "Taikokuka suru Indo: Chugoku to no taihi" [India's Emergence as a Superpower: A Comparison with China], *Gaiko* 6 (2011): 110–17.

the government could pay the estimated $600 billion reconstruction bill without running out of domestic savings and causing interest-rate jumps and inflation. The rating service Standard & Poor's was already so concerned that in January 2011 it lowered the rating for Japan's sovereign debt from AA to AA- and revised its outlook in April 2011 from stable to negative, even though opinion polls showed that the Japanese public was willing to pay taxes or buy bonds to rebuild.[70] The second burden was from the failure of the Fukushima Daiichi nuclear plant. The Japanese public and the world watched in horrified fascination as Self-Defense Force helicopters and Tokyo Electric Power Company engineers risked their lives to cool exposed fuel rods that were threatening to melt down. The longer-term effects of radiation leakage created an anxiety that is difficult to quantify or put to rest. The Fukushima disaster will also force a re-examination of Japan's larger energy strategy and likely a downgrading of reliance on nuclear power (currently responsible for 20% of power generation in Japan). The third burden was weak political leadership. When Japan needed a Winston Churchill (or a Yoshida or Koizumi) to rally the public and restore confidence, it instead had an irascible and unpopular politician with the support of about 20% of the public in the polls and a term in office that the press was measuring in weeks before the disaster hit. Following the disaster, on average 60% of the public disapproved of Kan's performance but also concluded, according to polls, that it would not be a good idea to replace him until the recovery was underway.[71] Already facing capacity problems, the DPJ government appeared set to stumble through the rest of 2011 overwhelmed by the crisis.

There is no doubt that this triple disaster will have a huge impact on the Japanese psyche. Almost 30,000 were killed, strong tremors continued for weeks afterward, and supply chains were interrupted for months. In terms of strategic Asia, there are two relevant questions. First, will Japanese

---

[70] Takahira Ogawa and Elena Okorotchenko, "Ratings on Japan Lowered to 'AA-'; Outlook Stable," Standard and Poor's, January 27, 2011, http://www.standardandpoors.com/ratings/articles/en/us/?assetID=1245286301728. Standard & Poor's revised its outlook from "stable" to "negative" on April 27, 2011. See "S&P Cuts Japan Rating Outlook to Negative on Fiscal Worry after Quake," *Nikkei Shimbun*, April 27, 2011, http://e.nikkei.com/e/fr/tnks/Nni20110427D27JF287.htm. Three polls published on April 18, 2011, showed public support for a tax increase: 69% in *Nikkei Shimbun*, 59% in *Asahi Shimbun*, and 58% in *Mainichi Shimbun*. See "Polls Find Japanese Unhappy with Crisis Response," *Voice of America News*, April 18, 2011, http://www.voanews.com/english/news/asia/east-pacific/Polls-Find-Japanese-Unhappy-With-Governments-Crisis-Response-120051679.html.

[71] Polls were published on April 18, 2011, by *Yomiuri Shimbun*, *Nikkei Shimbun*, *Asahi Shimbun*, and *Mainichi Shimbun* and generally revealed frustration with the Kan government's response to the crisis. The *Mainichi Shimbun* survey found that 26% wanted Kan to resign immediately, 56% thought he should step down after the first phase of reconstruction is completed, and 14% believed he need not resign at all. "Higashi Nihon dai shinsai: fukko zozei sansei, 58%—*Mainichi Shimbun* yoron chosa" [Great East Japan Earthquake: 58% Support Tax Increase for Reconstruction], *Mainichi Shimbun*, April 18, 2011, 1.

political, economic, or strategic performance deteriorate as a result of the crisis, or will it perhaps be transformed? Second, will March 11 change the trajectory of Japan's new strategic approach to China and India?

The answer to the first question is more difficult. In the near term, the malaise in Japanese politics, energy shortages, production interruptions, and the tragically slow process of identifying remains of the missing will put a downward pressure on Japanese confidence and international activism. On the other hand, the triple disaster highlighted the depth of respect for Japan around the world, with 145 countries offering aid and countries such as Korea and Thailand raising more donations for Japan than for any prior crisis in their histories. Nor is there compelling evidence that Korea, China, or other competitors are poised to replace Japan as the primary supplier of high-end technological components such as silicon wafers, despite the delays in production caused by the earthquake. (Japanese companies are likely to build redundancy by producing more abroad, but that is another matter.) Japan's defense forces performed superbly, as did U.S. forces working with Japan on humanitarian relief in Operation Tomodachi. This example will make it politically easier to relax constraints on the military's rules of engagement in the future. Political performance was weak among veteran DPJ members, but a number of emerging DPJ politicians stood out for their competence in the crisis, including Chief Cabinet Secretary Yukio Edano and Deputy Chief Cabinet Secretary Goshi Hosono. The Japanese public hungers for decisive and competent leadership, and it is possible that a more dynamic generation of political leaders will take the helm after Kan serves out his time overseeing the immediate recovery.

The impact of March 11 on Japan's strategic response to the rise of China and India will be less dramatic. China responded positively to the disaster by sending a small search and rescue team and offering a hospital ship. (Tokyo declined the latter, possibly because Beijing had refused Japan's offers to send C-130s to help after the 2008 Szechuan earthquake.)[72] However, within weeks of the crisis, the Japanese media was reporting another encounter between Japanese and Chinese patrol vessels, expressing dismay at China's insensitive attitude in the wake of Japan's national tragedy.[73] At most, the March 11 tragedy took some of the boil off of the overheating Sino-Japanese relationship, but it did not change the basic dynamics. India also responded

---

[72] "Acceptance of China's Emergency Rescue Team," Ministry of Foreign Affairs of Japan, March 13, 2011, http://www.mofa.go.jp/announce/announce/2011/3/0313_02.html.

[73] "Chinese Helicopter Approaches MSDF Vessel in East China Sea," Associated Press, March 26, 2011, http://www.breitbart.com/article.php?id=D9M70UAG0&show_article=1.

quickly to the crisis with offers of blankets for the displaced in Tohoku.[74] However, the devastating impact of the crisis on the credibility of Japan's nuclear power industry could put a crimp in Tokyo's plans for exporting nuclear power plants, including to India. Much will depend on whether the government's investigation of the nuclear disaster is seen as objective and contributing to stronger reactor safety standards in the future.[75] Overall, it appears that the events of March 11 are likely to have an impact on the trajectory of Japan's economic and political choices, but not on the current trajectory of Japan's strategic approach to China and India.

Looking Ahead

Although never referenced in official bilateral statements, the reality is that Japan's response to the rise of India is largely a function of Japan's response to the rise of China. The future direction of the burgeoning Japan-India strategic relationship will be one important indicator of the degree to which U.S. allies and partners within Asia are prepared to align more closely with each other to maintain a favorable strategic equilibrium in the region as Chinese power grows relative to that of the United States. Thus far, the indications from Japan-India relations are that there will continue to be pronounced, if measured, external counterbalancing by China's neighbors in the years to come. Certainly Japan's external balancing strategy vis-à-vis India has weathered changes in government and now a massive natural disaster. While the dynamics of the Japan-China-India triangle are becoming more pronounced, it is also important to note the centrality of the United States in both India's Japan strategy and Japan's India strategy. Japan's opening to India followed the Bush administration's U.S.-India strategic partnership, and India's approach to Japan has often involved the United States as an additional partner.[76]

While the direction of Japan-India balancing behavior toward China appears well set for the foreseeable future, there are five variables that will determine its content and pace:

---

[74] "Reception of Emergency Relief Supplies from India," Ministry of Foreign Affairs of Japan, March 15, 2011, http://www.mofa.go.jp/announce/announce/2011/3/0315_03.html.

[75] "Press Conference by Prime Minister Kan," Prime Minister of Japan and His Cabinet website, May 10, 2011, http://www.kantei.go.jp/foreign/kan/statement/201105/10kaiken_e.html.

[76] "Foreign Secretary Holds Wide-Ranging Consultations in Tokyo," Indian Ministry of External Affairs, April 8, 2011, http://meaindia.nic.in/mystart.php?id=530217528. It was with the objective of facilitating three-way communication between the states that CSIS began an annual "Track 1.5" U.S.-Japan-India strategic dialogue in 2006, anticipating Secretary of State Clinton's call for an official trilateral strategic dialogue in her January 2010 speech on the future of Asian regional architecture at the East-West Center in Hawaii and the decision in April 2011 to formally commence an official dialogue.

1. *Japanese and Indian perceptions of Chinese power and purpose.* If Beijing continues pursuing strategies aimed at anti-access and area denial in Japan's sea lanes and power projection into the Indian Ocean (including basing and access arrangements in the famous "string of pearls"), then Indo-Japanese maritime cooperation, and security cooperation more generally, will likely accelerate.

2. *Indian economic reform.* Economic reform and anti-corruption efforts within India will need to continue for the country to remain the top destination for new Japanese FDI beyond 2010. If New Delhi can satisfy Japanese industry concerns, then there could be significant increases in FDI, as the JBIC surveys suggest. The strategic relationship will be stronger with an economic leg.

3. *China's economy.* Indigenous innovation strategies, rising labor costs, labor protest mobilization, rare earth metal embargos, and political risk will accelerate Japanese diversification of trade and investment away from China and toward India and other countries in Asia. In contrast, greater Chinese transparency and predictability could dampen the enthusiasm for diversification, particularly if the Indian investment environment remains challenging for Japanese corporations.

4. *Japanese economic reform.* Japan's ability to execute trade agreements with India and other countries around China will depend on the current debate in Tokyo over participation in the TPP; Japan's overall power will also depend on whether economic reforms can be executed to build up the economy.

5. *Domestic political stability in Japan and India.* Thus far, Japan-India relations have survived the transition of power to the DPJ and weak leadership from both the LDP and DPJ governments, not to mention changes of power in New Delhi. However, both Indian and Japanese ruling parties may continue suffering the debilitating effects of having to rely on coalition governments. Under weak governments, rent-seeking and ideology can trump grand strategy. Failure to overcome opposition to a Japan-India peaceful nuclear agreement would be a particular setback in bilateral relations.

Perhaps the single most important variable in the Japan-India-China triangle will be the relative power and influence of the United States. Japan-India alignment has been enabled by the U.S.-India strategic partnership, but it also reflects the efforts of both New Delhi and Tokyo to compensate for perceived shifts in relative power between China and the United States. Leaders in both capitals have made quiet calculations that continued U.S. preeminence enhances their power, though it remains perhaps more critical to Japan than to India. Would a precipitous decline in U.S. power and influence in Asia (through failure to continue trade liberalization or maintain forward-deployed forces, for example) accelerate Japan-India strategic convergence or distract from it? Would a U.S.-China condominium, unlikely though that may seem now, lead to India-Japan convergence or weaken the Tokyo–New Delhi axis as Asia reordered around a bipolar U.S.-China accommodation? These are more difficult questions to answer, in part because the current dynamics of Japan-China and Japan-India relations are premised on the assumption that Beijing is unable to challenge U.S. global or regional hegemony for the time being. To the extent that the relationship between Japan and India continues on its current trajectory, it will reinforce a strategic environment that dissuades China from revisionist challenges to U.S. leadership. Importantly, closer Japan-India alignment has the potential to play this role without creating a security dilemma, because Tokyo and New Delhi are not formal allies and each shares important and mutually non-threatening economic interests with China. For these reasons, encouraging and facilitating Japan-India strategic trust and cooperation should be a central pillar of the United States' own China strategy.

EXECUTIVE SUMMARY

This chapter assesses Korean efforts to maximize a range of security and economic interests with the major powers of the Asian strategic landscape—especially China and India—without weakening South Korea's central alliance with the U.S. or loosening its growing linkages with the international system.

MAIN ARGUMENT:
Since the 1950s, Seoul's foreign policy has been driven principally by deterrence and defense requirements vis-à-vis North Korea. This dynamic has accelerated South Korea's economic development through robust international trade and ameliorated the harsher vestiges of Northeast Asia's brutal geopolitics. How South Korea chooses to define and operationalize its national security strategies in the new geopolitics of the 2020–30 timeframe, when transitions are likely to have occurred in the North, will also likely determine the trajectory of a potentially unified Korea.

POLICY IMPLICATIONS:
- South Korea should continue modernizing and upgrading its central alliance with the U.S. to coshape a mutually beneficial "smart power" grid in Northeast Asia, including key ties with China and Japan.

- Seoul should pay greater attention to matching U.S. and Chinese capacity-building related to nonlinear transitions on the Korean Peninsula and work to enhance the peninsula's role as a facilitator of intraregional cooperation.

- South Korea must sustain military reforms to address the modernized power-projection platforms possessed by its more powerful neighbors while adhering fully to a non-nuclear posture.

- Seoul must demonstrate its ability to forge a comprehensive policy conducive to ensuring a globalized Asia as one of the principal pillars of the emerging world order.

Coping with Giants: South Korea's Responses to China's and India's Rise

Chung Min Lee

The confluence of historically unparalleled centripetal and centrifugal forces is the defining characteristic of the early 21st century—a quandary most aptly captured by the fact that more than two decades since the end of the Cold War the world is still in the midst of a "paradigm lull." Yet from the viewpoint of geopolitics, the cumulative rise of Asia and the resurgence of its two continental giants—China and India—are an important strategic driver that will continue to shape geopolitics and geo-economics well into this century, based on the magnitude, intensity, and strategic longevity of China's and India's rise relative to Asia and the rest of the world.

There is little doubt that the world economy will be affected significantly by the growth of China and India, but there is also a fundamental tension of opposites paralleling their simultaneous rise: unprecedented opportunities and opportunity costs regardless of whether these two civilizational powers succeed or falter in sustaining their respective positions at the heart of the emerging world system.[1] As a strategically consequential middle power that lies at the epicenter of Asia's continental and maritime divide, South Korea's response to China's and India's rise (particularly the former) poses unique challenges across Seoul's foreign policy spectrum. Moreover, as a middle power, South Korea's engagement with China and India—not to mention other major powers such as the United States and Japan—is by definition asymmetrical. Yet, in the age of globalization, exploiting such asymmetries

Chung Min Lee is Dean of the Graduate School of International Studies and the Underwood International College at Yonsei University. He can be reached at <cmlee@yonsei.ac.kr>.

[1] *Global Trends 2025: A Transformed World* (Washington, D.C.: National Intelligence Council, 2008), 29–30.

for maximum mutual benefits is becoming a new *sine qua non* of South Korean foreign policy. The Republic of Korea (ROK) has accrued significant dividends over the past two decades from its growing linkages with China, but this relationship is also characterized by the sheer magnitude of China's rise and its corresponding influences over the Korean Peninsula. In contrast, while the strategic stakes for South Korea are significantly lower vis-à-vis India, given the out-of-area nature of India's involvement in Northeast Asia, the Seoul–New Delhi partnership has all the hallmarks of becoming a mini–Blue Ocean relationship.

Throughout much of the Cold War era, South Korea contended primarily with a two-tiered geopolitical grid: maintaining deterrence and defense against the North and sustaining strategic coupling with the United States. Today, however, the reintroduction of China into the Asian strategic equation, the globalization of Asian security, and more complex notions of key national interests have significantly heightened opportunity costs for Seoul. In addition, if these challenges were not enough, South Korea must also contend with worsening strategic trends in North Korea and the Pandora's box that will be opened if reunification dynamics shift from the conceptual to the operational realm.

On balance, South Korea has gained significant dividends from China's rise, including unprecedented economic linkages, a seemingly more balanced Chinese policy toward the two Koreas, and Beijing's recognition of Seoul's key role in maintaining stability and prosperity in Northeast Asia. It is difficult to imagine today, but until the early 1990s South Korea's interactions with the People's Republic of China (PRC) were defined by Cold War legacies, including China's massive intervention in the Korean War. Thus, South Korea's current attitudes and strategies toward China evoke unparalleled mutual gains but also ambivalence and latent anxiety. Conversely, while the Korean-Indian relationship is much newer and the strategic context differs significantly from the ROK's interactions with China, shared democratic values, the absence of historical conflicts, and increasingly convergent and complementary political and economic interests suggest that, if approached correctly, both sides can accrue significant "boutique dividends."

Thus, how Seoul chooses to manage the rise of both China and India can be seen as a litmus test for determining how it will define and align itself in the emerging Asian balance of power. This challenge is all the more poignant at a time when the linchpin of South Korean security— namely, the ROK's critical alliance with the United States—is arguably more successful than at any other time since the Korean War. Therefore, ensuring sustained alliance cohesion, even as South Korea grapples with a foreign policy template that resembles a Rubik's cube or the weight and complexity of the new geopolitics, will test South Korea's foreign policy acumen as never before.

This chapter is organized into four main sections. The first section lays out the key forces that are likely to determine South Korea's foreign policy choices, such as a shift from "old geopolitics" to "new geopolitics" and the growing complexity of how South Korea and its more powerful neighbors maintain and manage their national capabilities and interests and attendant priorities. The second section examines South Korean perceptions of China and the determinants involved in contemporary South Korean–Chinese relations. The third section examines the ROK's growing relations with and perceptions of India and the potential of this relatively recent relationship. The chapter concludes by assessing Seoul's ability to strike balances and maneuver in a neighborhood crowded with major powers.

One common theme that permeates South Korea's emerging security template is the beginning of the end of a status quo that placed a premium on stability. This is not to suggest that instability, convulsions, and massive dislocations will be the new normal, but rather that the conditions for maintaining stability will become much more complex, owing to the convergence of three key forces: (1) enhanced vulnerabilities stemming from a globalized economy that limits intrinsically national policy choices, (2) the growing value of economic interests (e.g., high dependence on trade and external energy and food supplies) that have to be balanced increasingly with adherence to international norms such as respect for human rights, UN Security Council resolutions, and other multilateral regimes, and (3) a policymaking process, including the bureaucracy and body politic, that has become unduly accustomed to preserving a static balance.

The Beginning of the End of the Status Quo

As on so many occasions in the past, Korea's central security dilemmas have been shaped by the country's inability to extricate itself from the iron grip of geography. For the past two millennia, especially after the "hermit kingdom's" forced entry into the modern world system 150 years ago, Korea's strategic culture has been driven and shaped by accommodating, thwarting, or mitigating to the best of its abilities the curses of geography and great-power politics. Until the downfall of Korea's Joseon Dynasty in 1910 and China's Qing Dynasty in 1911, Korea's dominant *weltanschauung* and foreign policy choices were synonymous with Sinocentric strategic alignment. In turn, such a paradigm resulted in three fundamental distortions: profound political rigidity or strategic groupthink that foreclosed alternative security options, inability to fully consider modern development strategies with commensurate state capacity-building, and bureaucratic inertia that prevented systematic reforms. With the ROK unable to defend itself while maintaining political independence in the face of rapid regional power transitions, the cumulative consequences for Korea, which reverberated well into the middle of the twentieth century, were brutal, systemic, and long-lasting: 35 years of Japanese colonial rule, the post-1945 partitioning followed by a devastating fratricidal war, the world's most pronounced Cold War conflict, and a broken, bankrupt economy.[2] The old geopolitics was not just present on the Korean Peninsula but came to define it with a vengeance.

From afar, the pronounced features of South Korea's search for a strategy in the early 21st century appear consistent with its historical record of structural rigidity, limited ability to influence decisively the prevailing regional balance of power, and deeply ingrained anxieties. In no particular order, Korea's security angst stems from a combination of centuries of great-power encroachment, overdependence on allies, the imposition of external security guarantees, and estrangement or intervention by its more powerful neighbors. Such conflicting strands in South Korean foreign policy have not been fully ameliorated, much less negated, but there is a qualitative difference today.

Old and New Geopolitics

For the first time since the country's founding in 1948, South Korea's significantly enhanced international profile has partially offset the roughest consequences of unbridled geopolitical competition in and around the Korean Peninsula. Seoul has garnered greater strategic maneuverability on account of its growing economic prowess and a more internationalized worldview. Its hosting of the group of twenty (G-20) summit in November 2010 is the latest example of South Korea's own rise. However, barely two weeks later, North Korean artillery shelled Yeonpyeong Island—the first bombing of South Korean territory since the Korean War. Therefore, even as the ROK celebrates the fruits of accelerated development, Seoul's security policymakers continue to be overwhelmingly focused on maintaining a precarious South-North balance, managing ties with the four major powers (the United States, China, Japan, and Russia) and its all-important alliance with the United States, and maintaining a paradoxical inter-Korean policy pursuing simultaneous deterrence and engagement. As Paul Kennedy

---

[2] For an insightful treatment of the shaping of Korean foreign policy in the context of its more powerful neighbors, see Sung-Hack Kang, *Korea's Foreign Policy Dilemmas* (Kent: Global Oriental, 2011), especially chap. 1–2.

has surmised, in an expanded version of Korea's historical branding as "a shrimp amongst whales,"

> the blunt fact is that South Korea's geopolitical (and thus economic) future is much more dependent on the actions of other, larger states than it is upon its own impressive endeavors. So long as the "Big Four" stay in harmony, South Koreans are free to follow their path to wealth. But they are genuinely concerned about the regional consequences of the rise of China (even if that can never be mentioned for fear of upsetting Beijing), hate the idea of leaning toward Japan, don't think much of Russia's current capacities in the region, and are anxious about America's willingness to stay in East Asia over the next decade or two.[3]

Yet, the continuing relevance of such structural constraints notwithstanding, rapid industrialization, accelerated democratization, and irreversible globalization have also resulted in the broadening of Seoul's foreign policy menu and greater self-confidence. Moreover, although Korea has been deeply affected by Northeast Asia's rigid political geography, as Kim Kyung Won argues, "it also stands to reason that structures aren't permanent and neither are prevailing dogmas," and "what is therefore required is a higher level of historical appreciation, philosophical harmonization between existent realities and desirable objectives, and policy capabilities that can creatively transform inter-Korean relations."[4]

Major Security Drivers

South Korea has sought to incrementally expand its security partnerships through greater attention to multilateral security mechanisms such as the Association of Southeast Asian Nations (ASEAN), participation in the ASEAN Regional Forum (ARF), and observer status in the Organization of Security and Co-operation in Europe (OSCE) and the South Asian Association for Regional Cooperation (SAARC). More importantly, despite its understandable preoccupation with North Korea, Seoul has begun to pay closer attention to global issues, driven by the South Korean economy's growing dependence on global trade and stable energy supplies; spillover from North Korea's WMD programs, such as Pyongyang's international WMD network with Pakistan, Iran, Syria, and potentially Burma; and, importantly, a pluralistic, democratized policymaking process that emphasizes stronger adherence to international norms. Consonant with the ROK's standing as one of East Asia's most robust democracies, it is becoming increasingly problematic for Seoul

---

[3] Paul Kennedy, "Why South Korea Isn't Asia's Switzerland," *New York Times*, August 27, 2010, http://www.nytimes.com/2010/08/28/opinion/28iht-edkennedy.html.

[4] Kim Kyung Won, "Jeonwhan shidaeui sengjon jeolryak" [Survival Strategy in an Era of Transformations] (Seoul: Salm Gwa Koom Publishers, 2005), 255.

to decouple key commercial interests from support for universal values and international norms. As an example, in August 2010 Seoul announced partial financial sanctions against Iran based on UN Security Council Resolution 1929, including placing 102 organizations and 24 individuals on a blacklist, which South Korean officials described as "similar but looser sanctions" compared with those of the European Union (EU) or Japan.[5]

More than any other previous government, the Lee Myung-bak administration came into office in February 2008 with the express view of accentuating "global Korea" as a key foreign policy platform based on two key pillars: strengthening and upgrading the alliance with the United States and implementing a "new Asian diplomacy."[6] In one of the most significant developments attesting to South Korea's expanding foreign policy profile, President Lee and then Australian prime minister Kevin Rudd agreed in a March 2009 ROK-Australia joint statement to substantially upgrade and institutionalize bilateral and multilateral security cooperation. This was South Korea's first real attempt at forging a "virtual security alliance."[7]

Thus, four major drivers are likely to significantly affect Seoul's security outlook well into the second decade of the 21st century. First, Asia's cumulative rise and a shifting balance of power, marked by China's enlarged footprint in East and Northeast Asia, will enrich but also complicate South Korea's external economic and security strategies. Second, ensuring a more nimble and sustainable foreign economic strategy will require a long-term supply of key energy and natural resources, a reduction in South Korea's overwhelming dependence on foreign trade (which presently constitutes 85% of the country's $1.4 trillion GDP), and stronger institutional ties with key emerging economies such as India, Indonesia, and Vietnam.[8] Third, South Korea must forge a more robust and resilient national security framework that takes into account the potential for nonlinear transitions in North Korea as well as the major security and economic challenges associated with a potentially reunified peninsula or a shift from defense by

---

[5] Jang Taeg Dong and Yun Wan Jun, "Jeongbu, Iran Danche 102got-Gaein 24 myung daesang geumyoong georae jehan" [Government Imposes Financial Sanctions on 102 Organizations and 24 Individuals in Iran] *Donga Ilbo*, September 9, 2010, http://news.donga.com/view.php?id=Print_Donga|3|20100909|31065342|1.

[6] Korean Ministry of Foreign Affairs and Trade, *2010 Diplomatic White Paper* (Seoul, July 20–22, 2010).

[7] The agreement entails regular high-level security consultative meetings, intelligence exchanges, defense technology cooperation, and joint coordination on security issues such as nuclear terrorism and WMD proliferation. See "Joint Statement on Enhanced Global and Security Cooperation between Australia and the Republic of Korea," Australian Department of Foreign Affairs and Trade, March 5, 2009, http://www.dfat.gov.au/fta/akfta/090305_joint_statement.html.

[8] South Korea depends on foreign oil imports for nearly 100% of its oil and spent $67 billion importing 872 million barrels in 2010. Of these imports, 83% are from the Gulf states and the Middle East. See "Gugka byul seokyoo suip tongae" [Statistics on Oil Imports by Country (as of December 2010)], Korea Petroleum Association, December 2010, http://www.petroleum.or.kr.

denial to a more proactive deterrence posture.[9] Fourth, the ROK will seek to exploit new security relationships and partnerships.

A critically related but also separate driver is how long China will be able to sustain its current level of economic growth. For an economy that has become increasingly dependent on the Chinese market, projecting China's economic future is a critical task. The general consensus today is that China's accelerated economic growth is sustainable for the next two to three decades and that, if current projections hold, China will eventually overtake the United States as the world's largest economy. In 2010, China surpassed Japan as the world's second-largest economy, and Goldman Sachs now projects that it will overtake the United States by 2027.[10] But, at the same time, the Chinese economy is fraught with deeply rooted structural problems such as rising inflation, underemployment and unemployment of college graduates, labor shortages, massive environmental problems, rising income gaps between the coastal and inland economies, endemic corruption, growing vulnerability to external shocks such as rising energy prices, and the possibility of political instability.[11] As one China watcher has commented recently:

> China has emerged as the endpoint of the East Asian assembly chains, and not as the center of the East Asian economy...China is highly competitive as a point of final assembly, but in the final analysis, other locations, particularly in Southeast Asia, could also perform these activities at reasonable cost. The same cannot be said for Japanese technological sophistication.[12]

Moreover, Kim Jin Hyun, a former minister of information and one of Seoul's most respected current affairs commentators, asserts that while Asia's

---

[9] Sangwoo Rhee, "Hankuk eui gukbang hyundawha gwaje" [South Korea's Defense Modernization Goals], 38th KIDA Defense Forum Proceedings, Korea Institute for Defense Analyses, January 2011, 26–27. The Lee Myung-bak administration has tabled a number of changes to the rules of engagement, command, and control and upgraded comprehensive response packages in the event of another major North Korean provocation like the sinking of the *Cheonan* in March 2010 and the bombing of Yeonpyeong Island in November 2010. One of the most important aspects of the new doctrine lies in ensuring that in the event of an attack South Korean forces will respond with situation-specific measures to dissuade North Korea from undertaking additional attacks.

[10] By 2050, the world's three largest economies are forecast to be China ($70 trillion), the United States ($40 trillion), and India ($35 trillion). Goldman Sachs projects, however, that China's annual growth will taper down from 7.9% in 2011–20 to 3.6% by 2041–50, while India will continue to register relatively high growth rates of 6.5% in 2011–20 and 5.8% in 2041–50. See Jim O'Neil and Anna Stupnytska, "The Long-Term Outlook for the BRICs and N-11 Post Crisis," Goldman Sachs, Global Economics Paper, no. 192, December 4, 2009, 21–23, http://www2.goldmansachs.com/ideas/brics/long-term-outlook-doc.pdf.

[11] For a discussion of the economic challenges facing China, see Bob Davis, "In Fast-Growing China, Dangers Threaten to Hamper Its Success," *Wall Street Journal*, April 11, 2011, http://online.wsj.com/article/SB10001424052748704415104576251070088286358.html.

[12] Barry Naughton, "The Dynamics of China's Reform-Era Economy," in *China's Rise in Historical Perspective*, ed. Brantly Womack (Lanham: Rowman & Littlefield, 2010), 138.

rise as the "center of gravity" is without question, it is not synonymous with China's rise and, moreover, that "China will never become a leader of a new order or create a *Pax Sinica*," as it did before the 19th century.[13] Kim provides three reasons why China will not emerge as the preponderant power in Asia and the world. First, in order for China to surpass the United States, it must become the "greatest country in the world or establish a continental coalition with Russia and India, or reorganize the G-20 into an organization lead by the BRICs [Brazil, Russia, India, and China]....However, as globalization proceeds and education, information, and communication becomes more widespread, no single country will be able to bear the cost of world hegemony and leadership. China is no exception."[14] Second, world hegemony cannot be established by hard power alone, since it must be "supported by values, attractiveness, and passion." China's "idiosyncratic socialism and the 'Beijing Consensus' cannot compete with the attractiveness of human rights, the welfare system, [and] democracy."[15] Third, the most important reason why a new *Pax Sinica* is impossible is because of China's "absolute shortage of life resources [such as critical food supply chains and sustainable development capacity] and the lack of forestry." While 1.8 global hectares of per capita biocapacity are needed on average, China only has 1.0 compared to the 3.9 for the United States, 5.7 for Russia, 3.0 for France, 14.9 for Canada, and 14.7 for Australia.[16]

As noted above, the common denominator in these four major strategic drivers is the de facto ending of the status quo that has come to characterize much of South Korea's national security and foreign policy for the past six decades. Attempts at maintaining a stable inter-Korean strategic balance have already been foiled by North Korea's nuclear capabilities and rising systemic inconsistencies. Traditional deterrence and defense strategies toward the North are becoming increasingly outdated, based on the growing probability of a range of scenarios for low-intensity conflicts and military operations other than war. Transforming South Korea's all-important alliance with the United States to include a broader regional and global mandate also entails major conceptual and political hurdles that portend the ending of the status quo in alliance-management dynamics. Last but certainly not least, ensuring South Korea's long-term economic prosperity will require Seoul to continue to exploit the Chinese market but also diversify its export markets. South Korea must also continue to secure

[13] Kim Jin Hyun, "Pax Sinica? Impossible!" Center for Strategic and International Studies (CSIS), Pacific Forum, PacNet, no. 10, February 8, 2011, 1, http://csis.org/files/publication/pac1110.pdf.

[14] Ibid.

[15] Ibid.

[16] Ibid.

stable energy supplies and strategic resources.[17] In essence, although Seoul has largely overcome its main source of traditional security angst other than the ongoing South-North stand-off—namely, the constant pull between overdependence on and abandonment by the United States—growing ties with an increasingly powerful China have fostered a new source of tension. South Korea faces the threat of being drawn progressively into China's strategic orbit, even as it benefits from a deepening economic relationship, or at a minimum of being increasingly perceived by China as one of its core "near-abroad" states deserving selective intervention or strategic denial.

Peninsular Futures and Seoul's Emerging Security Matrix

The status quo on the Korean Peninsula may be coming to an end, particularly if systemic political transitions take place in North Korea. Kim Jong-il has begun to transfer power to his third son and anointed heir, Kim Jong-un, who is 28 and holds the office of vice chairman of the National Defense Commission—the most important organ in North Korea—making him only second in influence to his father. Despite a saturation of state propaganda on the "scientific merits" and "ideological unity" of dynastic succession, speculation abounds on the leadership qualities of Kim Jong-un, given the growing uncertainties associated with Kim Jong-il's health, the long-term sustainability of the regime, North Korea's systemic economic failures, and the possibility of Chinese intervention in the event of regime or state collapse.

Whether North Korea ultimately implodes, suffers a long and drawn-out "collapse in slow motion," or enacts structural reforms along the lines of China and Vietnam is difficult to predict. Thus far, however, the regime has proved to be highly resilient due to two main factors: unparalleled state control and repression, befitting the world's last Stalinist outpost, and sustained Chinese support. Since 1948, a "triangular compact" has preserved the Kim dynasty—the absolute loyalty of the nomenklatura to Kim Il-sung and then Kim Jong-il, a military that owes its allegiance to the Kim family, and an omniscient party machinery that demands and grudgingly receives support from the masses in return for a minimal standard of living.

Yet the sustained longevity of such a compact is becoming increasingly tenuous, even with Chinese aid that amounts to over 70% of North Korea's

---

[17] South Korea's third-largest trading partner in the Middle East is Iran. Trade between the two countries in 2010 totaled $9.7 billion, of which $5.8 billion comprised oil imports. Seoul announced financial sanctions against Tehran in September 2010. For additional details, see Lee Sung Hoon, "Giro ae seon joongdong waekyo" [Middle Eastern Policy at a Crossroads], *Chosun Ilbo*, August 5, 2010, http://news.chosun.com/site/data/html_dir/2010/08/05/2010080500173.html.

fuel and food supplies. For now, China is unlikely to decouple itself from North Korea because Beijing continues to accrue key strategic dividends through its alliance with the North, which serves as a strategic buffer against South Korea, Japan, and U.S. strategic interests in Northeast Asia. The prevailing consensus among China watchers is that "China does not believe that the current situation on the peninsula or in the DPRK is stable or conducive either to regional stability or China's own national security, economic growth, or other national interests. For Beijing, enhancing stability is critical."[18] That said, despite China's primary emphasis on stability, it bears noting that even China is unlikely to effectively guide or steer the flow of events in the post–Kim Jong-il era.

China's response to developments in North Korea, particularly during a period of political transition, is an acutely sensitive issue for Koreans on both sides of the 38th parallel, given the perceived weight of Chinese influence throughout the process that could eventually culminate in a reunified Korean state. For the vast majority of Koreans in the South and the North, reunification remains the ultimate national goal. Nonetheless, highly charged issues persist, including the terms of reunification, the likely responses of the major powers directly affected by a unified Korea (the United States, China, and, to a lesser extent, Russia and Japan), and major policy choices such as the national security platform of a future, unified Korea. Whatever the ultimate outcome, however, maintaining the status quo is unlikely to prevail as the basic policy of inter-Korean relations and the strategy of the surrounding powers.

In essence, South Korea's hope for success must be tempered by the emergence of formidable challenges. For the first time, Asia's geopolitical and geo-economic spaces are being shared simultaneously by three indigenous great powers: China, Japan, and India. Moreover, unparalleled intraregional economic growth and cooperation driven by China's and India's accelerated rise have significantly enhanced the importance of economic interests in South Korea's foreign policy. At the same time, India's and China's increasing resources are resulting in more robust power-projection capabilities and creating new security dilemmas.

Political and policy permutations are bound to increase with sharper opportunity costs for all of Asia's strategically consequential states. Yet many strategic analysts in Seoul believe that the stakes are considerably greater for South Korea, given that its external calibrations must accomplish three essential goals. First, South Korea must accommodate, balance, and minimize China's growing capabilities while not endangering its critical

---

[18] David Shambaugh, "China and the Korean Peninsula: Playing for the Long Term," *Washington Quarterly* 26, no. 2 (Spring 2003): 45.

alliance with the United States. Second, the ROK must expand its strategic space by forging new security linkages with key emerging powers (notably, India, Indonesia, Vietnam, and Australia) and strengthening key bilateral economic relationships through free trade agreements (FTA) such as the ones signed with the United States, the EU, India, Japan, and China over the past five to ten years. Third, South Korea must maintain maximum independence throughout the process leading up to reunification, when preserving the status quo no longer dominates peninsular politics.

Perceiving China: A South Korean View

South Korea's perception of the major powers has traditionally been marked by intensely ingrained historical legacies and misperceptions, the pull between dependence and estrangement, major power interventions and support for and against eventual reunification, and shifting domestic determinants. China is not an exception, although an added dimension colors South Korea's dilemmas vis-à-vis China's rise: ensuring strategic independence while deepening economic, political, and societal relations. Since official ties were established in 1992, two-way trade between South Korea and China jumped from $6.3 billion to $188 billion in 2010, which is 21% of South Korea's $891 billion total trade volume. By 2020, total ROK-China trade is expected to reach $300 billion. Conversely, ROK-India trade in 2010 reached $17 billion, which is just 1.9% of South Korea's total trade volume, although South Korean firms have moved into the Indian market with greater acumen than other Asian economies such as Japan.[19]

The elevation of South Korea's relationship with China into a "strategic cooperative partnership" in 2008 signaled how far bilateral relations had grown since official ties were established in 1992. Nevertheless, one of the most important barometers of South Korean perceptions of China is the level of concern about the possibility, however remote it may seem at this juncture, of the ROK being redrawn into China's strategic orbit. Still, the need to maintain South Korea's most important economic relationship will continue to drive a significant portion of Seoul's policy toward Beijing in the early 21st century. In addition, Seoul will continue to solicit Chinese support for a peaceful resolution to the North Korean nuclear conundrum

---

[19] "Gugka byul suchulipshiljeok (Indo 2010)" [Import/Export By Country (India 2010)], Korea Customs Service, Trade Statistics, http://www.customs.go.kr/kcsweb/user.tdf?a=user.newTradestatistics.New TradestatisticsApp&c=1006&mc=STATS_INQU_TRADE_030.

and, most importantly, take steps to ensure that its core strategic interests going into the "unification tunnel" remain relatively intact.[20]

Seoul's China Prisms

Of the major power relations South Korea has to manage, the Seoul-Beijing relationship is among the most beneficial and complex. There is no single, overarching model or prism through which South Korea gauges China but rather a series of intertwining windows throughout the policymaking process, including government officials, the national assembly, the media, opinion leaders, and even NGOs. To be sure, such multi-tiered perceptions are also shared by the vast majority of powers who engage with China, but South Korean sensitivities are markedly higher based on China's critical influence in shaping peninsular balances, its strong historical legacies, and Korea's own heightened sensitivity to China's growing footprint. For example, while South Korea believes that China should become a more responsible stakeholder in the international system, it does not necessarily believe that China is a revisionist or anti–status quo power, but neither does it fully subscribe to China's "harmonious rise."[21]

From a global perspective, China's rise and unparalleled interactions with the global system are generally perceived favorably by South Korea, although Seoul remains wary of any prolonged or deep schisms in the U.S.-China relationship. If U.S.-China relations deteriorate significantly, owing to a progressively debilitating strategic rivalry, many South Korean Sinologists believe that any major fallout would be felt almost immediately in South Korea, given its acute dependence on these two great powers. In turn, such a development could convince China to buttress its geopolitical posture in Northeast Asia, including on the Korean Peninsula. China might then pursue a more forceful strategy of attempting to "reabsorb" South Korea into its sphere of influence, as it did in the seventeenth century or akin to the approach Japan adopted in the late nineteenth century.[22] At the regional and local levels, South Korean perceptions of China are being affected by China's significantly enlarged strategic footprint and choices vis-à-vis the Korean Peninsula.

---

[20] That is, Seoul must ensure that its strategic interests remain intact when key political and policy choices need to be made, owing to shifting and worsening internal dynamics in the North that could result in a post–Kim dynasty leadership and either accelerate rapprochement or political integration.

[21] Han Suk-Hee, "Joonguk eui busang gwa chekim daeguk ron" [The Rise of China and the Responsible Stakeholder Debate: Conceptual Differences between the West and China], *Korean Journal of International Affairs* 44, no. 1 (2004): 197.

[22] Park Hong Seo, "Naejaehwa den wison? Joonguk jeok saegaejilseoeui hyunshiljuijeok jaehaeseok" [Internalized Hypocrisy? Realist Reassessment of "China's World Order"], *Korean Journal of International Affairs* 50, no. 4 (2010): 12–13.

Historical memories also contribute significantly to South Korean perceptions of China, given its centuries of absorption into the "Sinic Zone" of states and other entities along China's periphery—including Korea, Vietnam, and the Uighur territories—marked by a highly institutionalized system of suzerainty that lasted from approximately the thirteenth century to the mid-nineteenth century.[23] Most importantly, geographic proximity meant that wrenching transitions in China, i.e., dynastic transitions and follow-on foreign policy changes, usually entailed immediate and long-lasting repercussions for Korea. While transferring such historical templates into contemporary Seoul-Beijing relations can only be case-specific, centuries of truncated autonomy shaped by Korea's place at the core of China's historical sphere of influence are never far from the surface.

Public Perceptions

South Korean public perceptions of China in the second decade of the 21st century perhaps can be best characterized as a mixture, in equal doses, of converging interests and deeply ingrained anxieties. The need to manage South Korea's growing China portfolio while resisting or ameliorating Chinese influence is an abiding hallmark of public perceptions of China, as illustrated by recent opinion polls. For example, an October 2010 survey conducted by the Asan Policy Institute in Seoul showed that, on a 1–10 scale, the average favorability rating for the United States was 5.9, followed by China with 4.5 and Japan with 4.2.[24] But a more striking result can be seen in a 2010 survey by the Pew Global Attitudes Project. When asked whether China was a partner or an enemy, only 23% of South Koreans responded that it was a partner, while 35% said China was an enemy and 38% responded that it was neither. Overall, 56% of respondents had "unfavorable" views of China, while 38% gave "favorable" ratings.[25] Indeed, from 2002 to 2010, South Koreans' favorable rating of China slipped from 66% to 38%. South Korea's deep ambivalence about its ties with China is also reflected in the mixed views on growing Chinese economic and military power. As noted above, 21% of the ROK's total trade is with China. Yet despite significant dividends from closer economic ties, South Koreans continue to be wary: 45% responded that a growing Chinese economy was a "good thing," while 49% responded

[23] Park, "Naejaehwa den wison? Joonguk jeok saegaejilseoeui hyunshiljuijeok jaehaeseok."

[24] Poll data cited in "Hankook-in 68% Cheonanham sakeon eun Bukhan soheng" [68% of Koreans Believe That the Cheonan Was Sunk by North Korea], October 19, 2010, *Chosun Ilbo*, http://news.chosun.com/site/data/html_dir/2010/10/19/2010101901014.html.

[25] "Strengthen Ties with China, but Get Tough on Trade," Pew Research Center, January 12, 2011, 2–4.

that it was a "bad thing." As for Chinese military power, only 7% believe it is a "good thing," while 86% view it as a "bad thing."[26]

Given South Korean perceptions of pervasive U.S. influence and the ebb and flow of popular support for the United States, one could assume that South Koreans today harbor equally unfavorable views toward the United States. Yet from 2000 to 2007 the average U.S. favorability rating was 55%, and this figure continued to climb in 2008 (70%), 2009 (78%), and 2010 (79%), with the United States ranking noticeably higher than Japan in those same years (50%, 59%, and 66%, respectively).[27]

In the Asan Policy Institute poll, 68% of South Koreans responded that they had "generally positive" feelings toward the Korea-U.S. relationship, while 27% responded that they had "generally negative" views toward the United States. As for whether the ROK-U.S. alliance should continue to be maintained, 87% said it was necessary (14.2% "very necessary" and 73.1% "somewhat necessary"), while 13% replied that the alliance was either "absolutely not necessary" or "not really necessary."[28] Finally, according to a 2010 *BBC* survey, 57% of South Koreans view U.S. influence as "mainly positive," while only 29% feel the same way about Chinese influence. Most surprisingly, 64% responded that Japan's influence was "mainly positive," an even higher rating than the United States received. As for how the world perceives South Korean influence, favorable ratings were highest in China (57%), followed by the United States (46%) and Japan (36%).[29]

Economic, Social, and Cultural Linkages

Shifting public attitudes notwithstanding, one of the most striking changes in South Korean foreign policy since the end of the Cold War has been driven by the unparalleled growth in South Korean–Chinese economic relations. Just short of two decades after normalization in 1992, bilateral trade in 2010 reached $188 billion. According to Chinese statistics, trade with South Korea in 2010 reached a slightly higher figure of $200 billion, which placed it in fourth place behind the United States

---

[26] "Obama More Popular Abroad Than at Home, Global Image of U.S. Continues to Benefit," Pew Research Center, Pew Global Attitudes Project, June 17, 2010, 53.

[27] See "Obama More Popular Abroad," 1. South Korea's higher favorable ratings for the United States stem from a number of factors, including Barack Obama's victory in 2008 and Lee Myung-bak's concerted efforts to upgrade the alliance with the United States. Conversely, the disagreement between the United States and Japan over the Okinawa base issue, coupled with rapid turnover in Japanese administrations, was the likely reason behind Japan's falling public support for the United States.

[28] "2010 Korean Society Survey on Public Attitudes," Asan Policy Institute and Media Research, September 2010, 27–28.

[29] "Global Views of United States Improve While Other Countries Decline," *BBC World Service*, April 18, 2010, 3, 8, 22, http://www.worldpublicopinion.org/pipa/pipa/pdf/apr10/BBCViews_Apr10_rpt.pdf.

($380 billion), Japan ($296 billion), and Hong Kong ($227 billion), and came in second ($138 billion) in imports. From 2004–9, South Korean investment in China spiked from $3.7 billion to $44.6 billion. Over the same period, Chinese investment in South Korea also grew, but at a much slower rate (from $1.1 billion to $3 billion), which amplifies South Korea's growing dependence on the Chinese market.[30] Exports to China account for approximately one-fourth of Samsung's and LG's total exports, while the Chinese market constitutes 30% of Hyundai Motor's worldwide sales.[31] Indeed, other leading South Korean firms such as Pohang Iron and Steel Company (POSCO), Doosan, CJ, and Hanwha have chosen China as one of their main investment destinations.

No single factor explains South Korea's deepening economic relations with China; rather, a confluence of forces triggered one of Asia's most dynamic economic partnerships. Soon after China's economic reforms began in earnest in the early 1980s, and despite the absence of official ties, Beijing's economic planners began to benchmark South Korea's export-led development model. However, bilateral economic ties did not begin to flourish until after the early 1990s when other factors came into play, such as South Korea's geographic proximity, Seoul's desire to counterbalance the Beijing-Pyongyang relationship, rising protectionist sentiments in key traditional markets (such as the United States), increasing labor costs and disputes, and, most of all, China's influence as the world's leading manufacturing giant. Korean watchers of the Chinese economy generally agree that three major features characterize the Seoul-Beijing economic partnership.

First, horizontal and vertical expansion across almost all industries has spurred complementary interests, but, commensurate with China's growth as the world's second-largest economy and the rapidly narrowing technology gap between South Korea and China, the Chinese government has focused more strongly on technology transfers and joint ventures. As the Chinese economy confronts major structural challenges such as rising labor costs and the need to spur its domestic market, South Korea will have to diversify its economic portfolio from re-exports, which now account for 50% of bilateral trade.

Second, despite the unprecedented growth in bilateral economic ties and an underlying assumption in South Korea that rising economic linkages would lead to more balanced Chinese approaches to the two Koreas, Beijing

---

[30] See "Juyo kyungjae mit mooyeok tongae" [Major Economic and Trade Data], Korean Ministry of Foreign Affairs and Trade, February 2011, 29, 32.

[31] Yu Gwang Yeol, "Hanjoong kyungjae kwankae eui yeokdongjeok byunwha jindan" [Assessing Dynamism and Change in the South Korean–Chinese Economic Relationship], Briefing on the Chinese Financial Market, January 2011, 2.

has steadfastly supported North Korea. Indeed, Beijing's refusal to criticize North Korea for the March 2010 sinking of a South Korean naval vessel and the November 2010 bombing of Yeonpyeong Island, while providing overt political support for the ongoing power transition in North Korea, came as a major wakeup call for the South Korean government and public. Such actions are compelling evidence that deepening economic ties will not necessarily translate into a more nuanced Chinese posture toward the two Koreas.

Third, and in a more positive vein, the growing bilateral economic relationship has spurred new areas of cooperation, such as currency swaps, as both sides seek to mitigate global financial repercussions through the acceleration of Chiang Mai Initiative Multilateralization (CMIM) and the establishment of the ASEAN +3 Macroeconomic Research Office (AMRO) to monitor economic developments in the region and activate reserve funds during a financial crisis.[32]

Growing economic ties have also spurred growth in two other areas: educational exchange and tourism. Of 83,842 foreign students studying in Korea in 2010, an overwhelming majority of students (57,783, or 68%) were from China, followed distantly by Japan (3,876, or 5%), Mongolia (3,333, or 4%), and the United States (2,193, or 3%).[33] China is also the second-leading destination for South Koreans studying overseas. In 2010, out of a total of 251,887 students, 64,232 (25.5%) went to China, while 75,065 (29.8%) went to the United States, together accounting for more than half of all South Koreans studying overseas. The overall trend in the past decade indicates very starkly that China and the United States are the two top destinations for South Korean students. Of the 124,833 students studying in Asia, 92,197 went to China and Japan (64,232 and 27,965, respectively); however, the vast majority (73%) were language students, compared to only 13% of those studying in the United States or Canada. Although postgraduate job security and competitiveness in South Korea is increasingly equated with proficiency in English as the dominant global language, Chinese is quickly becoming the second most popular foreign language in South Korea.[34]

People-to-people exchange is not just marked by an increasing number of commercial and educational contacts but also by increased tourism. The overall market for tourism in South Korea is considerably smaller than in other countries. Tourism revenue in 2010 was $9.7 billion, whereas

---

[32] Yu, "Hanjoong kyungjae kwankae eui yeokdongkjeok byunwha jindan," 4.

[33] "2010nyundo gukwae hangukin yoohakseng tongae" [2009–2010 Foreign Student Statistics], Korean Ministry of Education, Science and Technology, April 26, 2010, http://www.mest.go.kr/web/268/ko/board/view.do?bbsId=35&boardSeq=22594.

[34] Ibid.

outbound spending was $13.1 billion. Out of 12.7 million overseas tourists in 2010, 4 million traveled to China—for comparison, 2.4 million Koreans travelled to Japan and 1 million to the United States—whereas 1.8 million Chinese tourists visited South Korea in the same year.[35]

The depth and speed of economic, social, and cultural exchanges between South Korea and China over the past two decades have been nothing short of transformational for the relationship. South Korean prime minister Kim Hwang-sik stated during an April 2011 visit to Beijing that "bilateral ties in a span of little less than 20 years have grown into a relationship without historical parallel."[36] Although such rhetoric is certainly not unusual for political leaders, the sheer magnitude of South Korean–Chinese exchanges since the early 1990s illustrates the depth of this increasingly important relationship. Yet in spite of such growing linkages, a key issue is that the political and security relationship continues to be constrained above and beyond the North Korean factor. South Korean sensitivities toward China, even as Seoul continues to bandwagon on China's rise, are likely to become a prominent feature of South Korea's long-term angst.

The China Security Challenge

For South Korea, the depth and direction of China's power projection is emerging as a key concern, although in the near term Seoul will continue to be consumed with meeting a range of military threats from the North. While the global and regional security grids created and led by the United States in the post–World War II era will not be replaced fully by a Sinocentric security and economic order anytime soon, neither will the United States be able to lead its security consortium with as much freedom as it has for the past six decades—a point that is going to be felt more acutely by U.S. treaty allies such as South Korea. But even if China will not yet displace the United States as the preeminent global power, Beijing's more assertive regional presence increases its ability to counterbalance or selectively deny sustained U.S. access. As one leading commentator has noted:

> Over the longer term, we are witnessing a transition of power from the United States to China, which might well involve intense rivalry and potentially even war. China's rise raises questions about America's ability to adjust to Beijing's enhanced influence; about how China will use its newfound strength; and

---

[35] "2011 chulipguk mit kwankwang suji" [2011 Inbound/Outbound Tourist and Tourism Spending/ Earnings Analyses], Korea Tourism Board, Tourism R&D Center, April 1, 2011, 2, 10.

[36] Hwang Sang-Wook, "Kim Chongri Jungguk bangmoon etul jae, Wen Jiabao Chongri Hwaedam" [Prime Minister Kim's Visit to China and Meeting with Chinese Premier Wen Jiabao], *Media Daum*, April 13, 2011, http://media.daum.net/breakingnews/view.html?cateid=100000&newsid=20110413 190015068&p=akn.

about whether its military modernisation will set off an arms race in Asia, with all the attendant concerns associated with a security dilemma.[37]

In this context, the role played by U.S. power and the U.S. Asian security strategy remains as vital as during the Cold War, if not more so. The key strategic question facing the United States and its allies in the region is whether the United States can "preserve stability in Asia, protect its allies there, and limit the emergence of a Greater China while avoiding a conflict with Beijing."[38] Over the longer term, however, one core source of concern for U.S. allies in Asia, including South Korea, is whether "the United States, the hegemon of the Western Hemisphere, will try to prevent China from becoming the hegemon of much of the Eastern Hemisphere. This could be the signal drama of the age."[39] As an Australian strategist has noted:

> Increased East Asian energy vulnerability has stimulated plans for naval expansion and brings with it the unsettling prospect of naval rivalry over access through the Malacca Strait and Indian Ocean. The rivalry may also involve South Korea which has announced an intention to develop a naval capability to protect its oil imports and sea borne trade…As China, which is already concerned about the security of its energy supplies, engages in naval expansion for the above reasons it justifies and triggers similar responses from Japan, and also from India.[40]

Even in such an instance, some have maintained that it is unlikely that "China will ever manage to overtake the Western order."[41] Conversely, other analysts have asserted that "although the United States needs to coordinate with China to respond to global challenges, elevating the bilateral relationship is more likely to lead to a quagmire, with recriminations flying back and forth, than to a successful partnership. To escape this downward spiral, Washington must solicit the help of the rest of the world."[42] More worrisome for South Korea and other regional middle powers, such as Vietnam, Australia, and Indonesia, is the fact that China's response may become increasingly synonymous with a "virtual veto" that could constrain the strategic maneuverability of these states.

---

[37] Rosemary Foot, "China and the United States: Between Cold and Warm Peace," *Survival* 51, no. 6 (December 2009–January 2010): 123–24.

[38] Robert D. Kaplan, "The Geography of Chinese Power," *Foreign Affairs* 89, no. 3 (May/June 2010): 39.

[39] Ibid., 41.

[40] Leszek Buszynski, "Emerging Naval Rivalry in East Asia and the Indian Ocean: Implications for Australia," *Security Challenges* 5, no. 3 (Spring 2009): 90–91.

[41] G. John Ikenberry, "The Rise of China and the Future of the West," *Foreign Affairs* 87, no. 1 (January/February 2008): 36.

[42] Elizabeth C. Economy and Adam Segal, "The G-2 Mirage Subtitle: Why the United States and China Are Not Ready to Upgrade Ties," *Foreign Affairs* 88, no. 3 (May/June 2009): 19–20.

At the same time, some U.S. analysts argue that if China's economic growth continues into the foreseeable future, the United States and China could "engage in an intense security competition with considerable potential for war" and that "most of China's neighbors, including India, Japan, Singapore, South Korea, Russia, and Vietnam, will likely join with the United States."[43] Conversely, others assert that the advent of nuclear weapons significantly reduces the threat of war among great powers, and that "the Chinese leadership appears much more flexible and sophisticated than many previous aspirants to great-power status."[44] At the very least, however, China's growing military capabilities and the political willingness to demonstrate them have triggered strategic responses that may prove to be inimical to China's long-term interests—namely, by providing a tailored *raison d'être* for military build-up by its neighbors. Indeed, as China becomes increasingly confident of its power-projection capabilities, "Japan feels itself caught between the reality of Chinese power and questions about U.S. commitments in East Asia."[45]

For the time being, full-fledged ROK–Japan defense cooperation is not feasible, owing to outstanding political sensitivities, but Washington has consistently supported closer defense cooperation between Seoul and Tokyo—as has Japan, given rising Japanese concerns about North Korea and regional insecurity. Still, China's lukewarm response to North Korean provocations and much more aggressive response to ROK-U.S. and U.S.-Japan defense cooperation have pushed trilateral security and defense coordination between South Korea, the United States, and Japan in a new direction, although South Korea continues to prefer informal trilateral ties.[46]

All three countries have voiced growing concerns over the enhanced naval capabilities of the People's Liberation Army (PLA), as evinced by the PLA Navy's sustained modernization efforts and anti-access force demonstrations. In March 2010, for example, the commander of U.S. forces in the Pacific, Admiral Robert F. Willard, testified to the House Armed Services Committee that "China's rapid and comprehensive transformation of its armed forces is affecting regional military balances and holds implications beyond the Asia-Pacific region" and that "of particular concern is that elements of China's military modernization appear designed to

---

[43] Zbigniew Brzezinski and John J. Mearsheimer, "Clash of the Titans," *Foreign Policy*, January/February 2005, 47.

[44] Ibid., 49.

[45] Martin Fackler, "With Its Eye on China, Japan Builds Up Military," *New York Times*, February 28, 2011, http://www.nytimes.com/2011/03/01/world/asia/01japan.html.

[46] Kim Sang Hyun and Hong Sung Kyu, "Hanil Kunsa Hyupryeok Ganeunhanga," *Seoul Shinmun*, December 13, 2010. http://www.seoul.co.kr/news/newsView.php?id=20101213003020.

challenge our freedom of action in the region."[47] The PLA Navy has the "largest force of principal combatants, submarines, and amphibious warfare ships in Asia," and, according to the U.S. Department of Defense, the PLA has an "active aircraft carrier research and development program [and] the PRC shipbuilding industry could start construction of an indigenous platform by the end of this year [2010]."[48] Just when China's joint operational capabilities are likely to reach a tipping point is uncertain, although the PRC has begun to flex its military muscle with increased openness around the Korean Peninsula. For South Korea and the United States, an equally significant concern is the potential for Chinese military intervention in North Korea following regime collapse or prolonged instability following the de facto end of the Kim dynasty.

More immediately, South Korea has to contend with a China that is more willing than ever to directly contest the ROK-U.S. presence on the Korean Peninsula. For instance, Beijing strongly opposed U.S.–South Korean military exercises in the aftermath of North Korea's shelling of Yeonpyeong Island as well as the sinking of the *Cheonan*.[49] China's foreign ministry spokesman Qin Gang remarked in July 2010 that "we are firmly opposed to foreign military vessels engaging in activities that undermine China's security interests in the Yellow Sea or waters close to China."[50] Major General Luo Yuan, deputy secretary general of the PLA Academy of Military Sciences, gave five major reasons why China opposes ROK-U.S. military exercises in the Yellow Sea: (1) the United States should not conduct exercises along China's coasts; (2) as part of its preventive diplomatic strategy and strategic thinking, "China should take into account the worst possibility and strive to seek the best results"; (3) since the Yellow Sea is the gateway to Beijing, China is sensitive to "military exercises conducted by any country in an area so close to China's heartland"; (4) China supports peaceful solutions on the Korean Peninsula, but the United States and

[47] Bill Gertz, "Admiral: China's Buildup Aimed at Power Past Asia," *Washington Times*, March 26, 2010, http://www.washingtontimes.com/news/2010/mar/26/admiral-chinas-buildup-aimed-at-power-past-asia/.

[48] "Annual Report to Congress: Military and Security Developments Involving the People's Republic of China, 2010," Office of the Secretary of Defense, 2010, 2.

[49] "Chinese FM Relays Concern Over Upcoming S. Korean–U.S. Joint Naval Exercises," Yonhap News Agency, November 26, 2010, http://english.yonhapnews.co.kr/national/2010/11/26/22/0301000000 AEN20101126009400315F.HTML. See also "S. Korea, U.S. Start Naval Exercise in West Sea," *Chosun Ilbo*, July 8, 2010, http://english.chosun.com/site/data/html_dir/2010/11/29/2010112901222.html. During November 24–28, 2010, South Korea and the United States conducted a major air-naval exercise involving the USS *George Washington*, Aegis cruisers and destroyers, FA-18 C/D and E/F fighters, and surveillance aircraft in response to the November 2010 attack on Yeonpyeong Island.

[50] See Jung Sung-ki, "Korea, U.S. Firm on Naval Exercise Despite China's Protests," *Korea Times*, July 9, 2010, http://www.koreatimes.co.kr/www/news/nation/2010/12/205_69147.html.

South Korea are causing a new crisis; and (5) these exercises "pose a threat to China."[51]

Accustomed as it has been to focusing on the North Korean threat for much of the past six decades, South Korea has little choice but to factor in China's growing presence in and around the Korean Peninsula as a key element of peninsular dynamics. In partial response to such a development, South Korean–Chinese military cooperation has increased incrementally since the early 1990s, including through the establishment of military attaché offices, ad hoc defense ministers' meetings (the first held in January 2000), high-level military exchanges, and regular bilateral defense cooperation conferences.[52] For South Korea, however, despite elevated military-to-military discussions and ties with China, the ROK-U.S. alliance remains the main conduit for counterbalancing Chinese influence on the Korean Peninsula. At the same time, coping with the pressures of a G-2 template in Northeast Asia will require a much more nuanced external security and defense cooperation strategy. In this regard, South Korea should continue to increase its relative leverage within Northeast Asia by expanding and deepening both its alliance with the United States and selective defense cooperation with Japan, while also enhancing security cooperation with other key regional partners, such as Australia and Indonesia, and even traditionally out-of-area powers such as India.

Perceiving India: A South Korean View

If South Korea's ties with and perceptions of China are marked by powerful and contrasting strands, Seoul's relationship with India is characterized by the potential for jumping over two historical hurdles: the tyranny of distance and mutual disinterest. Managed adroitly, the relationship could produce strategic dividends, but to date it has been an important supplement to Seoul's foreign policy rather than a driving factor. Therefore, forging a long-term strategic partnership that is more than just platitudes and political rhetoric will require sustaining top-level political attention in Seoul and New Delhi, establishing matching economic and political instruments, and exploiting the opportunities for maximizing each other's relative political and economic advantages in South and Northeast Asia. As a case in point, growing commercial and energy interests mean that

---

[51] Luo Yuan, "Why China Opposes U.S.-South Korean Military Exercises in the Yellow Sea," *People's Daily*, July 16, 2010, http://english.peopledaily.com.cn/90001/90780/91342/7069743.html.

[52] "Hanjoong kwankjae kekwan" [Key Facets of South Korea–China Relations], Embassy of the Republic of Korea in China, http://www.koreanembassy.cn/contents/politics/serv2-71-01.aspx?bm=2&sm=3&fm=1.

freedom of the seas in the Indian Ocean and Western Pacific—including key strategic chokepoints and waters such as the Strait of Hormuz, the Bay of Bengal, the Strait of Malacca, and the South China Sea—is an issue on which both countries can cooperate actively and accrue joint benefits. Therefore, where India's "look east" and South Korea's "look west" policies overlap, both can gain significant strategic dividends if bilateral ties can be more fully institutionalized.

India accrues a major strategic advantage from being perceived by South Korea as the only one of Asia's major powers that is starting from a clean slate. Indeed, South Korea understands that India has the potential to significantly enlarge its strategic space in South Asia and beyond. At the same time, India can pursue a more nimble look east policy by exploiting the opportunities tendered by a growing partnership with South Korea. If Seoul's recent forays into India are any guide, concomitant with New Delhi's concerted effort in upgrading ties, Indian–South Korean relations contain all the essential ingredients of a win-win partnership across virtually all areas of common interest. Such a transition is noteworthy, if only because decades of minimal interaction, mutual ideological mistrust (as India's nonaligned foreign policy conflicted with South Korea's alignment with the United States), and limited strategic interests were the hallmarks of bilateral relations throughout the Cold War.

India's founding leader Jawaharlal Nehru declared that "we shall take care not to align ourselves with one group or another for temporary gains.... We want to be friendly with every country and follow our own line or policy on every question that may arise."[53] At the same time, India's traditional foreign policy strategies, including decades of strategic tilt toward the Soviet Union during the Cold War, outlived their utility, as evinced by New Delhi's sustained engagement with the United States beyond the 2008 Indo-U.S. civil nuclear cooperation agreement. But if the end of the Cold War was a watershed moment for Indian foreign and economic policies, it also coincided with two key transformations: China's leapfrogging entry into the world and South Korea's search for a more globalized Asian strategy. As Harsh Pant writes:

> The China factor in India–South Korea ties cannot be underestimated. India's tensions with China have increased in the past few years, with Beijing aggressively asserting its territorial claims on their shared frontier. At the same time, South Korea, too, is re-evaluating its ties with China...As they carefully assess the evolving strategic environment in the Asia-Pacific region, New Delhi and Seoul need to advance their political ties so that a mutually beneficial and long-term partnership can evolve between the two sides. The

---

[53] As cited in Lawrence K. Rosinger, "India in World Politics," *Far Eastern Survey* 18, no. 20 (October 1949): 229.

resulting relationship could be as important for greater regional stability as it is for Indian and South Korean national interests.[54]

South Korea and India share a range of complementary interests above and beyond their mutual concern over China's rise. These include (1) a high degree of still largely untapped economic potential, (2) coping with a major failed state with nuclear capabilities on their borders (Pakistan and North Korea) and the threat posed by Islamabad's and Pyongyang's mutually reinforcing WMD partnership, and (3) securing sea lines of communication (SLOC) in the Indian and Pacific oceans, given India's and South Korea's growing dependence on open sea lanes.[55] Finally, while one should not overemphasize the role of shared values in shaping core foreign policy strategies, another key advantage that India enjoys over China is its discordant but vibrant democracy.

Public Perceptions

For the majority of South Koreans, India is a recent discovery, and the same is true vice versa. Consequently, measuring Korean and Indian perceptions of each other is largely a task still in its infancy. South Korean views of India are on the whole quite positive, whereas Indian perceptions of South Korea are for the most part less positive. In a joint poll conducted by Seoul's East Asia Institute (EAI) and *JoongAng Ilbo* in June 2006, 56% of South Koreans held positive views of India.[56] Likewise, in a Pew Global Attitudes poll released in October 2010, 50% of South Koreans viewed India positively, compared to 34% who held a negative view, and 68% replied that the Indian economy has a positive influence, compared to only 17% who replied that its influence is negative.[57] Growing bilateral economic interactions since the mid-1990s are likely to have influenced perceptions of India, particularly since a majority of South Koreans continue to perceive such ties as nonthreatening. In a *BBC* poll released in March 2011, 66% of South Koreans had favorable views of India, a 10% increase from a

---

[54] Harsh V. Pant, "China's Rise Adds Urgency to India–South Korea Ties," World Politics Review, September 7, 2010, http://www.worldpoliticsreview.com/articles/6340/chinas-rise-adds-urgency-to-india-south-korea-ties.

[55] Lee Dae-Woo, "Indo eui talnengjeon anbojeongchek kwa kukjae kwankae" [India's Post–Cold War Security Policy and International Relations], *Sejong Policy Review* 6, no. 2 (2010): 496–97.

[56] "Hangukin eui euishik josa" [How South Koreans View the World (I): Perceptions on Seven Asia-Pacific Countries], East Asia Institute, EAI Issue Briefing, no. 2, July 2006, 17.

[57] "Indians See Threat from Pakistan, Extremist Groups," Pew Research Center, Pew Global Attitudes Project, October 20, 2010, http://pewglobal.org/2010/10/20/indians-see-threat-from-pakistan-extremist-groups/3/.

similar 2010 poll. Most interestingly, South Koreans gave India the highest favorable rating of any country in the survey.[58]

Perceptions of Indian leadership, however, are different, as reflected in a November 2010 Gallup poll on the performance of twenty Asian leaders. In this poll, 23% of South Koreans said they approved of Indian leadership (compared to 36% for Chinese leadership and 55% for the United States), while 21% responded that they did not approve. Most importantly, however, 56% had no opinion.[59] In other words, a majority of South Koreans are probably unaware of India's global role, given that the lion's share of South Korean public opinion vis-à-vis the world continues to be dominated by the United States, China, Japan, and leading EU countries. For example, in a February 2008 poll conducted by the EAI on the perceived influence of fourteen major countries, the United Kingdom came out on top with 77% followed by Germany (71%), the EU and France (65%), India (54%), Russia (50%), and the United States and China (49%).[60] This poll, however, came at the tail end of growing negative perceptions of the United States in South Korea from the early 2000s until 2007–8. Since that time, perceptions have improved dramatically. For example, according to the 2010 Pew poll, 79% of South Koreans had a favorable view of the United States.[61]

World views on South Korea's own international standing face similar challenges. In a poll surveying seventeen countries worldwide conducted by the EAI and its foreign partners in April 2010, only 32% of respondents perceived South Korea's international standing as positive, while nearly equal percentages thought it was negative (29%) or were uncertain (39%).[62] As for the Indian public, only 19% had a positive perception of South Korea's international standing (compared to 60% who held a negative view), which coincides with the findings of a *BBC* poll that included Indian perceptions of South Korea.[63]

---

[58] "BBC World Service Country Rating Poll: Country-by-Country Results," *BBC World Service*, March 7, 2001, http://www.bbc.co.uk/pressoffice/pressreleases/stories/2011/03_march/07/poll.pdf.

[59] Cynthia English, "U.S. Leadership More Popular in Asia Than China's, India's," Gallup, November 5, 2010, http://www.gallup.com/poll/144269/Leadership-Popular-Asia-China-India.aspx.

[60] Seo Sang Min, "Jupyun guka duleui Hangukin euishik josa" [South Korean Perceptions of Its Neighboring Major Powers], EAI, EAI Issue Briefing, no. 25, February 7, 2008, http://www.eai.or.kr/type_k/panelView.asp?bytag=p&catcode=1101210008&category=24&code=kor_report&idx=7091.

[61] "Obama More Popular Abroad."

[62] Lee Nae-Young and Jeong Han Ul, "2010 Saegaehyunan josa/17gae paweoguka eui soputoo paweo" [2010 Global Poll: 17 Major Powers and Soft Power], EAI, EAI Issue Briefing, no. 76, April 26, 2011, 4.

[63] "BBC World Service Country Rating Poll," 16.

Discovery and Convergence

For five decades, mutual disinterest and latent suspicion characterized the state of South Korean–Indian relations. India's perception of itself as a major power remaining aloof from either the Soviet Union or the United States reinforced its perception of South Korea as an extension of U.S. strategic interests rather than a potential economic or strategic partner.[64] South Korea viewed India's nonalignment both as a de facto tilt toward its archrival North Korea and as closely tying India to the Soviet Union, as evinced by the 1971 Indo-Soviet Friendship Treaty.[65] Additionally, the dearth of economic interaction between India and South Korea limited the potential for a fundamental breakthrough, even if both sides had desired to engineer one.

The key tipping point that broke the ice between South Korea and India occurred in the early 1990s, not only because of India's economic reforms but due to growing mutual concern about the pace and depth of Pakistani–North Korean collaboration on WMD proliferation. Moreover, the fact that Pakistan and North Korea were critically tied to China (the latter through a formal friendship treaty or de facto military alliance) raised the specter of security spillovers into India and South Korea. For New Delhi and Seoul, the emerging Pakistani–North Korean WMD axis was a *seiche* that was not readily visible from the surface but had the potential for devastating consequences, especially if it eventually involved other extraneous forces such as terrorist groups.[66]

The Pakistani–North Korean partnership most likely began in the mid-1980s, when Pakistani ballistic missile engineers began to work with their North Korean counterparts on missile technology transfer. North Korea's Rodong missile was probably reverse engineered by Pakistan into the Ghauri-1 missile. More active cooperation is believed to have begun in the 1990s, including the transfer of P-1 centrifuges from Pakistan to North Korea between 1997 and 2000.[67] President Pervez Musharraf admitted in September 2005 that A.Q. Khan exported "probably a dozen" centrifuges to North Korea, although in the same interview Musharraf added "that after two years of interrogations there was still no evidence about whether the expert

[64] David Brewster, "India's Developing Relationship with South Korea," *Asian Survey* 50, no. 2 (March/April 2010): 404.

[65] Ibid.

[66] For more on the impact of the Pakistan–North Korea relationship, see Chung Min Lee, "The Evolution of the North Korean Nuclear Crisis: Implications for Iran," IFRI Security Studies Center, Proliferation Papers, Winter 2009, 12–13.

[67] Sharon A. Squassoni, "Weapons of Mass Destruction: Trade between North Korea and Pakistan," Congressional Research Service, CRS Report for Congress, RL31900, November 28, 2006, 8, 10.

also gave North Korea a Chinese-origin design to build a nuclear weapon."[68] While Musharraf's 2005 statement was the first time that any Pakistani authority admitted to Pakistani–North Korean nuclear collaboration, U.S. intelligence had been tracing the relationship since the 1990s. According to a *New York Times* report in November 2002, the CIA tracked a secret shipment of ballistic missile parts from North Korea to Pakistan in July 2001.[69] Ironically, if "negative attraction" such as the Pakistani–North Korean WMD partnership first brought together India and South Korea, it has now become an important, but by no means dominant, facet of the bilateral relationship.

The Economic Rationale

While a memorandum of understanding (MOU) on bilateral trade was first signed in April 1964, Indian–South Korean trade was negligible until the 1990s. By the late 1970s, however, as South Korea's economy began to venture into the Middle East and South Asia in earnest, Seoul began to pay greater attention to India with the launching of the first Korean-Indian Joint Economic Consultative Meeting in June 1977 and the founding of the Korean-Indian Economic Cooperation Council in May 1979.[70] Still, the relatively closed nature of the Indian economy until the early 1990s foreclosed opportunities for major Korean investments. As shown in **Table 1**, in 2010 Korea's trade with India was under one-tenth of its trade with China ($17 billion and $188 billion, respectively). Yet considering that total trade between the ROK and India in 1991 was only $560 million, the potential for growth is clearly evident. Indeed, since 2003, bilateral trade between the two countries has grown at an annual rate of 25%. Nevertheless, two-way trade amounted to just 1.9% of South Korea's total trade in 2010 and has never topped 2% of India's trade, accounting for just 1.7% in 2007.[71]

Korean investments in India accelerated sharply from the late 1990s until the early 2000s, gaining "first mover" advantages in the world's second-largest consumer market. Notable successes included efforts led by Korean giants such

[68] David E. Sanger, "Pakistan Leader Confirms Nuclear Exports," *New York Times*, September 12, 2005, http://query.nytimes.com/gst/fullpage.html?res=9D00E2D81031F930A2575AC0A9639C8B63&ref=nuclearprogram.

[69] David E. Sanger, "In North Korea and Pakistan, Deep Roots of Nuclear Barter," *New York Times*, November 24, 2002, http://www.nytimes.com/2002/11/24/world/threats-responses-alliances-north-korea-pakistan-deep-roots-nuclear-barter.html.

[70] "Indo Gaehwang, urinara waeui kyungjae-tongsang kwanke" [Introduction to India and Korea's Eonomic-Trade Ties], Embassy of the Republic of Korea in India, June 2010, http://ind.mofat.go.kr/kor/as/ind/affair/relation/index.jsp.

[71] See Pravakar Sahoo, Durgesh Kumar Rai, and Rajiv Kumar, "India-Korea Trade and Investment Relations," India Council for Research on International Economic Relations, Working Paper, no. 252, December 2009, 4.

TABLE 1   South Korea's trade with China and India, 1991–2010 (in $ thousands)

	1991	1995	2000	2005	2010
India	560	1,192	2,300	6,700	17,000
China	6,378	16,561	31,252	100,562	188,410

SOURCE: Trade Statistics, Korea Customs, 2011.

as Samsung Electronics, LG Electronics, and Hyundai Motors. A major victory for South Korea's leading steel company POSCO (the world's third largest) occurred in January 2011, when the Indian government approved a $12 billion steel investment plan in the state of Orissa after a six-year struggle between the company, environmental activists, and the Indian government.[72] This is the single-largest FDI project in India, and while the Indian government placed 60 new environmental conditions in the agreement, most analysts expect POSCO to comply.[73]

The POSCO announcement comes in the aftermath of the conclusion of a major FTA between South Korea and India—the Comprehensive Economic Partnership Agreement (CEPA)—on March 29, 2010. According to South Korea's trade minister Kim Jong-hoon, CEPA, which entered into force on January 1, 2011, will eliminate or reduce tariffs on 85% of Korean exports and 90% of Indian imports over the next eight to ten years. It is the first FTA that Korea has signed with a BRIC nation, as well as the first de facto FTA that India has signed with an Organisation for Economic Co-operation and Development (OECD) country.[74] At the signing, Indian commerce minister Anand Sharma highlighted the growing complementarities between the two economies, particularly in the fields of IT, alternative energy, and knowledge-based services, and mentioned that 400,000 South Korean cars produced in India were shipped to Europe in 2010.[75]

When Lee Myung-bak visited India in January 2010, bilateral ties were elevated from a "long-term cooperative partnership for peace and prosperity"

---

[72] Amy Kazmin, "India Agrees to $12bn POSCO Steel Plan," *Financial Times*, January 31, 2011, http://www.ft.com/cms/s/0/b0a9763c-2d6b-11e0-8f53-00144feab49a.html.

[73] "POSCO, India's Biggest FDI Project, Finally Cleared by Jariam," *Times of India*, February 1, 2011, http://articles.timesofindia.indiatimes.com/2011-02-01/india/28369388_1_captive-port-posco-plant-biggest-fdi-project.

[74] Yoo Soh-jung, "Korea and India Sign CEPA," *Korea Herald*, March 30, 2011, http://www.koreaherald.com/business/Detail.jsp?newsMLId=20090808000010. India concluded an FTA with Japan on February 15, 2011, a few days after it was reported that China had officially surpassed Japan as the world's second-largest economy. See Andrew Monahan, "Japan, India Sign Free-Trade Pact," *Wall Street Journal*, February 16, 2011.

[75] Yoo, "Korea and India Sign CEPA."

to a "strategic partnership," with the two leaders pledging to increase their trade to $30 billion by 2014. President Lee and Prime Minister Manmohan Singh also agreed to upgrade defense cooperation (such as India's consideration of South Korea's KT-1 trainer) and nuclear energy development.[76] The two countries are also on the verge of concluding a civilian nuclear agreement with an emphasis on R&D and civil nuclear plants. South Korea is actively seeking to become a major exporter of nuclear power plants, as evinced by its December 2009 sale to the United Arab Emirates.[77]

Despite enormous potential in the bilateral economic relationship, however, South Korea's overall share of FDI in India has fallen sharply from the early 2000s. South Korea registered as the sixth-largest investor in India from 1991 to 2005 but fell to twentieth from 2005 to 2009. From 1968 to 2009, 84% of Korean investment in India was in manufacturing (automobiles composed 62.5%; metals, 7.8%; machinery and equipment, 6.5%; food and beverages, 5.1%; and electronics and IT, 3.4%), followed by small- and medium-sized businesses (8.7%), finance and insurance (2.8%), and construction (1.3%).[78] Yet despite ebbs and flows in the Korean-Indian economic partnership, it should not be forgotten that this relationship began to take off a full decade after the ROK-China relationship commenced in earnest in the late 1980s. Although manufacturing and consumer electronics continue to dominate South Korean investments in India, green growth, IT, steel, energy, and defense/security are likely to become high-growth areas for Korean-Indian cooperation in the 2020–30 timeframe.[79]

As Seoul ponders the future of economic relations with New Delhi, the Samsung Economic Research Institute has outlined four major strategies: (1) deeper localization of consumer electronic investments in India, given the 20% annual growth in the Indian market, (2) a much more aggressive focus on developing business-to-business networks in the Indian auto market to both meet accelerating demand in one of the fastest-growing markets among the emerging economies and use India as an automobile

---

[76] "Korea, India Now Each Other's 'Strategic Partners,'" Cheong Wa Dae, Office of the President, January 26, 2010, http://english.president.go.kr/pre_activity/summit/diplomacy_view.php?uno=2545.

[77] Sandeep Dikshit, "Nuclear Pact with South Korea," *Hindu*, February 15, 2011, http://www.thehindu.com/news/national/article1455896.ece. External Affairs Minister S.M. Krishna visited Seoul in June 2010 to accelerate progress on an Indian-Korean nuclear agreement. See "South Korea Awarded UAE Nuclear Power Contract," *BBC*, December 27, 2009, http://news.bbc.co.uk/2/hi/8431904.stm.

[78] Yim Jeong Sung, "Hanguk kieopdeuleui Indo tooja, saeroeun daean" [South Korean Firms' India Investment: New Alternatives], *Chindia Journal* 41 (January 2010): 24.

[79] According to 2009 data, Hyundai Motors had a 23% share of the Indian auto market, while LG and Samsung had a commanding lead in the Indian consumer electronics market—45% of televisions (including 63% of LCD units) and on average 44% of air conditioners, microwaves, and washing machines. See Greg Scarlatoiu, "ROK-India Summit Meeting: South Korea's 'New Asia Initiative' Converges with India's 'Look East Policy,'" Korea Economic Institute, Korea Insight, February 1, 2010, 4.

hub for the Middle Eastern and European markets, (3) joint public and private sector participation in Indian infrastructure modernization, and (4) enhanced R&D and joint development in biotechnologies, clean energy, and nuclear power.[80]

Security Plus

As an add-on to the burgeoning economic relationship, but also important on its own merit, bilateral security cooperation is another area that has been pried open by the two sides. In September 2010, Indian defense minister A.K. Anthony reached a five-year defense cooperation agreement with Seoul during the first visit to South Korea by an Indian defense minister. The agreement calls for institutionalized cooperation in three main areas: defense technology transfers, joint production, and R&D.[81] India and South Korea began discussions in the mid-2000s on a range of potential defense cooperation efforts, including India's purchase of 5,000-ton frigates, armored vehicles, and KT-1 trainers from Korea. But for the time being, Korean-Indian defense and security cooperation is likely to be pursued by cross-checking key areas of interest collusion, such as maritime cooperation and growing Chinese naval power in the Western Pacific, including the all-important South China Sea, the Strait of Malacca, and the Bay of Bengal. As Harsh Pant observes:

> South Korea is one of the world's leaders in naval ship-building technology, and India would like to tap into South Korean naval capabilities to augment its own. As a result, naval cooperation is rapidly emerging as a central feature of bilateral defense cooperation, with the two navies cooperating in anti-piracy operations in the Indian Ocean region and the Gulf of Aden. Both states also share a strong interest in protecting the sea lines of communication in the Indian Ocean region.[82]

Although it makes little sense for Seoul or New Delhi to oversell the bilateral security relationship or to brand the partnership as a de facto anti-Chinese coalition, Indian strategists realize the potential for harnessing bilateral cooperation to help virtually counter China's "string of pearls" strategy. One Indian analyst has surmised:

---

[80] "Samsung kyungjae yeonkuso Indoshijangeui busangkwa Hanguk kieopeui jinchul jeolryak" [SERI Assessments on the Indian Market and the Strategy of South Korean Firms], Newswire, March 2, 2011, http:www.newswire.co.kr/modules/etc/print_news.php?no=529721.

[81] "India, S Korea Sign 5-year Defence Co-op Agreement," Press Trust of India, September 3, 2010, http://www.business-standard.com/india/news/india-s-korea-sign-5-year-defence-co-op-agreement/107610/on. The agreement also listed cooperation on humanitarian assistance, maritime issues, and peacekeeping activities.

[82] Pant, "China's Rise Adds Urgency."

> Coming against the backdrop of reports of a massive Chinese military build-up in Gilgit-Balistan, the northern area of Pakistan-administered Kashmir... India is looking to effectively counter the Chinese "string of pearls" strategy and Anthony's visit to South Korea should be looked at in that larger context...If indeed some kind of "axis" is being formed between China, Pakistan, and Myanmar, it would seem legitimate for India to sculpt a similar "axis" with Japan and South Korea as a counterpoise to China's design. China's "string of pearls" strategy is clearly designed to control maritime interests in the Indian Ocean Region (IOR) by building bases or partnering with countries such as Pakistan (Gwadar) and Sri Lanka (Hambantota) in securing sea routes for maritime commerce.[83]

South Korea's rationale for deepening security cooperation with India reached a crucial juncture in August 2008. Seoul supported India's request for an exemption from the Nuclear Suppliers Group (NSG) even though it continues to be concerned about the implications of U.S.-Indian nuclear cooperation on the North Korean nuclear problem.[84] Given South Korea's desire to enter more fully into India's civilian nuclear power program over the long term, as well as the fact that India has been a strong advocate of nuclear nonproliferation, Seoul adopted a flexible stance on New Delhi's nuclear policy. This decision was also likely driven by the depth of WMD collaboration between North Korea and Pakistan, as well as by North Korea's expanding threat envelope through defense relationships with Iran and Syria.

Conclusions

When South Korea was founded as a modern republic in August 1948, none of its leaders would have been able to predict that by the early 21st century it would rank as Asia's fourth-largest economy and host a summit of the world's twenty principal powers. While numerous factors highlight the story of postwar Korea, three key elements stand out.

The first element is a national strategy that embedded South Korea firmly into the post–World War II international order shaped and led by the United States, as both a functioning democracy and a market economy. To be sure, until the outbreak of the Korean War in June 1950, South Korea's net strategic utility from the viewpoint of the United States was marginal at best or it was seen as a supporting column for the more important task of bolstering Japan as a linchpin of the United States' emerging Cold War strategy in the Asia-Pacific. The Korean War, however, triggered a major

---

[83] Rajaram Panda, "Fruits of Antony's Visit to South Korea: Defence Ties Strengthen Further," Institute for Defense Studies and Analysis, IDSA Comment, September 7, 2010, 1.

[84] Brewster, "India's Developing Relationship with South Korea," 421.

turnaround in U.S. strategy, both in Asia and in Western Europe, given that the conflict came to symbolize the emerging Cold War. For South Korea, extricating itself from one of the most pronounced consequences of the globalization of the Cold War was not a viable option, since the divided peninsula was a microcosm of the broader East-West conflict. Nevertheless, if South Korea's linkages with the United States were grudgingly accepted on the U.S. side due to the necessities of Cold War politics, the alliance has been transformed and maintained not only on the basis of necessity but increasingly on the basis of mutual choice. Since then, the alliance, and by extension South Korea, has gained unprecedented dividends from this "unnatural" trans-Pacific partnership, including the ROK's ability to focus on accelerated economic development under a security umbrella provided by the United States and its broader Asian alliances. While the ROK-U.S. relationship has endured its share of difficulties, the alliance enabled "South Korea's transformation as a leading economic power and its transition from authoritarianism to a vibrant democracy [and] has created opportunities for practical cooperation in new areas that extend well beyond the peninsula."[85] Despite intermittent expressions of intense nationalism, South Korea today is irreversibly linked with the rest of the world, owing in no small measure to the relationship it forged with the United States in the midst of war.

Second, Korea's centuries-old alignment with China was disrupted in the early twentieth century, and for nearly half a century, from the late 1940s until the early 1990s, Seoul's perceptions of and ties with the PRC were shaped by Beijing's supportive relationship with the South's nemesis, North Korea. Since the end of the Cold War, however, South Korea's ties with China have grown to the point where China is now its largest trading partner. Moreover, on virtually all the core security policies that directly impinge on South Korea's key national interests—maintaining deterrence and engagement with the North, attempting to resolve the North Korean nuclear problem, buttressing its alliance with the United States, forging new ties with Japan, and expanding its "global Korea" footprint—the China factor is ever present. As a country that has a lengthy history of strategic interaction with China, South Korea's overlapping interests with China are certainly not a new phenomenon. But the stakes today are considerably larger than before, given that even as Seoul continues to receive major dividends from its growing ties with Beijing, it does not want to be reincorporated into a Chinese sphere of influence. How to cope with shifting dynamics in the North, ideally with minimal strategic

---

[85] Stephen Flanagan, Michael J. Green, Nicholas Szechenyi, and Scott Snyder, *Pursuing a Comprehensive Vision for the U.S.–South Korea Alliance* (Washington, D.C.: CSIS, 2009), 1.

fallout from systemic transformations there, is also emerging as one of the central over-the-horizon issues confronting Seoul and Beijing.

Third, ensuring South Korea's long-term economic growth, along with commensurate political maneuverability as a strategically consequential middle power, means that Seoul has no choice but to seek newer, niche dividends driven by the imperatives of the new geopolitics and South Korea's ability to fully exploit the opportunities provided by the rise of powers such as Indonesia and India. Here, the Korean-Indian relationship illustrates one of the most interesting developments in Korean foreign policy since the end of the Cold War, considering that mutual disinterest more than any other factor characterized the bilateral relationship until India's opening to the world in the early 1990s. By happy coincidence and a budding realization that both New Delhi and Seoul would be able to jointly make relative but significant gains, the Korean-Indian relationship has the potential to become a key niche partnership well into the 21st century. Still, Seoul's preoccupation with the vestiges of the old geopolitics is never too far from the surface, particularly in the context of China's unprecedented rise and the attendant implications for the inter-Korean strategic balance, even as South Korea continues to accrue major dividends from a new partnership with China.

On balance, the emerging foreign policy challenge for South Korea lies in exploiting the opportunities tendered by the simultaneous rise of Asia's two major civilizations while retaining and upgrading the successful bilateral alliance with the United States. That Seoul has to cope with giants is hardly a novel tenet of its foreign policy, given that it is the only Asian power that has and continues to live in the midst of the world's largest and most powerful neighbors. The difference today is that the costs of failure and the benefits of success in managing the realities of a new strategic Asia are without precedence for a country that has achieved an impossible postwar mission: rising from the ashes of war as one of the world's most successful but existentially vulnerable middle powers.

EXECUTIVE SUMMARY

This chapter examines Australia's response to the rise of China and India, including tensions among economics, security, and values, as well as implications for U.S. strategy in Asia.

MAIN ARGUMENT:

For Australia, the rise of China and India combines vast economic gain with challenges in security and values. The Asian giants have become principal markets for Australia's resources, major sources of human capital, and critical strategic players in the region. China brings Australia greater economic benefits than does India, but its growing military power, combined with differences over values, poses fundamental security anxieties. India, meanwhile, is seen as a potential—albeit frustrating—strategic partner. Thus, Canberra has tried to intensify diplomatic engagement and economic enmeshment with both powers, yet is also revealing a hedging strategy against Chinese power. This involves strengthening Australia's navy, as well as enhancing the U.S. alliance and forging links with Asian partners.

POLICY IMPLICATIONS:

- The Australia-U.S. alliance will need to adapt to an Indo-Pacific era of Chinese and Indian power. The U.S. will benefit from further coordinating its strategies toward China and India with those of Australia. Beyond candid bilateral dialogue and possible trilateral talks or activities with Australia and India, this could mean placing U.S. equipment or even forces in Australia.

- Above all, Canberra will be sensitive to any change in Washington's Asia strategy that leaves allies vulnerable to Chinese coercion. Yet Australia will also be wary of being drawn into an unnecessary confrontation with China as well as of seeing its interests sidestepped in a U.S.-India partnership. Either way, it will be important for the U.S. to engage Australian society beyond traditional policy elites when addressing the rise of China and India.

Grand Stakes: Australia's Future between China and India

Rory Medcalf

Australia is at a difficult juncture. For the first time in its history, this mid-sized democracy at the southern edge of maritime Asia is confronted by the simultaneous rise of two Asian great powers, China and India. In 2009, China overtook Japan to become Australia's top trading partner, the first time this status has been held by a state that is not also Canberra's security guarantor, or that ally's ally, and that does not share Australia's democratic values. The potential for a contested Asia, in which China and India loom large, poses critical new challenges to Australia's security, long-reliant on an open and stable regional order underwritten by U.S. dominance.[1] For now, Australia is enjoying the best of both worlds. The rapid economic growth of China and India provides massive markets for the country's abundant mineral and energy reserves, while U.S. preeminence underwrites Australian security. But questions are emerging about how long these good times can last and whether the nation has a strategy for an Indo-Pacific era of Chinese and Indian strength.

In this context, Australia is beginning to face uncomfortable strategic challenges and decisions. These primarily involve potential choices between

Rory Medcalf is Director of the International Security Program at the Lowy Institute for International Policy. He can be reached at <rmedcalf@lowyinstitute.org>.

[1] This chapter defines Australia's region as the Indo-Pacific, rather than adopting a more traditional Asia-Pacific formulation, in recognition of Australia's two-ocean geography and of the growing integration of the Western Pacific and Indian Ocean regions into one strategic system. The 2009 Australian defense white paper suggested that "over the period to 2030, the Indian Ocean will join the Pacific Ocean in terms of its centrality to our maritime strategy and defence planning." Australian Department of Defence, *Defending Australia in the Asia Pacific Century: Force 2030* (Canberra, 2009), 41–45, http://www.defence.gov.au/whitepaper/docs/defence_white_paper_2009.pdf.

its security ally, the United States, and its premier economic partner, China, a nation that buys almost a quarter of Australian exports and has deepening links through business, migration, education, and tourism.[2] The starkest questions revolve around whether and how the alliance with the United States might one day be invoked in a possible military confrontation with Beijing. More broadly, there is the question of whether Australia might differ with the United States or others in how far it would be willing to see Chinese interests accommodated in the regional order. Canberra's recent reaffirmation of the alliance suggests that a near-term divergence between Australia and the United States on this front remains unlikely, even if some analysts argue that it is a serious risk in the longer term.[3]

The rise of India makes Asia's power dynamics more complicated but also potentially more beneficial for Australia. India has become Australia's fourth-largest export market and one of its fastest-growing, at an average of 20% a year.[4] India buys about 7% of Australian exports, and Canberra is eager to complement this with a serious strategic partnership. But Australia is encountering frustrations here, including in establishing political trust and strategic relevance, despite common democratic values and shared security interests. Progress will probably require awkward policy choices in Canberra, including ending its ban on uranium sales to India. Looking ahead, Australia faces challenges in simultaneously engaging China and India while adapting its U.S. alliance. The time may come when Canberra must choose not only between Beijing and Washington but also between Beijing and New Delhi.

Thus, there are both parallels and great contrasts between Australia's relations with China and India. Relations with both involve economic enmeshment. Societal links are also growing rapidly through migration, business, tourism, and education. Yet qualitative differences between Australia's relations with China and India are emerging on security and values-based issues.

This chapter is divided into four sections. The first provides an overview of how Australia perceives its national interests—with reference to economics, security, and values—and how these interests are likely to be affected by the rise of China and India. The second and central part of the chapter

---

[2] "Speech to the Australia-China Economic and Cooperation Trade Forum," Prime Minister of Australia, Press Office, April 26, 2011, http://www.pm.gov.au/press-office/speech-australia-china-economic-and-co-operation-trade-forum-beijing.

[3] See, for example, Hugh White, *Power Shift: Australia's Future between Washington and Beijing*, Quarterly Essay 39 (Collingwood: Black Inc., 2010).

[4] Department of Foreign Affairs and Trade of the Australian Government, *Composition of Trade Australia 2010* (Canberra, 2011), 29, 31, http://www.dfat.gov.au/publications/stats-pubs/composition_trade.html.

surveys Australia's historical interactions with China and India in terms of geopolitics, economics, society, and security, including military and nuclear issues. This is followed by an assessment of whether Australia's efforts to protect national interests in response to the rise of China and India amount to a coherent strategy. It will be argued that the rudiments of a strategy are becoming clear, but that questions remain over how coherent, sustained, and effective this approach will be. These responses are influenced by a mix of economic, security, and values-based drivers, which sometimes reinforce and sometimes cut across one another. Australia's resulting approach is a hybrid one: economic and diplomatic enmeshment combined with a hedging strategy against the unknown ways China might use its future power. This hedging strategy involves increasing Australia's own military weight, intensifying the U.S. alliance, and building security links with large democratic Asian partners, including India. The chapter concludes by considering the policy implications for Washington of Canberra's response to the rise of China and India and presenting ways in which the United States might further coordinate its strategies toward China and India with those of its antipodean ally.

Australia's Strategic Interests: Why China and India Matter So Much

To grasp the profound impact of the rise of China and India on Australia's interests, it is necessary to appreciate how Canberra perceives those interests. Australia has singular geopolitical circumstances. It is the only nation in the world to possess an island continent, which bestows strategic depth, vast maritime jurisdiction, and globally important natural resource deposits. Australia is the world's largest exporter of iron ore and coal, has the largest uranium deposits, and is also a major supplier of natural gas, gold, and other commodities.[5] This is combined with high per capita wealth, a stable democratic system, a resilient and multicultural society, a small but advanced defense force, and a diplomatic record of strong global

---

[5] Besides being the largest exporter of iron ore, Australia is the world's number one coal exporter, shipping 28% of world exports in 2008–9. In that year, Australia was also the third-largest producer of uranium, with 15.7% of the global market. In addition, it has the world's fifteenth-largest reserves of natural gas and is the seventh-largest exporter of liquefied natural gas (LNG). "The Australian Coal Industry - Coal Exports," Australian Coal Association, http://www.australiancoal.com.au/the-australian-coal-industry_coal-exports.aspx; "Statistics and Balances," International Energy Agency, http://www.iea.org/stats/index.asp; "Iron Ore," Geoscience Australia, http://www.ga.gov.au/minerals/mineral-resources/iron-ore.html; "Uranium Production Figures, 2000–2010," World Nuclear Association, April 2011, http://www.world-nuclear.org/info/uprod.html; "Australian Uranium Industry," Australian Uranium Association, http://www.aua.org.au/content/resources.aspx; and "Oil and Gas Overview," Austrade, http://www.austrade.gov.au/Oil-Gas-overview/default.aspx.

and regional engagement.[6] Australia's geography bestows economically advantageous proximity to Indo-Pacific Asia but also a large maritime barrier against any regional adversary.

Still, in spite of the country's exceptional national endowments, Australian strategic culture contains a strong thread of insecurity. This has origins in modern Australia's beginnings as a thinly populated British outpost near populous Asia, as well as later exposure to great-power rivalries and Japanese aggression in World War II. Such insecurity is reinforced by proximity to a sometimes unstable Indonesia.[7] Australia continues to have a small population relative to its territory, and the continent's dry environment restricts population growth. This means a limited base for defense recruitment and, despite substantial immigration, a gradually graying demographic profile, which will restrict economic growth and government revenues, including for defense.

Crucially, Australia's strengths are entwined with external dependence on commodity exports, sea lines of communication (SLOC), stability in Asia, a rules-based global order, and the protection of a powerful ally. These strengths and dependencies help define national interests. Australia's security interests include protecting its extensive territory, resources, and maritime zones; maintaining its independence and democratic political system; and preserving a stable, peaceful, and rules-based international order.[8] Its economic interests include maximizing prosperity through exports to major markets and are obviously affected by the growing wealth and power of China and India.

On the positive side, China's growth supports a vast and expanding market for Australian commodities, especially iron ore, and provides indirect payoffs by increasing the economic activity of Australia's other trade and investment partners.[9] India also provides an important market for Australian exports, and one, moreover, with great potential for further

---

[6] In 2009, Australia had the world's thirteenth-largest economy by exchange rate measures and the world's fourteenth-highest defense budget. *SIPRI Yearbook 2010: Armaments, Disarmament and International Security* (New York: Oxford University Press, 2010), 203.

[7] Rory Medcalf, "Australia: Allied in Transition," in *Strategic Asia 2008–09: Challenges and Choices*, ed. Ashley J. Tellis, Mercy Kuo, and Andrew Marble (Seattle: National Bureau of Asian Research, 2008), 233; and Hugh White, "Australian Strategic Policy," in *Strategic Asia 2005–06: Military Modernization in an Era of Uncertainty*, ed. Ashley J. Tellis and Michael Wills (Seattle: National Bureau of Asian Research, 2005), 306.

[8] Australian Department of Defence, *Defending Australia in the Asia Pacific Century*, 41–45.

[9] In 2010, China imported A$34.6 billion worth of Australian iron ore and concentrates. "China Fact Sheet," Australian Department of Foreign Affairs and Trade, June 2011, http://www.dfat.gov.au/geo/fs/chin.pdf.

growth.[10] The rise of the Asian giants has thus protected Australia from the contemporary travails of most developed economies, although the country's reliance on mineral exports may prove a long-term vulnerability.

On the negative side, the rapid growth of Chinese military power is confronting Australians with an unfamiliar tension between their economic interests, on the one hand, and their security interests and democratic values, on the other. Australia fears risks to a stable Asian order; these include not only U.S.-China confrontation but also potential conflict between China and others. Canberra has come to see China's rise as the central strategic challenge in the Indo-Pacific region, and it has thus become a major driver of Australia's maritime force modernization, reflected in the 2009 defense white paper and confirmed in leaked conversations involving former prime minister Kevin Rudd.[11] This marks a long-term shift in Canberra's defense thinking, given that from the 1970s to the 1990s Australian planners did not identify China as a major potential threat.[12]

Canberra is also concerned about the potential for Chinese coercion of other nations in the region. The threat or use of force by Beijing against any of its neighbors, for instance over disputed sovereignty in the South China Sea, would be seen in Canberra as a sign of the way China might use its future power. Worries are even beginning to emerge in Australia about the possibility that China might pose some future direct threat to Australian security interests, for instance, through cyberattacks or in the maritime domain, even though the idea of a Chinese military threat to Australia's territory, sovereignty, or democratic way of life has long been regarded as radical within the Australian foreign and security policy discourse.[13] Nonetheless, from a marginal position some years ago, the notion of a "China threat" now appears to be taken seriously by much of the Australian public.[14] Although Australian

---

[10] In 2010, India imported approximately A$6.8 billion worth of Australian coal. "India Fact Sheet," Australian Department of Foreign Affairs and Trade, June 2011, http://www.dfat.gov.au/geo/fs/inia.pdf.

[11] Australian Department of Defence, *Defending Australia in the Asia Pacific Century*; and Greg Sheridan, "The Realist We Need in Foreign Affairs," *Australian*, December 9, 2010, http://www.theaustralian.com.au/news/opinion/the-realist-we-need-in-foreign-affairs/story-e6frg6zo-1225967870772.

[12] Richard Smith, "The Long Rise of China in Australian Defence Strategy," Lowy Institute for International Policy, Perspectives, April 2009, http://www.lowyinstitute.org/Publication.asp?pid=1023.

[13] Ross Babbage, "Australia's Strategic Edge in 2030," Kokoda Foundation, Kokoda Papers, no. 15, February 2011, http://www.kokodafoundation.org/Resources/Documents/KP15StrategicEdge.pdf; and Paul Dibb and Geoffrey Barker, "Panicky Response Would Harm Our Interests," *Australian*, February 8, 2011, http://www.theaustralian.com.au/news/opinion/panicky-response-would-harm-our-interests/story-e6frg6zo-1226001745570.

[14] In a 2010 opinion poll, 46% of respondents said they thought China would become a military threat to Australia within twenty years. Fergus Hanson, *The Lowy Institute Poll 2010* (Sydney: Lowy Institute for International Policy, 2010).

security thinkers also recognize the potential for a strong Chinese military to contribute to global security public goods, such as antipiracy, evacuations, and disaster relief, this perception is becoming overshadowed by worries about the destabilizing impact of Chinese martial might.

India's perceived net impact on Australia's strategic interests is considerably more benign. India is the country's fastest-growing major trading partner and could offer a limited degree of economic insulation against a deterioration of relations with China. On the security front, Australia sees a strengthened India as in part a balancer to Chinese power, as well as a partner against terrorism and in zones of shared interest, notably the Indian Ocean.

It would be a mistake, however, to imagine that India's expanding interests, ambitions, and responsibilities will always benefit Australia; rather, there are limits to the convergence of the two countries' strategic interests. India's energy needs will keep it looking west as well as east. Australia is also concerned about the wider impact from confrontations in which India may become embroiled, notably with Pakistan. Growing Indian naval power may not always reinforce Canberra's interests unless it can be coordinated with Australian or U.S. activity.[15] In addition, Canberra is not yet convinced about the effectiveness or predictability of India's diplomacy, its readiness to act as a great power, or the depth of its strategic role in East Asia. Still, Australia sees a rising India much more as a potential strategic partner and a net contributor to public goods than as a cause for concern.

One long-term Australian concern about China and India is the way they might interact as their power and interests expand and, in particular, the possibility that their current state of competitive coexistence might descend into active rivalry. This would have spillover effects for Australia's interests and place Canberra in situations where it would need to make potentially painful choices between Asia's giants.

Dealing with Giants: Australian Interactions with China and India

The rise of China and India confronts Australia with new dilemmas and risks, as well as opportunities. But in order to understand how novel and complex these challenges are, it is worth surveying Australia's historical and recent record in dealing with the Asian giants across geopolitical, economic, societal, and security dimensions.

---

[15] David Brewster, "Australia and India: The Indian Ocean and the Limits of Strategic Convergence," *Australian Journal of International Affairs* 64, no. 5 (November 2010): 549–65.

History

Australia's geographic closeness to Asia has only recently translated into comprehensive interaction with China and India. From their establishment in the late 1700s and the 1800s, the British colonies in Australia were isolated and vulnerable. This settler society was conscious of its distance from Europe and feared being overwhelmed by Asian powers or populations. To be sure, there were some early and fruitful connections with China and India. Australia had regular social and commercial contact with British India, and its first coal exports, in 1799, went to Calcutta. Meanwhile, thousands of workers came to Australia from China to join nineteenth-century gold rushes, establishing substantial communities. Attitudes of racial exclusion grew within Australia, with the labor movement in particular seeking tight curbs on Asian immigration.[16] This became formalized as the "White Australia" policy shortly after the colonies became a federal nation in 1901—a policy that was not fully dismantled until 1972, after already having caused lasting damage to the nation's reputation.

China and India began to matter more to Australia as it came to grips with the decline of the British Empire, Indian independence in 1947, and the establishment of the People's Republic of China (PRC) in 1949. Although Australia recognized the need to engage the two awakening giants, the conservative governments of the 1950s and 1960s soon became wary of what Communist China and nonaligned India meant for Australia's interests, values, and, from 1951, alliance with the United States. Fear of Beijing worsened with the Korean War, in which Australians directly fought Chinese forces.[17] Australia-India ties, meanwhile, stalled over differing Cold War alignments, India's closed economy, the lingering White Australia policy, and a clash of personalities and worldviews between Indian prime minister Jawaharlal Nehru and the conservative prime minister Robert Menzies.[18] Impetus for change came in the 1970s. Efforts under Labor prime minister Gough Whitlam to reach out to the developing and Communist worlds coincided with the U.S. opening to China. Australia-China trade

---

[16] David Dutton, "A British Outpost in the Pacific," in *Facing North: A Century of Australian Engagement with Asia – Volume 1: 1901 to the 1970s*, ed. David Goldsworthy (Canberra: Department of Foreign Affairs and Trade, 2003), 29–39.

[17] Lachlan Strahan, *Australia's China: Changing Perceptions from the 1930s to the 1990s* (Cambridge: Cambridge University Press, 1996), 125–59; and Michael Wesley, "Australia-China," in *Australia as an Asia-Pacific Regional Power: Friendships in Flux?* ed. Brendan Taylor (London: Routledge, 2007), 61–62.

[18] Meg Gurry, *India: Australia's Neglected Neighbour? 1947–1996* (Brisbane: Centre for the Study of Australia-Asia Relations, 1996), 17–18; and Meg Gurry, "Leadership and Bilateral Relations: Menzies and Nehru, Australia and India, 1949–1964," *Pacific Affairs* 65, no. 4 (Winter 1992–93): 510–26.

and diplomatic relations improved steadily after Mao Zedong's death, but Australia-India ties remained fitful.[19]

Although relations between Canberra and Beijing were impeded by the Tiananmen Square massacre in 1989, when Canberra gave political asylum to thousands of Chinese students, the trading relationship continued. Political and security dialogue again expanded as Australia, under Labor prime minister Paul Keating and foreign minister Gareth Evans, encouraged China to become a constructive player in Asia's post–Cold War security order. Following a 1996 crisis over the support of the conservative John Howard government for the U.S. naval deployment against Chinese intimidation of Taiwan, Canberra's ties with Beijing settled into a pattern of mutual respect that would work for more than a decade: sidestepping differences over security and values to take advantage of economic complementarity. Chinese business and societal links to Australia increased. The changed place of China in Canberra's worldview was underlined in 2003, when President Hu Jintao addressed the Australian Parliament the day after President George W. Bush.[20] There followed brief confusion about whether Australia's alignment in Asia was changing as a consequence of China's rise. This uncertainty was heightened by comments from Foreign Minister Alexander Downer in 2004 that Australia would not necessarily join the United States in a war with China over Taiwan, though Howard moved swiftly to reaffirm the alliance.[21]

With India, meanwhile, Australia's achievements were less spectacular. Both nations failed to create real diplomatic traction out of commonalities such as democracy, the English language, and the sport of cricket. Differences intensified following India's 1974 nuclear test, given Australia's outspoken support of the Nuclear Non-Proliferation Treaty (NPT). Security mistrust further increased in the 1980s over each country's naval posture. By the mid-1990s, however, Australia had begun to recognize India's potential following New Delhi's economic liberalization reforms in 1991. The bilateral relationship was set back by India's 1998 nuclear tests and Australia's response, which included cutting defense ties for almost three years. Still, since about 2001, the relationship has made impressive progress, particularly in trade, which grew about 28% a year between 2002

---

[19] Gurry, *India: Australia's Neglected Neighbour?*

[20] Evan Medeiros et al., *Pacific Currents: The Responses of U.S. Allies and Security Partners in East Asia to China's Rise* (Santa Monica: RAND Corporation, 2008), 211–12.

[21] Hamish McDonald and Tom Allard, "ANZUS Loyalties Fall under China's Shadow," *Sydney Morning Herald*, August 18, 2004.

and 2007 and a staggering 55% in 2009.[22] At an inaugural bilateral strategic dialogue in 2001, each country publicly proclaimed the other a force for regional stability,[23] and the events of September 11 and after—including the deaths of many Australians in the 2002 Bali bombings—emphasized a new common cause against terrorism. By the last phase of the Howard government, Canberra had clearly recognized New Delhi's potential as a strategic partner, demonstrated by Howard's surprise move in 2007 to overturn a decades-old ban on uranium exports to India.

When former diplomat Kevin Rudd defeated Howard in the November 2007 election, expectations were high that he could build on his predecessor's achievements in major-power relations. Howard had ranked his success in simultaneously strengthening Australia's relations with China and deepening the U.S. alliance as his greatest foreign policy achievement.[24] Yet while trade continued to rocket along, official relations with both China and India became strained.[25] With China, the issues included Rudd's failed experiment in seeking to position Australia as a plain-speaking friend seemingly able to reconcile Western and Chinese worldviews,[26] Australia's identification of China as a potential threat in its 2009 defense white paper, controversy over Chinese state investments in Australian resources, Australia granting a visa to a Uighur activist, frank official comments from Australia about China's harsh treatment of Uighur protesters, Rudd's speech marking the twentieth anniversary of the Tiananmen Square massacre, and Beijing's arrest of a Chinese-Australian mining executive. Rudd's ambitious diplomacy fell victim to Beijing's false expectations that his deep knowledge of China, as the first Mandarin-speaking leader in the Western world, would translate into a heightened respect for Chinese policy priorities. His idiosyncratic style of personal diplomacy and policy management appears to have been another factor.[27]

With India, the Rudd government's main differences were over uranium sales, crimes against Indian students in Australia, wider policy failures in

[22] "The Growing Importance of Australia-India Trade," Australian Department of Foreign Affairs and Trade, http://www.dfat.gov.au/trade/focus/080606_aus_io_trade.html.

[23] "India-Australia Strategic Dialogue," Australian High Commission, Media Release, August 30, 2001, http://www.india.embassy.gov.au/ndli/PA_12_01.html.

[24] Paul Kelly, *The March of the Patriots: The Struggle for Modern Australia* (Melbourne: Melbourne University Press, 2010), 452.

[25] Rowan Callick, "Dysfunctional Diplomacy," *Australian*, January 15, 2010.

[26] Kevin Rudd, "A Conversation with China's Youth on the Future" (speech at Peking University, Beijing, April 9, 2008); and Kevin Rudd, "A Conversation with the Prime Minister of Australia the Hon. Kevin Rudd MP" (presentation at the Brookings Institution, Washington, D.C., March 31, 2008), http://www.brookings.edu/events/2008/0331_australia.aspx.

[27] Callick, "Dysfunctional Diplomacy."

the education relationship, and the Indian media's sensationalist reporting of these issues. Another problem was mutual misperception regarding China policy. Indian concerns about the Rudd government's supposed tilt toward China were heightened in 2008 when Australian foreign minister Stephen Smith publicly rejected Canberra's participation in a quadrilateral dialogue with Washington, New Delhi, and Tokyo during a press conference with his Chinese counterpart. In sum, the Rudd government's difficulties illuminated long-term policy challenges for Australia's engagement with both China and India.

Geopolitics and Diplomacy

Australia's contemporary interactions with China and India—since 2010 under Labor prime minister Julia Gillard, with Rudd as foreign minister— have been informed by some basic geopolitical realities. One is the scale and pace of economic growth in the two rising powers. The second is the strategic consequences of that growth: the heft it brings to India's and China's militaries and diplomacy, and the interests, responsibilities, vulnerabilities, expectations, and risks that come with such power. These massive changes in the external environment have a direct bearing on Australia's interests.

The unprecedented challenge for Canberra has been to craft a set of responses constituting a coherent strategy that can satisfy the country's economic interests, security interests, and values. Whether such a strategy exists, or is even possible, has become a matter of public debate in Australia, at least in relation to China.[28] The debate within the government would not appear to be on the same stark terms as that in the public domain. What is clear, however, is that Canberra has been trying to respond to Asia's changing power equations along multiple tracks—diplomatic, economic, security, and societal—and that tensions exist between those tracks.

The contemporary logic of Australia-China and Australia-India relations is based on the assumption that China's and India's power and impact will keep growing. Events in recent years, both involving China's regional assertiveness and in the turbulent relationship between Canberra and Beijing, have fueled Australian concerns about Beijing's power. At the same time, Australia seeks to do much more than trade with China; the bilateral relationship is multifaceted, and Canberra has been working to enmesh Beijing in a multilateral diplomatic architecture. Above all, Canberra recognizes the centrality of U.S.-China relations to regional security. Australia has strong geopolitical interest in guarding against

---

[28] Alan Dupont, "Living with the Dragon: Why Australia Needs a China Strategy," Lowy Institute for International Policy, Policy Brief, June 2011, http://www.lowyinstitute.org/Publication.asp?pid=1614.

Chinese regional dominance and considers that such a possibility could be forestalled by a combination of inclusive regional multilateralism, U.S. forward presence and alliances, and balancing strategies by other regional players—notably India, Japan, South Korea, and Indonesia.

Australia's prosperity and security are embedded in the fate of the big Northeast Asian economies (China, Japan, and South Korea), which makes the reckless actions of North Korea, and China's role in tolerating them, so troubling. Still, given Australia's geography, Canberra is also very concerned about China's geopolitical influence in maritime Southeast Asia and the South Pacific and will be watchful for any future Chinese strategic presence in the Indian Ocean. Despite the mixed results of China's charm offensive with the Association of Southeast Asian Nations (ASEAN), Australia is still conscious of a great-power contest for influence, with India potentially replacing Japan as China's main Asian rival. In East Timor, Papua New Guinea, and the island states of the South Pacific, it is Australia whose influence is being challenged. Here Canberra has long been the primary partner in development, trade, security, and diplomacy. Although Australia remains the largest aid donor in the South Pacific, China is now vying with the United States for second place.[29] Of particular concern is the fact that China's aid and engagement activities are typically unconnected or at odds with improved governance and transparency.[30]

Geopolitical interaction between Australia and India is more limited but potentially more positive. Beyond the precedent of a strategic embrace between the United States and India over the past decade, Canberra has many reasons for wanting to engage New Delhi as a strategic partner: India's democratic achievement and relative stability; its growing naval capability; its potential as latent balancer against China; common interests in combating terrorism; shared concerns about instability in Pakistan and Afghanistan; New Delhi's growing diplomatic, economic, and security role in East Asia; and the existence of common zones of direct security interest, notably the Indian Ocean. All these points informed Canberra's initiative to craft a 2009 security declaration with India, a step that can be seen as part of an emerging web of bilateral security links among U.S. allies and partners.[31]

---

[29] In 2009, Chinese aid in the Pacific was an estimated $209 million, while Australian aid was more than $650 million. Fergus Hanson and Mary Fifita, "China in the Pacific: The New Banker in Town," Lowy Institute, Policy Brief, April 2011, 5, http://www.lowyinstitute.org/Publication.asp?pid=1546.

[30] Lindsay Murdoch, "Relations Strained as East Timor Buys Chinese Navy Boats," *Sydney Morning Herald*, June 10, 2010; and Fergus Hanson, "The Dragon Looks South," Lowy Institute, June 2008, http://www.lowyinstitute.org/Publication.asp?pid=814.

[31] "India-Australia Joint Declaration on Security Cooperation," Australian High Commission, New Delhi, November 12, 2009, http://www.india.embassy.gov.au/ndli/pa5009jsb.html; and David Brewster, "The Australia-India Security Declaration: The Quadrilateral Redux?" *Security Challenges* 6, no. 1 (Autumn 2010): 1–9.

Australia and India intend to work together multilaterally, including in the East Asia Summit (EAS), where they are regional outliers. Globally, Australia supports India's bid for a permanent seat on the UN Security Council. Moreover, after an experiment in "minilateralism," notably through the core group of four countries that convened to lead relief efforts after the 2004 tsunami and later formed the quadrilateral dialogue, it is conceivable that future crises may prompt more cooperation between Canberra and New Delhi, perhaps involving additional parties such as their common maritime neighbor Indonesia or, of course, the United States.

For their part, China and India have difficulty fitting Australia into their worldviews and crowded diplomatic agendas. Nonetheless, China appears to pay more attention to Australia than does India, presumably due to the former's larger resource needs, security concerns about U.S. alliances, and strategic approach to external policy.[32] This attention has been exhibited in positive and negative ways. China has variously agreed in principle to negotiate a free trade agreement, called for an undefined "strategic" partnership, pushed for closer defense relations, and invested in soft-power efforts, such as funding Confucius Institutes at Australian universities. Yet on other occasions Beijing has tried to block Australian entry to the EAS, made diplomatic demarches against the quadrilateral dialogue, moved slowly on high-level visits, been accused of conducting large-scale espionage and harassment of dissidents in Australia, and dismissed Australian human rights concerns.[33]

The government of India, meanwhile, has been slower to engage Australia, although this is changing in light of booming resources trade and the 2009 student furor. But most of the initiative in building bilateral ties has been left to Canberra or the private sector. There remains difficulty in persuading New Delhi to treat Australia as a diplomatic priority. Lingering misperceptions about Australia's degree of independence from the United States may be a factor, although the U.S. defense partnership with India could make the Australia-U.S. alliance a channel for better Australia-India relations. Another part of this problem could simply be the challenges faced by New Delhi—with its notoriously undersized foreign service—in pursuing strategic priorities with any country. Yet by neglecting Australia, India may miss opportunities to deepen ties with a substantial, globally

---

[32] Linda Jakobson, "China Chary, Gillard on Guard ahead of Talks with Hu and Wen," *Australian*, April 25, 2011.

[33] Craig Skehan, "Chen's Pitch to Congress May Fuel Row with China," *Sydney Morning Herald*, July 20, 2005, http://www.smh.com.au/news/national/chens-pitch-to-congress-may-fuel-row-with-china/2005/07/19/1121538975641.html; and "China Questions Aussie Human Rights Record," *Age*, April 27, 2011, http://news.theage.com.au/breaking-news-national/china-questions-aussie-human-rights-record-20110427-1dvah.html.

connected regional partner.[34] No Indian prime minister has visited Australia since Rajiv Gandhi in 1986 and Manmohan Singh's decision not to attend the British Commonwealth summit in Perth in October 2011 has caused fresh disappointment in Australia.[35]

Economics

Economics have a huge bearing on the evolving strategic relations between Australia and the Asian giants. This is mainly due to the complementarity of their economic growth and Australia's resource endowments, though Australia's institutional stability and geographical proximity are also factors.[36]

China is now firmly entrenched as Australia's largest export market and trading partner, and the trading relationship is growing at an average of 27% a year.[37] In 2010, almost a quarter of Australia's total exports went to China. The scale of the two-way trading relationship, which passed A$100 billion in 2010, is ahead of Australia's other major bilateral trading relationships with Japan, India, South Korea, and the United States by an order of magnitude.[38] Although the balance is in Canberra's favor, Australia also imports billions of dollars worth of Chinese goods. Australia's main exports are resources and energy, including coal, natural gas, uranium, and iron ore, which dwarfs all else. The country is China's largest iron ore supplier (followed by Brazil and India), and China is overwhelmingly the main destination for Australian ore. China accounts for 71% of Australia's total iron ore exports, a trade dominated by a few corporations such as BHP Billiton and Rio Tinto and focused in the Pilbara region in northwest Australia. Export earnings from this trade have grown rapidly, thanks to Chinese demand as well as to a series of dramatic price rises, which have raised political concerns in China. Given that Australia's economic health is connected to China's construction boom, a collapse in Chinese demand

---

[34] Rory Medcalf, "Australia-India Relations: Hesitating on the Brink of Partnership," East-West Center, Asia-Pacific Bulletin, no. 13, April 3, 2008.

[35] "Indian PM Pulls Out of CHOGM," *Sydney Morning Herald*, August 11, 2011, http://news.smh.com.au/breaking-news-national/indian-pm-pulls-out-of-chogm-20110811-1int9.html.

[36] In 2010, merchandise exports to China were valued at A$58.3 billion and accounted for 25.3% of all Australian exports. Iron ore, the country's top export, made up the largest share of this figure at A$34.6 billion. In the same period, Australian exports to India brought in A$16.4 billion and made up 7.1% of total merchandise exports. At A$6.8 billion, coal was Australia's biggest export to India, while exports of gold were second-largest at A$5.3 billion. "Country and Region Fact Sheets," Australian Department of Foreign Affairs and Trade, June 2011, http://www.dfat.gov.au/geo/fs/.

[37] Department of Foreign Affairs and Trade of the Australian Government, *Composition of Trade Australia 2010*, 29, 31.

[38] Julia Gillard, "Speech to the Australia-China Economic and Co-operation Trade Forum," Prime Minister of Australia, Press Office, April 26, 2011, http://www.pm.gov.au/press-office/speech-australia-china-economic-and-co-operation-trade-forum-beijing.

for steel would leave Australia scrambling, and India remains far from ready as a replacement market. It is little wonder that Australia has begun trying to diversify into greater services trade with China, such as in finance, education, tourism, and environmental management.

Where the economic relationship has encountered trouble is in Chinese state-owned corporations' investment in Australia. The level of such investment has grown rapidly: in the past five years China has invested more in Australia than in any other country, concentrated in the resources sector.[39] In 2008–9, China was the second-largest foreign investor in Australia, and in 2009–10 it became the third largest.[40] Canberra has accepted the overwhelming majority of Chinese and other foreign investment bids, either outright or with amendments.

Political tensions arose, however, over the failure of the contentious bids by Chinese state-owned enterprise (SOE) Chinalco to increase its stake in Rio Tinto in 2008 and 2009, aimed in part at strengthening China's position in price negotiations for iron ore. The ultimate decision by Rio Tinto to reject the bid and opt instead for a partnership with rival BHP was not an act of government. But it came after BHP's reported lobbying of Canberra against a Chinalco–Rio Tinto alliance and amid heightened public concern about the potential impact of large Chinese state investments in strategic sectors of the Australian economy.[41] The collapse of the Rio Tinto–Chinalco talks relieved Canberra of having to show its hand, but perceptions in Beijing of a less-than-compliant Australian government were reinforced by other developments: the special scrutiny accorded to SOEs and sovereign wealth funds by the nation's foreign investment rules and the curbs placed on other Chinese resource investment bids, including one related to rare earth deposits and others involving sensitive military locations. Nonetheless, Chinese investment in Australia is expected to continue, including in infrastructure to expand capacity for resource exports. The Australian government and business community, meanwhile, have become increasingly frustrated at Beijing's much greater restrictions on foreign investment in China.

---

[39] Rowan Callick, "We Are No Threat, China Seeks to Assure," *Weekend Australian*, February 12–13, 2011.

[40] According to Australian government statistics, the United States was the largest source country for foreign investment in Australia in 2009–10 at A\$39.1 billion, followed by the United Kingdom (A\$28.6 billion) and China (A\$16.3 billion). In the previous year, China was the second-largest foreign investor after the United States at A\$26.6 billion. Foreign Investment Review Board, *Annual Report 2009–2010* (Canberra, 2011), http://www.firb.gov.au/content/Publications/AnnualReports/2009-2010/_downloads/2009-10_FIRB_AR.pdf; and Foreign Investment Review Board, *Annual Report 2008–2009* (Canberra, 2010), http://www.firb.gov.au/content/Publications/AnnualReports/2008-2009/_downloads/2008-09_FIRB_AR.pdf.

[41] "BHP 'Lobbied to Scuttle Rio-Chinalco Deal,'" *Sydney Morning Herald*, December 11, 2010, http://news.smh.com.au/breaking-news-world/bhp-lobbied-to-scuttle-riochinalco-deal-20101211-18tm8.html.

India's economic relationship with Australia is markedly smaller than China's: the two-way Australia-India trade relationship is less than a quarter of the two-way Australia-China trade relationship. Nonetheless, bilateral trade with India has been fast-growing and weighty in its own right. The country has become Australia's fourth-largest export market and has the potential to overtake South Korea and eventually Japan for second place. India receives half of Australia's gold exports and about 15.8% of its coal and is considered the best growth prospect for the latter industry.[42] Australia is also beginning to sell natural gas to India. In addition, the Labor Party could withdraw its opposition to uranium exports to India, although the damage to the reputation of the nuclear industry following the 2011 Fukushima disaster may make moving on this issue politically difficult for Canberra.[43] There has also been strong bilateral trade in services, especially education, although the number of Indian students studying in Australia has declined after recent controversies, particularly over safety.

Investment levels are also rising in both directions, including investments by Australian service and construction companies in India and a growing—and generally welcome—flow of Indian investors in Australian resources and related infrastructure such as ports.[44] In contrast to the experience with China, such investment is not perceived in Australia as posing strategic challenges, coming as it does from the Indian private sector rather than from the SOEs of a one-party state. Although the practices of some Indian entrepreneurs have left a sour taste, others have revived flagging industries and become local heroes.[45]

Societal Links and Perceptions

The societal dimension figures prominently in Australian relations with China and India, and Australia's nature as a multicultural society of immigrants means that this factor can only grow. People of Chinese and of Indian origin now constitute Australia's largest migrant communities after British and New Zealanders and are among the fastest-growing

---

[42] Australian coal exports to India were worth A$6.8 billion in 2010. "India Fact Sheet," Australian Department of Foreign Affairs and Trade, June 2011, http://www.dfat.gov.au/geo/fs/inia.pdf; and author's personal communication with the Department of Foreign Affairs and Trade, July 14, 2011.

[43] Katharine Murphy, "Nuclear Rethink Over before It's Begun," *Sydney Morning Herald*, March 17, 2011, http://www.smh.com.au/opinion/politics/nuclear-rethink-over-before-its-begun-20110316-1bx94.html.

[44] Dinakar Sethuraman, "Adani Selected to Develop Coal Port in Queensland, Australia," *Bloomberg Businessweek*, July 12, 2010, http://www.businessweek.com/news/2010-07-12/adani-selected-to-develop-coal-port-in-queensland-australia.html.

[45] Colin Kruger, "The Ammonia and Acrimony Remain," *Sydney Morning Herald*, January 29, 2011; and "Indian Mining Firm to Invest $500 Million in NSW Coal Mines," *Australian Mining*, March 12, 2010, http://www.miningaustralia.com.au/news/indian-mining-firm-to-invest-500-million-in-nsw-co.

demographic groups. By early 2011, Australia's population of 23 million included an estimated 700,000 people of Chinese descent,[46] more than half of whom were first-generation immigrants. The Indian community is smaller—in 2009, there were 308,000 Indian-born Australians—but its numbers are increasing rapidly. In 2009 the Indian population grew by 17%, whereas the Chinese community grew by only 9%.[47] India has become Australia's second-largest source of skilled professionals after the United Kingdom.[48] Of note also is the concentration of Chinese-Australians in Sydney, the country's largest city, as well as their above-average levels of wealth and education.

Another large part of the human element of Australia's relations with China and India is the role of tourists and students. The numbers of Chinese and Indian tourists visiting Australia have been growing by roughly 20% a year. China is expected to overtake the United Kingdom, the United States, and Japan to become Australia's largest and most lucrative source of tourists, while India is on track to become the fifth-largest source.[49] Likewise, China, followed by India, is the largest source of foreign university students in Australia. In 2010, there were 167,000 Chinese students enrolled in Australian universities, compared to 128,000 in the United States.[50] Meanwhile a different cohort of Indian students—from provincial and aspirational backgrounds—filled Australian vocational courses when this was briefly permitted as a shortcut to legal residency in order to fill labor gaps. At its peak in 2009, an estimated 120,000 fee-paying young Indians enrolled in Australian vocational colleges and universities.[51] These numbers have declined after controversies over violent crime and the standards of some vocational courses, as well as after a tightening of

---

[46] Julia Gillard, "Speech to the Australian Council of Chinese Organisations Dinner in Celebration of Australia Day and Chinese New Year," Prime Minister of Australia, Press Office, January 22, 2011, http://www.pm.gov.au/press-office/speech-australian-council-chinese-organisations-dinner-celebration-australia-day-and-ch.

[47] "Country of Birth," Australian Bureau of Statistics, http://www.abs.gov.au/AUSSTATS/abs@.nsf/Lookup/92C0101965E7DC14CA25773700169C63?opendocument.

[48] "Indian Community in Australia," High Commission of India in Australia, http://www.hcindia-au.org/indian_in_australia.html.

[49] "Key Facts: Australian Tourism Sector," Australian Department of Resources, Energy and Tourism, http://www.ret.gov.au/tourism/Documents/Tourism%20Statistics/Tourism_Key_Facts_web.pdf; "Chinese Tourists Top Monthly Visits to Australia for First Time," China Daily, April 6, 2011, http://www.chinadaily.com.cn/business/2011-04/06/content_12278248.htm; and "Minister Opens Tourism Office in India," Australian Minister for Tourism, Press Release, November 3, 2008, http://minister.ret.gov.au/MediaCentre/MediaReleases/Pages/MinisterOpensTourismAustraliaOfficeinIndia.aspx.

[50] Gillard, "Speech to the Australia-China Economic and Co-operation Trade Forum"; and "Around 128,000 Chinese Students Study in U.S.," People's Daily, November 16, 2010, http://english.peopledaily.com.cn/90001/90776/90882/7201401.html.

[51] "Ministerial Statement on the Australia-India Relationship," Stephen Smith, Australian Minister for Foreign Affairs, February 9, 2010, http://www.foreignminister.gov.au/speeches/2010/100209_australia_india.html.

visa rules to control the quality of education-related migrants. Reports of criminal attacks, including a few with racist overtones, against some Indian students stirred nationalist outrage and sometimes hysterical criticism of Australia in the Indian media.[52] The diplomatic fallout and lasting damage to Australia's image demonstrate that even the combination of large-scale societal interaction and shared democratic values does not automatically make for a positive bilateral relationship with a rising India. Indeed, the gulf of cultural misunderstanding between India and Australia appears in some ways greater than between Australia and China.[53] In a media-charged environment of societal mistrust between two democracies, the role of governments in implementing good policy and devoting resources to public diplomacy is becoming critical.

So far the foreign policy and strategic impacts of the Chinese and Indian diasporas in Australia have been relatively modest. Generally, neither community has organized or mobilized to effect major change in Canberra's external orientation in the way that Indian-Americans, for example, lobbied for the 2008 India-U.S. nuclear deal. But this can be expected to change as these communities grow. Questions remain about the influence growing Chinese and Indian communities may wield in Australia or the positions they will take, including whether their view toward one another will be primarily competitive, cooperative, or indifferent. Also unknown is whether ideological, interest-based, or cultural divisions within these communities might prevent their acting as cohesive political forces.

Chinese and Indian communities could influence Australian policy through parliamentary channels, as was perhaps seen with the swing of Chinese-Australian voters against the Labor Party in 2010, following its removal of Kevin Rudd as prime minister.[54] But the impact of these communities may also develop through extra-constitutional means. In 2008, many Australians were disturbed by the spectacle of perhaps 10,000 pro-Beijing demonstrators—many of them Chinese students—at the Olympic torch relay in Canberra, noisily drowning out small Tibetan and human rights protests. There have been credible allegations of China's official orchestration of this activity.[55] By contrast, the largest mobilization of Indians in Australia consisted of spontaneous protests by Indian students

---

52 Ashok Malik, "No Longer Out of Focus," *Hindustan Times*, June 7, 2009, http://www.hindustantimes.com/No-longer-out-of-focus/Article1-418970.aspx.

53 Mutual allegations of racism or disrespect have featured in multiple controversies between India and Australia, including on the cricket field and during the 2010 Commonwealth Games.

54 Imre Salusinszky, "Liberal MP John Alexander Unseats Maxine McKew in Bennelong," *Australian*, August 21, 2010.

55 Ben English, "Chinese Embassy 'Helped Get Rent-A-Crowd' to Relay," *Daily Telegraph*, April 25 2008.

against alleged racial violence in Melbourne in 2009—an outcry which initially drew considerable Australian public sympathy. These protests, amplified by the Indian media, compelled New Delhi to pressure Canberra and thereby influenced Australian policing, education standards, and visa rules. But the experience also left Australian authorities wary of the Indian media, whose sensationalist coverage stereotyped Australians as racist, and may have had a negative impact on how many Australians view India. At the same time, an increase in high-level political attention to the bilateral relationship may have offset any short-term damage to mutual perceptions.

Despite growing engagement with people of Chinese or Indian nationality or descent, Australians appear to be generally unsentimental about both countries. They welcome their own economic gains from these nations' growth, yet worry about China's strategic impact. In opinion polls, most Australians indicate feeling neither particularly warm nor cold toward Asia's rising giants.[56] A similar degree of ambivalence is reflected in the low level of trust many Australians accord India and China to act responsibly in the world.[57]

Australians' mistrust of a rising China, in particular, is sharpening. Only 35% of Australians were worried about a potential threat from China's growing power in a 2005 poll, a figure that had fallen to 19% by 2007.[58] Yet in 2008 this trend began to reverse, seemingly in line with broader concerns about Beijing's actions and image. That year, 34% of Australians regarded China as a "critical threat," and this number rose to 40% in 2009. Furthermore, the percentage of Australians believing that China's aim was to "dominate Asia" rose from 60% in 2008 to 69% in 2010.[59] By 2010, 55% of Australians supported the view that Canberra "should join with other countries to limit China's influence," and in early 2011 56% expressed the view that Australia should help South Korea in the event of war with North Korea, even if China supported the North.[60] Many Australians appear to attach value to the U.S. alliance because of such concerns about Chinese power. Between 2005 and 2007, as public concern about China waned, the

---

[56] Hanson, *The Lowy Institute Poll 2010*, 19.

[57] In polls between 2006 and 2009, just under half the respondents indicated low levels of trust in China and India. Fergus Hanson, *The Lowy Institute Poll 2009* (Sydney: Lowy Institute for International Policy, 2009), 7.

[58] Ivan Cook, *The Lowy Institute Poll 2005* (Sydney: Lowy Institute for International Policy, 2005), 1; Ivan Cook, *The Lowy Institute Poll 2006* (Sydney: Lowy Institute for International Policy, 2006), 38; and Allan Gyngell, *The Lowy Institute Poll 2007* (Sydney: Lowy Institute for International Policy, 2007), 8.

[59] Fergus Hanson, *The Lowy Institute Poll 2008* (Sydney: Lowy Institute for International Policy, 2008), 10; and Hanson, *The Lowy Institute Poll 2009*, 10; and Hanson, *The Lowy Institute Poll 2010*, 10.

[60] Hanson, *The Lowy Institute Poll 2010*, 10; and Brendan Nicholson, "Aussie Troops Should Defend South Korea," *Australian*, April 25, 2011, http://www.theaustralian.com.au/national-affairs/aussie-troops-should-defend-south-korea/story-fn59niix-1226044204452.

number of poll respondents who regarded the alliance as "very important" declined. Similarly, coinciding with increasing apprehension about China's intentions, there was a notable lift in support for the alliance, with the percentage of Australians who termed it "very important" growing from 42% in 2008 to 56% in 2010.[61]

At the same time, Australians hold overwhelmingly positive views about China's economic impact. In 2010, 73% still felt that "China's growth has been good for Australia." Admittedly, most of the public believes the government has not done enough to pressure China on human rights, leading some observers to argue that many Australians seem willing to sacrifice some economic benefit in the name of democratic values.[62] Nonetheless, the Australian business community is by and large an advocate for the bilateral relationship and would be loath to see it jeopardized.[63] There is thus the potential for real tension between the business community's enthusiasm about China and the greater wariness found among the security establishment and much of the public.

Security Relations

The security dimension of Australia's interaction with China and India involves active efforts to build constructive military engagement with both powers. With China, although limited cooperation may eventually be possible, the main objective is to establish mutual understanding and transparency. Despite professional cordiality, the military relationship involves undercurrents of mistrust based on the recognition of potentially conflicting security interests and values. With India, Australia's goal is more ambitious: to move from dialogue to practical cooperation under a formal strategic partnership, including in Indian Ocean maritime security.[64] Yet convergent security interests and values have not ensured rapid progress in military trust and cooperation between Canberra and New Delhi.

Australia is ahead of most democracies in its defense relations with China, with the two countries holding a range of annual talks up to the level of chief of defense force, as well as performing occasional bilateral exercises. In September 2010 an Australian frigate took part in China's first-ever live fire exercise with a Western navy, prompting some quiet consternation in

---

[61] Gyngell, *The Lowy Institute Poll 2007*, 13; and Hanson, *The Lowy Institute Poll 2008*, 9.

[62] Andrew Shearer, "Sweet and Sour: Australian Public Attitudes towards China," Lowy Institute for International Policy, Analysis, August 2010.

[63] The main relevant body and lobby group, the Australia-China Business Council, represents more than seven hundred companies. For further details, see the council's official website at http://www.acbc.com.au/default.asp?id=1,1,0,1.

[64] Australian Department of Defence, *Defending Australia in the Asia Pacific Century*, 95–96.

Japan and even reportedly within parts of the Australian government.[65] In early 2011, Prime Minister Gillard declared the aim of expanding defense relations with China.[66] Canberra has a mix of reasons for this objective, including a recognition of the potential impact of growing Chinese military power both as a destabilizing force and as a provider of public goods, demonstrated by the antipiracy naval taskforces China has been sending to the Gulf of Aden.

Australia uses such military-to-military relations as a channel to assess China's strategic intentions and to influence Beijing on issues such as transparency and confidence-building measures in order to reduce the risks from incidents at sea. The maintenance of an Australia-China defense dialogue during periods of disruption in U.S.-China, Japan-China, or indeed India-China security relations could provide an avenue to relay messages to and from China on these issues. Notably, Canberra and Beijing sustained defense talks and activities in 2010, a time of heightened tension in these other relationships. Nonetheless, like these other relationships, Australia's defense engagement with China is vulnerable to political winds. Some observers argue that China cooled down defense relations in 2009 to signal displeasure about the perceived "China threat" message of the Australian defense white paper. For a brief phase, it was Canberra that seemed to need Washington as a diplomatic bridge to Beijing.[67] Even so, China did not suspend military ties entirely, suggesting that it places a special value on keeping lines of communication open with Canberra.

With India, Australia has again had difficulty converting shared interests and values into a strong security relationship. To be sure, defense ties have grown respectably since their suspension over Indian nuclear tests. There are now national security adviser and ministerial talks, political-military dialogues, meetings between defense force and service chiefs, staff college exchanges, and ship visits. But the tempo of exercises remains slow, and their content and scale generally modest. Little progress, and indeed some regression, has occurred regarding shared participation in advanced multilateral exercises. For example, Australia has not taken part in a U.S.-India Malabar exercise since a five-nation

[65] Author's interviews with Japanese scholars and officials, Tokyo, October 2010; John Garnaut, "Rudd Secures Human Rights Dialogue," *Sydney Morning Herald*, November 5, 2010, 1; and "Royal Australian Navy Joins China in Live Fire Exercise," Royal Australian Navy, Press Release, September 24, 2010, http://www.navy.gov.au/Royal_Australian_Navy_joins_China_in_live_fire_exercise.

[66] Simon Benson, "Our China Plates—Julia Gillard Seeks Closer Defence Links to Chinese Military," *Daily Telegraph*, April 28, 2011, http://www.dailytelegraph.com.au/news/national/our-china-plates-gillard-seeks-closer-defence-links-to-chinese-military/story-e6freuzr-1226045883726.

[67] John Garnaut, "Rudd Secures Human Rights Dialogue"; and Jonathan Pearlman, "Australia, U.S. Call on China for War Games," *Sydney Morning Herald*, September 3, 2009, http://www.smh.com.au/world/australia-us-call-on-china-for-war-games-20090902-f8h4.html.

drill in 2007 that also involved Japan and Singapore, and in 2008 India declined an Australian invitation to join a Kakadu multilateral naval exercise. Moreover, despite apparent Australian enthusiasm, progress has been slow in deepening the security relationship in other areas, such as logistics, industry, and intelligence-sharing, although counterterrorism cooperation at the 2010 Commonwealth Games may help convince India of Australia's special capabilities. The 2009 joint security declaration anticipates cooperation in many of these areas, but implementation seems to have been obstructed by wider problems, particularly Indian dissatisfaction over Australia's refusal to export uranium, which New Delhi appears to define as a barometer of trust. And there are other potential irritants in the security area. One is India's efforts to sell Brahmos antiship cruise missiles in Southeast Asia, a zone where Australia wants to retain a capability edge. Another is Australian counterinsurgency training for Pakistani military officers.

Nonetheless, solid bilateral defense cooperation is likely a matter of time, given the range of interests and concerns the two democracies have in common, including the situations in Afghanistan-Pakistan, Southeast Asia, and the Indian Ocean and regarding Chinese military modernization. Both also share British-inspired traditions of naval diplomacy. India's widening acquisition of U.S. platforms and systems—a mainstay of Australia's technological edge—will add a capability imperative to these convergent threat perceptions. Both nations, for instance, are purchasing P-8 Poseidon surveillance and submarine-hunting aircraft, which will operate in adjoining or overlapping subregions of the Indian Ocean, creating potential opportunities for cooperation in training and maintenance as well as in building a shared operational picture. Both countries could also benefit from exchanging insights into their maritime force modernization efforts. In particular, India could benefit from Australia's specialized facilities and capabilities, such as in submarine training and rescue. The parallel deepening of the U.S.-India defense partnership and the Australia-U.S. alliance could likewise open new doors for positive interaction between the Australian and Indian militaries.

Nuclear Nonproliferation

One security issue that sharply illuminates Australia's dilemmas in dealing with the rise of China and India is nuclear nonproliferation and arms control. Here Australia has struggled to reconcile its status as a major uranium supplier, champion of nonproliferation, and U.S. ally.[68] A 2006 agreement opened the way for Australia to export safeguarded uranium to China for civilian purposes. Yet, the brief 2007 shift by Howard notwithstanding, Canberra has refused to do the same for India on the grounds that India has not acceded to the NPT. Australia would seem to have failed to achieve any particular nonproliferation leverage from sales to China, given that Beijing has been less than wholehearted in pressuring Iran and North Korea to abandon their nuclear weapons ambitions and has not even declared that China has ceased producing its own fissile material. There is limited common ground between Australia and China on most nuclear issues, other than in obvious areas such as NPT membership and disarmament rhetoric. Australia is a recipient of U.S. extended deterrence, a strong advocate of the entry into force of the Comprehensive Nuclear-Test-Ban Treaty and the commencement of negotiations on a Fissile Material Cutoff Treaty, and broadly supportive of U.S. policies on most nuclear issues, including the Obama administration's efforts to begin a strategic stability dialogue with China.

Turning to India, differences over the NPT and uranium exports remain a major thorn in the bilateral relationship. The Labor government, which since 2010 has been informally allied with the anti-nuclear Greens party, has not changed its policy of prohibiting uranium exports to India, despite Australia's support for the U.S.-India deal and subsequent Nuclear Suppliers Group waiver. Canberra and New Delhi have had limited success in finding common ground on other nuclear and arms control issues, despite Canberra's increased willingness to acknowledge India's good nonproliferation record and the parallels between both countries' nuclear disarmament agendas.[69] In late 2010, the Obama administration leapt ahead of the government in Canberra in calling for Indian admission to export control regimes, even though this was one area where Australia could have taken the lead without breaching the letter of the Labor Party's non-export policy. The conservative opposition in Australia, meanwhile, has long shifted from seeing India as part of the global proliferation problem to seeing it as part of the solution and now openly backs uranium sales to India. By early 2011, even some Labor ministers were openly calling for

---

[68] "Australia," in *Preventing Nuclear Dangers in Southeast Asia and Australasia*, ed. Mark Fitzpatrick (London: International Institute for Strategic Studies, 2009).

[69] A global panel of experts sponsored by the Australian and Japanese governments supported much of the Indian nuclear arms control agenda—for instance, the advocacy of a "no first use" policy. See Gareth Evans and Yoriko Kawaguchi, *Eliminating Nuclear Threats: A Practical Agenda for Global Policymakers* (Canberra/Tokyo: International Commission on Nuclear Non-proliferation and Disarmament, 2009), http://www.icnnd.org/Reference/reports/ent/contents.html.

a change to their own government's position.[70] Thus, it is probably only a matter of time before Australia exports uranium to India, whether as a result of a debate within the Labor Party or simply the next change of government. The delayed timing of any such policy shift—at least six years after the U.S. nuclear deal with India—means that Canberra's gains in securing Indian political trust and goodwill are likely to be modest.

Australia's Strategies

The rise of China and India poses unprecedented dilemmas for Australia in reconciling its security interests, democratic values, and economic well-being. Each of these policy drivers can in some circumstances reinforce the others, as is typically the case in Australia's engagement with the United States or India. But in other situations the drivers can cut across each other, especially in relation to China.

The scale and impact of the rise of China and India, combined with the tensions among Australia's policy drivers, raise a series of questions about Canberra's future response. The key question is whether all three drivers can be integrated into a coherent national strategy. Even if this could be achieved, how sustainable would such a strategy be if China-U.S. relations, China-India relations, or both became locked in patterns of strategic competition or confrontation? On the other hand, if an integrated strategy proved either impossible or unsustainable, which one or two of the three drivers might predominate in defining Australian policy choices? Would the U.S.-allied security alignment, democratic values, or primacy of economics determine Canberra's direction in an era of a powerful China and India?

None of these questions has yet been fully resolved in Australia's deliberations. A debate is developing about how to respond to the rise of China, and a mature policy discussion is beginning to take shape on the rise of India. But there has been little sophisticated public discourse so far on how Canberra's China and India policies might interact, or on how Australia may need to reshape itself to prepare for a contested region of multiple Asian great powers.[71] What debate does occur in Australia will fluctuate and evolve in response to changes in domestic politics as well as in the international environment. Australian politics entered a phase of

---

[70] "Labor Must Lift Ban on Uranium Sales to India," Liberal Party of Australia, Press Release, October 10, 2010, http://www.liberal.org.au/Latest-News/2010/10/28/Labor-must-lift-ban-on-uranium-sales-to-India.aspx; and Katharine Murphy, "Sell India Uranium, Minister Says," Age, February 16, 2011, http://www.theage.com.au/national/sell-india-uranium-minister-says-20110215-1av4i.html.

[71] Michael Wesley, There Goes the Neighbourhood: Australia and the Rise of Asia (Sydney: New South Books, 2011).

deep uncertainty when the cliffhanger August 2010 election result led to the formation of a minority Labor government under Prime Minister Gillard.[72] In these circumstances, Canberra has become more vulnerable than usual to a political agenda influenced by opinion polls and the media, encouraging short-term solutions and even policy paralysis.[73] These are hardly ideal times to be fashioning a long-term strategy to cope with major geopolitical change.

Some observers claim that Australia is failing to shape much of a strategy at all or that it has failed to gain leverage from its economic advantages—for instance, through extracting diplomatic benefits from major powers in return for a privileged supply of resources.[74] On the security side, one prominent view is that any approach based on unconditionally siding with Washington militarily while relying on China economically is bound to fail. According to this perspective, following current trajectories, Australia's interests as an economic partner with China will clash with its interests as a U.S. security partner. Australia would, therefore, be wise to encourage the United States to accommodate Chinese power and minimize risks of confrontation.[75] What is not clear from such arguments, however, is precisely what kind or level of accommodation is being proposed—for instance, over the status of Taiwan or the South China Sea—and what the wider strategic effects might be.

Australian leaders, meanwhile, have publicly asserted that their country does not need to make an ultimate choice between seeking security against China and securing prosperity in partnership with it. Howard, for instance, sought to run relations with China on two parallel tracks: one involving close economic ties and diplomatic mutual respect, the other involving security and values alignment with the United States. Rudd briefly tried to combine the two tracks in a relationship of frankness with China, whereas Gillard and her successors will likely try to revert to the logic and even rhetoric of the Howard era, as suggested by talk of "mutual respect" and the low-key references to human rights during her business-oriented visit

---

[72] This election took place shortly after Gillard replaced Rudd in an internal party coup. From then through the time of writing, Labor has had an uneasy grip on government in an informal alliance with the left-wing Greens party and three independent parliamentarians. Rudd has remained as foreign minister, and there appear to be persistent differences within the cabinet about foreign policy that cannot easily be confronted because the party needs Rudd's support to retain its fragile majority in parliament. See Dennis Shanahan, "Allies Confused by 'Two Policies,'" *Weekend Australian*, March 12–13, 2011.

[73] George Megalogenis, *Trivial Pursuit: Leadership and the End of the Reform Era*, Quarterly Essay 40 (Collingwood: Black Inc., 2010).

[74] Richard Leaver and Carl Ungerer, *A Natural Power: Challenges for Australia's Resources Diplomacy in Asia* (Canberra: Australian Strategic Policy Institute, 2010), 16–21.

[75] White, *Power Shift*.

to Beijing in April 2011.[76] The challenge will be to make this approach work in a more challenging context, involving growing levels of Chinese power, Sino-Australian enmeshment, Australian public anxieties, and Sino-U.S. strategic competition.

Furthermore, Asia's strategic environment is characterized by wider changes no middle power can control: shifting power balances, the decisions of major powers, and the recklessness of other states, such as North Korea. Sooner or later, these may force painful choices upon a reluctant Australia. The most fundamental and obvious is the question of Australian support for the United States in a military confrontation with China, but India's rise means that less familiar dilemmas may also emerge. There is little appetite so far in Australia for taking sides on bilateral issues between China and India. For example, when asked to declare Australia's position on the status of Arunachal Pradesh, officials have attempted to not offend China or India, at the risk of annoying both.[77] It may become more difficult for Australia to stay aloof if Chinese behavior toward India fits a pattern of assertiveness seen elsewhere in the Indo-Pacific region (for instance, against Japan or Southeast Asian states). Looking to the future of the Indian Ocean, eventually a larger Chinese military presence could confront Australia with a clear choice: to support possible Indian or U.S. efforts to limit Chinese influence or to work with India and the United States to find ways to accommodate China's legitimate security interests as a maritime trading nation without compromising vital interests.

Despite all the reasons why Australia might be reluctant or ill-prepared to make strategic decisions, the contours of a strategy are emerging. Canberra is beginning to reveal some significant choices in response to China's and India's rise. If sustained, these will provide building blocks for an integrated national approach. Two broad elements can be identified. The first is enhanced diplomatic engagement and economic enmeshment with China and India. The second is a security strategy of hedging against the impacts of Chinese power through modernizing Australia's maritime forces, intensifying the U.S. alliance, and building security links with other Asian powers, including India.

Engagement and Enmeshment

China is a priority diplomatic partner for Australia across the board, from economics—with Australia keen to finalize a free trade agreement—to

---

[76] Gillard, "Speech to the Australia-China Economic and Cooperation Trade Forum."

[77] "After Helping China, Australia Says Arunachal Belongs to India," *Zee News*, September 24, 2009, http://www.zeenews.com/news566108.html.

science, education, culture, and tourism. The political, personal, and soft-power contacts between Australia and China are generally more advanced than those with India. Australia's ambitions for defense engagement with China, though real, have built-in limits owing to strategic differences. In contrast, Canberra's strategy toward India involves greater alignment of trade, security, and values. Australia has substantially increased efforts to engage with its fellow Indian Ocean democracy by trying to affirm Australia's value to India, including through offers of security cooperation and the 2010 opening of negotiations on a free trade agreement. Australia is additionally investing in a large diplomatic presence, public diplomacy campaigns, and scientific collaboration.

Conscious of the limits of its bilateral heft as a middle power, Canberra is also seeking to entangle the giants in multilateral institutions.[78] Regionally, it has worked to expand the EAS to include all key powers. Globally, Australia has promoted the group of twenty (G-20) summit, thus involving itself, as well as China and India, in what it sees as the new preeminent world summit. Nonetheless, Australian policymakers are realistic about the limits of multilateralism. A seemingly idealistic effort by Rudd to promote an Asia-Pacific community of nations soon yielded to the much more limited goal of supporting U.S. and Russian admission to the EAS. And while Australia also dutifully supports the ASEAN Regional Forum and the new ASEAN Defense Ministers' Meeting Plus Eight—and has called for these, along with the EAS, to be venues for discussing serious interstate security problems such as the South China Sea—Canberra is under no illusions that major powers will allow such meetings to mediate their core differences. Moreover, although it is working with New Delhi to revive the moribund regionalism in the Indian Ocean,[79] Canberra is unlikely to entrust that region's security primarily to such forums and their motley membership. Australia knows well the limits of multilateralism to engage the giants, as Chinese and Indian obstructionism at the Copenhagen climate change summit demonstrated in late 2009.

Balancing: A Stronger Military, the U.S. Alliance, and the Asian Security Web

The 2009 defense white paper called for a large increase in Australia's maritime strategic weight by 2030. This was a marked shift for defense policy,

---

[78] Scott Dewar, "Australia and China and the United States: Responding to Changing Great Power Dynamics," Australian Centre on China in the World, Research Paper, August 2011, http://ciw.anu.edu.au/research_papers.

[79] "Australia-India Foreign Ministers' Framework Dialogue," Australian Minister for Foreign Affairs, http://www.foreignminister.gov.au/releases/2011/kr_mr_110120.html.

which has traditionally aimed for a balanced force, designed as much for transnational challenges as for interstate conflict. The proposed "Force 2030" includes doubling the submarine fleet to twelve boats of a new and advanced design, acquiring larger surface combatants, equipping ships and submarines with land-attack cruise missiles, improving maritime surveillance, and proceeding with the Howard government's proposed major purchases, notably one hundred F-35 Joint Strike Fighters, three Aegis air warfare destroyers, and two 27,000-ton flat-deck amphibious ships.[80] It is an ambitious plan for a new force structure, and one that is unlikely to materialize in full. The proposal has been criticized for both being poorly costed and ignoring existing deficiencies, such as technical problems and crew staffing shortfalls in the current fleet of six submarines. In light of such challenges, it would take a major external shock for Canberra to heed the suggestions of strategists who have called for a radically stronger Australian military, one that might be capable of single-handedly deterring a major power.[81]

The Australian defense white paper also reaffirmed an enduring U.S. alliance, involving greater interoperability with U.S. forces and U.S. extended nuclear deterrence. In late 2010 and again when Prime Minister Gillard visited the United States in early 2011, Canberra and Washington publicly agreed to adapt and strengthen the alliance for future challenges in Asia. Their steps include renewed joint efforts in intelligence, surveillance, and reconnaissance, as well as in the space and cyber domains.[82] In a significant departure, Australia has signaled a willingness to consider greater U.S. military access to its territory in the context of the global force posture review. There is speculation about an increased tempo of ship visits and exercises, logistics hubs, and even the possibility of an eventual U.S. military presence in Australia.[83] Some observers have also suggested that there might be mutual interest in Australian forces operating out of U.S. facilities, such as Guam.[84]

In tandem with this alliance, Australia is strengthening bilateral security relations with other key regional players—namely, Japan, South Korea,

---

[80] Australian Department of Defence, *Defending Australia in the Asia Pacific Century*.

[81] Ross Babbage, "Learning to Walk Amongst Giants: The New Defence White Paper," *Security Challenges* 4, no. 1 (Autumn 2008): 13–20, http://www.securitychallenges.org.au/ArticlePages/vol4no1Babbage.html.

[82] "AUSMIN 2010 Joint Communique," Australian Minister of Foreign Affairs, http://www.foreignminister.gov.au/releases/2010/kr_mr_101108.html.

[83] Phillip Coorey, "Gillard Keen for Closer Military Ties with the U.S.," *Sydney Morning Herald*, March 9, 2011, http://www.smh.com.au/world/gillard-keen-for-closer-military-ties-with-the-us-20110308-1bmo5.html.

[84] Thomas G. Mahnken and Andrew Shearer, "Leading in the Indian Ocean," *Wall Street Journal*, March 10, 2011, http://online.wsj.com/article/SB10001424052748704132204576190052669099280.html.

India, and Indonesia—through formal declarations supported by regular dialogue and practical activities. Additionally, Canberra has experimented occasionally with combining such partnerships with the U.S. alliance, or indeed with each other, to achieve minilateral dialogues or activities, of which the Trilateral Strategic Dialogue with Japan and the United States has been the most enduring and effective. In the years ahead, Australia might consider other such functional arrangements involving India.

Implications for the United States

Australia's policy tensions and dilemmas amid the rise of China and India have large implications for the United States as it adjusts its own Asia policy. Plainly, the Australia-U.S. alliance will need to adapt to an Indo-Pacific era of Chinese and Indian power. U.S. policymakers should keep in mind a range of questions as they assess how Australia relates to the United States' China strategy. What exactly is the nature of Australia's chief security concerns about China's rise? Is it potential Chinese coercion of others or perceived long-term possibilities of Chinese threats against Australia? Is it, correspondingly, the regional vulnerabilities that may be left behind were Washington to diminish the United States' strategic presence and alliance commitments in Asia? Is it the risk of miscalculation or misperception, leading perhaps to unexpected conflict with the United States, Japan, India, Vietnam, or others? Or are Australian concerns centered on the possibility that in some future hardening of U.S. Asia policy, a refusal to concede any ground to Chinese security interests might lead to an avoidable confrontation or conflict that would both draw in a reluctant Australia and destroy national and regional prosperity? All these questions feed into Australian policy debates.

What is clear, however, is that Australian security concerns about the impact of China's rise are growing and that Canberra is taking steps to deepen the U.S. alliance. This suggests that, above all, Australia will be sensitive to any change in U.S. strategy toward Asia that leaves any ally vulnerable to Chinese pressure. Broadly speaking, Washington has a window to explore practical and creative ideas with Canberra for enhancing the alliance. This could include not only an increased tempo of ship visits and joint training but also bolder steps such as the creation of logistics hubs and perhaps even a permanent U.S. presence in Australia to take advantage of its two-ocean geography.[85] Basing U.S. naval ships on the coast

---

[85] James Holmes and Toshi Yoshihara, "U.S. Navy's Indian Ocean Folly?" *Diplomat*, January 4, 2011, http://the-diplomat.com/2011/01/04/us-navy's-indian-ocean-folly/.

of Western Australia or the Northern Territory would allow flexible access to the Indian Ocean and Southeast Asia from a highly secure location, while tangibly registering Washington's commitment to Australia in an Indo-Pacific era of growing Chinese and Indian power. It could also better enable U.S. and Australian forces to exercise together, including perhaps with third nations such as India or Indonesia. There might also be scope to pre-position fuel or equipment, including for humanitarian operations such as disaster relief.[86]

The United States also has opportunities to further coordinate with Australia its efforts to engage China in security dialogue and cooperation, bilaterally and in multilateral forums. For instance, Canberra's bilateral defense engagement with Beijing might provide markers about the prospects (and limits) for Washington's own engagement strategy. Australia-China defense relations will also continue to provide a useful additional channel for communicating with China, including during times of tension in Beijing's relations with Washington or other powers.

At the same time, there remain some open questions about how far Canberra is willing to go to contribute to the alliance in the Indo-Pacific. Australia has been understandably coy about publicly indicating precisely how its strengthened maritime capabilities might work within U.S.-led coalitions in future contingencies, such as a maritime conflict with China. In terms of particular capabilities, Australia remains cautious about how far it would cooperate with the United States and Japan on missile defense, an issue on which the Labor Party remains divided.

Turning to New Delhi, Washington should not assume a precise congruence between its partnership and the one Canberra is trying to forge. Nor should it assume that Australia will be in lockstep with its every move to engage the South Asian giant. The United States needs to be aware that Australia continues to face challenges in building a relationship of strategic cooperation with India, even though Australian and U.S. views of India's future role in the world are broadly similar. There may be occasions when Canberra could use Washington's help in making headway in security relations with New Delhi, such as through trilateral talks and military exercises or advance notice of any further major Indo-U.S. security initiatives. What U.S. policymakers will want to avoid is a situation in which Australia harbors concerns about its own formal alliance becoming less valuable to Washington in light of the growing importance the United States has come to place on India, a non-ally strategic partner.

---

[86] Rory Medcalf and Andrew Shearer, "PM Faces Challenge of Deeper Alliance," *Australian*, March 7, 2011, http://www.theaustralian.com.au/news/world/pm-faces-challenge-of-deeper-alliance/story-e6frg6so-1226016729247.

Overall, the United States would benefit from further coordinating its strategies toward China and India with those of its Australian ally. Of course, Washington and Canberra already engage in regular and candid dialogue across the whole spectrum of major strategic issues among senior officials and military chiefs and in the annual AUSMIN consultations, which are "two plus two" combined meetings between the secretaries of state and defense and their Australian ministerial counterparts. These venues would be ideal for deepening the conversation on how to coordinate national efforts to engage China and India, as well as for ensuring that each side fully understands the reasons for the other's China and India policies and has the opportunity to anticipate any major changes to them. Canberra will continue to use these forums to ensure that the United States takes due account of Australian views when formulating its China, India, and wider Asian strategies. After all, these may affect Australian interests in ways not readily apparent in Washington. Despite the two countries' many commonalities in worldview, Washington should not assume that Canberra understands or agrees with the full logic of its Asia strategy at any given time. Moreover, Australia has both official and scholarly expertise on regional affairs, particularly in relation to East Asia, that can provide useful alternative assessments to the United States' own.[87]

There would also be value in the United States looking beyond the traditional policy elites of the cabinet ministries, bureaucracy, and military in its efforts to understand and perhaps influence Australia's evolving response to the rise of China and India. Washington would be well-advised to engage more directly on this issue with the Australian business community, media, and parliamentarians of all political hues. The broad continuities of Australia's policies toward China and India, despite some variations under Rudd, suggest a degree of national consensus. This interpretation may not, however, be sufficient to anticipate and respond to possible changes in Australia's stance. For instance, some leaders of the main conservative opposition party, the Liberal Party, would not appear to share the level of anxiety over China that informed the Rudd government's 2009 defense white paper.[88] The Greens party is in loose alliance with the

---

[87] This is likely to expand with the establishment of an A\$53 million China center at the Australian National University. Rowan Callick, "Rudd Announces New ANU China Centre," *Australian*, April 24, 2010, http://www.news.com.au/national/rudd-announces-new-anu-china-centre/story-e6frfkvr-1225857681148.

[88] Malcolm Turnbull, Liberal leader in 2008–9, has rejected the notion that China could become a threat to Australia. See Phillip Coorey, "Turnbull Sees Red on Rudd China Policy," *Sydney Morning Herald*, May 1, 2009, http://www.smh.com.au/national/turnbull-sees-red-on-rudd-china-policy-20090430-aozf.html. Tony Abbott, Liberal leader since 2009, has been openly confident about China's inability to challenge U.S. strategic primacy. See Tony Abbott, *Battlelines* (Melbourne: Melbourne University Press, 2010), 159–61.

Gillard Labor government and has held the balance of power in the federal parliament since mid-2011. The Greens party is deeply critical of China on human rights grounds, opposes uranium sales to India, and wants in effect the abolition of the U.S. alliance. Though typically ignored by the cabinet on foreign policy, the party's 12% share of the popular vote, including many ex-Labor supporters, worries Labor electoral strategists. The business community, meanwhile, is generally in favor of closer economic (including investment) ties with China, although it may also become increasingly concerned about the downsides of that relationship, such as vulnerability to Chinese espionage and cyber threats.[89]

Australian public attitudes might in some instances complement U.S. policy priorities in Asia, while on other occasions complicating them. On China, public opinion has shifted twice in the past decade—first seemingly to welcome Beijing's influence, then to reject it—whereas on India a clear pattern cannot yet be discerned. The United States would do well to be mindful of any such trends, especially as the percentage of the Australian population that is of Chinese or Indian descent continues to rise. Australia is a democracy with Western origins but also with a future heavily bound up in Asia's rise. Thus, the study of the country's response in trying to integrate security, economics, and values while dealing with an increasingly strong and confident China and India will help inform the United States' own policies.

---

[89] Jennifer Hewett, "Miners Fear Secrets Stolen by Chinese Cyber-Spies," *Australian*, April 20, 2010, http://www.theaustralian.com.au/business/mining-energy/miners-fear-secrets-stolen-by-chinese-cyber-spies/story-e6frg9df-1225855718533.

EXECUTIVE SUMMARY

This chapter examines Russian perceptions and policies regarding the rise of two Asian giants: one near neighbor, China, and one long-time ally, India.

MAIN ARGUMENT:
The rise of China and India confronts Russia with many challenges, while also offering several opportunities. These challenges and opportunities include:

- rethinking Russia's traditional Eurocentrism and opening the country to Asia, including by creating international arrangements with the region's principal players—notably China and the United States—that would make Russia's position in the Asia-Pacific more secure

- developing the Russian Far East and integrating it with the rest of the country, while also developing ties with Northeast Asia and the North Pacific

- filling market demand where Russia has comparative advantages, such as in energy, water, and transportation

- striking a new balance in relations with China

- re-energizing relations with India by transforming the relationship into a technological partnership and a security pillar, particularly with regard to Central Asia and Afghanistan

POLICY IMPLICATIONS:
- Russia should use preparations for the 2012 APEC summit in Vladivostok to map a strategy toward the Asia-Pacific.

- Moscow needs to keep relations with Beijing on an even keel, upgrade the partnership with New Delhi, and demilitarize relations with Washington.

- Russia must think strategically about Japan and work to transform the relationship into one like the current Russo-German partnership. Likewise, Moscow should build a long-term relationship with Seoul, supporting it on Korean reunification and engaging it in Russia's modernization effort.

Challenges and Opportunities:
Russia and the Rise of China and India

Dmitri Trenin

The rise of China and India has confronted Russia with a number of new challenges and opportunities. Adequately responding to the former and successfully taking advantage of the latter require a fundamental rethinking of Moscow's foreign policy, as well as major elements of its domestic policies. For the time being, no such rethinking has taken place; rather, there is a process of adjustment to the new realities that is proceeding haphazardly and unevenly. This is evident in the slow upgrading of Pacific Asia in the Russian strategic mind, which chips away at Russia's traditional Eurocentrism; in the difficult search for balance in Russia's relations with China and the use of the energy card as one such balancer; in efforts to modernize the venerable but fraying relationship with India; in a cautious reassessment of the U.S. role in Asia; and in the moves to integrate the provinces in the Russian Far East with the rest of the country, while still using them as a foothold to reach out to the wider Asia-Pacific.

This chapter will consider the impact of China's and India's rise on Russian foreign and domestic policies and, more broadly, the Russian political mind and society at large. Section one will start by setting out the historical context for the relationship and demonstrating its relevance for the present. The highlight of this section is the dramatic change in Russia's and China's historical fates at the close of the twentieth century, which established China, for the first time in modern times, as the more powerful, dynamic, and successful of the two countries. For Russia, this is nothing short of a political earthquake; the earth has moved, sending China way

Dmitri Trenin is Director of the Carnegie Moscow Center and a Senior Associate of the Carnegie Endowment for International Peace. He can be reached at <dtrenin@carnegie.ru>.

up and placing Russia partly in its shadow. The rise of India, by contrast, has had far less of an impact on Russia, although it was unambiguously welcomed by Russians.

The next section will discuss the geopolitical and geostrategic aspects of the relationship. Russia sees China as both an opportunity—thanks to a fundamentally improved and vibrant relationship—and a challenge. The former holds out a chance for Russia to develop its Far Eastern territories and use that foothold to integrate the country into the Asia-Pacific region. The latter contains the prospect of Russia turning itself, starting with Siberia, into a raw materials appendage of China, and possibly also its political client. India can be a close partner to Russia, but the fate of the partnership depends on Moscow's ability to be interesting and attractive to New Delhi, including beyond the relatively narrow scope of intergovernmental relations.

The third section will examine the energy-heavy and formerly arms-heavy economic relations between Russia and China, with the two countries' roles fundamentally reversed from the middle of the twentieth century. Russia, which has become a major energy exporter for the EU countries, is looking for a similar, if scaled-down, role in Asia, with China being its principal customer. China, for its part, has an interest in having overland routes for supplying itself with oil and gas. There is far less economic interdependence between Russia and India, whose two-way trade is a fraction of the Sino-Russian exchange.

A discussion of military cooperation and nuclear issues will follow. These security-related issues have been central to Russia's relationships with both China and India, historically among the main purchasers of Russian arms. The opening of the Chinese arms market in the early 1990s allowed the struggling Russian defense industry breathing space, although now China is exporting arms and equipment based on Russian technologies. New Delhi's arms relationship with Moscow goes back to 1962, and Russia has always dominated the Indian arms market.

The fifth section addresses Russian perceptions of the rise of China and India and Moscow's reactions, including realignment and balancing efforts. China's new assertiveness, although not aimed at Russia, makes Russians think about what this portends for the long-term future. By contrast, Russians are more welcoming toward India's rise, see Indian national interests as compatible with their own, and view India's foreign policy as constructive and friendly. The chapter then considers the cultural attitudes toward the two Asian nations that underlie Russia's policies and strategies. Until recently, direct contacts with the Chinese and Indians had not been particularly strong, but this is changing. One vehicle of such change is ethnic Chinese migration into Russia, which, though still rather moderate, nevertheless leads to fears and suspicions. Similarly, many ordinary Russians are visiting China as tourists, professionals, or businessmen, which gives the relationship a wholly new flavor. The relationship with India is undergoing similar changes, but on a smaller scale. For example, there is no significant Indian diaspora in Russia.

The next section will describe Russian strategies toward India and China—or at least the building blocks for such strategies. It also examines the internal differences of interests and opinions within the Russian establishment and the public regarding the strategies to be pursued vis-à-vis Beijing and New Delhi. The chapter's final two sections will broaden the focus to include Russia's views of the Asia-Pacific as a whole and the implications of Moscow's policy moves toward Beijing and New Delhi for the United States.

The Historical Context

Historical Interactions with China

Russia's patterns of historical interaction with China and India have been markedly different. On the China front, as the seventeenth century Tsardom of Muscovy was pushing its frontiers eastward from the Urals toward the Pacific, it came into its first contact with the Manchus, who then ruled China. The first encounters in the 1680s were unfortunate for the Cossacks, but the Russian colonization of Siberia all the way to the Pacific coast continued unabated. During the next 150 years, the Russian empire modernized its state administration on the European model, built a new army and started a navy, consolidated its control of Siberia, and even extended its rule across the Bering Strait into Alaska, known then as "Russian America." During the same period, the Chinese empire stagnated and became easy prey for European powers, led by Great Britain. Russia entered the competition in the 1850s and 1860s by extending its borders all the way to the Amur and the Ussuri rivers, annexing territories whose inhabitants heretofore had been tributaries of the Manchus. In 1860, Russia founded Vladivostok, whose name literally means, "rule the East." To the Chinese, the treaties of 1858, 1860, and 1864, which added some 1.5 million square kilometers (km) to the Russian empire, are known as "unequal."

In the late nineteenth century, Russian expansion focused on Manchuria, which became a Russian zone of influence. The more ardent Russian imperialists even invented a name for the new acquisition, "Yellow Russia." Russian soldiers took part in a collective European intervention in Beijing (1900); Russian sailors built a naval base at Port Arthur (Lüshun) and a commercial port at Dalny (Dalian) on the Yellow Sea (1898); and Harbin, in the center of Manchuria, was founded in 1898 as a Russian city and remained predominantly Russian well into the 1930s. Russia's advance was finally checked by its imperialist rival, Japan, which defeated the Russian forces in the 1904–5 war and displaced the Russians from southern Manchuria. The Chinese to this day consider these events to be a story of two colonialist predators preying on a weak and almost prostrate China.

Soviet Russia at first renounced its tsarist-era privileges but soon afterward became deeply involved in China's civil war and defense against Japanese aggression. Moscow, at the same time, sought to control the Chinese Communist Party (CCP) and also supplied arms to Chiang Kai-shek's Nationalist Party. Eventually, Stalin backed Mao in his bid for ultimate power and befriended the newly proclaimed People's Republic of China (PRC), giving it massive aid but treating it as a junior partner. With Stalin's death, the Soviet-Chinese bloc started to unravel. Divergences led to a split in 1960 and then to a veritable Cold War, complete with a military stand-off, which lasted for nearly three decades and was interspersed with border conflicts. During that period, Russia rediscovered the "yellow peril," and China had to live with the "threat from the north."

The confrontation ended in 1989 when the last Soviet leader, Mikhail Gorbachev, essentially agreed to the Chinese demands for Moscow's geopolitical retrenchment and troop reduction. In the two-plus decades that followed, China and Russia dramatically reversed their historical roles. Russia's GDP, still on par with China's in 1990, was only a quarter of its neighbor's in 2010. Russian exports to China are now mostly composed of raw materials, while its imports from China are increasingly made up of manufactured goods, including machinery. Today's China is more dynamic and, despite its overriding interest in national development, increasingly outward-looking. By contrast, Russia is growing at a far slower speed and is largely focused on itself, despite all the noises its elites make. In a tale of two cities, richly replicated along the Sino-Russian frontier, Russian towns that once proudly looked down on Chinese villages across the river are now dwarfed by the glitz of China's urban modernity.

Looking back on the history of the Sino-Russian relationship, what is striking is that the two countries, despite all the tensions and conflicts, never waged a large-scale war against each other. Moreover, they formed various types of alliances, however short-lived.[1]

---

[1] Alexei Voskresensky, *Kitay i Rossiya v Evrazii: Istoricheskaya dinamika politicheskikh vzaimovliyaniy* [China and Russia: Historical Dynamics of Reciprocal Political Influence] (Moscow: Muravey, 2004), 520.

Historical Interactions with India

Russo-Indian interactions have a shorter and far less rocky history. Soviet Communist leaders saw India's independence as a major blow to Western imperialism. Even though they did not have much time for Jawaharlal Nehru's Fabian socialism, they nonetheless appreciated New Delhi's policies of nonalignment. In reality, nonalignment turned out to favor Moscow. Beginning in the mid-1950s, the Soviet Union politically supported India against Pakistan, a U.S. Cold War ally, and from the early 1960s supplied it with a wide range of military hardware. Soviet-era maps even identified the whole of Kashmir as part of India. Although Prime Minister Alexei Kosygin mediated a peace deal between India and Pakistan in 1966, for Moscow relations with Pakistan were always secondary to relations with India. In the 1962 Sino-Indian border conflict in the Himalayas, the Soviet Union's sympathies were with India rather than with former ally China. In 1971, Moscow and New Delhi signed a friendship treaty, which the former saw as a geopolitical instrument aimed at both the United States and China. With the demise of the Soviet Union, a new Russo-Indian friendship treaty was signed in 1993.

In 1979–80, India was one of the few countries around the world that refused to condemn the Soviet invasion of Afghanistan. In the mid to late 1980s, Gorbachev attempted to create a model partnership with India's Rajiv Gandhi, an attempt that failed due to the assassination of Rajiv and the rapid decline and fall of the Soviet Union itself. The Russian Federation, however, continued the tradition of friendly rhetoric toward India, which remained one of its principal arms clients. In the early 1990s, Russia was ready to sell rocket engines to India, and only desisted under pressure from the Clinton administration. Many in Russia saw this as a humiliation and resolved to never let it happen again. Despite U.S. protests, Russia undertook the construction of a nuclear reactor at Koodankulam, Tamil Nadu. Further, in 1998, Moscow—in contrast to Washington—did not censure India for its nuclear weapons tests, apparently considering its long-time ally a safe bet in terms of proliferation and a useful addition to the nuclear balance in Asia. Rather, Moscow's concerns were with Pakistan, due to its perennial political instability, record of proliferation, Islamist radicalism, and history of unfriendly relations with the Soviet Union.

Yet despite the good feelings on both sides, Russo-Indian relations have shown signs of decline in the past two decades. The relationship's material base—Russian arms sales and a few joint projects, such as Koodankulam—is too narrow and continues to shrink. Private business in each country has displayed only modest interest in the other, while high-sounding reaffirmations of eternal friendship and strategic partnership are not supported by close strategic collaboration on practical issues, such as Afghanistan. Unless that decline is reversed, the Russo-Indian relationship will become increasingly hollow, an empty shell without much substance.

Before it can start responding to the challenges of China's and India's rise, Moscow needs to form an integral, comprehensive view of its interests in East and South Asia and the Pacific. The next section assesses Russia's geopolitical position and the implications for national strategy.

Geopolitics and Geostrategy

Today's post-imperial Russia is inward- rather than outward-looking. Its challenges in Asia begin at home. The most serious issue with respect to Russia's position in Asia is the underdevelopment of Eastern Russia, which includes eastern Siberia and the Pacific seaboard from Vladivostok to the Bering Strait. There is a consensus within the Moscow establishment that unless Russia manages to integrate those vast but sparsely populated territories—with a population of less than 30 million east of the Urals and just over 6 million in the Russian Far East[2]—into a common economic and social space with the rest of the country, it will see them gravitating toward China. In much of the Far East, local entrepreneurs look at China more pragmatically as a source of wealth.[3]

Constructing an essential equilibrium in its relations with Beijing is Moscow's prime policy goal. At the same time, across Eastern Russia, and especially through the Pacific coast territories, Russia has an opportunity to integrate itself into the world's most dynamic economic region and use that integration to spur its own growth and development. In Asia beyond the Pacific, Russia has a need, and an opportunity, to build its time-honored but recently neglected relationship with India into a full partnership, with vibrant strategic, economic, and cultural dimensions. Finally, Moscow has an interest in contributing to the emergence of a system of international checks and balances in Asia, above all to protect Russia's eastern flank.

Constructing Equilibrium in Relations with Beijing

Geopolitically, China represents the biggest challenge for Russia but also an important opportunity. No two major countries in recent times have changed places in peacetime vis-à-vis each other more dramatically and

---

[2] The national population of Russia in 2010 was 142 million. In the two previous decades, Russia suffered a net population decline of 5 million.

[3] Alexander Ivanter, "To, chto oslabevaet, usilitsya" [What Gets Weaker, Will Grow Stronger], *Expert*, March 8–14, 2010, 36–44.

quickly than have the Soviet Union/Russian Federation and China between 1990 and 2000. As Russia was plunging in terms of its world influence, China was soaring. Stunningly, Moscow did not lose its nerve and avoided the extreme reactions of either hostility toward China or kowtowing to it. Instead, Russia chose to adjust to the reversal of fortunes. It helped that China desisted from crowing over the demise of its former mentor and rival. The adjustment continues, even as the gap between China and Russia continues to widen, making the challenge facing Moscow ever bigger and more complex.

Above all, Russia needs to find a credible way to reaffirm its strategic independence relative to a rising China and to keep the relationship on a good, neighborly keel. Russians are afraid of losing their status as a global and regional player and of being sidelined by China attracting the interest of the Western world.[4] Specifically, the Russian government needs to find a way to ensure political, economic, social, and military stability along the Chinese border; better balance economic exchanges with China, which at present make Russia a raw materials resource for its neighbor; and stabilize and start reversing the demographic decline of Eastern Russia, even as the country as a whole has to accept more immigrants from Asia. In a nutshell, Russia's task is both to ensure that the current border with China— enshrined in a series of agreements signed in 1991, 1994, 1996, and 2004— stays permanent and to engage China as a factor promoting economic development along the Russian side of the border.

Politically, Moscow needs to fashion a relationship with Beijing that reaffirms good-neighborliness and partnership, reflected in the 2001 treaty that replaced the 1950 Sino-Soviet pact, while allowing Russia freedom to maneuver in order to ensure that it does not get sucked into China's real or potential conflicts with neighbors and other major Asian powers, such as Japan and India. At the same time, Moscow must find a way to balance China through reaching out to New Delhi and others, such as Hanoi, in a way that strengthens its position relative to Beijing without unnecessarily provoking China.[5] The most important and sensitive issue here is Russia's need to position itself vis-à-vis the increasingly complex Sino-U.S. relationship, which has already begun to define Asian and, to a significant degree, global geopolitics in the 21st century.

---

[4] *Rossiya i mir: 2011 ezhegodny prognoz* [Russia and the World 2011: An Annual Forecast] (Moscow: Institute for World Economy and International Relations, 2010), 111.

[5] Alexander Lukin, "'Kitayskaya mechta' i budushchee Rossii" [The Chinese Dream and Russia's Future], *Russia in Global Affairs*, June 19, 2010, http://www.globalaffairs.ru/number/Kitaiskaya-mechta-i-buduschee-Rossii-14857.

When Russians think of China, they first think of the Russo-Chinese border, the scene of an armed conflict in 1969. Extending for almost 4,500 km, it is one of the longest borders in the world. With the end of Sino-Soviet confrontation, border talks resumed, leading to a series of agreements on the delimitation and demarcation of the border that were finally fully implemented in 2008. Solving the border problem with China has been one of the most important accomplishments of Russia's post-Soviet diplomacy. In an effort to conclude the agreement, President Vladimir Putin eventually agreed to hand over some large islands on the Amur and Ussuri rivers. Russians are becoming concerned, however, over recent publications in the Chinese government-controlled media referring to the current border as a result of the nineteenth century "unequal treaties," thus rendering it implicitly illegal. Moscow finds disingenuous Beijing's characterization of these publications as "marginal" and suspects that it may have a hidden agenda.

Even apart from the border issue, the growing economic and social gap between Russia's Far East and China's northeast is a major risk and even a potential threat to the Russian Federation. Speaking in 2000 in the border town Blagoveshchensk, Putin publicly wondered what language the future population of the area will speak.[6] That looming problem, however, is the product of Russia failing to develop and integrate the Far East rather than of China planning a "demographic aggression."

At the subregional level, Russia faces different challenges from China in former Soviet Central Asia as well as in Northeast Asia. Central Asia is an area of Chinese economic and political activism and, at the same time, Moscow's post-imperial backyard. So far, Beijing has managed to quietly displace Moscow from the region without provoking Russia's ire and open resentment. Thus, China, through an agreement with Turkmenistan, has broken Gazprom's monopoly on gas deliveries from the region. Kazakhstan pumps its oil to Xinjiang and plans to link the country's former and present capitals with a Chinese-built high-speed railway. In addition, Kyrgyzstan has been overwhelmed by Chinese goods. China has been able to displace Russia in these ways by outwardly respecting Moscow's sensitivities as a "great power"—a hollow term to Beijing—and staying clear of those areas, such as military security, that Russians consider to be their preserve. China has thus focused on developing commercial and investment links with Central Asia.[7]

---

[6] Vladimir Putin, "Introductory Remarks at a Meeting on the Prospects of the Development of the Far East and the Trans-Baikal Region," President of Russia, Kremlin, website, July 21, 2000, http://archive.kremlin.ru/eng/speeches/2000/07/21/0000_type82912type82913_127800.shtml.

[7] Eugene Rumer, Dmitri Trenin, and Huasheng Zhao, *Central Asia: Views from Washington, Moscow, and Beijing* (Armonk: M.E. Sharpe, 2007).

A similar pattern in kind, but in a much starker form, can be observed in Mongolia, a Russian protectorate from 1911 and then a Soviet client state until 1991. After the fall of the Soviet Union, the Russian Federation immediately lost interest in that country, which gravitated economically toward Beijing and had to use political relations with Japan and the United States for geopolitical balance. When Moscow began to rediscover Mongolia—essentially from a business perspective—in the 2000s, it could only be a minor player there.

In Northeast Asia, Moscow, left without much leverage in Pyongyang and not particularly influential with Seoul, found itself in the 2000s following Beijing's policies on North Korea. More recently, Russia has started to craft a more independent approach to the region. It has a more relaxed attitude than Beijing to such issues as U.S. presence and military activities in the area, the format of Korean reunification and South Korean–U.S. military ties, and Japan's defense efforts—whose main thrust has recently shifted from the north to the southwest—and military alliance with the United States. Moscow has also taken a harsher line than Beijing on Pyongyang's military provocations and refusal to abide by UN Security Council (UNSC) resolutions.

Maintaining a "Friendship for All Times" with New Delhi

Unlike China, India is geographically remote from Russia, even more so after the collapse of the Soviet Union. This reduces the intensity of exchanges but also eliminates the usual causes of friction. In the 1990s, as Moscow became focused on the West, it neglected relations with India. This relationship recovered in the 2000s, however, with Moscow unreservedly welcoming India's rise. It helps of course that, in contrast with the Anglo-Indian colonial administration that feared a Russian threat and engaged in a "great game" to thwart it, the successive governments of independent India have viewed the Soviet Union/Russian Federation as a friend and ally.

Thus, strategically the Indo-Russian relationship is not merely peaceful but virtually problem-free, a rare case between two major powers. For Moscow, New Delhi seems to be a "friend for all times." Even India's emergence as a nuclear power was met in Moscow with understanding befitting a great and responsible friendly power and virtually no criticism. However, the relationship now confronts new challenges: the situations in Afghanistan and Pakistan, the rise of China, the rapprochement between New Delhi and Washington, and the weak economic foundation and primitive infrastructure of Russo-Indian ties.

These challenges, if properly addressed, could lead to a revitalization of the old relationship. The gradual withdrawal of the United States and NATO from Afghanistan calls for more active Russian involvement there in the political, security (non-military), and economic spheres. Naturally, both Moscow and New Delhi would benefit from coordinating their policies and activities on the Hindu Kush.

Pakistan is a more sensitive issue. Russia has relatively few contacts and little influence there, and New Delhi certainly does not want Moscow to become any closer to Islamabad. While Russia sees India's red lines, such as arms sales to Pakistan, and is closely watching the development of Islamabad's relations with Beijing,[8] it clearly wants to keep the channels of communication open. The Kremlin has even managed to form a "quad" group with Afghan, Pakistani, and Tajik leaders to discuss the regional context of the Afghan conflict. Some in New Delhi hope that this new Russian activism will lead to cooperation with Moscow not only on Afghanistan but on Pakistan as well.[9]

The question now is whether Moscow can remodel its old relationship with New Delhi and use it as the basis for a full partnership in the 21st century. To do so, Russia would have to redefine the relationship, giving a much bigger role to business ties and engaging India in practical regional cooperation, particularly by helping to stabilize Afghanistan politically and contributing to the economic development of Central Asia. Close relations with New Delhi, of course, have an impact on Moscow's relations with Beijing. India is openly wary of China; Russia is, outwardly at least, less so. While remaining formally neutral in the Sino-Indian border dispute, Russia could be using its India connection to softly balance growing Chinese power.

So far, Russia has viewed India's new de facto alliance with the United States rather calmly. Of course, Washington is a powerful competitor to Moscow in a number of areas, from arms sales to nuclear energy. However, on the more important issue of grand strategy, Moscow is more relaxed. It views India as a strategically independent country, its new closeness with the United States notwithstanding. At the end of the day, Moscow believes New Delhi will only do what it thinks is best for India and will not just do Washington's bidding. Russian views of Pakistan's policies and prospects are not nearly as strident as India's views, but Russia is genuinely concerned about Pakistan. As to New Delhi's ambitions in South Asia and the Indian Ocean, Russia sees them as natural for an emerging great power. It helps, of course,

---

[8] See, for example, Vladimir Shcherbakov, "Kitaysko-Pakistanskiy dalniy pokhod" [The China-Pakistan Long March], *Nezavisimoe Voennoe Obozrenie*, April 22–28, 2011, 8–9.

[9] Smita Purushottam, "Russia in India's National Strategy," Institute for Defence Studies and Analyses (IDSA), 2010.

that Russia's own ambitions do not reach that far and that, in the post-Soviet era, Moscow's foreign relations have become increasingly dominated by economics rather than traditional geopolitical or security issues.

Economic Relations

China: A Destination for Natural Resources

In the 1950s, Soviet aid to China compared in terms of scale to the Marshall Plan for Europe. Then, for about 30 years there were no significant economic exchanges between the two countries. Bilateral trade with China picked up in 1990, when the cross-border flow of cheap Chinese consumer goods and food products helped sustain the suddenly impoverished Russian population across the border in the Far East, which had suffered from the breakdown of economic links to the rest of the country. Now Russians see economic relations with China not only as valuable in their own right but also as a basis for integrating their country into the Asia-Pacific.

At the same time, Russo-Chinese commercial relations reflect the new complementarity of the two economies, which many Russians resent. Russia has become a raw materials and energy resource base for the booming economy of China, whose own exports to Russia are increasingly made up of manufactured goods, including machinery. There are two important exceptions to this. For two decades now, Russia has also been the principal supplier of arms to China, and Rosatom has undertaken to build nuclear power plants there.

The Sino-Russian trade turnover grew tenfold in ten years to reach just under $60 billion in 2008, before dipping in 2009 and rising again to $55.5 billion in 2010. However, this is still a fraction of China's trade with the United States, Japan, or South Korea. China's massive trade links with the rest of the world support the view among Russians that Beijing is interested in a stable, secure, and rapidly developing economic area in East Asia and the Pacific. China has become Russia's biggest trading partner as a country, even though the latter's trade with the European Union as a whole is several times bigger, but Russia's own place among China's commercial partners is a modest fourteenth, behind Australia, Malaysia, and Thailand.

Yet Russia is nevertheless important to China in the energy field, as its fourth-biggest energy supplier. What is particularly important is that Russian oil—and potentially natural gas in the future—flows overland, across the common border, and thus is immune from possible sanctions or interdiction from the U.S. or Indian navies. In 2009 a deal was struck under which Russia will supply China with 110 million barrels of oil over a period of twenty years, ending in 2030, and China agreed to lend $25 billion in credits to the Russian state-owned company Rosneft and the pipeline operator Transneft. Thus, Russian companies received much-needed cash, and China was able to enhance its energy security. In 2010 a pipeline was built to transport Siberian oil to China. Significantly, for the first time, China was given access to two oil fields in Eastern Siberia.[10]

For Russian energy companies, exports to China represent an effort to diversify their trade away from overreliance on Europe—a lucrative, but essentially stagnant market. The Russian government's current energy strategy calls for raising the share of the Asian market for Russian crude oil from 8% to 20%–25% by 2030 and for natural gas from currently zero to about 20%. China is viewed as a major potential market for Russian gas, but plans of laying pipelines to China have so far been stymied by Beijing's refusal to pay a competitive price. Unlike trade, cross-investment between China and Russia is still undeveloped. Russia's investment climate is notoriously inhospitable. Chinese companies would like to invest in Russia's energy business, but the Russians fear being taken over by companies actually acting on behalf of the Chinese government.

Modest Trade with India

Despite the superior political relationship and a record of Soviet development assistance in the 1960s–1980s, Russo-Indian trade is puny by comparison with Sino-Russian exchanges. Although trade had grown six times in a decade, it was just shy of $8 billion in 2010. India is Russia's 24th-largest trading partner, with bilateral trade being only 0.8%–0.9% of each country's global turnover. Russian exports include a relatively high percentage (over 40%) of machinery and transportation equipment, which is in part due to the arms trade. In the past, Russia was crucial to India for importing weapons, but with the warming of U.S.-Indian relations, Russian arms manufacturers have faced stiff competition in the Indian market. Other major Russian exports are chemicals (around 20%) and metals (10%). India, for its part, exports to Russia mainly pharmaceuticals (30%), foodstuff (20%), and textiles (10%).[11]

The energy element in the relationship is rather modest but growing steadily, with India's Oil and Natural Gas Corporation (ONGC) having

---

[10] For an excellent in-depth analysis of Moscow's energy policies in Asia, see Vagif Guseinov, ed., *Neftegazoviy Kompleks Rossii: tendentsii razvitiya (2000–2010)* [Russia's Oil and Gas Complex: Development Trends (2000–2010)] (Moscow: Krasnaya Zvezda, 2011), 357–72.

[11] "Rossiyssko-Indiyskoe torgovo-ekonomicheskoe sotrudnichestvo" [Russo-Indian Trade and Economic Cooperation], Ministry of Foreign Affairs of the Russian Federation, February 14, 2011, http://www.mid.ru/ns-rasia.nsf.

participated in the Sakhalin-1 project since 2001. Sakhalin oil has been flowing to India since 2006. India has also won exploration rights to an oil and gas field in Tomsk, Siberia. Gazprom, for its part, is looking for gas in the Gulf of Bengal. The first nuclear reactor at Koodankulam, built with Russian assistance, is due to be launched in 2011. Altogether, Rosatom plans on building twelve reactors in India.

Finally, investment links between the two countries are not particularly strong. Apart from ONGC, India's principal investor in Russia is SUN Group, a private equity fund manager with $1 billion of investments in the country. Russia's leading investor, Sistema, is active in India's telecommunications. There are plans to increase the volume of trade between India and Russia to $20 billion by 2020,[12] but even then Indo-Russian trade will trail Russian trade with China by a great distance. Whatever Moscow's plans and hopes, so far its economic relations with both New Delhi and Beijing have been dominated by arms exports.

Military Cooperation and Nuclear Issues

Arms Sales and Military Relations with China: Growing Competition

China and India have historically been among the premier purchasers of Russian arms. Stunningly, Moscow resumed arms shipments to Beijing in 1992, just 3 years after the end of their 30-year confrontation. For over a decade and a half since then, Russia sold China between $1–1.5 billion worth of arms and military equipment per annum. Throughout the 1990s, this constituted about 20% of the bilateral trade turnover and around 40% of Russia's weapons exports. The opening of the Chinese arms market in the early 1990s allowed the struggling Russian defense industry breathing space. The Russian government also hoped at the time that this arms trade would institute a patron-client relationship with China in the defense area. Mindful of the need to maintain a military balance, Russia imposed internal restrictions on what could be transferred to China.

There is no question that deliveries of Russian aircraft, air defense systems, missiles, naval ships, and key components such as aircraft engines helped increase the firepower and overall capabilities of the People's Liberation Army (PLA).[13] In the post-Tiananmen atmosphere, Russia was also the only major arms producer willing to sell to China. The EU countries

---

[12] Nikolay Surkov, "Moskvu i Delhi interesuet naukoyemkoe partnerstvo" [Moscow and Delhi Are Interested in Hi-Tech Partnership], *Nezavisimaya Gazeta*, February 1, 2011.

[13] Vassily Kashin, "Voenny budget KNR: Otsenki masshtabov i veroyatnye prioritety" [PRC Defense Budget: Assessment of Scale and Likely Priorities], *Export Vooruzheniy* 3 (2009): 36–42.

imposed an arms embargo, and Israel stopped arms sales in 2003–4. By the mid-2000s, however, Beijing's interest in massive off-the-shelf purchases from Moscow had waned. China had managed to reverse engineer its own clones of Russian weapons systems, such as the Su-27 fighter jet, renamed J-11B. In addition, these systems, mostly designed in Soviet times, were also becoming obsolete. In 2009, proceeds from Russian arms sales to China were about $800 million, just 10% of Moscow's overall weapons exports.[14] Having stopped large-scale imports from Russia, China is now exporting arms and equipment based on Russian weapon systems. This has led to Sino-Russian competition in the world arms market, where the Chinese undercut Moscow by offering lower prices. Moscow has protested to Beijing over the infringement of intellectual property rights, but to no avail.[15]

Joint Russo-Chinese military exercises are a more recent phenomenon than arms trade. The first antiterrorism maneuvers were held in China's Shandong Province and the Yellow Sea in 2005. The timing was significant, marking the start of a serious deterioration in U.S.-Russian relations under George W. Bush. Since then, the Chinese military has practiced with Russia in 2007 in the Urals, in 2009 in China, and in 2010 in Kazakhstan. These regular exercises, codenamed "Peace Mission," are officially held under the auspices of the Shanghai Cooperation Organisation.

Arms Sales and Military Relations with India: Long-standing Cooperation

Historically, India has bought more Soviet and Russian arms than any other country ($50 billion). In the 1990s and the early 2000s, New Delhi and Beijing together accounted for 80% of Russian arms exports.[16] New Delhi's arms relationship with Moscow goes back to 1962 and has never been interrupted.[17] For a long time, the Soviet Union was able to dominate the Indian arms market as a result of the Western embargo following the 1965 Indo-Pakistani war. By the mid-1990s, as much as 70% of the Indian army, 80% of the air force, and 85% of the navy arsenals were made up of Russian military hardware, from tanks and artillery pieces to fighter and bomber planes to naval frigates, destroyers, and diesel and nuclear

---

[14] Igor Chernyak, "Kalashiy ryad [Kalashnikov Stall]: An Interview with Anatoly Isaykin, Director General of the Russian Weapons Export Agency," *Rossiyskaya Gazeta*, April 10, 2010.

[15] Jeremy Page, "China Clones, Sells Russian Fighters," *Wall Street Journal*, December 6, 2010, A1.

[16] Chernyak, "Kalashny ryad."

[17] "The Russian-Indian Arms Trade: New Threats and New Opportunities," *Eksport Vooruzheniy* 5 (September–October 2007), http://www.cast.ru/eng/journal/2007/.

submarines.[18] Generally, Russian weaponry proved itself well in the battles that India had to wage. Not all arms sales, however, went smoothly. Alongside the perennial problems with spare parts, maintenance, and support,[19] the transfer to the Indian Navy of the Russian aircraft carrier *Admiral Gorshkov*, renamed *Vikramaditya*, and the nuclear submarine *Nerpa* has notoriously stalled.

Very importantly, this arms relationship with Russia has allowed India to develop its own capabilities. The two countries have jointly developed and produced an antiship supersonic missile, the Brahmos.[20] They are also cooperating on fifth-generation fighter aircraft, multi-role transport aircraft, and other weapons systems. Another advantage of this relationship for New Delhi is that Moscow has proved itself resistant to sanctions and other restrictions that have been applied to India,[21] as well as assisted India in developing its space program. Currently, India is seeking to diversify its arms purchases in order to reduce reliance on Russia, which some experts regard as the most important irritant in the bilateral relationship.[22]

Russian and Indian army units have been exercising together since 2005—initially, as in joint exercises with China, under the rubric of antiterrorism cooperation—and the first naval exercise was held in 2007. In 2009, joint INDRA (India and Russia) exercises were staged in the Indian Ocean, with the participation of the Russian aircraft carrier *Pyotr Veliki*. In 2010, INDRA maneuvers were held on land in Uttar Pradesh. These strong military links with New Delhi, as with Moscow's ties to Beijing, have an impact on Russia's stance on the nuclear issues relevant to India and China, which will be discussed in the next section.

Nuclear Technology and Nonproliferation

The Soviet Union was an early backer of the Chinese nuclear weapons project. This support ended abruptly in 1958, when Beijing risked a conflict with the United States over Taiwan without consulting Moscow. This episode, as much as anything else, led to the break in relations two years

---

[18] T.L. Shaumian, ed., *India segodnya* [India Today] (Moscow: Russian Academy of Sciences, Institute of Oriental Studies, 2005), 413.

[19] These problems are fully admitted in Russia. See, for example, Nikolay Novichkov, "Akhillesova pyata aviaproma" [The Achilles' Heel of the Aviation Industry], *Nezavisimoe Voennoe Obozrenie*, April 22–28, 2011, 3.

[20] Mikhail Barabanov, "'Vikramaditya,' 'Brahmos,' 'Trishul' i drugie proekty dlya Indii" [Vikramaditya, Brahmos, Trishul and Other Projects for India], *Nezavisimoe Voennoe Obozrenie*, April 8–14, 2011, 8–9.

[21] Gurmeet Kanwal, "Otnosheniya, proverennye vremenem" [Time-Tested Relations], *Nezavisimoe Voennoe Obozrenie*, April 1, 2011.

[22] Purushottam, "Russia in India's National Strategy."

later. When in the 1960s China finally developed nuclear weapons of its own, the Soviet Union viewed it as a potential adversary. In the late 1960s, a nuclear war between the USSR and the PRC was considered imminent.

In the 21st century, Russia's consistent desire has been to involve China in the U.S.-Russian nuclear arms control process in view of China's growing capability for nuclear arms build-up. Yet Beijing has so far expressed no inclination to participate. Thus, Moscow must live with the uncertainty of a China potentially capable of enhancing its presently modest nuclear arsenal even as Russia is downsizing its own. Russia and China, however, have been cooperating with the United States, South Korea, and Japan on the issues of the North Korean and Iranian nuclear programs. On both counts, Russian and Chinese views have been fairly close, particularly in their rejection of the use of force or harsh sanctions against Pyongyang and Tehran.

Although Russia has been long concerned about Pakistan's nuclear program, to which China contributed massively, Moscow has never expressed any special anxiety over India's nuclear efforts. To the contrary, the Soviet Union helped India in the development of its civilian nuclear industry. After the 1998 nuclear tests the Russian Federation not only refused to join U.S. sanctions against India but concluded a ten-year deal with New Delhi on military and technological cooperation. In 2010, Moscow and New Delhi signed an agreement on the peaceful uses of nuclear energy. In fact, Russia had started building nuclear power plants in India well before the relaxation of the Nuclear Suppliers Group restrictions in 2008. The excellent overall quality of Indo-Russian relations, the close strategic and military links between the two countries, the transparent and predictable nature of the Indian political system, and the relatively low risk of proliferation from India have been the principal factors behind Moscow's favorable attitude. Nuclear weapons being symbols of national power, this attitude reveals a lot about how Russia views China's and India's rise.

Russian Perceptions of and Reactions toward China's and India's Rise

Reversing Global Status with China and Welcoming India's Rise

In 1979, China's GDP was 40% of the GDP of the then Russian Soviet Republic. In 2010, China's GDP was almost four times bigger than Russia's. To say that Russians are stunned would be an understatement. However, China's remarkable growth presents opportunities too, inasmuch as China's appetite for resources drives world commodity prices up, which benefits the

Russian federal budget. If that growth falters, Russia will immediately suffer economically. On the other hand, Russians have no experience of living with a strong China, and some are understandably worried. Beijing has sought to put those worries to rest by adopting a relatively cautious policy toward Moscow. Sergei Razov, Russia's ambassador to China, observes:

> Unlike some other countries, the PRC has not pursued a consistently anti-Russian policy; it does not claim the territories which belong to us; it does not move the infrastructure of politico-military blocs to our borders; it does not install Russia-unfriendly regimes along our borders. On the contrary: it supports us on a number of key domestic and foreign policy issues. Objectively speaking, China is one of the few genuinely strategic partners our country has.[23]

It is only very recently that this feel-good attitude has become a bit more reserved. The worsening in 2010 of Sino-U.S. and Sino-Japanese relations in particular has led Russian officials to conclude that the Chinese leadership has set aside Deng Xiaoping's policy of assuming a low international profile. China's new assertiveness, although not aimed at Russia, makes Moscow think about what this portends for the long-term future of Russo-Chinese relations. Moscow knows dealing with Russia is not presently Beijing's priority, but it suspects that Russia may be already on the list. The references in official Chinese media to the "unequal treaties" with imperial Russia give some Russians pause. However, those who have studied the history of China's foreign policy point out that China's approach is markedly different from that of the European great powers, or the Soviet Union and the United States. China will "curve the geopolitical space" in its favor by means of increasing its own weight and using soft power to create the kind of "harmony" in the world that Beijing appreciates.

India's rise, by contrast, is applauded without reservation as ostensibly benign. Senior Russian academics place India in a different category from China: they regard it as a third-tier power—after the United States, which is at the very top, and the EU and China in the second tier—in the good company of Brazil, Indonesia, or Russia itself. India's many domestic problems, these analysts believe, will not allow it to match China's power and status.[24] Russians thus have trust in Indians that they still do not have for the Chinese. They see Indian national interests as fully compatible with their own and New Delhi's foreign policy as constructive and friendly. They welcome India as a global power and hope to benefit from its political, as well as economic, ascendancy. Moscow was an early supporter

---

[23] Interview with Sergei Razov, the Russian ambassador to China, in *Rossiyskaya Gazeta*, October 13, 2009.

[24] Alexander Dynkin, ed., *Strategichesky globalny prognoz 2030* [Global Strategic Forecast 2030] (Moscow: Institute of World Economy and International Relations), 2011.

of New Delhi's bid to become a permanent member of the UNSC. Having India in the world's top league, Russian strategists believed, would help stabilize the global balance and give international development a more positive direction.

Power Balancing in Asia and Beyond

Moscow is no stranger to power balancing. True, what Russia mostly needs now is domestic development, particularly in Siberia and along the Pacific coast. However, this task has an external aspect. Ideally, Moscow would like Japan to become a "Germany in the East," a modernization resource and a political partner in Asia. A strong relationship with Tokyo would also give Moscow more room to maneuver with Beijing. Moscow's efforts to stimulate competition between Beijing and Tokyo as it was pondering whether the oil pipeline from Eastern Siberia should go to Northeast China or to the Sea of Japan is sufficient evidence that Moscow understands the stakes involved.[25] However, Russo-Japanese political relations continue to be in a deep freeze over the Kuril Islands. In 2010–11 the issue turned into a political football in both capitals.[26] Thus, the opposite happened. In 2010, Moscow played along with Beijing to put pressure on Tokyo during the anniversary of the end of World War II, and Moscow's 2011 offer for foreign companies to invest in the southern Kurils could be exploited by China to drive a serious wedge into Russo-Japanese relations. At the same time, however, China's growing might and new assertiveness has already started to "concentrate the minds" in both Moscow and Tokyo. Eventually, this may drive the two countries to resolve their territorial issue.

Russian–South Korean relations are also relevant to China. Wedged between China and Japan, South Korea may see some value in a partnership with Russia. Another piece of the Eastern Asian chessboard is Vietnam. Given the legacy of the Soviet era, Moscow views Hanoi as potentially its premier economic partner in Southeast Asia. Hanoi's relations with Beijing are complicated, yet Moscow will hardly pass up the opportunity to bolster its engagement with Vietnam in order to balance China's power on the PRC's southern flank.

Russian leaders and thinkers usually point to the double-headed eagle of the state emblem as a symbol of the country's bi-continental character

---

[25] In the end, it was decided that the pipeline would run to the Sea of Japan, with a spur to China to be built first. Russian oil started flowing to China in 2011.

[26] See, for example, Sergei Strokan, "Yuzhye Kurily ne delyatsya, a umnozhayutsya" [Southern Kurils Do Not Divide, They Multiply], *Kommersant*, February 9, 2011; and Yuri Tavrovsky, "Problema severnykh territoriy—yashchik Pandory" [The Northern Territories Issue: The Pandora's Box], *Nezavisimaya Gazeta*, February 7, 2011.

and intimate involvement in the affairs of both Europe and Asia. This popular view notwithstanding, Russian elites have always been Eurocentric. Traditionally, Asia has been a backyard and an afterthought. This is now changing, however. The drivers of change include Russia's post-imperial loss of power and status, and the general reversal of its dynamic from outward expansion to inward-looking preoccupation with its own problems; the EU's initial consolidation and expansion, now followed by apparent stagnation; and, as far as Asia itself is concerned, the rise of China and the emergence of India as a great power. Even as Russia reaches out to Europe economically and socially, it is becoming increasingly aware of the growing strategic importance of Asia, which is starting to dominate Russian strategic thinking for the first time. Although Russians sometimes pride themselves on being "Eurasian"—that is, capable of understanding equally well the peoples of the West and the East[27]—engaging Asia's two biggest nations presents a serious challenge to Moscow.

Cultural Links

China: A Civilizational Divide

Russians usually become more aware of their European cultural origin when they meet with their neighbors in Asia (above all China) than when they deal with other Europeans, who do not always treat Russia as "one of us." The Russo-Chinese border is a clear civilizational divide. In cultural terms, the Russian Far East is an extension of Eastern Europe, not of East Asia. Foreign visitors, whether Secretary of State Henry Kissinger, who travelled to Vladivostok for the U.S.-Soviet summit in 1974, or the EU Commission president José Manuel Barroso, who arrived in Khabarovsk in 2010 for an EU-Russia summit, are struck by that fact.[28] What is amazing is how little presence Asia has in Eastern Russian cities, from Blagoveshchensk to Irkutsk, often only a few dozen or a couple hundred km from the Chinese or Mongolian border.

Despite the occasionally alarmist talk of Chinese immigration into Russia, the number of resident Chinese there is relatively small, totaling at most 500,000 and being concentrated in Russia's cosmopolitan capital, Moscow, as well as in St. Petersburg and a handful of other major cities. By contrast, the number of Chinese at any one time in Primorie, which has a

---

[27] See, for example, Karen Brutents, "Rossiya i Aziya" [Russia and Asia], *Mezhdunarodnaya Zhizn*, no. 3 (March 2011): 120–37.

[28] Henry Kissinger, *Years of Upheaval* (New York: Little Brown and Co., 1982); and author's personal conversations with Jose Manuel Barroso's staff.

population of 2 million, is only between 25,000 and 27,000.[29] And yet even though there is no evidence of Chinese "colonization" of the Russian regions lying just across the border from China, which some Chinese still hold to have been unlawfully annexed by the Russian empire, that continues to be the principal fear in the popular Russian mind. This fear, while deep-seated, has not yet reached the stage of paranoia. Instead, Russian public opinion polls reflect generally positive attitudes toward China. In a 2009 survey, Russians ranked China fourth among the countries friendliest to Russia (with 18% of respondents calling it friendliest) and only fourteenth among potential adversaries (only 3% of Russians saw it as a likely enemy). India, for its part, was ranked below China among Russia's friends (likely owing to the more distant relationship between the countries) but was nowhere to be found on the list of would-be adversaries.[30]

The recent rise in Russia of xenophobia, chauvinism, and racism has largely focused on Muslim immigrants from Central Asia and the North Caucasus. So far, there have been relatively few—though well-publicized—incidents involving the Chinese or Indian populations. The Chinese have escaped such hostility by keeping a generally low profile and living in tightly-knit, inward-looking communities with very few points of contact with the wider world, which gives them a degree of protection. Chinese communities in Russia have a highly developed infrastructure, with banks, hotels, and newspapers catering to the needs of the local Chinese residents.

The opening of the Sino-Russian border in the early 1990s resulted not only in an influx of Chinese traders and workers in the Far East but also in a parallel stream of Russian visitors to China. They arrived first as shuttle traders, hoping to make a bit of money by buying cheap consumer goods in neighboring Chinese cities and reselling them in Khabarovsk, Vladivostok, and Irkutsk, among other places. Later, Russians travelled to China for more sophisticated business deals and eventually for holidays and vacations. From Beidaihe on the Yellow Sea to subtropical Hainan, Chinese beaches are increasingly populated by Russian tourists. In 2010, they numbered 2.4 million, which, though fewer than in 2008, is still many more than the 700,000 Chinese who visited Russia.[31]

---

[29] Ivanter, "To, chto oslabevaet, usilitsya," 39.

[30] *Obshchestvennoe mnenie 2009* [Russian Public Opinion 2009] (Moscow: Levada Center, 2010), 162–63, tables 19.9 and 19.10.

[31] *Rossiyskiy turizm v Kitae: rost na 36%* [Tourism from Russia in China Grows in 2010 by 36%], RIA Novosti, February 24, 2011, http://rian.ru/tourism/20110224/338323158.html.

India: Limited Cultural Ties

Russo-Indian cultural links are weaker, but relations are warmer. Ordinary Russians have no fear whatsoever of Indians and a great deal of sympathy for them. The number of Indian residents in Russia is about 15,000, of which some 5,000 are students and 500 are businessmen.[32] Those Indian residents are widely dispersed in Moscow and other major centers. Most Russian travelers to India visit Goa and other tourist destinations. In order to promote cultural links, the Russian government has held "year of Russia" celebrations in both China and India, while organizing Chinese and Indian festivals in Russia, including a "year of the Chinese language," starting in 2006. While people-to-people links represent the future of Russo-Chinese and Russo-Indian relations, the past and the present have been dominated by military-technical ties, which for different reasons are now losing their primacy.

In the 21st century, Russia should define itself as a Euro-Pacific country rather than a Eurasian one. The principal difference lies in the emphasis on integration with Europe and the Asia-Pacific rather than domination of either, as in the past ("a great power in Europe and a great power in Asia"). If accepted, this would constitute a fundamental change of strategy. Russia is probably moving in that direction anyway, but its establishment as a whole is not there yet. This makes strategizing both immensely important and exceedingly difficult.

Russia's Strategies toward China and India: Internal Differences and Consensus

Leadership and Societal Perceptions of China's and India's Rise

Russia's top leadership, still essentially westward-looking, sees China as a major partner, of course, but not as a pole of attraction. India is a friend, but the United States and the EU matter much more. President Dmitry Medvedev seeks to assure Russia's security in the Euro-Atlantic, and Prime Minister Putin champions a common economic space with the EU through asset swaps with Europe's leading multinationals.[33] For Gazprom and Rosneft, even despite the $15 billion loan that the latter received from Beijing in 2009,

---

[32] "Indian Community in Russia," Embassy of India, Moscow, March 25, 2011, http://www.indianembassy.ru/cms/index.php?option=com_content&task=view&id=22&Itemid=540.

[33] Vladimir Putin, "Von Lissabon bis Wladiwostok" [From Lisbon to Vladivostok], *Sueddeutsche Zeitung*, November 25, 2010. See also Vladimir Putin, "Vystuplenie predsedatelya pravitelstva RF v gosudarstvennoy Dume RF" [The Prime Minister's Annual Report to the State Duma], April 21, 2011.

China remains an alternative, or secondary, market, which should bolster the Russian state companies' positions vis-à-vis European countries.

On China, the Russian political class as a whole is more sharply divided. The diehard opponents of the United States among government bureaucrats, the official media, and retired veterans, who still resent the way the Cold War ended, fancy China as the United States' nemesis. Some of them hope that Russia can be to China what Great Britain was, or at least tried to be, to the United States in the course of the twentieth century: sort of a new Athens to a latter-day Rome. These Russians define such a role as that of "an elder sister."[34] This group also includes those elements in the defense industry and its affiliates that blame the United States for stealing their traditional Soviet-era markets, refusing to allow them access to the arms markets of U.S. allies, and having thus effectively confined them to the "China-India ghetto."

Others, sometimes no less skeptical of the U.S. global role than the former group, view China with a wary eye. The Federal Security Service (FSB in Russian) has been regularly and publicly reporting on captures of Chinese agents engaged in military-technological espionage in Russia. The security community also has imposed restrictions on what arms and equipment can be sold to China. Russian technology transfers to China are being subjected to particularly stringent regulations. This has bred discontent in Beijing, where off-the-shelf purchases are no longer regarded as essential. Chinese arms manufacturers have learned to copy (clone) Russian-made weapons systems, much to the chagrin, of course, of Russian defense industrialists. As for the Russian armed forces, in 2010 they staged their biggest military maneuvers in Siberia and the Far East since the downfall of the Soviet Union.[35]

Russian society as a whole is ambivalent toward China and the Chinese. According to a Russian FOM (Public Opinion Foundation) poll in October 2009, 44% saw China as a threat to Russian interests, compared to 39% who did not. The former group argued that China's power is growing, thanks to Russian resources, while Russia is losing its edge. As noted above, China's threat to Russia, as opposed to its interests, is rated by the bulk of the Russian public as fairly low.

India, on the contrary, is almost universally seen as a good, problem-free, friendly country. To many within the Russian establishment, India is the only major power that can be Russia's genuine ally. The military industrial complex has fewer reservations about sharing sensitive technologies with

---

[34] See, for example, Andrey Devyatov, interview with *Finam FM*, May 15, 2009.

[35] Oleg Falichev, "'Vostok-2010': Nachalo, kulminatsiya, epilog" ["Vostok-2010": The Beginning, Apex, and Epilogue], *Voenno-Promyshlenniy Kurier*, July 14, 2010.

India than it does with almost any other country. A comparison between the Su-30MKI (the fighter's export version for India) and Su-30MKK (the modification for China) graphically shows that even the weapons systems that Russians sell to India are more advanced than similar ones that are earmarked for the Chinese market. There is virtually no group within Russia that is opposed to closer ties with India. The problem is developing the right strategy for cultivating those ties and committing the necessary resources toward such a strategy. Incidentally, this is also true with regard to Russia's approach to China.

Policies and Strategies toward China and India

Russia has a set of policies toward China but hardly a long-term strategy. The policies include resolving the border issue and ensuring that the resolution is final; keeping the relationship friendly and stable; honoring Beijing's three core interests (Taiwan, Tibet, and Xinjiang); avoiding anything that might provoke Beijing's ire, such as extending an invitation to the Dalai Lama (who was last permitted to enter Russia in the 1990s) or attending the Nobel Peace Prize ceremony in 2010 in honor of a Chinese dissident; using the Chinese market to diversify Russia's energy exports; and supplying China with military hardware to tie it to Russia, but not with more advanced military technology that might make China too strong too soon.

Russia's leaders, who now meet their Chinese counterparts several times a year in both bilateral and multilateral settings, seem to realize that the Chinese look at Russia very pragmatically, as both a geopolitical rear that has freed China from the "threat from the north" and as a resource base rich in raw materials and water. Some leaders are also aware of the contempt that a number of present-day senior Chinese feel toward Russia and the Russians.

Russia's strategic approach to India is based on the notion that the "problem-free" relationship can be turned into a functioning strategic partnership, bordering on an alliance. The way to that essentially lies in expanding and diversifying the economic ties between the two countries, transforming the arms relationship into one of defense industrial integration, and translating the general agreement on strategic goals into practical cooperation in the region, beginning in Afghanistan and Central Asia. The question is whether there is enough capacity in the Russian government bureaucracy not only to develop and articulate such a strategy but, more importantly, to stick to it. At a different level, country strategies need to be harmonized and integrated into a more general strategic framework related to Asia that will be implemented in both bilateral and multilateral contexts.

Russia's Emerging Multilateralism

A Multipolar Global Order

Since the mid-1990s, Beijing, New Delhi, and Moscow have adopted broadly parallel visions of the global order. All were unhappy, albeit to a different degree, about Washington's "unipolar moment," and all came up with their own versions of multipolarity instead. All spoke in favor of upholding traditional post–World War II international law, with its respect for state sovereignty and territorial integrity and rejection of outside interference in other countries' internal affairs, particularly regarding the use of force. As permanent, veto-wielding members of the UNSC, Russia and China supported the leading role of the UN.

In the course of the past two decades, Russia and China have consistently adopted similar positions at the UNSC, sometimes blocking motions by the Western powers, led by the United States. Moscow and Beijing agree on the following principles:

1. Only those decisions which are adopted by the UNSC—i.e., to which Moscow and Beijing do not object—are legal in terms of international law.

2. There should be minimal interference by the world body in the internal affairs of member states; this concerns, above all, military intervention and the removal of governments.

3. Human rights, in particular, should be no reason for outside intervention as long as violations do not constitute a threat to world peace and security.

Before Russia's war with Georgia, China and Russia also appealed to the principle of the territorial integrity of states. Even when Moscow later recognized Abkhazia and South Ossetia, which had broken away from Georgia, Beijing stuck to its old position of the inviolability of borders.

During the Kosovo crisis in 1998–99, Russo-Chinese opposition prevented the United States, Britain, and France from winning UNSC approval of the military intervention against Yugoslavia. Moscow, Beijing, and Paris similarly refused to support the U.S.-UK invasion of Iraq in 2003 and instead sought to mediate between Saddam Hussein and the international community prior to the invasion. Russia and China have been consistently more conciliatory toward North Korea and Iran, Russia's trading partners. They have occasionally agreed to calibrated sanctions against Pyongyang and Tehran while continuing to reject the threat of force. Each country, however, is pursuing a policy geared to its own interests. China views North Korea in the wider geopolitical context of Northeast Asia and through the prism of the PRC's relations with the United States. Russia, arguably, does the same vis-à-vis Iran.

Sino-Russian cooperation at the UN is not absolute, however. When, in the atmosphere of improved U.S.-Russian relations following their "reset," Moscow decided in 2010 to toughen its stance on Iran, Beijing was suddenly denied a useful cover and compelled to make a hard choice: either to be left alone at the UNSC or to bandwagon on what was becoming a common great-power position. It chose the latter. Likewise, on the issue of UNSC reform, Moscow and Beijing take different positions. Russia, like the United States, supports permanent Security Council membership for India, a longtime ally and friend. China, which views India as a competitor, adamantly opposes its bid.

Although India's less elevated status at the UN prevented it from taking center stage in Security Council discussion of these issues, its actual position on them was close to the positions of Beijing and Moscow. After joining the Security Council as a non-permanent member in January 2011, India took the same position as Russia, China, Brazil, and indeed Germany on the military intervention in support of the UNSC's no-fly zone resolution on Libya. Despite all their glaring differences and disparities, the BRIC countries (Brazil, Russia, India, and China) have managed to display solidarity and a degree of policy coordination.

As of 2011, the BRIC group has held three summits and numerous foreign ministers' meetings. The group expanded in April 2011 to include South Africa (BRICS from now on). Although the BRIC format was initiated by Moscow, Russia itself is the odd man out in that group. The issue is not only that its economy is not growing as fast as China's or India's, or that it is primarily an energy producer, while the others are consumers. Russia does not consider itself an emerging country. It is a historical great power, a past military superpower, and a former colonizer rather than a former colony. Few among Russia's political elite would naturally identify themselves with the likes of Brazil, not to mention South Africa.

Russia, of course, enjoys having a foot in different camps. Apart from the UNSC and BRICS, it is a member of the group of eight (G-8), is oriented toward strategic partnership with NATO, and is an observer at the Organization of the Islamic Conference. Since the late 1990s, Russia has also been promoting the idea of a triangular partnership with India and China (known as RIC).[36] That idea is particularly attractive to Moscow because Russia has much better relations with each of the Asian giants than China and India have with each other. This gives Moscow an advantage as long as it has a valid objective, a well-conceived strategy, and particularly flexible and resourceful diplomacy. So far, RIC, which by early 2011 had held ten meetings at the foreign ministers' level, has been more of a protocol event than a real policy tool.

Multilateral Organizations and Activities in Russia's Own Neighborhood

Even in the mid-1990s, Moscow supported Beijing's initiative to institutionalize the border talks mechanism between China and the successor states of the Soviet Union. Originally named the Shanghai Five, the group later became known as the Shanghai Cooperation Organisation (SCO). It presently includes China, Kazakhstan, Kyrgyzstan, Russia, Tajikistan, and Uzbekistan as full members; India, Pakistan, Iran, and Mongolia are observers. Moscow's decision to go along with the Chinese idea was probably based on the assumption that the SCO would give Russia a degree of transparency and a measure of control regarding China's westward expansion. India's inclusion in the SCO was made on Moscow's initiative. Pakistan was simultaneously added by Beijing for balance.

At the same time, Russia has sought to strengthen its own presence and influence in Central Asia through the Collective Security Treaty Organization (CSTO), the Eurasian Economic Community, and the Customs Union with Kazakhstan (and Belarus). Moscow has made clear that it envisages only a limited role for the SCO in the field of regional security, which it views as its own preserve, and instead prefers to rely on the CSTO. Moscow likewise does not embrace the idea of turning the SCO into an organization for regional development, a field where China has a clear advantage. As a result, the SCO is still little more than a platform for regional dialogue and a chapeau for various contacts, from military exercises to transportation projects.

In Northeast Asia, Russia has long been calling for transforming the six-party talks on the North Korea nuclear issue into a regional security arrangement. This is a long shot, however. Meanwhile, Russia and the

---

[36] This idea belongs to Yevgeny Primakov, Russia's foreign minister (1996–98) and prime minister (1998–99). See R.N. Das, "Russia-China-India Trilateral: Calibrating a Fine Balance," IDSA, IDSA Comment, November 15, 2010, http://www.idsa.in/idsacomments/ RussiaChinaIndiaTrilateralCalibratingaFineBalance_rndas_151110.

United States have just joined the East Asia Summit,[37] which will discuss security issues in Pacific Asia. On the North Korea issue, Moscow first sought to perform the role of a mediator between Pyongyang and the West; having failed in that, it aligned its approach closely with that of Beijing, before more recently moving closer to Seoul. This trajectory suggests that Russia views South Korea, and in the future a united Korea led by Seoul, as a useful partner vis-à-vis both Japan and China. In Southeast Asia, Russia has participated in a regular dialogue with Association of Southeast Asian Nations (ASEAN) countries.

Finally, Russia in 2012 will host the Asia-Pacific Economic Cooperation (APEC) summit in Vladivostok. This decision had a lot to do with Putin's desire not only to promote Russia as a Pacific country but also to use the preparation for the summit to spur the development of the city and the area. Yet another reason behind the move was to highlight Russia's sovereignty over the region, acquired through the 1860 treaty with China. The more flags wave in Vladivostok, the higher flies the Russian tricolor. The concluding section will discuss the relevance of these activities for the United States.

Conclusion and Outlook

Becoming a Euro-Pacific Country

At present, Moscow's Asia-wide strategy is still in gestation at best.[38] The rise of India and especially China, which present different challenges to Moscow, can help the process. The 2012 APEC summit in Vladivostok will be propitious for setting out Russia's policy ideas for the Asia-Pacific. Moscow has realized that in the early 21st century its foreign policy must primarily serve the interests of domestic development, and vice versa: Russian foreign policy will only be as strong as the country's economic, demographic, and scientific potential will allow. Consequently, Russians think less of projecting power in Asia and more of spurring the development of their own eastern, "Asiatic" provinces.

The concept of Eurasianism, which vacillated between open confrontation with the West and balancing between the West and China, is irrelevant for the issues facing Russia today and should be replaced by the concept of Russia as

---

[37] Heretofore, the East Asia Summit included the ASEAN countries, China, Japan, South Korea, India, Australia, and New Zealand.

[38] One can point to a 2010 policy speech by Medvedev in Khabarovsk. See Dmitri Medvedev, "Excerpts from Transcript of Meeting on the Far East's Socioeconomic Development and Cooperation with Asia-Pacific Region Countries," July 2, 2010, President of Russia, Kremlin, website, http://eng.news.kremlin.ru/transcripts/547.

a Euro-Pacific country.[39] This means, in practice, the establishment of a Euro-Atlantic security community as well as economic integration with the EU in the west and close economic relations with the Pacific Rim countries in the east. Russia would not split into two in the process; rather, both European and Pacific countries would be encouraged to invest in all Russian regions. The real problem is how to make Russia attractive to investors—that is, how to ensure the rule of law, property rights, and transparency in decisionmaking.

Along its European flank, Russia would be right to pursue a strategy of economic integration, complete with a free trade area and a common economic space built on an energy partnership. In the Pacific, a concept that would be particularly useful for Russia's modernization and geopolitical balance would be that of a North-Pacific region embracing Alaska and the U.S. west coast, Canada, Japan, South Korea, China, and Pacific Russia and eastern Siberia. Unlike the more familiar concept of Northeast Asia, a North Pacific region would include China but not be dominated by it.

At present, Russo-Chinese relations are better than at any time in history, and they are likely to remain so and perhaps improve further in the foreseeable future. However, as China's power continues to grow, Moscow's policy toward Beijing should steer clear of both confrontation and overdependence. Moscow needs to enhance mutual confidence through a dialogue with Beijing and build trust through collaboration, but it should not compromise on key interests. Domestically, Russia must avoid harboring both inordinate fears and illusions about its mighty neighbor. While increasing economic cooperation with China, Russia should begin to gradually raise the technological level of its exports. In the political sphere, Track 2 and 1.5 dialogues should support and enliven the rather stale official exchanges. In the cultural sphere, Russia needs to dramatically expand Chinese studies and gain new expertise through student and professional exchanges.

Russia should also be prepared for the eventuality of China's growth slowing down and even faltering, which might result in Beijing adopting a more belligerent foreign policy in order to bolster the regime's legitimacy. Then, Russia might find itself affected. In view of this eventuality, Moscow needs to make sure that its deterrence capacity is credible and that the regional and global international environment is favorable to Russia.

Even under current stable conditions, strengthening relations with other Pacific countries, such as Korea, Japan, and the United States, would

[39] It is telling that the concept of Russia as a Euro-Pacific country, first proposed by the author, has by now found its way into internal documents prepared for Medvedev's 2010 policy speech in Khabarovsk. See Vyacheslav Nikonov, "Tikhookeanskaya strategiya Rossii" [Russia's Pacific Strategy] (unpublished manuscript).

increase Russia's position vis-à-vis China. Here, relations with India are of particular importance. Not only is India the natural balancer on the Asian continent, but it is also a useful partner for Russia in Central Asia and, potentially, the Middle East. Moscow must take advantage of the largely untapped reservoir of economic cooperation and sense of cultural affinity between the two countries to help broaden societal support for the bilateral relationship. The prospects for Indo-Russian collaboration are only limited by the capacities of both countries to sustain such collaboration. In the next couple of decades, Russia is likely to become more like India than China in terms of the influence it exercises in the world—that is, more a major regional power than a global force.

The United States will have a very important impact on Russian policies in Asia. Unlike in the case of Europe, Moscow does not object to U.S. politico-military presence in Northeast Asia and the Western Pacific, which it feels has a restraining effect on Beijing. Even more importantly, U.S. investments in Pacific Russia and Siberia, should they occur in a significant volume, could strengthen the economic foundation of the Russian state and its position in Asia. While the United States is not the ultimate guarantor of Russia's military security in the Far East (the Russian nuclear deterrent is), good relations with Washington are a clear asset for any potential eventuality.

Implications of Russia's Asia Policies for the United States

With Russia possessing vast geopolitical space and rich natural resources, its China policy is among the most important factors in Asian power balancing. Nonetheless, the days when Russia seeks to dominate China and claim a leading role in the bilateral relationship are history, not to be repeated. At the same time, Moscow is not yet an independent and active player in the Asia-Pacific. If such were the case, it would probably help sustain a more balanced security environment in the region. By contrast, a Russia that is China's de facto vassal creates a massive imbalance and thus contributes to insecurity in Asia and the Pacific. Russia will not join any coalition to contain China. That much is clear, and calls by individual Americans to build a U.S.-Russian partnership to resist the rise of China are met with skepticism or suspicion.[40] Only if China were to turn against Russia and start threatening it would Moscow start campaigning for an international effort to pressure Beijing.

---

[40] Yevgeny Bazhanov, "Luchshe druzhit' s Kitaem, a ne protiv nego" [Better to Make Friends with China, Not Be Against It], *Nezavisimaya Gazeta*, February 14, 2011.

An enlightened U.S. foreign policy must first make sure that Russia, with its resources and geopolitical position, is not driven into an overt anti-U.S. alliance with China. Tactical maneuvering is one thing; a strategic alignment is another. This agrees with Russia's own natural inclination, which is toward Europe and, more broadly, the West—as a coequal member, not a client or a ward. Reorienting the U.S.-Russian strategic relationship from residual post–Cold War adversity toward a non-adversarial model is a prerequisite for Russia's modernization. By contrast, Russia's strategic isolation and rivalry in the West would probably make it move far closer to China than would otherwise be necessary, just for the sake of geopolitical balance.

Russia's India policy runs parallel to that of the United States. Although outwardly it may appear that Moscow is competing with Washington for New Delhi's favors, in reality, unlike in the days of the Great Game or the Cold War, this is not a zero-sum game. In many areas, Russia simply cannot compete with the United States; in many more, it would not. As for India, it will seek to benefit from good relations with both its new powerful friend, the United States, and its long-term ally, Russia. Of course, there may be perceived gains and losses, as in the areas of arms sales or civilian nuclear energy. Yet Moscow's general respect for New Delhi will probably prevent it from misinterpreting strengthened India-U.S. ties as a sign of India letting down Moscow to curry favor with Washington.

The United States, India, Russia, and China share a number of important interests and can surely find a way to cooperate. Afghanistan is one obvious opportunity for cooperation. As the U.S.-NATO operation there is phased out, the importance of big-power cooperation in the region increases. Narcotics, terrorism, and regional instability in Central Asia are potential areas for joint engagement. In Northeast Asia, the six-party talks and the East Asia Summit could lay the foundation of an inclusive security arrangement embracing all the main players in that part of the world.

STRATEGIC ASIA 2011–12

REGIONAL STUDIES

EXECUTIVE SUMMARY

This chapter explores the competition for influence in Central Asia between China, India, and other powers, as well as Central Asian responses.

MAIN ARGUMENT:
The strategic dynamic created by the interplay of large powers—China, India, the U.S., and Russia—and the smaller, resource-rich Central Asian states is complex and constantly shifting. China's robust economy and geographic position tilt the competition in its favor and offer opportunities available to no other actor. India is at a disadvantage, but its fortunes could change depending on its relationships with Russia and the U.S., growing demands for Indian technology, and a generational change in Central Asia that results in a greater appreciation for India's democratic values. Russia remains the critical balancer in the Central Asian competition, and significant advantages will accrue to any future Russian partner.

POLICY IMPLICATIONS:
- China's advantage in Central Asia is large and growing. Beijing has cornered vital energy resources and used its abundant funds to promote their transport to China. But this strategy contains inherent contradictions and could prove fragile.

- India's presence in Central Asia has been tentative, and its strategy seems piecemeal. India trails China in the competition for Central Asian energy, and New Delhi's security relationship with Tajikistan lacks deep roots, although its position in Kazakhstan and Turkmenistan may be strengthening.

- In Central Asia, only Kazakhstan stands out for its strategic thinking. Kyrgyzstan, Tajikistan, and Turkmenistan are largely reactive to other actors in the region. Uzbekistan could be a game changer, but it remains isolated. Central Asian countries have yet to work together to advance common interests in the face of large-power competition, and there is little prospect of this happening in the near future.

Great Games in Central Asia

S. Enders Wimbush

In the shadow of Asia's rising powers and on the margins of Asia itself, the states of Central Asia—Uzbekistan, Kazakhstan, Kyrgyzstan, Tajikistan, and Turkmenistan—are in play in a deepening competition for access and influence between China and India, among others. This chapter explores, first, how Chinese and Indian strategists might think about the shape and dynamics of that competition in Central Asia and the character of their strategies, to the extent that such strategies exist. Second, it examines the competition from the standpoint of the Central Asian countries themselves, seeking to associate their reactions to the strategies of the larger powers and the strategies they create in response, at least where they might be visible. Third, the chapter attempts to broadly understand how the interplay of large-power strategies and small-country responses could affect the emerging strategic landscape in Asia.

To understand the trajectories and dynamics of the new competition in Central Asia—and especially the region's response to nearby rising powers China and India—analysts must first jettison the notion that Central Asia is a single strategic piece forged from the experience of being the object of Russia's foreign policy for several centuries. That Russia was able to seal Central Asia for so long enhanced this notion, despite the inconvenient fact that much of Central Asia lay outside Soviet political boundaries. The individual states now constituting post-Soviet Central Asia are not an amalgam of shared strategic interests and objectives, despite having much in common with each other. Increasingly they are designing their own strategies to pursue objectives that are sometimes shared but sometimes

S. Enders Wimbush is Senior Director, Foreign Policy and Civil Society, at the German Marshall Fund of the United States. He can be reached at <ewimbush@gmfus.org>.

in conflict with their Central Asian neighbors. The Central Asia they see—as well as the character of the competition enveloping it—is not foremost the Soviet Central Asia of yesteryear, but rather the larger Central Asia encompassing states beyond the former Soviet Union and dynamics that are largely external to the former Soviet space. That said, some countries see the emerging strategic architecture better than others; some simply react to it.

China encompasses a good portion of Central Asia and shares ethnic and historical populations, languages, and cultures with the former Soviet states it borders. This is true of most of the states proximate to the old Soviet empire (for example, Iran, Afghanistan, and Turkey). The historical and cultural roots of India's Mughal civilization are likewise in Central Asia, a theme found frequently in the analysis of contemporary Indian experts on the region.[1] Islam links these groups to a greater or lesser degree from Russia's Middle Volga region to India's Punjab, and from the fractious North Caucasus to China's Xinjiang Province. Even Tibet can claim a historical attachment to Central Asia.

The competitive context in Central Asia is formed primarily by two larger dynamics that sometimes overlap, intersect, converge, or collide. The first dynamic is created by outsiders. Central Asia is a cauldron of large actors, including not only China and India but also the United States, the Gulf Arab states, Turkey, and, to a lesser extent, Europe. Russia's strategic interests in the region continue; indeed, they have intensified as the presence of other actors has become more pronounced. But Russia is itself now an outsider, though one possessing an insider's feel for the leitmotifs of societies it once ruled and for the local political cultures still dominated by Soviet-generation leaders.

The second dynamic is created by insiders. Central Asia today is a dynamic mix of local actors redefining themselves along both vertical and horizontal strategic axes. The states of post-Soviet Central Asia today adopt very different attitudes toward larger competitors, including India and China, to the extent that they adopt any attitude at all. Relations among these states are at best cautious, at worst hostile; they affect and project different attitudes about their affinity for or antipathy to the West and East. While their strategic visions are often opaque or difficult to identify, little suggests that Central Asian states see themselves on a common pathway to the same future.

---

[1] Emilian Kavalski, "An Elephant in a China Shop? India's Look North to Central Asia…Seeing Only China," in *China and India in Central Asia: A New "Great Game"?* ed. Marlène Laruelle, Jean-François Huchet, Sébastien Peyrouse, and Bayram Balci (New York: Palgrave MacMillan, 2010), 42.

Of these two dynamics, the former is probably still the more powerful, although this is changing. Indeed, to a large extent the first dynamic drives the second, in the sense that Central Asian countries tend to establish objectives and design strategies to pursue these objectives reactively or opportunistically in response to their perceptions of the larger actors' strategies, especially those of China, Russia, and, to a much lesser extent, India and the United States. Their foreign policies generally attempt to accommodate the objectives and strategies of outsiders rather than boldly define pathways for achieving well-understood national interests. It probably is the case, too, that most see China as the emerging hegemon in the region. Russia, in contrast, remains a force to be mollified despite being eclipsed by China across most measures of power and influence. India remains in the distant background, a rumor of economic power and technological accomplishment. It is not in the same league as China or Russia, nor half so visible, but is potentially a future balancer of either or both.

Unlike in the Soviet period, when strategic thinking was centered in Moscow, today Central Asian leaders and their foreign policy establishments for the most part exhibit a mixed understanding of the strategic context and dynamics of large-power competition in Central Asia. Old-guard leaders such as Uzbekistan's Islam Karimov, Kazakhstan's Nursultan Nazarbayev, and Turkmenistan's Gurbanguly Berdymukhamedov dominate all aspects of thinking and planning in their respective strategic spheres. However, in each state a younger generation of specialists, often working in newly created national institutes or in U.S. or European institutions, is emerging as the cultures of isolation that characterized these societies in the immediate post-Soviet years are confronted by a variety of new influences. As the actuarial tables claim most of today's Central Asian leaders, the tempo and direction of the competition described below will almost certainly change.

Giants on a Roll

China's Strategy

China is on everyone's mind. A Chinese strategist in Beijing surveying the challenges and opportunities in Central Asia might construct the following list of strategic objectives:

1. The emerging contest for competitive advantage in Central Asia has many parts. Securing overland energy supplies from Central Asia that cannot be interdicted during long maritime voyages from West Africa or the Persian Gulf by the United States, Japan, or India is an immediate requirement and a long-term strategic interest for

China. China can free-ride on the U.S. protective domination of the sea lanes only so long without other options. What might happen if Washington suddenly decided not to protect Chinese energy from the Gulf but to interdict it?

2. The march of Islamic radicalism from Arab lands, Pakistan, and Russia's Middle Volga or North Caucasian regions into China's restive Xinjiang Province via Central Asia is a real problem. Already these antisocial ideas resonate among the Muslims of China. We need to build barriers to this infestation because Russia and the Central Asian states have little resistance. How do we stop this scourge at China's borders?

3. Russia is economically weak, but it continues to have influence in Central Asia. China must soft-pedal Russia by luring it into agreements that allow time for its economy to deteriorate and its demographic position to become irretrievable. Meanwhile, we will engage the Central Asian states so as to erode Russia's dominance and blunt its influence.

4. China's powerful economy provides many instruments for contesting Russia's historical influence in the region, including along its sparsely populated flank in Siberia and the Russian Far East. If we take our time and do not overreach, Central Asia will drop into our lap, which will make it all but impossible for Russia to hold these eastern territories. They could eventually become part of China.

5. The United States' interest in Central Asia is superficial and fleeting, easily countered by China's expanding political influence and physical presence, which flow naturally from its economic power. Where our money goes, so do our people. The Americans have never been particularly good imperialists, and their presence in Central Asia is no different. They will go home soon, chastened and vowing never to return.

6. India will have no chance in Central Asia once the Americans are gone. It has neither the strategic will nor the economic depth to exercise much influence there. By the time New Delhi realizes that its "look north" policy is really nothing more than looking to the Americans to help it acquire strategic positioning, we will have outflanked India totally in Eurasia, right through Iran to the Gulf. Our goal must be to keep Pakistan bubbling without boiling over, which will effectively keep India focused on Pakistan at the expense of developing a larger Central Asian presence.

These objectives, to the extent that they represent official Chinese strategy, are a complex and interactive mix of defense and offense. China was quick to establish relations with the newly independent states of former Soviet Central Asia for purely defensive purposes to protect against the possibility that Taiwan might preempt Beijing in adding the new states to its stable of anti-Chinese diplomatic allies. China successfully negotiated a series of lingering border disputes—it shares borders with Kazakhstan, Kyrgyzstan, and Tajikistan—to inoculate its new sovereign neighbors against visions of influencing co-ethnics and co-religionists in adjoining Xinjiang Province, a kind of "security through normalization of relations."[2]

There is no doubt that acquiring proprietary access to Central Asia's substantial energy resources is a key Chinese strategy, by now documented extensively.[3] Energy is at the core of China's immediate needs in Central Asia, and much that Beijing does can be wrapped in an energy explanation. At the same time, China would have important strategic interests and objectives in Central Asia even if the Eurasian heartland were to contain no energy whatsoever. One should not lose sight of these non-energy objectives, which conduce to strengthening China's geostrategic position against all Eurasia's powerful states, Europe, and the United States. The imperative of having to compete for Eurasia's principal energy sources accelerates and focuses Chinese strategy for the region and establishes tactical milestones.

China's strategy for Central Asia is also captured in the organizations it has created specifically for this purpose, beginning with the Shanghai Five in 1996—consisting of China, Kazakhstan, Kyrgyzstan, Russia, and Tajikistan— which evolved in 2001 into the Shanghai Cooperation Organisation (SCO) with the inclusion of Uzbekistan.[4] Originally conceived as a mutual security arrangement, the SCO now initiates large infrastructure projects (e.g., in communications and transport) and hosts meetings of members' representatives across many interest areas, including antiterrorism, banking, and culture, in addition to hosting joint military exercises. Over time, the success of China's leading role in this multilateral initiative has become evident. The SCO has become the premier international forum for discussions of Central Asia's political and economic future, and much of China's bilateral dialogue with Russia—frequently focused on Central Asian issues of mutual interest—is conducted within the SCO's structure. Not

---

[2] Jean-Pierre Cabestan, "Central Asia–China Relations and Their Relative Weight in Chinese Foreign Policy," in Laruelle, Huchet, Peyrouse, and Balci, *China and India in Central Asia*, 26–27.

[3] For a useful synopsis of China's early efforts to gain and then expand a foothold in Central Asia's energy competition, see Xuanli Liao, "Central Asia and China's Energy Security," *China and Eurasia Forum Quarterly* 4, no. 4 (November 2006): 61–69.

[4] See, for example, Michael Clarke, "China and the Shanghai Cooperation Organization: The Dynamics of 'New Regionalism', 'Vassalization', and Geopolitics in Central Asia," in *The New Central Asia: The Regional Impact of International Actors*, ed. Emilian Kavalski (London: World Scientific Publishing Company, 2010).

surprisingly, India deduced that the SCO is a forum from which the country could not afford to be absent and still hope to remain competitive in Central Asia. It applied for and received "observer" status in 2010.

At the same time, China has developed economic enterprises and trade routes into Central Asia,[5] which the Chinese see as an important barrier to prevent both Islamic militancy and the incipient nationalism of the newly independent states from piercing China's borders and infecting Uighurs, Kazakhs, Kirghiz, Uzbeks, and other Central Asian Muslims living within China. Using a strategy that appears paradoxical, China has set about trying to accomplish two seemingly contradictory objectives.

The first is to strengthen the Chinese state's control in these outlying frontier regions, which have a long history of separatist activities and resistance to Beijing's rule. This part of the strategy is reminiscent of the old one, which included flooding Xinjiang with Han Chinese so as to dilute the non-Han presence; aggressive, forced assimilation of local non-Han inhabitants into Chinese norms and culture; and the permanent and, when necessary, brutal application of force by security organs. There is nothing new here. In the post–September 11 political environment, Chinese authorities increasingly conflate terrorism with ethnic nationalism, and their aggressive responses to any opposition—described variously as "zero tolerance" or "strike hard" campaigns—are well documented.[6]

But the second part of this strategy is new. "With the Soviet menace to its western frontiers gone," argues Michael Clarke, "Xinjiang's geopolitical position at the crossroads of Eurasia need no longer be viewed as an obstacle to be overcome in search of integration but rather as an important asset to achieve it."[7] This Chinese "epiphany," attached to Deng Xiaoping's "reform and opening" policies, set in motion a new dynamic strategy to secure Xinjiang's internal stability by guaranteeing its economic development through integration with the larger, hitherto untouchable Central Asia. This is a high-risk game for China, not to be entered into half-heartedly or with half measures. And by all indications, China has successfully doubled down on it.

---

[5] The dimensions of Chinese trade in Central Asia are analyzed in Martin C. Spechler, "Why Does China Have No Business in Central Asia?" *China and Eurasia Forum Quarterly* 7, no. 2 (May/June 2009): 3–15. He argues that China's business in Central Asia results mostly from smuggling and "shuttle trade," and that China actually has developed little "normal commercial business" (see p. 4).

[6] For an excellent historical overview of China's reaction to separatist forces in Xinjiang in the post-Soviet period, see Michael Clark, "China's Post-9/11 Strategy in Central Asia," Griffith Asia Institute, Regional Outlook Paper, no. 5, 2005, http://www.griffith.edu.au/__data/assets/ pdf_file/0015/18231/regional-outlook-volume-5.pdf; and also the excellent collection of essays in Colin Mackerras and Michael Clarke, eds., *China, Xinjiang and Central Asia: History, Transition and Crossborder Interaction into the 21st Century* (New York: Routledge, 2009).

[7] Michael Clarke, "China's Deepening Ties with Central Asia," *Businessweek*, May 26, 2010, http:// www.businessweek.com/globalbiz/content/may2010/gb20100526_156952.htm.

The Central Asian states' reluctance to become involved in, or even vocal about, the July 2009 separatist turmoil in Xinjiang suggests that the bet is paying off. Uzbekistan, Kyrgyzstan, and Kazakhstan all host substantial Uighur communities whose sympathies are known to lie strongly with Xinjiang's restive Uighurs.[8] Yet the SCO's engineered position was neutered. It took note of the suffering caused by the turmoil in Xinjiang but quickly defined away the problem by asserting that the matter was internal to China. Beijing, meanwhile, worked through the SCO and bilaterally to pressure Central Asian governments to crack down on Uighur nationalist sympathizers at home and extradite a number of Uighur "separatists and terrorists" to China.[9]

A casual stroll today down the main streets of most of Central Asia's large cities reveals the unmistakably growing economic preponderance of China. The shops are stuffed with inexpensive Chinese consumer goods, and both legal and illegal Chinese merchandise is sold throughout Central Asia's bazaars. Hotels boast large contingents of Chinese businesspeople, many with direct ties to China's government. Chinese music can be heard routinely in bazaars and on 24-hour radio stations. Mandarin is taught in an expanding network of Confucius Institutes, as fluency in Mandarin is the passport to a good job in either the public sector or private industry.[10]

In Turkmenistan, Kazakhstan, Uzbekistan, and Afghanistan, China has embarked on massive purchases of strategic resources and hydrocarbons, mostly gas, which it works to transport directly to China by pipeline, most recently through the Turkmenistan-China Gas Pipeline. The amounts of energy involved are substantial, as is the size of Chinese investments in energy fields and pipeline infrastructure.[11] Kazakhstan is a particular target, with fifteen majority-Chinese companies and many more with minority stakes at work in the energy and resource industries (e.g., zinc, copper, titanium, aluminum, silver, and gold, in addition to oil, gas, and coal). In 2009, trade between China and the five new Central Asian states stood somewhere around $25 billion.

---

[8] The author witnessed this sympathy first hand while leading a Radio Liberty delegation to Central Asia in 1992, just after the collapse of the Soviet Union. My personal assistant and translator for that trip was Erkin Alptekin, son of the famous late Issa Yusuf Alptekin, head of the First Turkestan Republic in Kashgar in the early 1930s and a leading advocate of Turkestan independence thereafter. Word had passed that Erkin was in the delegation, and at every stop we were met by hundreds of local Uighurs wanting to see and hear the heir apparent.

[9] Clarke, "China's Deepening Ties."

[10] Sébastien Peyrouse, "Comparing the Economic Involvement of China and India in Post-Soviet Central Asia," in Laruelle, Huchet, Peyrouse, and Balci, *China and India in Central Asia*, 167.

[11] See, for example, Florian Pantazi, "China's Investment Strategy in Central Asia," Spotlight on Geopolitics, May 10, 2010, http://florianpantazi.blogactiv.eu/2010/10/chinas-investment-strategy-in-central-asia/.

China sweetens its purchases with soft loans, direct payments, and in some cases advanced technologies. It has signed dozens of investment agreements and credit contracts across the region, worth billions of dollars, in the last decade. Perhaps most attractive of all, China's assistance comes without the political criticism of the region's inbred authoritarian, anti-democratic tendencies that often prefaces trade and development assistance from the United States and Europe. Its agreeable arrangement with Central Asia is not about "democracy or development or transparency," observes analyst Cholpon Orozobekova. "It is all about money."[12]

Beijing's strategy of investing in Central Asia as a way to integrate it with Xinjiang is not without apparent risks to both sides, though it is doubtful that either side thinks of this as a Faustian bargain. The Chinese description of the country's efforts as building a "continental Eurasian land bridge" leaves out the less digestible graphics of the bridge being used as a conduit for people and ideas, perhaps even arms, capable of threatening Xinjiang's tenuous stability. For Central Asians, the bridge from east to west already groans with thousands of Chinese following the fertile opportunity trail extending beyond China's own frontier into Central Asian countries. Whole Chinese communities are springing up, and many more are likely, given the velocity of Chinese investment and the state's preference for ensuring it with lots of Chinese on the ground. Chinese state-directed migrants have occasionally demonstrated a remarkable cultural tone-deafness in other regions of Chinese interest—for example, in Africa and the Middle East—and opposition to China has arisen despite its pecuniary largesse.[13] This should be a cautionary tale to Beijing, lest it be repeated in Central Asia. Having only recently scrubbed much of Russia's heavy veneer from their politics and cultures, Central Asians are unlikely to stand quietly as their fragile, emerging national societies are challenged by a new, albeit richer, imperial power. For the time being, however, China's bargain with Central Asia is paying off, positioning it as the next dominant power in the region.

India's Strategy

In contrast to China, India's movement is more tentative: hesitant and less persistent, yet with a great sense of urgency that to date lacks a strong strategic focus. In private and frequently in academic forums, Indians articulate an acute awareness of the shape and dynamics of the competition

---

[12] Cholpon Orozobekova, "Beijing's Stealthy Expansion in Central Asia," Radio Free Europe/Radio Liberty, January 12, 2011, http://www.rferl.org/content/beijing_stealthy_expansion_central_asia/2274062.html.

[13] See, for example, Rafael Marques de Morais, "The New Imperialism: China in Angola," World Affairs 173, no. 6 (March/April 2011): 67–74.

in Central Asia. Official India seldom reflects these views. An Indian strategist musing in New Delhi on his state's involvement in Central Asia might identify a number of desirable objectives and strategies:[14]

1. China must not be allowed to outflank India in Central Asia through its commercial activities and close political and security relationship with Pakistan. This could have injurious implications for India's access to energy and resources, as well as its ability to influence the larger strategic competition with China in Iran, the Middle East, and Africa.[15]

2. Pakistan and Afghanistan are in danger of failing as states. State failure would cause instability and Islamic radicalism to spread in all directions, including via Afghanistan into Central Asia, where India has fundamental strategic and security interests, and from Central Asia via Afghanistan and Pakistan to India's large Muslim population. Therefore, it is in India's interest to contain this spillover by expanding the country's influence and presence in Central Asia, including some military presence. India lacks a common border with any of the new Central Asian states, but Tajikistan is a mere twenty kilometers from Pakistani-administered Kashmir.

3. Russia is an old friend who, however weakened, still occupies a central position in Central Asians' considerations of their own objectives and strategies. Russia and China may forge tactical alliances to advance their respective competitive advantages in Central Asia—for example, the kind of "mutual security" cooperation championed by the SCO—but in fact they are by nature adversaries. India's strategy for Central Asia should focus on ways to discourage any permanent Sino-Russian strategic alliance. Is it possible, for example, for India to become the "strategic middleman" between Russia and the United States for a focused security discussion on the perils of allowing China's influence to expand unopposed in Central Asia?

4. India needs energy, which Central Asia has in abundance, and must find ways to bring it back to India, notwithstanding the turmoil in Afghanistan and Pakistan. Oil (Kazakhstan), gas (Turkmenistan), and hydropower (Kyrgyzstan and Tajikistan) all figure in this mix. Uzbekistan, the largest and most powerful Central Asian state, has a mix of hydrocarbon resources and must be engaged. Large Western and

---

[14] A good summary of India's strategy is available in Teresita C. Schaffer and Vibhuti Haté, "India's 'Look West' Policy: Why Central Asia Matters," Center for Strategic and International Studies, South Asia Monitor, no. 110, September 5, 2007.

[15] For further remarks on India's policy toward Iran, see "Iran Is the Key to India's 'Look West' Policy: Foreign Secy," *Asian Age*, July 6, 2010.

Russian energy firms have locked up most of the major hydrocarbon fields. Competition for the rest is likely to be between India and China. Indeed, although Indians have managed to cooperate with the Chinese occasionally on energy exploitation, in practice we are intense competitors for most raw materials in Central Asia.[16] This is unlikely to change.

5. Washington must be kept involved in Central Asia at all costs, because without the United States Afghanistan is doomed, which means that Pakistan is doomed. This would lead to a range of other nightmares. But U.S. involvement is a mixed blessing, for, on the one hand, Washington seems keen to keep India distant from Central Asia out of concern for how a larger role for India might upset its "ally" Pakistan. On the other hand, the United States has reorganized diplomatically to align Central Asia and South Asia in a way that underlines common interests and levels of strategic convergence between India and United States at the expense of both Chinese and Russian influence. In this sense, Central Asia is a larger testing ground for the burgeoning Indo-U.S. alliance. This will require delicate diplomacy on India's part.

India's efforts to expand politically, culturally, and economically into Central Asia—"restoring traditional linkages to its extended neighborhood"[17]—have, like China's efforts, for the most part been welcomed by the region's major states. Like China, India does not mind dealing with Soviet-era authoritarian leaders; indeed, it knows most of them intimately. But unlike China, India lacks a geographic attachment to Central Asia's new states. To the contrary, New Delhi's strategies for Central Asia must first contend with hostile Pakistan as a large barrier against direct trade and energy flows between Central Asia and the subcontinent.[18] Put differently, Central Asians have no direct access to India's substantial market. Moreover, India has access to few multilateral institutions capable of facilitating economic and cultural cooperation with the region, and

---

[16] Jean-François Huchet, "India and China in Central Asia: Mirroring Their Bilateral Relations," in Laruelle, Huchet, Peyrouse, and Balci, *China and India in Central Asia*, 108–10.

[17] Gulshan Sachdeva, "India's Attitude towards China's Growing Influence in Central Asia," *China and Eurasia Quarterly* 4, no. 3 (August 2006): 23.

[18] The Trans-Afghanistan-Pakistan-India (TAPI) pipeline, proposed but not yet built, could change attitudes toward political impediments to Central Asia–India trade. Long in planning, a framework to proceed with TAPI was signed with Turkmenistan by Afghanistan, Pakistan, and India in December 2010. The natural gas pipeline will run more than one thousand miles across territory once thought too hostile for such a project. See Bruce Pannier, "TAPI Pipeline Signed, Sealed—Not Yet Delivered," Radio Free Europe/Radio Liberty, December 15, 2010, http://www.rferl.org/content/feature/2248838.html.

its largely private economy lacks the powerful state driver of China's commercial activity.[19]

Comparisons reveal the extent of China's advantage. Its trade with Central Asia was more than 18 billion euros in 2008, while India's was a mere 247 million euros. China is Kyrgyzstan's largest trading partner, Uzbekistan's and Tajikistan's second largest, Kazakhstan's third largest, and Turkmenistan's seventh largest. By contrast, India ranks 20th, 16th, 22nd, 19th, and 20th, respectively.[20] Although India has enjoyed success in exporting its pharmaceuticals to Central Asia, capturing perhaps as much as 30% of the regional market, the Central Asian market is too immature to draw heavily on India's knowledge and technology economy. That will have to await the future.

Without transport infrastructure to link South and Central Asia via Pakistan, India will remain at a permanent disadvantage to China in the region. Its efforts to go around the Pakistan bottleneck led India to join with Iran and Russia in 2000 to propose the North-South Transport Corridor, a planned network of highways, railroads, and shipping lanes intended to move goods between South Asia and Europe via Central Asia, the Caucasus, and Russia. Infrastructure deficiencies have limited the project's potential, to date.[21] Even when Pakistan's assent is forthcoming—for example, to build a Turkmenistan-Afghanistan-Pakistan-India (TAPI) pipeline to bring Turkmenistan's gas to the subcontinent—other potentially lethal issues (such as finance and security) arise.[22] This on-again, off-again project would bring as much as 45 million cubic meters of natural gas per day to India. India's experience with the SCO has likewise been less than gratifying for political and economic reasons evidently associated with China's lukewarm embrace of India as even an observer member.[23]

India's approach to Central Asia lacks the single-mindedness of China's state-driven economic development to create a security buffer among those Central Asia states bordering China by embracing them economically. For India, commercial development and security seem to connect accidentally more often than purposefully. In some critical sectors (banking, for

---

[19] Peyrouse, "Comparing the Economic Involvement," 155–56.

[20] Ibid.

[21] "Trade Corridor Flounders on Infra Bottlenecks," *Business Standard*, February 13, 2008, http://www.businessstandard.in/india/news/trade-corridor-floundersinfra-bottlenecks/313607/; and "Central Asia: Turkmenistan Pushing North-South 'Trade Corridor' with Iran," Radio Free Europe/Radio Liberty, June 20, 2007, http://www.rferl.org/content/article/1077234.html.

[22] "Difficulties Remain for a Turkmen-China Energy Deal," Stratfor, March 4, 2011, http://www.stratfor.com/analysis/20110303-difficulties-remain-turkmen-china-energy-deal; and Jeff Smith and Ilan Berman, "Central Asia's Energy Bazaar," *Wall Street Journal*, January 27, 2011.

[23] Sachdeva, "India's Attitude," 32–33.

example), India is virtually absent, while China's presence is growing. India has competed with some success for energy assets in the Caspian region, but it has also suffered some notable failures, such as being outbid in 2005 by the China National Petroleum Corporation (CNPC) in an attempt to acquire PetroKazakhstan. India has had more success in other areas of petrochemical development, but the bottom line is sobering. Among the leaders in oil and gas exploitation in Central Asia, India is not among the top ten, and the involvement of Western and Russian companies and China's aggressive competitiveness, underpinned by the state's resources, suggest that India will not quickly move up.[24]

Yet in its search for an extended security perimeter, India has copied China's enthusiastic engagement of contiguous Central Asian states. Of course, India is not immediately contiguous to any of the new states, but Tajikistan comes close to India's disputed territory of Kashmir, located approximately twenty kilometers away. Tajikistan is a linchpin in India's understanding of its security requirements in Central Asia. It borders China, Afghanistan, Uzbekistan, and Kyrgyzstan and provides an additional vantage point from which to monitor activities in Pakistan. In a conflict, a position in Tajikistan would offer India the possibility of striking Pakistan in its rear. Consequently, India turned to Tajikistan to acquire its first military base outside India—the airbase at Ayni, close to the Tajik capital Dushanbe. Ayni is a former Soviet airbase used during the war in Afghanistan, sitting idle since the collapse of the Soviet Union.[25] India set about refurbishing the base, making it operational in 2006, according to reports. Following a trilateral agreement, the Ayni base would rotate command among the three principals: India, Tajikistan, and Russia. The base is intended to host twelve to fourteen MIG-29s fighter jets and a squadron of India's Mi-17 V1 helicopters, as well as trainer aircraft allowed under a 2002 defense cooperation agreement for training Tajikistan's air force. India's assistance to Afghanistan is channeled through Ayni, avoiding Pakistan.[26]

The politics of India's effort to secure its presence at the Ayni airbase is a caricature of the larger competition in Central Asia among the key outside powers, the new Central Asian states, and nearby actors. China was quick to increase its political and economic activities in Tajikistan in response to India's foothold at Ayni, and it turned up the heat on Tajikistan in the

---

[24] Peyrouse, "Comparing the Economic Involvement," 158–59.

[25] India also supported a medical facility for the Northern Alliance against the Taliban at Farkhor, Tajikistan, until 2002.

[26] Shishir Gupta, "Tajik Air Base Is Ready, Gives India Its First Footprint in Strategic Central Asia," *Indian Express*, February 25, 2007, http://www.indianexpress.com/news/tajik-air-base-is-ready-gives-india-its-first-footprint-in-strategic-central-asia/24207/; and Sudha Ramachandran, "India's Foray into Central Asia," *Asia Times*, August 16, 2006.

SCO, where India holds only observer status. Russia, whose largest overseas military base is in Tajikistan, exerted pressure through the multilateral security organization it dominates in the region, the Collective Security Treaty Organization (CSTO), which includes Tajikistan. Chinese and Russian investment in Tajikistan far outstrips that of India by many orders of magnitude, especially in key infrastructure projects, a fact not lost on the Tajiks. Tajikistan also has close bilateral relations with Pakistan and Iran, both of which undoubtedly upbraided Tajikistan about the specter of a threatening new Indian military facility close by. Both the United States and France have reportedly also sought access to the base. This U.S. connection certainly complicates India's petition, as Russia and China have been vocal opponents of the emerging Indo-U.S. security alliance. This soup of colliding strategic objectives appears to have stalled India's momentum. At this time, according to Tajikistan's foreign minister, talks for use of the Ayni base are ongoing only with Russia. Ayni is thus in many ways a metaphor for India's dilemma in Central Asia more generally:

> The airbase negotiations and India's likely failure to secure the base—at least for the time being—implies that, first, Russia still plays the predominant security role in the region. Second, the absence of an Indian military foothold will diminish New Delhi's ability to influence the security dynamics in Afghanistan and the broader region. Third, without a significant economic presence, India will unlikely be able to project its military power in and from Central Asia any time soon, though lingering negotiations may still present it with a second chance. Finally, the air base talks clearly show Tajikistan's interest in balancing regional powers to secure financial and political support as it sees convenient.[27]

How to Play with Giants

At the center of the competition for Central Asia lie five states untethered from the defunct Soviet Union: Kazakhstan, Kyrgyzstan, Tajikistan, Uzbekistan, and Turkmenistan. Each entertains a "China question" that is specific to it, though some commonalities exist.[28] On some levels, one may distinguish the responses and reactions of the three border states—Kazakhstan, Kyrgyzstan, and Tajikistan—from those of the two non-border

---

[27] Roman Muzalevsky, "India Fails to Gain a Military Foothold in Tajikistan," Central Asia-Caucasus Institute and Silk Road Studies Program, Central Asia–Caucasus Institute Analyst 13, no. 2, February 2, 2011, http://www.cacianalyst.org/?q=node/5485.

[28] Marlène Laruelle and Sébastien Peyrouse, *China as a Neighbor: Central Asian Perspectives and Strategies* (Washington, D.C.: Central Asia–Caucasus Institute and Silk Road Studies Program, 2009), http://www.isdp.eu/images/stories/isdp-main-pdf/2009_laurelle-peyrouse_book_china-as-a-neighbor.pdf.

states, Uzbekistan and Turkmenistan. States in the former group feel the hot breath of geographic proximity in their dealings with China, and indeed each has negotiated complex border treaties with its giant neighbor. There is a strong sense that the border territories over which they currently have sovereignty might still be at risk if China begins to wield its regional heft aggressively and that eventually China might threaten their national unity through any number of opportunities physical contiguity offers it. These fears are heightened by private-enterprise trade flows from China into these three states, all attended by migrations of Chinese into their territories.

In contrast, Uzbekistan and Turkmenistan share no borders with China. Their economic relations with China are for the most part limited to official agreements between large companies. Few private trade exchanges exist, and consequently the cross-border migratory flow of Chinese into these states is more limited. Similarly, the flow of Uzbek and Turkmen traders toward markets in China is currently small, although this is changing as Uzbekistan's petty traders discover the opportunities in borderland trading towns such as Kyrgyzstan's Kara-suu, which has become a hub for re-exporting Chinese goods to Uzbekistan. Shops in Tashkent and other Uzbek cities already boast large selections of Chinese goods.[29]

Turkmenistan traditionally has been drawn in the direction of its long border with Iran and the Caspian Sea, as well as toward its relations with Turkey. But China nonetheless looms large on Turkmenistan's commercial radar through its strong entry into Turkish and Iranian markets and, to the extent that Chinese penetration of Uzbekistan accelerates, across the long Turkmenistan-Uzbekistan border. China is aggressively courting Turkmen energy markets (mostly gas) and, according to one analyst, possesses a comprehensive strategy going far beyond simply oil and gas. Kevin Rosner reports that "since 2000 China-Turkmenistan trade has multiplied by a factor of 40; thirty-five enterprises are working in Turkmenistan today with Chinese capital. Chinese companies are active in sectors of the Turkmen economy as diverse as oil and gas, telecommunications, transport, agriculture, textile, chemical and food industries, healthcare, and construction."[30] The "game changer" is the new Turkmenistan-China gas pipeline, exceeding four thousand miles in length, that is expected to export up to 60 billion cubic meters of gas to China when completed in 2012, though this forecast could be overly optimistic. China's substantial technological achievement breaks

---

[29] Ablat Khodzhaev, *Kitaiskii faktor v Tsentral'noi Azii* [The Chinese Factor in Central Asia] (Tashkent: FAN, 2007); and Ablat Khodzhaev, "The Central Asian Policy of the People's Republic of China," *China and Eurasia Forum Quarterly* 7, no. 1 (February 2009): 9–28.

[30] Kevin Rosner, "China Scores Again in Energy: Russia & Central Asia," Institute for the Analysis of Global Security, Journal of Energy Security, January 12, 2010, http://www.ensec.org/index. php?option=com_content&view=article&id=230.

Russia's transport monopoly of both Turkmen gas and Kazakh oil, while providing China with a strategically significant energy supply that avoids the long maritime journeys from the Persian Gulf or West Africa, which are vulnerable to interdiction by hostile forces. Turkmen president Gurbanguly Berdymukhamedov has publicly applauded China's multifaceted strategy in his country, noting that all facets "are positive in context."[31]

The border–non-border distinction in trade and economic activities has a political parallel. Kyrgyzstan allows many public freedoms, while Kazakhstan and Tajikistan allow considerable diversity of opinion and information flows despite their more authoritarian character. Their "China questions" receive public attention and discussion at many levels.[32] Such public discussion is much rarer in Uzbekistan and Turkmenistan, where information is more often repressed. In this sense, the border states are prompted to think about China strategically in ways that the outliers seldom do.

The two poorest and most fragile states, Kyrgyzstan and Tajikistan, tend to see China as a positive feature in their relations in and beyond Central Asia because of China's preeminence among Central Asia's large competitors in supporting things that enhance state stability and prosperity—for example, transport infrastructure and bank loans. China's luminescence in this regard is heightened by its interaction with both states in the SCO. Not surprisingly, many Kyrgyz and Tajiks are inclined to think of China as the best choice among those competing for their favor, since none of the other competitors has invested in them to such a degree. Kyrgyzstan is the Central Asian state most heavily penetrated by China, with some 30,000 Chinese living in Kyrgyz cities and towns in 2009; in 2008, 6,000 work permits were issued to Chinese citizens.[33] Tajikistan is in a similar position. China supplies about 20% of its imports but receives little trade in return, though Tajikistan's potential lies in its water resources and the possibility of substantial hydroelectric energy exports to China in the future.[34]

This "China first" predisposition of Kyrgyzstan and Tajikistan—it seems far short of a real strategy—carries acknowledged risks with respect to China's growing political influence over their sovereign affairs as well as over their relations with other Central Asian states and large suitors, such as India, Russia, and the United States. Tajikistan's preference for China is especially

---

[31] Rosner, "China Scores Again in Energy."

[32] Askar Abdrakhmanov and Adil Kaukenov, "Otnosheniia Kitaia i stran Tsentral'noi Azii glazami Kazakhstanskikh ekspertov" [The View of Kazakhstani Experts on the Relations between China and the Countries of Central Asia], *Kazakhstan v Global'nykh Protsessakh*, no. 3 (2007): 119–28.

[33] Amantur Zhaparov, "The Issue of Chinese Migrants in Kyrgyzstan," *China and Eurasia Forum Quarterly* 7, no. 1 (February 2009): 79–91.

[34] Spechler, "Why Does China Have No Business in Central Asia?" 6.

pronounced. Tajiks are linguistically and culturally Persian, in contrast to the dominance of Turkic languages and culture throughout Central Asia, and recognize in China's forceful rejection of the separatist aspirations of Xinjiang's largest Turkic nationality, the Uighurs, an ally against a tide many Tajiks fear could eventually submerge them in Central Asia.[35]

The "Chinese question" in Kazakhstan has long been debated, often in the context of fear that illegal Chinese migration could ultimately fill the vacuum of Kazakhstan's vast uninhabited spaces. This concern is heightened by the explosive arrival of many Chinese in recent years, often to support Chinese companies engaged in Kazakhstan's industrial and energy sectors.[36] President Nursultan Nazarbayev recently added new energy to this conundrum when he revealed that Chinese agricultural companies had agreed to lease one million hectares of Kazakhstan's territory. This triggered a vibrant media debate, a strong nationalist backlash, and even demonstrations outside the Chinese consulate in Almaty.[37] Yet the little available data on public opinion in Kazakhstan suggests a complex, sometimes contradictory set of attitudes toward China. On the one hand, fear that Chinese labor will compromise the local labor market is high. On the other hand, Chinese workers are seen as reliable and are admired for their prodigious capacity for hard work.[38] Young people have more tolerant attitudes than their elders toward China, and at least one survey concludes that the more familiar people become with the Chinese, the more they value them.[39] Media in Kazakhstan, perhaps at the direction or urging of that country's leadership, are thought to manipulate the "Chinese threat" to serve ascendant policy

---

[35] Saodat Olimova, "The Multifaceted Chinese Presence in Tajikistan," *China and Eurasia Forum Quarterly* 7, no. 1 (February 2009): 61–77.

[36] See, for example, Sébastien Peyrouse, "Chinese Economic Presence in Kazakhstan," *China Perspectives*, no. 3 (September 2008): 18; Klara Khafizova, "Transgranichniye otnosheniya Sin'tzyan'—Kazakhstan" [Cross-border Relations between Xinjiang and Kazakhstan], *Central'naya Asiya i Kavkaz*, no. 3 (2000), http://www.ca-c.org/journal/cac-09-2000/12.Khafizov.shtml; Ludmila Piskorskskaya, "Bol'shiye 'glaza' kitaiskoi ekspansii" [The Large "Eyes" of Chinese Expansion], Zakon, April 19, 2010, http://www.zakon.kz/169690-legendy-i-mify-kitajjskojj-jekspansii-v.html; and Elena Sadovskaya, "Chinese Migration to Kazakhstan: Causes, Key Trends, and Prospects," *Central Asia and the Caucasus* 49, no. 1 (2008): 156.

[37] Dilbegim Mavlonii, "Mimohodnoye zayavleniye Nazarbayeva privelo aktivistov k Kitaiskomu konsul'stvu" [An Offhand Comment by Nazarbayev Draws Crowds to the Chinese Consulate], Radio Azattyq, December 11, 2009, http://rus.azattyq.org/content/Kazakh_lands_rent_to_China_/1901588.html.

[38] Syroyezhkin Konstantin Lvovich, "Kitaiskaia migrasiia v Kazahstane: Voobrazhayemyie i real'nyie ugrozy" [Chinese Migration to Kazakhstan: Imaginary and Real Threats and Challenges], *Mezhdunarodnyie Issledovaniya: Obshchestvo, Politika, Ekonomika*, no. 1 (2009), http://www.ispr.kz/files/magazine_1.pdf, 117–28.

[39] Svetlana Kozhirova, "Vnutrennie i vneshnie aspekty sovremennoi Kitaiskoi migratsii" [Domestic and Foreign Aspects of Contemporary Chinese Migration], *Analitic*, no. 6 (2008): 45–52; and Elana Sadovskaia, "Kitaiskie migranty v Kazakhstane: Otnosheniia Kazakhstankikh grazhdan (po resul'tatam sotsiologicheskogo issledovaniia)" [Chinese Migrants in Kazakhstan: The Attitudes of Kazakhstan's Citizens (Results of a Sociological Survey)], *Analitic*, no. 5 (2007): 23–24.

interests. Most of the reactions and responses from Central Asians toward China are more visceral than strategic. Indeed, serious research on these attitudes is rare, and the application of results to strategic planning, to date, seems almost nonexistent.

Perhaps alone among the five Central Asian states, Kazakhstan has entertained an ongoing assessment of its relative strategic position in Central Asia—often involving local and outside specialists—that seeks to identify its competitive advantages and vulnerabilities relative to China.[40] Unlike Uzbekistan, which entertains and seems to relish frequent disputes with the United States and Europe, Kazakhstan welcomes positive attention from Western powers—emblemized by its holding the presidency of the Organization for Security Co-operation in Europe (OSCE) in 2010—as well as from Russia.[41] Its diplomats speak openly of balancing competing foreign interests in Kazakhstan's mineral wealth and preventing China from monopolizing political influence in Central Asia.

It is of course possible to hold more than one view of China, and indeed many Central Asians do. Fear of China and appreciation for China coexist in Kazakhstan and the rest of Central Asia. Surprisingly, public attitudes on China and the Chinese are not often tested—or perhaps are not allowed to be tested. Some information exists from Kazakhstan, Kyrgyzstan, and Tajikistan (the bordering states), but public opinion surveying in Uzbekistan and Turkmenistan on China questions—or for that matter on most questions—is inaccessible, if it exists at all. Where research does exist, it is revealing, if dated. For example, a 2005 survey conducted in Tajikistan, Kyrgyzstan, and Kazakhstan determined that in the competition among large powers for influence in Central Asia the most trusted competitor by far was Russia. China lagged by more than 40%, with trust ratings of 80% for Russia and 38% for China, in Tajikistan, the most pro-China state in Central Asia. In Kyrgyzstan, China was trusted by only 26% of those surveyed, and by only 19% in Kazakhstan. But on the anxiety scale the results are reversed. China raises the blood pressure of only 5%

---

[40] The author has participated in many such discussions.

[41] Vladimir Paramonov and Aleksei Strokov, "Ekonomicheskoe prisutstvie Rossii i Kitaia v Tsentral'noi Azii" [Economic Involvement of Russia and China in Central Asia], Defence Academy of the United Kingdom, Conflict Studies Research Center, Central Asian Series, July 12, 2007, http://www.da.mod.uk/colleges/arag/document-listings/ca/07%2812%29VPRussian.pdf; Andrea Schmitz, "Kasachstan: Neue führungsmacht im Postsowjetischen raum?" [Kazakhstan: The New Leading Power in the Post-Soviet Region?], Stiftung Wissenschaft und Politik, SWP Research Papers, no. 7, 2009, http://www.isn.ethz.ch/isn/Digital-Library/Publications/Detail/?id=116948; and B.K. Sultanov, *Evraziiskaia strategiia suverennogo Kazakhstana* [The Eurasian Strategy of Independent Kazakhstan] (Almaty: KISI, 2005).

in Tajikistan, 26% in Kyrgyzstan, and 32% in Kazakhstan.[42] A more recent survey confirms Tajikistan's benign view of China, while acknowledging that these attitudes are based on an almost total ignorance of it.[43]

The Tajiks' favorable view of China apparently owes little to their familiarity with the country or the people but rather to the favors China bestows on Tajikistan. The same is not the case in Kyrgyzstan and Kazakhstan, the two countries most intimate with the Chinese. China's popularity appears to suffer in both places, according to admittedly scant survey data. But this may be further evidence of a recurring pattern in China's involvement beyond its borders, seen in places such as Africa and the Middle East,[44] where China's culture has little resonance with local folk and growing concentrations of Chinese tend to irritate local sensibilities.

In contrast to every Central Asian state's having a "China discussion," discussions of India are much rarer among Central Asians. Historically, India enjoyed closer relations with Uzbekistan and Tajikistan, where many Indians studied at technical institutes during the Soviet period, than to the three other states in the region. Yet with Uzbekistan, India's relations have proved more difficult than might have been expected, given Uzbekistan's close ties to Afghanistan, where Pakistan seeks to distribute its influence.[45] To the contrary, the Karimov government's warm relations with Pakistan, particularly in the 1990s, heightened concerns in India.[46] Uzbekistan's growing isolationism and its unfavorable investment climate discouraged Indian private firms from establishing a strong base in the country. Responding to suggestions that Uzbekistan would benefit strategically from closer relations with New Delhi,

---

[42] Vilia Gel'bras, "ShOS na fonde obshchestvennykh nastroenii naseleniia Rossii, Kazakhstana, Kirgizii, Tadzhikistana i Kitaia" [The SCO According to Public Opinion in Russia, Kazakhstan, Kyrgyzstan, Tajikistan, and China], in *ShOS: Stanovlenie i perspektivy razvitiia* [The SCO: Current State and Development Prospects], ed. M. Ashimbaev and G. Chufrin (Almaty: Institute for World Economy and Politics, 2005), 186.

[43] Olimova, "Multifaceted Chinese Presence in Tajikistan."

[44] See, for example, Moises Naim, "Help Not Wanted," *New York Times*, February 15, 2007; and Nicholas Kristof, "China's Genocide Olympics," *New York Times*, January 24, 2008. For a contrary view, see Deborah Brautigam, "Africa's Eastern Promise," *Foreign Affairs*, January 5, 2010, http://www.foreignaffairs.com/articles/65916/deborah-brautigam/africa's-eastern-promise.

[45] At the time of writing, India may be moving to close this distance. See Maria Abi-Habib and Amol Sharma, "As Delhi Sidles Up to Kabul, Pakistan Feels the Pinch," *Wall Street Journal*, May 13, 2011; Irina Komissina, "Will India Become a Full-Fledged Participant in the Big Game in Central Asia?" *Central Asia and the Caucasus* 49, no. 1 (2008): 57–69; and Emilian Kavalski, "Partnership or Rivalry between the EU, China and India in Central Asia: The Normative Power of Regional Actors with Global Aspirations," *European Law Journal* 13, no. 6 (2007): 839–56.

[46] Fazal-ur-Rahman, "Pakistan's Evolving Relations with China, Russia, and Central Asia," in *Eager Eyes Fixed on Eurasia, Vol. 1: Russia and Its Neighbors in Crisis*, ed. Iwashita Akihiro (Hokkaido: Slavic Research Centre, Hokkaido University, 2007), 211–29; Shahram Akbarzadeh, "India and Pakistan's Geostrategic Rivalry in Central Asia," *Contemporary South Asia* 12, no. 2 (2003): 219–28; and Meena Singh Roy, "Pakistan's Strategies in Central Asia," *Strategic Analysis* 30, no. 4 (October 2006): 798–833.

including security cooperation that might balance potential influence from China and Russia, Uzbek authorities often express either ignorance or a studied unawareness of India's burgeoning potential.[47]

Tajikistan's response to India is similar. Although Tajikistan is conceived as India's gateway to Central Asia, this relationship has produced neither political influence nor an economic presence.[48] As noted earlier, the Tajik embrace of India's venture at the Ayni military base has been anything but open-armed.[49]

Kyrgyzstan, with no cultural or historical ties to India and lacking resources or other assets coveted by the great powers, reveals no particular interest in India, its economic or political potential, or its balancing potential with regard to the other great powers. For the Kyrgyz, India seems an afterthought.

Turkmenistan has remained largely closed to Indian interests, both economic and political, although there has been a resurgence of interest toward India from Ashgabat since the gradual reopening of the country began in 2007, when a new political regime assumed power in Turkmenistan. The previously noted TAPI pipeline, if built, could positively affect this largely stagnant relationship. But that is in the future, if ever.

Kazakhstan stands out as the Central Asian actor most aware of India's potential both as an economic partner and as a possible balancer to China's growing presence or to a Russia-China coalition that pinches Kazakhstan from all directions. In 2009, Astana and New Delhi signed a strategic partnership agreement confirming this shared understanding of the region's emerging competitive dynamics.[50] Kazakhstan's political and foreign policy elite possess a fluid comprehension of India's potential on many fronts, a realization that contrasts sharply with their counterparts in the other Central Asian states.[51]

---

[47] These are the author's personal observations based on frequent contact with Uzbek elites in Uzbekistan and abroad in the post-Soviet period.

[48] Mahavir Singh, ed., *India and Tajikistan: Revitalizing a Traditional Relationship* (New Delhi: Anamika, 2003).

[49] Stephen Blank, "Russian-Indian Row over Tajik Base Suggests Moscow Caught in Diplomatic Vicious Cycle," Eurasianet, January 11, 2008, http://www.eurasianet.org/departments/insight/articles/eav011108f.shtml.

[50] P. Stobdan, "India and Kazakhstan Should Share Complementary Objectives," *Strategic Analysis* 33, no. 1 (January 2009): 1–7; and Suchandana Chatterjee, "The Steppe as a Regional Potential," in *Eurasia Regional Perspectives: Proceedings of an Indo-Kazakh Workshop, Almaty, 2007* (Kolkata: Maulana Abul Kalam Azad Institute of Asian Studies, 2008), 13–23.

[51] This observation is based on the author's personal experience.

Central Asia's Emerging Strategic Crucible

If the competition for influence, position, resources, and advantages in Central Asia were a simple binary contest between Asia's rising powers, China and India, then the game would appear to be largely over, or at least so radically tilted in China's direction as to make further efforts by India little more than playing hopeful catch-up, at least for the foreseeable future. At this writing, China dominates every facet of the competition with India by having successfully and patiently choreographed its favorable geographic position, its robust economy and the state's ability to direct that economy strategically, its influence in the region's multilateral institutions, and its clear understanding of China's pressing security imperatives. Moreover, compared to India—and for that matter to the United States and Russia, the region's other large actors—China remains helpfully unencumbered by other conflicts requiring constant attention. Beijing has the luxury of space and time in Central Asia, and it has employed both effectively.

However, the competition in and for Central Asia is not a two-player game; rather, it is one of many moving parts, where the power of any part can be strategically greater than its apparent weight, depending on the context. Critical uncertainties abound. A political scientist will find in any analysis of Central Asia's many actors evidence of classic balancing and bandwagoning, but this kind of theoretical analysis is likely to miss the rapid movement from one side to the other or in both directions simultaneously. This is true among the large powers, between and among large powers and small states, and among the small states themselves. Central Asia is not unique in this regard, just very complicated.

Russia's role in framing the competition among Asia's rising powers is key. For China and India, Central Asia is a place where they labor to explain their current strategic objectives as an extension of a distant historical narrative. For Russia, in contrast, Central Asia embodies much of its living history for the last several centuries. Central Asia is Russia's backyard, it is often said, not least by the Russians themselves. This metaphor underscores the sovereignty Moscow enjoyed in the region until very recently; its parentage of the political cultures and elites in the new states, whose roots are deep in the Soviet experience; and the prevailing attitude among Russians of all kinds that Russia must protect its interests in Central Asia against all the encroaching imperial newcomers.

It is this same familiarity on the part of Central Asians that causes them to be fearful and resistant to Russian aims and activity in the new Central

Asia.[52] In discussions about their national problems, Central Asian elites predictably find a Russian villain lurking somewhere near their core. "The Kremlin is still inclined to think of Central Asia as an acquired zone of influence," notes Marlène Laruelle, "and the Central Asian governments feel this is disrespectful."[53]

Russia is not one of Asia's rising powers but the opposite. Yet since the collapse of the Soviet Union, Russia has managed to overcome its largely negative image to achieve a powerful position in Central Asia through trade, through its support for Central Asia's undemocratic regimes, and by convening joint security activities. Moscow has been courted by all the other key players, including China, India, and the United States. China and Russia have managed to resolve land and border issues since 2005, and Russia continues to see China as an important customer for its abundant energy resources. Likewise, India cooperates with Russia on several important energy projects, including one in Sakhalin, and on commercial nuclear activities. The Indian military also remains one of Russia's largest clients for aviation and naval arms. Vladimir Putin engineered a strategic partnership agreement with India in 2000 that included accelerated trade between the two countries, assistance to expand India's nuclear power industry substantially, military assistance to India's air force and naval assets, and expanded cooperation in energy, space, satellite navigation, agriculture, and other areas.[54]

The United States reset its relations with Russia after 2008, in part to gain Moscow's acquiescence to the presence of U.S. bases in Central Asia supporting the war in Afghanistan. How much this reset actually benefited the United States is open to different interpretations. What is less doubtful is that, though netting the Central Asian states some immediate investment from the United States for supporting its logistic efforts for the war in Afghanistan, the reset also signaled U.S. reluctance to assert particular interests in the region that might conflict with Russia's. As such, it suggested an unwillingness to compete aggressively in the Central Asian space, thus effectively ceding the field to others. By setting a deadline for withdrawal from Afghanistan, the United States further underlined local perceptions of its staying power in Central Asia. It is hard to find anyone in Central Asia brave enough to advance the proposition that the United States will

---

[52] Roland Dannreuther, "Can Russia Sustain Its Dominance in Central Asia?" *Security Dialogue* 32, no. 2 (June 2001): 245–58; and Andrei Kazantsev, "Russian Policy in Central Asia and the Caspian Sea Region," *Europe-Asia Studies* 60, no. 6 (August 2008): 1073–88.

[53] Laruelle and Peyrouse, *China as a Neighbor*, 13.

[54] Ibid., 14–18; and Zoglul Husain, "Putin's India Visit Revamps Russia-India Strategic Partnership," *Financial Express*, March 23, 2010.

compete in the region with either China or Russia beyond the next few years, while those who envisage a Central Asia without effective U.S. influence are plentiful.[55]

In one way or another, Russia influences the actions of China, India, and the United States in Central Asia and, consequently, the way Central Asians evaluate their opportunities and then make strategic choices. This is unlikely to change until Russia's influence has been fully eclipsed, plausibly by China, and all parties acknowledge that the strategic tectonic plates have shifted and a new political order reigns.

In the decade ahead, a number of forces and influences will be active in and on Central Asia that will affect the behavior of Asia's rising powers. First, the number of plausible contexts that might erode China's advantage, despite its long head start, are notable. For example, what if the United States had announced early in its involvement in Afghanistan that it envisioned a long stay in Central Asia and had then punctuated this declaration with serious efforts to acquire and hold military bases in Uzbekistan, Kyrgyzstan, or Kazakhstan? We know with certainty that some Central Asian regimes welcomed just this approach but that, for a variety of political and financial reasons, efforts fell short of a believable commitment, especially as U.S. leaders foreswore any long-term objectives in Central Asia. Even now, such a commitment almost certainly would affect how both large and small actors in Central Asia calculate their advantages, establish objectives, and design strategies. Another plausible counterfactual might link India and Russia in a new marriage of convenience—perhaps with the United States' blessing and participation—to forge a more dynamic competition with China in Central Asia than either partner could mount on its own. There are probably advocates for such an arrangement in New Delhi and Moscow, and even in Washington. Another version of this could be an Indo-U.S. strategy for Central Asia that foresees the collapse of Pakistan or failure in Afghanistan. Without predicting the future, it is already evident that these or other realignments are possible and that their impacts would likely change the objectives and strategies of many actors in Central Asia, some fundamentally.

Second, the Central Asian states themselves often possess outsize power to alter this context. Each is supported by some combination of rich resources, critical geostrategic positioning, and other assets such as

---

[55] Robert Guang Tian, "From Central Asia to Great Central Asia: The Goals and Adjustments of U.S. Central Asian Strategy," *Central Asia and the Caucasus* 57, no. 3 (2009): 58–71; and Mels Omarov, "Central Asia in the Foreign Policy of Russia, the United States, and the European Union," *Central Asia and the Caucasus* 57, no. 3 (2009): 71–78.

military bases that gives it persuasive clout in foreign policy matters.[56] They can control who receives access and at what price. As such, they should be able to act with unusual influence over the context in which Asia's rising powers and other outsiders must operate. But the reality is more nuanced. Kazakhstan, with a small population and large exposed territory, embraces a classic foreign policy of interests and uses its energy wealth as an effective instrument to achieve them. It behaves like a strategic actor. In comparison, Tajikistan, Kyrgyzstan, and Turkmenistan seem less certain of their direction or strategic possibilities. It is hard to detect anything akin to real strategy in the way they behave or make decisions. Uzbekistan, which alone borders all the other Central Asian states but does not border China or Russia, and which possesses the largest population, is a strategic enigma. It courts Pakistan over India, feuds with the United States, holds Russia at arm's length, and resists China's overtures. It quarrels with nearly all its neighbors, with some disputes involving highly personalized antagonism between leaders. Uzbekistan is alone and isolated, but perhaps it prefers things this way. What should be clear to everyone is that if Uzbekistan decides to embrace one side or the other in the strategic competition among outsiders for influence in Central Asia, its impact will be felt, perhaps decisively.

Third, the contours of China's current advantage are stark: more than 80% of Central Asia's exports to China are raw materials, such as oil, gas, and ferrous and non-ferrous metals. In return, the Chinese send Central Asia cheap finished products, such as electronics, shoes, clothing, and toys. As the Central Asian economies mature, India's technology and services sector will almost certainly make inroads in areas such as space and IT, in addition to pharmaceuticals and textiles.

Fourth, the optics of China's engagement are often negative. Small- and medium-sized Chinese enterprises are rare in Central Asia, and those that arrive from China often come complete with their own workers and equipment, thereby depriving local economies of employment opportunities and sparking resentment.[57] As noted, China's activities in other energy-rich states have brought or built on endemic corruption, shoddy work, and social tensions. Both dynamics could degrade China's advantage or offer India chances to improve its position.

Fifth, perhaps the largest critical uncertainty is embedded within China's overarching strategy for the region, namely to secure Xinjiang by

---

[56] Marlène Laruelle and Sébastien Peyrouse, L'Asie Centrale à l'aune de la mondialisation: Une approche géoéconomique [Globalization in Central Asia: A Geo-Economic Approach] (Paris: IRIS–Armand Collin, 2010).

[57] Peyrouse, "Comparing the Economic Involvement," 166–67.

integrating it economically with the surrounding Central Asian states. This is a high-risk strategy, potentially containing its own antidote. While China has apparently extracted pledges from the Central Asian states in the SCO and other forums to refrain from contributing to the nationalistic radicalization of Xinjiang, in practice some spillover from Kazakhstan, Kyrgyzstan, Tajikistan, and Uzbekistan is likely. The reality is that the new Central Asia, however authoritarian, offers fairly ready access to the world's media, modern communications, travelers and businesspeople, NGOs, and other conduits for ideas capable of penetrating Xinjiang. During the July 2009 anti-Chinese disturbances by Uighur nationalists in Xinjiang, Beijing proved that it could repress dissent by using brutality liberally. No doubt it will have cause to do so again, as the new strategy, despite its heavy emphasis on physical security, all but ensures that Xinjiang cannot be hermetically sealed.

Two final aspects of Central Asia's evolution are certain to shape the way that regional countries respond to Asia's rising powers. The first is the likelihood that on matters of mutual concern or interest the Central Asian states will find reasons to work together to enhance their competitive advantages, without recourse to large-power intermediaries such as China and Russia operating within multilateral structures like the SCO. Private discussions in capitals such as Astana and Tashkent increasingly evoke local leadership and urge ending the supplicatory culture of earlier times that survived the collapse of the Soviet Union. The question right now is who will lead. Some combination of leadership by Uzbekistan and Kazakhstan seems obvious, except perhaps to them. Mutual suspicions and outright hostility have often defined the relations between Central Asian states themselves and particularly their leaders. But this will change, as the incentives to cooperate pile up and the leadership changes.

The second new element, closely related to the first, is the certainty of generational change. Soviet-era leaders will be replaced by younger men and women whose formative experiences have taken place after or outside the former Soviet Union. Central Asia lags in this transition compared to other parts of the former empire, but it will catch up. Those who are in frequent contact with Central Asian governments and with local NGOs and private sector firms often remark about the good education, creative intelligence, and globalized awareness of the young people who work in them. How they might be impressed by Asia's rising powers is yet to be determined.

EXECUTIVE SUMMARY

This chapter discusses the responses of countries in South Asia to the rise of India and China.

MAIN ARGUMENT:
For Pakistan, the rise of India is a strategic nightmare, while the rise of China is an opportunity to curb India's advancement and reduce dependence on the United States. Afghanistan sees its ties with India and China, as well as with the U.S., as vehicles for blunting interference by its immediate neighbors, especially Pakistan. Bangladesh, Nepal, and Sri Lanka generally accept India's primacy in their region. Bangladesh and Nepal see their ties with China as a way of increasing their freedom of action against India; Sri Lanka sees both India and China as means to emphasize its independence from Western donors.

POLICY IMPLICATIONS:
- India's South Asian neighbors look on India and China with one eye on relations with the U.S. Most of these countries are seeking either to balance a hostile relationship or to hedge against excessive dependency on the U.S. or India.

- India is still the major player in South Asia, and is becoming more active in East Asia.

- China's security profile and economic heft in South Asia have risen dramatically in the past decade. India's economic growth will determine whether New Delhi maintains its influence in its own neighborhood.

- The Indian Ocean is the arena where the India-China rivalry will play out. U.S. strategic goals align well with India's, and U.S. interests would be well served by treating the Indian Ocean as a single policy space.

- The smaller South Asian countries, especially Sri Lanka, will play a greater role in the dynamics of the Indian Ocean region than traditional U.S. policy would indicate.

India Next Door, China Over the Horizon: The View from South Asia

Teresita C. Schaffer

South Asia has been an area of Indian preeminence since India and Pakistan became independent. Indian primacy is bitterly contested by Pakistan but accepted, with varying degrees of comfort (or discomfort), by Sri Lanka, Bangladesh, and Nepal. Afghanistan, unlike these three countries, is more in Pakistan's shadow than India's, and for tiny Bhutan and Maldives, India is one of many much larger neighbors that shape their environment. India's rise accentuates but does not change this basic dynamic.

China's rise, on the other hand, has brought Beijing into a more prominent role in the region. Its search for military access around the Indian Ocean is part of the reason; another is its larger economic engagement through both trade and aid. China has long been a counterweight to India's influence for all the countries in the region, especially for Pakistan. An enhanced economic profile will make this role more important. China has used its ties with India's neighbors to constrain Indian influence and try to keep India bottled up in South Asia.

Not surprisingly, India looks suspiciously on its neighbors' relations with China. India's neighbors also see the United States as a counterweight to India. However, with the expansion of U.S.-India relations after the Cold War, India's misgivings about U.S. ties with the smaller South Asian countries have abated, though its concerns about the implications of the U.S.-Pakistan strategic relationship remain sharp.

Teresita C. Schaffer writes and speaks on economic, political, security, and risk management trends in South Asia. She spent thirty years as a U.S. diplomat in Pakistan, India, and Bangladesh and as ambassador to Sri Lanka, and is co-author of the website South Asia Hand. She can be reached at <t.c.schaffer@comcast.net>.

This analysis will look first in some detail at Pakistan. Its security perceptions center on India as a mortal threat, the United States as an unreliable friend, and China as a steady ally. Pakistan is the one country in the region for which the rise of India and China is a major strategic consideration. The study turns next to Afghanistan, where the United States and Pakistan are deeply engaged, with India and China over the horizon. Strategically in Pakistan's shadow, Afghanistan has played its relations with India and Pakistan against one another for half a century, and will do so again when the opportunity arises. Finally, this chapter examines the view from the rest of the region. For Nepal, Sri Lanka, and Bangladesh, India has been the main external factor in their security. All three have traditionally sought to expand their margin for maneuver vis-à-vis India without contesting its regional dominance. Bhutan and Maldives have used different strategies for managing the international affairs of tiny states in an area where giants are active. For all these countries, the rise of India and China needs to be examined in light of their relationship with the United States, taking into account New Delhi's new partnership with Washington and the shifting relations between the United States and China.

For Pakistan: Danger from India, Opportunity in China

The rise of India represents the strategic challenge Pakistan has sought to avoid for its entire independent existence, and the rise of China is its major opportunity to balance Indian power and hedge against dependence on the United States.[1] Pakistanis see in a more powerful China an opportunity to neutralize India's current geostrategic advantage.

The Historical Perspective:
A Vulnerable Pakistan Seeks Outside Friends

Born in the trauma of Britain's partition of the subcontinent and created as the homeland for that region's Muslims, Pakistan's policy (and much of public opinion) starts from the proposition that India is an existential threat. Countering that danger is the quintessential task of Pakistan's army, diplomacy, and strategic thinking. This helps to explain why Pakistan has been ruled by generals for about half its life, and why the army has been the dominant political player as well as the largest expenditure in the

---

[1] In this discussion, "balancing" refers to efforts to neutralize the power of a larger rival or hostile country; "hedging" refers to efforts to mitigate excessive dependence on another country that is not necessarily hostile.

government's budget for much of the time that civilian governments have been in charge.

Pakistan's political strategy for dealing with this threat relied from the start on recruiting powerful extraregional friends who, Pakistan hoped, could neutralize India's greater size and larger military and economy. The first to play this role was the United States in 1954, when Pakistan agreed to join the U.S.-led Cold War alliance structure. The second to become involved was China about a decade later. That rapprochement began when Zulfiqar Ali Bhutto, then foreign minister and later prime minister, negotiated a settlement with China over their border within the old princely state of Jammu and Kashmir, an agreement India bitterly disputes.[2] Within a short time, Pakistan had enlisted China as a long-term friend.

The contrast between Pakistan's relations with these two giants led to another enduring feature of the country's geopolitical thinking. The United States, whose ties with Pakistan have had three periods of intense relations, two of them interrupted by dramatic break-ups—"three marriages and two divorces"—is seen as an unfaithful and unreliable friend.[3] Since about 2005, anti-American sentiment has been at historic highs, the result of this reputation and of a perception, widely shared and persistently reported in polling data, that the United States is anti-Muslim.[4] China, by contrast, is often described as "Pakistan's all-weather friend," discreet, reliable, and willing to support its most critical and controversial security plans, such as its nuclear arsenal.[5]

The expansion of U.S.-India relations after 2000 set off alarm bells in Islamabad. A subject of particular resentment was the U.S.-India agreement on civil nuclear cooperation, first announced in principle in July 2005 and formally completed with the passage of U.S. legislation in December 2008. The United States turned down Pakistan's request for a similar deal largely on account of Pakistan's track record of transferring nuclear know-how. But this unequal treatment fueled the already strong suspicion that the United

---

[2] "China-Pakistan Boundary," Office of the Geographer, Department of State, International Boundary Study, no. 85, November 15, 1968.

[3] Howard B. Schaffer and Teresita C. Schaffer, *How Pakistan Negotiates with the United States: Riding the Roller Coaster* (Washington, D.C.: United States Institute of Peace, 2011).

[4] Steven Kull, Clay Ramsay, Stephen Weber, Evan Lewis, and Ebrahim Mohseni, "Public Opinion in the Islamic World on Terrorism, al Qaeda, and U.S. Policies," World Public Opinion, February 2009, www.worldpublicopinion.org/pipa/pdf/feb09/STARTII_Feb09_rpt.pdf.

[5] For a fuller discussion of Pakistan's strategic perceptions, see Schaffer and Schaffer, *How Pakistan Negotiates*, especially chaps.1 and 2; and Dennis Kux, *Disenchanted Allies: The United States and Pakistan 1947–2000* (Washington, D.C.: Woodrow Wilson Center Press, 2001). See also Abdul Sattar, *Pakistan's Foreign Policy 1947–2005: A Concise History* (Oxford: Oxford University Press, 2007), which starts the first substantive chapter with the statement that "the foreign policy of Pakistan was to be molded in the crucible of interaction with its neighbor India" (p. 8). Sattar was twice foreign secretary of Pakistan and once its foreign minister.

States was tilting toward the more powerful and prosperous India and away from its erstwhile ally, Pakistan.[6]

This episode illustrates a singular feature of Pakistan's geopolitical response to India's growing power and political heft: while Pakistan's security perceptions are focused on the threat from India, its response to the rise of India and China is, to a significant extent, U.S.-centric. Pakistan views the improvement in India's previously thin and fractious relations with the United States as a threat to one of its two big balancing relationships.

Pakistani leaders see their role in Afghanistan as important leverage to keep the United States in their corner. This is consistent with the earlier pattern of U.S.-Pakistan relations. Islamabad has often dealt with Washington on the assumption that the United States needs Pakistan more than the other way around, and that Pakistan can therefore afford to play hardball when its goals diverge from those of the United States.[7]

By contrast, belief in China's faithfulness is a constant of Pakistan's foreign and strategic policy, rarely critically examined. China has provided vital assistance, the details of which are described below. But there are limits to China's support. China has not intervened militarily in Pakistan's wars, and its friendship did not prevent Pakistan from being divided in 1971, with the creation of an independent Bangladesh. More recently, China refused to support Pakistan's incursion into Indian-controlled territory at Kargil in 1999.[8] Commentaries on China-Pakistan relations, however, are strikingly devoid of the anxiety and resentment that are daily fare in similar speeches and writings on ties with the United States.[9] Officials and media seem to be willing to let such actions pass without comment—an option that would be inconceivable with respect to the United States. This probably represents a

---

[6] The clearest statement of this policy, and the most painful one for Pakistan, was in President George W. Bush's press conference at Aiwan-e-Sadr in Islamabad. See "Remarks by President Bush and President Musharraf of Pakistan," Islamabad, March 4, 2006, available from the Embassy of the United States–Islamabad, Pakistan, http://islamabad.usembassy.gov/pakistan/h06030401.html.

[7] Schaffer and Schaffer, *How Pakistan Negotiates*, especially chap. 6.

[8] In 1999, after Indian troops began fighting to repel the Pakistani forces that were on the Indian side of the Line of Control, Pakistani prime minister Nawaz Sharif flew to Beijing for what had been billed as a six-day visit. His return after only one and a half days made it clear that the Chinese had rebuffed his request for support, although none of this appeared in the public record of the visit. The tone of both official and unofficial comments on Pakistan-China relations is well illustrated by the joint communiqué at the end of Chinese premier Wen Jiabao's 2010 visit to Pakistan. See "China, Pakistan Sign Joint Communiqué to Consolidate Partnership," Xinhua, December 19, 2010, http://news.xinhuanet.com/english2010/china/2010-12/19/c_13655688.htm.

[9] For details on Pakistani prime minister Yusuf Gilani during Wen Jiabao's December 2010 visit to Pakistan, see "Pakistan, China Want Conflict-Free Region: Gilani," *Dawn*, December 18, 2010, http://www.dawn.com/2010/12/18/pakistan-china-want-region-free-from-conflict-says-pm. html; and "China-Pakistan Relations: 2011, Year of Friendship," Institute for Strategic Studies, Islamabad (ISSI), summary report of a conference held January 11–12, 2011, http://www.issi.org. pk/conference-seminar-files/1296625461_61212309.pdf.

shared inhibition about publicly airing any doubts regarding the country widely regarded as Pakistan's most stalwart defender, which shares its key strategic goal of hemming in India.

Pakistanis inside and outside the government thus share a strong conviction that China's rise is a strategic boon for Pakistan. This is intensified by the widespread belief that the U.S. commitment in Afghanistan will soon end, as will be examined more closely in the next section. Pakistan questions the staying power of U.S. engagement in Afghanistan and the long-term prognosis for U.S. power in the region. This reinforces Islamabad's attraction to China and admiration for its economic and strategic accomplishments.

Military and Security Ties

Willingness to take Pakistan's part against India is the standard by which Pakistan judges its "balancers." By that standard, as noted, Pakistan believes that China has been faithful and that the United States has fallen short.

Both countries have played a major role in arming Pakistan. All three of the "marriages" with the United States started with a security and arms supply relationship. Pakistan's first major military supply deal with the United States came soon after Pakistan joined the Cold War alliance system in 1954. The United States was a major military supplier to Pakistan for the next decade. In 1980, President Mohammad Zia ul-Haq famously rejected President Jimmy Carter's initial offer of economic and military aid as "peanuts." When he resumed negotiations after the election of Ronald Reagan, his gamble paid off: Reagan delivered a significantly larger package than Carter had contemplated.[10] After the September 11 attacks, the United States resumed and increased the military assistance that had been cut off in 1990. Security-related assistance between 2002 and 2010 came to an estimated $13.3 billion, compared to $6.2 billion in economic aid.[11]

Both U.S.-Pakistan "divorces," similarly, came about through termination of the security relationship. The United States cut off military supply to Pakistan in 1965 during its war with India.[12] Regular supply was not resumed until after the Soviet Union invaded Afghanistan in 1979. That period of U.S.-Pakistan collaboration ended a decade later. The legislation

---

[10] See Schaffer and Schaffer, *How Pakistan Negotiates*, chap. 7.

[11] Alan Kronstadt, "Direct Overt U.S. Aid and Military Reimbursements to Pakistan, FY2002–FY2011," and Alan Kronstadt, "Major U.S. Arms Sales and Grants to Pakistan Since 2001," analyses prepared for the Congressional Research Service, January 4, 2011. Coalition support funds, technically reimbursements rather than aid, accounted for $8.9 billion of the security assistance between 2002 and 2010.

[12] The United States also cut off arms supply to India, but India, with a more diverse set of suppliers, suffered little from the action.

enacted to permit assistance, the 1985 Pressler Amendment, required that such aid be cut off once the United States could no longer certify that Pakistan did not "possess a nuclear explosive device," a threshold the United States concluded that Pakistan had passed by October 1990. Pressler is still a byword in Pakistan for U.S. double-dealing and discrimination.[13]

This stormy history of U.S.-Pakistan security ties helps explain the importance Pakistan attaches to its military ties with China. The U.S. cut-off of weapons in 1965 launched Pakistan's military relationship with China. President Ayub Khan, who was a field marshal in the army, approached the Chinese soon after the United States announced its embargo. By October 1965, a Pakistani team, including pilots to be trained on the new F-6 aircraft, had arrived in China, and the first sale of 60 of these jets, the Chinese version of the MiG-19, was on its way. Military supply continued to be an integral aspect of Pakistan's growing links to China, although Pakistan had problems with the quality and safety of the equipment. One of the air force officers involved in the sale noted, for example, that the F-6s were "not pilot-friendly in an emergency," and that Pakistan lost a number of lives as a result. But the availability of supply and willingness to consider whatever Pakistan asked for has won China points and contributed mightily to the all-weather friendship that Pakistanis speak of with such appreciation.[14]

China has continued since then as a major supplier of military equipment to Pakistan, being the largest supplier during periods of U.S. embargo, and the second-largest during the years after September 11 when the United States had resumed defense sales. Other providers of high-profile equipment include Britain and France. China has also been willing to work with Pakistan on defense production: their joint development of the JF-17 fighter is a case in point.[15]

The most sensitive area of China-Pakistan collaboration is nuclear. While neither side has confirmed this, it is universally believed that China provided critical assistance, designs, and materials to help Pakistan develop its nuclear weapons. A U.S. Defense Department report states that "in the

---

[13] The Pressler Amendment actually set two standards: that Pakistan did not "possess a nuclear explosive device" and that the continuation of U.S. assistance would significantly reduce the likelihood of its doing so. The Pakistani government was deeply engaged in the drafting of the amendment, recognizing that it was the means by which the United States would resume a major assistance program. This history did not, however, prevent Pakistan from looking on the ammendment's "discriminatory" character as a security threat and an insult.

[14] For a fascinating first-person account of the first major arms deal, see Inam H. Khan, "The Origins of Pakistan-China Military Relations," All Things Pakistan, March 18, 2010, http://pakistaniat. com/2010/03/18/china-pakistan-military-relations/.

[15] Stockholm International Peace Research Institute (SIPRI), SIPRI Arms Transfers Database, available at http://www.sipri.org/contents/armstrad/output_types_TIV.html; and "Pakistan & China's JF-17 Fighter Program," Defense Industry Daily, November 22, 2010, http://www.defenseindustrydaily. com/stuck-in-sichuan-pakistani-jf17-program-grounded-02984/.

past, China supplied Pakistan with nuclear materials and expertise and has provided critical assistance in the production of Pakistan's nuclear facilities."[16] While Pakistan has obtained imported equipment and know-how from a number of countries, none but China has been willing to be officially associated with the nuclear weapons program. This goes a long way toward explaining Pakistan's confidence in the relationship with China and the invidious comparisons it makes with the United States. China's association with Pakistan's nuclear program is continuing: Beijing has pledged to supply two additional nuclear generators to Pakistan despite the fact that this would contravene the guidelines of the Nuclear Suppliers Group. For Islamabad, the politics of such a transaction would be even more important than the economic impact. China would in effect be offering Pakistan civil nuclear cooperation like what the United States granted India.

But the key to Pakistan's confidence in China is Chinese enmity toward India, which China bested in a war in 1962. Although Beijing does not regard India as a major rival, it has no interest in India's emerging as a more significant competitor. Islamabad sees in China a potential participant in Pakistan's most important strategic endeavor—cutting India down to size.

The Economic Stakes

Traditionally, Pakistan's major economic ties have been with the United States and the countries of the Persian Gulf. The United States is the country's major export market, purchasing about 19% of Pakistan's exports, and is a significant but less important source of imports.[17] The United States is also a major aid donor, providing $1.6 billion in economic assistance grants in 2010. This represented a steady increase over the decade since the two countries re-engaged following September 11. Taken together with U.S. security assistance, U.S. aid is comparable to the resources provided to Pakistan by the 2008 International Monetary Fund (IMF) program, currently suspended, and more than what flows from the World Bank.[18] Because Pakistan's balance of payments has been under severe pressure in

---

[16] See Office of the Secretary of Defense, *Proliferation: Threat and Response* (Washington, D.C., 2001).

[17] "Table 14.1, Value of Foreign Trade," Federal Bureau of Statistics, Government of Pakistan, http://www.statpak.gov.pk/fbs/sites/default/files/external_trade/14.1.pdf; "Table 14.6, Cumulative Exports by Major Countries," Federal Bureau of Statistics, Government of Pakistan, http://www.statpak.gov.pk/fbs/sites/default/files/external_trade/14.6.pdf; and "Table 14.7, Cumulative Imports by Major Countries," Federal Bureau of Statistics, Government of Pakistan, http://www.statpak.gov.pk/fbs/sites/default/files/external_trade/14.7.pdf.

[18] Kronstadt, "Direct Overt U.S. Aid"; "Pakistan: Lending by Volume," World Bank, http://www.worldbank.org.pk/WBSITE/EXTERNAL/COUNTRIES/SOUTHASIAEXT/PAKISTANEXTN/0,,menuPK:2204162~pagePK:51331374~piPK:2037600~theSitePK:293052,00.html; and "IMF Assesses Financing for Pakistan after Devastating Floods," IMF Survey, August 24, 2010, http://www.imf.org/external/pubs/ft/survey/so/2010/new082410a.htm.

recent years owing to rising prices for petroleum, which alone accounts for 30% of imports,[19] the aid relationship is economically very important. The major contribution of the oil-producing countries to Pakistan's economic well-being has been oil financing or occasionally oil payment forgiveness by the United Arab Emirates (UAE) and Saudi Arabia. Remittances from Pakistanis in the Gulf are the country's biggest foreign exchange inflow, accounting for an estimated $7.8 billion in 2008–9.[20]

As China's economy has grown, so has its economic relationship with Pakistan. Today China has a profile comparable to that of the United States in Pakistan's trade: China is the second-largest source of imports, with 14.6% of the market in 2010, and the fourth-largest export market, buying 6% of Pakistan's exports in that same year. Beijing has also become a major donor of economic aid, with 2010 aid commitments totaling $2.0 billion, exceeding U.S. aid levels. All the assistance is for infrastructure and, unlike aid from the United States, is in the form of loans. Loans for the nuclear power plants mentioned above total $1.6 billion. In the past, China has provided some critical and very welcome types of aid, including construction of two strategic transport links: the Karakoram Highway between northern Pakistan and China and a new port at Gwadar on the Arabian Sea close to the Iranian border. During Chinese premier Wen Jiabao's visit to Islamabad in December 2010, he announced $410 million in aid to victims of the floods that swept through Pakistan the preceding summer; buried in the press coverage was the fact that only $10 million of this was a grant.[21] This expanding economic profile makes China an even more attractive strategic partner than it was in the past.

Economic ties between Pakistan and India are trivial, with two-way trade estimated at $2 billion per year, much of it traveling through a third country.[22] Interestingly, trade liberalization has some support both in Pakistan's business community and in policy and academic circles. Several Pakistani economists have urged accelerated movement on trade. They describe candidly the obstacles to expanded trade on both sides: Pakistan's failure to extend nondiscriminatory "most favored nation" treatment to

---

[19] "Table 14.3, Imports by Commodity/Groups," Federal Bureau of Statistics, Government of Pakistan, http://www.statpak.gov.pk/fbs/sites/default/files/external_trade/14.3.pdf.

[20] Mushtaq Ali Hub, "Pakistan Economic Survey 2009–2010," Pakistan Ministry of Finance, 2010, 101, table 7.11, http://www.finance.gov.pk/survey/chapter_10/07_Balance_of_Payments.pdf.

[21] "Foreign Economic Assistance, Status Report on Commitments and Disbursements, July 2009–June 2010," Government of Pakistan, Economic Affairs Division, available at http://www.ead.gov.pk/; and "China Announces $410 Million for Flood Victims," Dawn, December 18, 2010, http://www.dawn.com/2010/12/18/china-announces-410-million-assistance-for-flood-victims.html.

[22] Estimate from Mohsin S. Khan, "Improving India-Pakistan Relations through Trade," East Asia Forum, April 19, 2010, http://www.eastasiaforum.org/2010/04/19/improving-india-pakistan-relations-through-trade/.

India and India's non-tariff barriers.[23] At the official level, however, Pakistan has resisted India's efforts to make trade liberalization an early agenda item in peace talks on the grounds that moving trade to the head of the queue could reduce the urgency behind Pakistan's commitment to the Kashmir problem. One of the side effects of this policy is to prevent economic ties between the two rivals from becoming a significant counterweight to the difficult aspects of their relationship.

Cultural Links

India and Pakistan share the same cultural space. Spoken Urdu, the national language of Pakistan, is so close to the most widely spoken language of India, Hindi, that one can carry on a conversation and scarcely know where one language ends and the other begins, although they do use different alphabets. Pakistanis and north Indians who are not vegetarian share a cuisine. Many traditions of dress, ceremony, family relationships, and the like are held in common. This gives a kind of schizophrenic quality to the two countries' rivalry. People from Punjab, one of two provinces in pre-partition India that were divided in two, comment with warmth and sentimentality on the wonderful reception they experience when traveling in the other part of Punjab. The Pakistani-Indian cricket rivalry is legendary, but big matches have also been the occasion for affectionate people-to-people encounters.

Such shared cultural links, however, do nothing to soften Pakistan's mistrust of India or blunt the impact of India's growing economy and expanding global political footprint. Pushing in the other direction is Pakistan's Islamic birthright. All Pakistanis agree on the importance of Islam to their identity. But there are sharply different views on which style of Islam Pakistan represents, or whether the country can comfortably accommodate more than one style. The Islamic identity is especially important to Pakistan's status as "the un-India."[24]

Whereas Pakistan defines itself as Islamic, India has traditionally seen itself as a secular, multireligious, multicultural state. India's roughly 15% Muslim minority is an integral part of this mosaic. To further complicate the picture, one of India's major political parties, the Bharatiya Janata Party, defines India as both secular and Hindu, and asserts that India's

---

[23] See, for example, Mohammad Waqas Sajjad, Mahwish Hafeez, and Kiran Firdous, "The Search for Peace—Pakistan and India," ISSI, Reflections, no. 7, 2010, http://www.issi.org.pk/publication-files/1298971430_39792596.pdf.

[24] For an especially insightful discussion of Pakistan's Islamic identities, see Farzana Shaikh, *Making Sense of Pakistan* (London: Hurst, 2009).

religious minorities—including Christians and Muslims—should consider themselves culturally Hindu.

With China, by contrast, Pakistan shares little common cultural heritage. Theirs is a relationship founded on common strategic interests and nurtured with great care by both governments. People-to-people contact is limited by distance and language, and there is no great effort on either side to expand it. Pakistan looks to China as a counterweight to India and a safety net against U.S. infidelity; nothing else matters. Beijing's support for Pakistan against India is sufficient to generate affection for China among the Pakistani people. From that perspective, a stronger China can only help.

The one factor that could provide a basis for closer ties at the popular level with some parts of China is Islam. In practice, this is, if anything, a complication. China is concerned that contact with Islamists in Pakistan and Central Asia might radicalize the sometimes restive Muslims of western China. It is a mark of the importance that Islamabad places on relations with the Chinese government that the Pakistan government has stayed aloof from China's Muslims despite the strong feelings of loyalty Pakistanis normally bear toward their coreligionists.

Afghanistan: A Theater for India-Pakistan Rivalry

Afghanistan has been at war since the late 1970s. The Afghan government is mainly interested in consolidating internal power, establishing internal security, and maintaining independence. Afghanistan is not strong enough to control its own security space, so its leaders pursue these objectives by manipulating and balancing internal rivals and interested foreign countries. This is a game at which the Afghan leaders who stay alive and in power are skilled and ruthless.

Historically, the major outside players in Afghanistan were Pakistan and Russia; today, they are Pakistan and the United States. India is a traditional friend, a country that can balance Pakistan, while China has not been a major player. But the most important objective of the Afghan leadership's maneuvering is internal: maintaining power. The Taliban are the major threat to that power, one that must be either overcome or co-opted. Afghanistan looks on its international friends through that prism.

Afghanistan as Buffer State

Afghanistan is an ethnic mosaic. It has never had a strong central government. Certain Pashtun tribes have traditionally ruled, though always in conjunction with other ethnic and tribal groups. For many years the country was a buffer between Russia to the north and the British Indian empire to the south. It shares ethnic and tribal ties across all its borders. Pashtuns, the largest ethnic group, have extensive ties of kinship and language in Pakistan. Among the smaller ethnic communities, the Uzbeks and Tajiks have family and linguistic links across the northern frontiers in Uzbekistan and Tajikistan, and the Hazaras share both ethnicity and Shia Islam with Iran to Afghanistan's west.

Pakistan looms large in Afghanistan's strategic world. The Pashtun tribes that straddle the border make competing demands on both national governments and have been involved in irredentist movements aimed chiefly against Pakistan. Some of these tribes initially opposed the partition of India and creation of an independent Pakistan. More recently, Islamabad has sought a dominant role and "strategic depth" in Afghanistan. Pakistan was the main conduit for aid to the anti-Soviet *mujahidin* and, after the Soviet army left in 1989, was one of only three countries that recognized the Taliban government. Afghanistan under the Taliban became a virtual client state, albeit one that frequently embarrassed its patron.

Following the implosion of the Taliban government in 2001, the Bonn Conference gave birth to a new constitution that put in place an Afghan government headed by a Pashtun, Hamid Karzai, and built around the Northern Alliance. This group, composed chiefly of non-Pashtuns, had resisted the Taliban to the end, with support from India and Russia. Pakistan regarded the change of government in Kabul as a strategic disaster. Determined not to return to the days when Afghanistan could be the other end of an Indian pincer movement, Islamabad reactivated relationships with groups the Karzai government saw as enemies. Not surprisingly, the Afghan government remains suspicious.

India, by contrast, saw the new Afghan dispensation as a strategic opportunity, a chance to leap beyond the restrictions Pakistan had placed on trade and transit between India and Central Asia and to thwart Islamist extremism aimed at India. The latter's involvement with Afghanistan has a long history. Karzai himself, like many other prominent Afghans, studied in India, and this history laid the groundwork for Afghanistan to play India off Pakistan. Karzai has cultivated relations with both countries. During visits to India, he has referred eloquently to the India-Afghanistan "strategic relationship" and publicly urged India to put pressure on the United States to end Pakistan's internal involvement in Afghanistan.[25] On the other hand, when visiting Islamabad, he has referred to India as a "brother"

---

[25] Rajeev Sharma, "Karzai on India and Pakistan," *Diplomat*, September 24, 2010, http://the-diplomat.com/indian-decade/2010/09/24/karzai-on-india-and-pakistan/.

but to Pakistan as a "conjoined twin."[26] Afghanistan is not strong enough to be able to dictate terms to Pakistan, but its leaders use the relationship with India to create some margin for maneuver. In similar fashion, Karzai has occasionally threatened to "join the Taliban" when pressure from the United States was getting uncomfortably heavy.

China has historically played a small role in Afghanistan, and its current profile is still not high. Where India represents a balancing force, China represents an opportunity for resources in the short term. If Afghan security improves enough to permit long-term strategic thinking, Afghanistan may come to see China as a potential future balancer of the United States, but that is still a distant prospect.

The Key: Security

The dominant features of Afghanistan after September 11 are fragmentation and insecurity. Addressing these issues is central to the government's efforts to stay in power and consolidate the country. Kabul is interested in working with whoever can help it achieve security and stability, trying to avoid creating new enmity, though it is not in a position to drive policy.

The United States, NATO, and a wider coalition have deployed over 130,000 troops from 48 countries in Afghanistan.[27] One of their primary objectives is to prepare the fledgling Afghan National Army to take over responsibility for the country's security, a task most observers regard as daunting. None of the primary players from the neighborhood have troops in this coalition.

Pakistan has a substantial intelligence presence and is working closely with the United States on the opposite side of the border. It is also determined to remain the most influential outside country in Afghanistan. There is substantial evidence that Pakistan has put its considerable weight behind certain Taliban factions that it would like to see in a future government. Islamabad fears that a premature departure of coalition forces could leave

---

[26] Irfan Ghauri and Sajjad Malik, "No Proxy Wars on Afghan Soil, Says Karzai," *Daily Times*, March 12, 2010, http://www.dailytimes.com.pk/default.asp?page=2010\03\12\story_12-3-2010_pg1_1; "India-Afghanistan Relations," Government of India, Ministry of External Affairs, Press Release, January 2011, http://www.meaindia.nic.in/meaxpsite/pressrelease/2011/01/bilateralafghanistan.pdf; "India and Afghanistan: A Development Partnership," Government of India, Ministry of External Affairs, External Publicity Division, 2009, http://meaindia.nic.in/staticfile/Report.pdf; Sandeep Dikshit, "Karzai, Manmohan Discuss Wide Ranging Issues," *Hindu*, February 4, 2011, http://www.hindu.com/2011/02/04/stories/2011020465501400.htm; and Peter Wonnacott, "India Befriends Afghanistan, Irking Pakistan," *Wall Street Journal*, August 19, 2009, http://online.wsj.com/article/SB125061548456340511.html.

[27] See "Troop Numbers and Contributions," International Security Assistance Force, http://www.isaf.nato.int/troop-numbers-and-contributions/index.php.

behind a chaotic situation harmful to Pakistan, and the country's security managers have devoted considerable attention to positioning themselves for such a contingency. In the words of one commentator:

> With the resurgence of the Taliban and constant reservations over U.S. war strategy, the situation in Afghanistan has reached a level where there is little hope of victory anytime soon. The U.S. withdrawal decision conveyed through the strategic dialogue has clearly exposed the weakening position of President Karzai at home. To save the Afghan government and the country from collapsing, President Karzai has realized the importance of Pakistan and the influential role it can play in stabilizing Afghanistan.[28]

India has no interest in a direct military role but does not want Pakistan to have uncontested primacy in Afghanistan. After years of unremitting hostility to any proposals for negotiations on Afghanistan that include the Taliban, India is now signaling that it recognizes that all parties must be involved in creating a peaceful Afghan future.[29] New Delhi would like to help build the Afghan armed forces through exchanges and training, in keeping with its pre-1979 role and in order to build up future relations. India's aims are regarded with great suspicion by Pakistan. The United States, convinced that it must work with Pakistan in order to achieve an acceptable end state in Afghanistan, has kept India at arm's length from the security effort. China is not involved in the security effort.

Rebuilding a Poor and Shattered Economy

The Afghan economy, which is based largely on horticulture and animal husbandry, is one of the poorest and least developed in the world, having been ravaged by three decades of war, internal violence, and massive population dislocation. Close to one-third of the country's prewar population fled to refugee camps in Pakistan and Iran during the 1980s, and only a small percentage of those people and their children have returned. Afghanistan is heavily dependent on foreign assistance. A UN official told this author in 2006 that Afghanistan financed the lowest percentage of its national budget from its own resources of any country in the world.[30]

Afghanistan's economy is dependent on transit, especially through Pakistan, for foreign commerce. A 2010 report by the U.S. Geological Survey estimated the value of Afghanistan's natural gas, copper, and other

---

[28] Humera Iqbal, "Pak-Afghan Ties in the Light of Pak-U.S. Strategic Dialogue," Institute of Regional Studies, Spotlight 29, no. 11, November 2010, http://irs.org.pk/PublSpotLight.htm.

[29] See, for example, Prime Minister Manmohan Singh's remarks during a May 2011 visit to Afghanistan. Manmohan Singh (remarks at a banquet lunch hosted by the President of Afghanistan, Kabul, May 12, 2011), http://meaindia.nic.in/mystart.php?id=530117621.

[30] Author's interview with UN official at a U.S.-sponsored briefing, Kabul, 2006.

minerals at $1 trillion.[31] Creating a functioning economy and getting international assistance to the places that need it are major challenges for the Afghans and their international supporters. Furthermore, exploiting the country's resources will require a major increase in security.

Both India and China have been involved in the effort to revive the Afghan economy. India is one of the top five donors, with pledges of $1.8 billion in the first decade after the new government was put in place. This is India's largest aid program, and one of only four that disburse significant funding. India has supported a mix of activities. These include high-profile projects that will provide favorable publicity in Kabul, such as construction of a hydropower facility and a new parliament building; community development; educational exchanges; linkages between Afghan and Indian NGOs; and road projects of strategic importance to Afghanistan. This assistance makes India a significant economic player and has also strengthened its political ties with the Karzai government. The Afghan government is trying to maintain a strong enough Indian connection to provide a margin for maneuver without antagonizing Pakistan.

China's economic aid to Afghanistan is relatively modest, estimated at $131 million, including some construction projects and training of mine detectors. Its most prominent contribution is an estimated $4 billion investment in the Aynak copper mine, the largest foreign investment in Afghanistan's history. China's profile is in line with its practice of developing a significant political presence in mineral-rich countries. Afghanistan's location—next to politically troubled parts of China, next to Pakistan, and at the outer rim of the Indian subcontinent—makes it strategically important to China, an added motivation to maintain a presence in a part of the Afghan economy that would in any event be interesting for Beijing.

Cultural Ties with the Surrounding Region

Afghanistan has been a cultural crossroads since at least the time of Alexander the Great. Its cultural ties with neighbors have led to external interference for centuries and continue to complicate the search for peace and stability. Relations with India and China are driven in part by Afghanistan's quest for cards to play against closer and more intrusive neighbors.

The most important neighbor is Pakistan, which sees the Pashtuns as the most friendly group in Afghanistan. At the same time, the sometimes irredentist claims of Afghanistan's and Pakistan's Pashtuns—including their unwillingness to accept the border demarcated in the days of the British

---

[31] Alissa J. Rubin, "Afghan Officials Elated by Mineral Report," *New York Times*, June 14, 2010, http://www.nytimes.com/2010/06/15/world/asia/15afghan.html.

Empire—have exacerbated the often hostile relations between the two countries. In the three decades since the Soviet army invaded Afghanistan, this ethnic linkage has become entangled in Afghanistan's conflicts, including deep involvement by Pakistan's intelligence services with certain Pashtun tribes and sanctuaries for Afghan insurgents in both Pakistan's largely ungoverned tribal areas and the chronically restive province of Balochistan. The Karzai government recognizes that it must work with Pakistan but has deep misgivings about Pakistan's meddling in ethnic and tribal politics and especially about its linkages with Afghan insurgents.

Other nearby countries also have cultural ties with Afghanistan. Iran is close to the Hazara community, the principal Afghan Shia population, and is deeply suspicious of Pakistan's designs on Afghanistan. Iran also has linguistic ties with the Tajiks in Afghanistan, who are well represented in the Karzai government. Likewise, Turkey has ties with the Turkic-speaking communities, notably the Turkmen and Uzbeks. Tajikistan and Uzbekistan also have ethnic compatriots in Afghanistan, with Uzbekistan being home to an Islamist insurgency that occasionally moves across its border with Afghanistan. Although none of these countries has the ability or in some cases the desire for involvement in Afghanistan on the same scale as Pakistan, they are part of the mosaic.

India and China, neither of which is a Muslim country, are "almost neighbors" with greater overall power than most of the immediate neighbors, but with less direct access to Afghanistan. From Karzai's perspective—or indeed from the perspective of any future government—keeping India and China, as well as the United States, involved in Afghanistan offers some hope of providing a counterweight to excessive meddling by others, especially Pakistan. Balancing and complicated bargaining are in most Afghans' political DNA. These are practically the only tools available to the leadership of a country whose economy and security have been undermined by three decades of war.

India's Remaining Neighbors

For the other countries in South Asia, India is the dominant power, sometimes supportive, sometimes overbearing, but, unlike the perspective from Pakistan, not a threat to their sovereignty. Nepal, Sri Lanka, and Bangladesh have all had ups and downs coexisting with India, and share the ambivalence that smaller neighbors frequently have toward much larger ones, whereas Bhutan and Maldives follow two very different models for conducting the international relations of very small states. Each of these countries' relationship with India and China has a slightly different dynamic. All, however, employ a combination of balancing and hedging strategies, using relationships with outside powers to enhance their margin for maneuver vis-à-vis India. Relationships with China and the United States are part of this game. One traditional concern is that the United States might outsource its South Asia policy to India. A result of improved U.S.-India relations is much greater and more candid consultation between the two countries on developments in the region. This is welcome in New Delhi but makes India's smaller neighbors uneasy.

Nepal: Between Two Giants

Sandwiched between the new global giants, Nepal and Bhutan face India, which has dominated them to a degree unimaginable in any of its other neighbors. India's role is buttressed by treaties that extend to it the preeminent role once enjoyed by the British in these Himalayan buffer states. Both countries' relationships with India have been modified in recent years. The advent of the Maoists to a share of national power in Nepal raises the question of whether China is becoming a more serious player. It also makes the rise of India and China a matter of even more than usual anxiety in Nepal.

Nepal was never colonized, and its landlocked mountain geography kept it isolated from the outside world until 1950. The country's special relationship with India reflects geography, powerful geostrategic interests, and close ties of culture and religion. India controls Nepal's access to the sea, and the India-Nepal border runs through the plains of the Terai, far easier to traverse than the Himalayas between Nepal and China. India and Nepal have an open border; nationals of both countries can cross and trade at will. The Indian Army has long recruited its elite Gurkha troops from Nepal, and pensions paid to Nepalese soldiers retired from the Indian Army are a significant source of foreign exchange. As the world's only other Hindu country, Nepal has a special place in India's conception of the South Asian neighborhood.

During Nepal's monarchy, India was close to the king and the army. Security interests took priority, and New Delhi fiercely defended its primacy among Nepal's foreign friends. In 1989, for example, reports that Nepal was talking to China about arms sales and road construction led India to suspend renewal of its trade and transit agreement, effectively blockading the country for nearly a year. Nepal was in no position to push back, recognizing that another move toward China would provoke even more damaging Indian retaliation.

A Maoist insurgency that garnered substantial rural support eventually caused massive changes both in Nepal's internal politics and in the India-China equation in Nepal. From 1996 onward, the Maoists profited from the disillusionment and ineffective governance that had already led a people's movement to demand constitutional restrictions on the monarchy in 1990. The insurgency spread, drawing added strength after the massacre of most of the royal family in 2001 by a disgruntled prince.[32] A year later, the new king dissolved the parliament and in the process doomed the monarchy. In 2006 an interim parliament was elected that included the Maoists, and in 2008 a newly elected Constituent Assembly abolished the monarchy.

The Maoists moved to strengthen relations with China. Within the first six months of his prime ministership in 2008, Maoist leader Pushpa Kamal Dahal (better known by his *nom de guerre* "Prachanda") visited China twice and received two Chinese military delegations.[33] Subsequent non-Maoist prime ministers, however, have not continued this appeal for closer ties with China. Jhalanath Khanal, who took office in February 2011, went out of his way to call for strengthening relations with India and to appeal to "good friends" India and China to respect Nepal's independence.[34] But with the government's survival fragile, its focus has been on solidifying its internal power base. Nepal was faced with a new requirement to balance its huge neighbors, and relations with China and India have become a factor in internal politics.

This upheaval profoundly influenced the way both India and China dealt with Nepal. India was determined to retain the primary outside influence, but its institutional ties with both the king and the army lost much of their value. China was ambivalent about the Maoists. Although their entrance into governing institutions was an opportunity, the violence and revolutionary ethos of the Maoists raised Chinese anxiety about the spread of disorder to adjacent areas in Tibet.

Nepal's trade and security relationships with India and China reflect these changes. New Delhi is still the most important player, but Beijing has risen in importance. India is Nepal's principal military supplier and is overwhelmingly its largest trading partner. The $923 million in trade in 2009 represented about two-thirds of Nepal's total trade, an increase of 75% since 2005. However, China has emerged in strong second place, with trade between the two countries increasing twenty-fold since 2005 to $414

---

[32] Chitra K. Tiwari, "Maoist Insurgency in Nepal: Internal Dimensions," South Asia Analysis Group, Papers, no. 187, January 20, 2001, http://www.southasiaanalysis.org/papers2/paper187.htm.

[33] "Prachanda Ready for Second China Trip," *Times of India*, December 3, 2008, http://articles.timesofindia.indiatimes.com/2008-12-03/rest-of-world/27935390_1_first-maoist-prime-minister-pushpa-kamal-dahal-prachanda-nepal-china.

[34] Jhalanath Khanal, interview by Prashant Jha, "We Are Aware of India's Interests," *Hindu*, February 14, 2011, http://www.thehindu.com/opinion/interview/article1413795.ece.

million in 2009, virtually all in exports to Nepal.[35] In the aid field, India leads by a substantial margin, providing an estimated $361 million in assistance in 2010–12, including road and rail projects through the Terai plains along the Indian border. China is emerging as a donor and pledged $22 million in assistance in 2009, including contributions to the hydropower industry, Nepal's major natural resource. By way of comparison, the United States provided $58 million in aid in 2010.[36]

India and China will continue to jockey for influence in Nepal over the next decade. India has the advantage of history, geography, and established linkages; China is motivated by concern about Tibet and interested in crowding India's strategic space. There is already talk of China extending the railway to Tibet and possibly building a rail connection to Kathmandu. Transit links that create north-south routes across Nepal are a potential security nightmare for India. Nepal's volatile internal politics could make pursuing an active balancing strategy difficult, but the country may have eager suitors, and some degree of hedging its dependence on India could be attractive. As China becomes more of an aid donor, Nepal will have new tools to pursue such a strategy.

Sri Lanka: Connecting Domestic and International Politics

India and China are both important for Sri Lanka, but for different reasons. Sri Lanka's principal linkage with India is the country's 18% Tamil population, which shares ties of ethnicity and language with the over 70 million Tamils in South India.[37] For decades, ethnic conflict was the most important problem Sri Lanka faced. Following the end of the civil war in 2009, repairing ethnic relations remains a crucial challenge. China, on the other hand, has long been an instrument and symbol of Sri Lanka's independent voice in international affairs, and frequently a foil for Colombo's relations with Washington. China has also been an important partner for trade and military supply.

---

[35] Figures on China are from the Ministry of Commerce, People's Republic of China (PRC), available at http://english.mofcom.gov.cn/. Figures on India are from the Department of Commerce, Government of India, available at http://commerce.nic.in/.

[36] Jyoti Thottam, "Nepal: Caught between India and China," *Time*, March 2, 2010, http://www.time.com/time/world/article/0,8599,1967859,00.html; "China Increases Aid to Nepal by 50 Percent," *Indian Express*, April 19, 2009, http://www.expressindia.com/latest-news/China-increases-aid-to-Nepal-by-50/448796/; and USAID Nepal, available at http://nepal.usaid.gov/our-work/publications-a-reports.html.

[37] "Background Note: Sri Lanka," Bureau of South and Central Asian Affairs, U.S. Department of State, June 2010, http://www.state.gov/r/pa/ei/bgn/5249.htm; and "Provisional Population Figures, Census 2011," Census of India, Government of India, Ministry of Home Affairs, http://www.censusindia.gov.in/2011-prov-results/data_files/tamilnadu/2-FIGURES%20AT%20A%20GLANCE-tn.pdf.

Sri Lanka's ties with India have been mercurial. Soon after Sri Lanka's independence, negotiations over the nationality of the "Tamils of recent Indian origin"—those whose grandparents had come from India as plantation workers during the days of the British Empire (about half the Tamil population)—strained relations, as did periodic internal crises over language use and political rights for the Tamils. India was always the major strategic and economic player in Sri Lanka. It has the largest navy in the region and is Sri Lanka's largest trading partner, supplying about 25% of imports in 2007.[38] An India–Sri Lanka free trade agreement signed in 1999 accelerated the growth of bilateral trade.

In 1987, during a particularly bloody period of the ethnic conflict, India stepped in as peacemaker and negotiated an agreement providing for expanded local self-governance, including for Tamil-majority areas. The Indian Peace Keeping Force (IPKF) went to Sri Lanka to supervise the ceasefire between the Sri Lankan army and the principal Tamil insurgent group, the Liberation Tigers of Tamil Eelam (LTTE), as well as the disarming of the latter. The disarmament agreement fell apart almost instantly, leaving the IPKF with a thousand dead after a shooting war with the LTTE. Two years later came the low point in Indo–Sri Lankan relations, when the Sri Lankan government publicly asked India to withdraw the IPKF. The backlash from this intervention kept India on the sidelines until the Sri Lankan government declared victory in the ethnic civil war in May 2009.

Reports of army atrocities during the bloody end to the war elicited international calls, led by Sri Lanka's Western aid donors (including the United States), for an investigation of possible war crimes. This appeal sounded hollow and hypocritical to a government that had just vanquished one of the world's worst terrorist groups. Sri Lanka responded by showcasing its non-Western relationships, and India was the first beneficiary of this ugly mood. Within six months, New Delhi announced a $100 million grant for resettling Sri Lanka's internally displaced people. Sri Lankan president Mahinda Rajapaksa's visit to New Delhi on June 9, 2010, spotlighted more commitments: an $800 million concessional credit for railway construction, including a line to Rajapaksa's home town of Matara; a $200 million line of credit for a joint power plant in Trincomalee; and additional unspecified amounts for infrastructure in the war-torn north of the island.[39] The two countries started a strategic dialogue and pledged military cooperation, and

---

[38] "Trade Statistics of Sri Lanka 2007," Sri Lankan Department of Commerce, 2007, http://www.doc. gov.lk/web/down/2.pdf.

[39] "India-Sri Lanka Joint Declaration," Ministry of External Affairs, Government of India, June 9, 2010, http://www.meaindia.nic.in/mystart.php?id=290015869; and "Power Push: Sri Lanka Gets More Indian Aid for Coal Power Plant," *Lanka Business Online*, November 26, 2010, http://www. lankabusinessonline.com/fullstory.php?nid=180007130.

India opened consulates in the Tamil city of Jaffna and in Hambantota in the Sinhalese deep south. The benefits to Sri Lanka were clear; so was the message to the West.

The other big beneficiary was China, which intensified India's eagerness. The China–Sri Lanka relationship has deep roots. It started in 1950 with a swap of Sri Lankan rubber for Chinese rice, a move that attracted China's gratitude and led the United States to cut off aid. Colombo's largest public auditorium and court building were built by China, and an immense statue of Buddha, much revered in this Buddhist-majority island, stands next to the Chinese Embassy downtown. China is a significant military supplier, primarily selling aircraft and radar, and a large trade partner.[40]

China's recent aid contributions are at least equal to India's in monetary value. The most important ones are infrastructure improvements: a port upgrade and new airport for Colombo, a power plant in the northwestern part of the island at Puttalam, and a new port costing an estimated $1 billion in Hambantota on the southeastern corner.[41] The latter project is the most worrisome from the Indian perspective. Indian security analysts describe the port as part of a Chinese "string of pearls," a collection of facilities around the Indian Ocean where the Chinese are creating naval access.

Sri Lanka is, in short, engaging eagerly with both India and China, and deriving significant benefits from both countries. Beijing and New Delhi are strategic rivals, but from Colombo's perspective, they are complementary inasmuch as both can be used to balance the West and enhance freedom of action. Sri Lanka's overtures to Iran and Libya have the same motivation.

Bangladesh: The Other Muslim Neighbor

Bangladesh's strategic priority is to protect its independence and obtain support for its poor but developing economy. Bangladesh owes its birth to India's intervention in 1971, but India, the classic big neighbor, has become a lightning rod in Bangladeshi politics. Relations with India are strongly influenced by Bangladeshi domestic politics. The Awami League, headed by Sheikh Hasina, whose father brought Bangladesh to independence, is closer to India. The Bangladesh Nationalist Party (BNP), by contrast, is more sympathetic to Pakistan and is often in electoral alliance with the Islamist

---

[40] SIPRI Arms Transfers Database. Sri Lanka's view of China as the "anti-Western friend" has one ironic historical footnote. In 1970 a Sinhalese Marxist insurgent group called the JVP (Janatha Vimukthi Peramuna, or People's Liberation Front) took up arms against the government. The then prime minister Sirimavo Bandaranaike sought military assistance from both the United States and China, the first time those two governments supported the same government against rebels.

[41] "Power Push: Sri Lanka Gets More Indian Aid for Coal Power Plant," *Lanka Business Online*, November 26, 2010, http://www.lankabusinessonline.com/fullstory.php?nid=180007130.

political parties. The relationship with China is free of this entanglement in domestic politics, but it is more a hedge against India than against the West.

Some 90% of Bangladesh's 2,700-mile external border is with India. Weak governance, forbidding terrain, and the fact that the border runs through insurgency-prone parts of India make it difficult to control movement across the border. India claims that millions of illegal Bangladeshi immigrants have slipped across, a number that swells with political turmoil or natural disaster. The flight of an estimated 9 million people into India in 1971 prompted an Indian intervention that resulted in the former East Pakistan becoming independent Bangladesh. A physical border that includes Bangladesh enclaves within India and vice versa adds to the tension. Although India and Bangladesh have enhanced their military and paramilitary cooperation along the border, there is no history of the kind of military cooperation that India has, for example, with Nepal.

New Delhi is convinced, with some justification, that Bangladesh is perhaps unintentionally hosting Pakistan-supported intelligence and subversion aimed at India.[42] The electoral alliance between the BNP and two Bangladeshi Islamist parties aggravated these concerns during the previous elected government, as did a series of simultaneous attacks all over the country by Islamic militants in 2005. Preventing militant sabotage from Bangladesh is India's top priority.

The most important economic link between Bangladesh and India is a natural one. The Ganges and Brahmaputra rivers, Bangladesh's lifelines, flow through India before their mouths intertwine and reach the sea in Bangladesh. As water has grown scarcer on the subcontinent, use of river waters has become more contentious and emotionally fraught. Bangladesh signed an agreement with India on the Ganges waters in 1996 under an Awami League government. The agreement has succeeded fairly well in alleviating tensions over that river system. However, opinions are starkly divided in Bangladesh about how and whether to attempt an agreement on the Brahmaputra system.

Since 2009, Sheikh Hasina's Awami League government has tried to revitalize ties with India. As her legacy, she would like to resolve chronic problems such as water use and road transit between the easternmost parts of India and the rest of the country (called "connectivity" in Bangladesh). Building on a partial free trade agreement reached under the BNP government that preceded her, Hasina is working to expand trade. But the

---

[42] See, for example, Sultan Shahin, "India Frets over Pakistan-Bangladesh Nexus," *Asia Times Online*, March 6, 2004, http://www.atimes.com/atimes/South_Asia/FC06Df02.html; and "ISI Behind Counterfeit Currency Racket, Says Bangladesh," Rediff News, January 30, 2010, http://news.rediff.com/report/2010/jan/30/pak-intel-agencies-behind-fake-currency-racket-bangladesh.htm.

asymmetric relationship and the intense hostility between the major parties in Bangladesh have made it almost impossible to develop a consensus on relations with India. No Bangladesh government has been willing to look seriously at energy cooperation, either through sales of Bangladeshi natural gas or through electrical grid-sharing. Even a private investment agreement proposed by Tata, one of India's most internationally renowned corporations, fell by the wayside. The reason in all these cases was the toxic politics of appearing to "give something away" to India.

Another powerful bond with India is cultural. Bengal was partitioned when the British Empire left the subcontinent, and Bangladesh still shares intimate bonds of culture, language, and history with West Bengal in India. These ties are far more compelling than the corresponding bonds between Indian and Pakistani Punjabis. The Bengali language and literature hold the emotions of all Bengalis. There is a significant Hindu community in Bangladesh and a Muslim one in West Bengal, and the populations have never been separated as rigorously as they were in the west. Calcutta is a cultural beacon for all Bengalis, and the same Bengali poets are revered on both sides of the border.

Security, economic, and cultural linkages make India the more important of the two rising powers for Bangladesh. However, to India's discomfiture, Bangladesh and China have carefully nurtured their relationship. China accounts for 80% by value of Bangladesh's military purchases since 2005, including an F-7 fighter aircraft deal.[43] On the economic side, trade between the two countries came to $4.5 billion in 2009, as China supplied 22% of Bangladesh's imports, about double India's market share. By way of comparison, Bangladesh's trade with China is about equal to that with the United States, except that the United States is primarily an importer from Bangladesh, whereas Chinese trade consists almost entirely of exports.[44]

Geography and culture will keep India and Bangladesh closely connected, but China's rapid economic rise will enhance Beijing's influence in Bangladesh, a prospect that concerns New Delhi greatly. The BNP, traditionally wary of India and ambitious in its negotiating goals, may at some point try to adopt a more assertive hedging strategy. This might garner trade and aid benefits from China, but would almost certainly also produce an increase in tensions with India.

---

[43] SIPRI Arms Transfers Database.

[44] UN Conference on Trade and Development (UNCTAD), UNCTADstat Database, http://unctadstat.
unctad.org.

Bhutan and Maldives: Tiny States Dealing with Emerging Giants

Bhutan and Maldives illustrate two very different ways that states with tiny populations and isolating geography manage their relations with much larger countries. Bhutan, tucked into the Himalayas between India and China and close to Nepal, has carefully tended a special relationship with India. Maldives, a group of atolls in the Indian Ocean, a thousand miles from the nearest landmass, has studiously avoided special relationships. Both have been quite successful in maintaining some margin for maneuver.

Bhutan's situation is a more extreme variant of Nepal's. Geography and history dictate a special relationship with India and a near-protectorate status, and the country has managed its affairs with considerable skill. In the 1980s, Bhutan began establishing diplomatic relations with countries other than India but carefully avoided establishing formal ties with any of the great powers in a clear effort to minimize Indian anxiety. In 2007, the government renegotiated a 60-year-old treaty that required Bhutan to take India's advice on foreign affairs and defense, replacing the treaty with one committing both countries to "cooperate closely with each other on issues relating to their national interests"—a much looser obligation.[45]

In contrast to Nepal, Bhutan's relationship with China has been troubled. Although the two signed their first international agreement in 1998, border talks have been difficult and inconclusive. Chinese incursions into Bhutanese territory in 2009 may have been intended as a signal to India but got Bhutan's attention as well. In short, the India-China game is a more intimidating one in Bhutan than in Nepal, and the hedging strategy relies on a gradually growing network of global relationships.[46]

Maldives, by contrast, has relished its "splendid isolation." Maldives maintains diplomatic relations with most countries in the world—a handful through resident embassies, and the rest through ambassadors resident in Colombo, Islamabad, or New Delhi. The country's small population—under 0.4 million people—means that donors can fund a meaningful project with a small amount of money, so aid has been easy to secure.[47] The Maldivian government carefully balances the economic or military assistance it receives from one country with comparable contributions from others in order to avoid the appearance that it is lining up either with great powers

---

[45] "Treaty between India and Bhutan, 2007," Druk National Congress, 2007, http://www.bhutandnc.com/Treaty.htm.

[46] Mohan Balaji, "In Bhutan, China and India Collide," *Asia Times Online*, January 12, 2008, http://www.atimes.com/atimes/China/JA12Ad02.html; and S. Chandrasekharan, "Bhutan's Northern Border: China's Bullying and Teasing Tactics: Update No. 82," South Asia Analysis Group, Note, no. 564, http://www.southasiaanalysis.org/%5Cnotes6%5Cnote564.html.

[47] "Background Note: Maldives," Bureau of South and Central Asian Affairs, U.S. Department of State, July 10, 2010, http://www.state.gov/r/pa/ei/bgn/5476.htm.

or with rivals from around the region. This policy of balancing foreign friends is designed not to manipulate the politics of the influential countries Maldives deals with but to preserve its freedom of action. The big threats to the islands, however, are not India and China. Maldives faces more serious dangers from climate change—the country stands to disappear if the level of the Indian Ocean rises—and from violent and lawless forces in the Indian Ocean, such as Somali pirates or Islamist militant groups who might wish to hide out in these otherwise peaceful and remote Muslim islands. This possibility represents a threat to the regional powers, as well as to the United States, and will keep them interested in and supportive of Maldives.

The Big Powers in South Asia

Each of the South Asian countries is trying to advance its own objectives as it responds to the rise of India and China. Most employ some form of triangular strategy, with the United States often serving as the third corner of the triangle. Pakistan's "external balancers" are intended to counter the Indian threat: the rise of China helps Pakistan balance India while hedging against excessive dependence on the United States. Sri Lanka too is interested in demonstrating its reduced reliance on the United States and more generally on the West; both India and China are partners in this hedging game. Bangladesh is hedging against excessive dependence on India, using both China and the United States as alternative sources of support.

For Afghanistan, Pakistan is both partner and threat. The United States is the principal provider of security today, but is seen as a short-timer. The rise of India and China offers two additional relationships that may expand Afghanistan's freedom of maneuver. In Nepal, the revolution that gave the Maoists a share of power also made China a player in a way that it never had been in the past. These two fragile states and the tiny states of Bhutan and Maldives have limited ability to drive a strategic bargain. All are basically takers rather than creators of their security environment. These states are looking for benign relationships and some room to maneuver.

India remains the primary Asian power engaged in the Indian Ocean and South Asian region. Since the end of the Cold War, its economic growth has accelerated dramatically, and the country's security managers have come to regard economic success as one of the drivers of foreign and security policy. This will ultimately determine India's ability to maintain primacy in its immediate neighborhood.

A key lesson of this study is that China has become a player in India's strategic space. China's military presence in the subregion is smaller than India's because it lacks India's permanent Indian Ocean naval presence.

But Beijing's security involvement in the Indian Ocean is growing as it acquires access to more ports and develops stronger military relationships. Its economic power is rising rapidly as well and now dwarfs India's on the global scale. Yet even as China is becoming more active economically and militarily in South Asia, India is expanding its interaction with East Asia. Throughout Asia, the two Asian giants deal with each other with a blend of engagement and rivalry. Their rivalry is likely to intensify, with each trying to maintain the upper hand in its traditional space.

If, as is anticipated, China continues to build up its presence and role in the Indian Ocean, this strategy is likely to bring more competition than cooperation with the United States. India and the United States have largely compatible strategic goals in Asia; both seek an equilibrium among major players. China, on the other hand, will eventually want to reduce the U.S. role and redefine the equilibrium. Both India and the United States are likely to resist such an effort. This does not necessarily presage conflict, but it does suggest that India and the United States will continue to conduct either cooperative or parallel strategies. China will in some degree be a competitor or problem for both countries.

Lessons for the United States

Relations with Pakistan and India drive U.S. policy in South Asia. Policy toward Pakistan starts from the conviction that without Pakistan's cooperation, there is no chance of a successful end to U.S. military involvement in Afghanistan. More broadly, U.S. policy toward Pakistan is motivated by the fear of how badly things could go wrong there. India, by contrast, is a strategic opportunity. India and the United States are increasingly conscious of their common interests as well as interested in engaging on Asia-wide issues. Their security ties are growing, though this heightened engagement is tempered by India's continuing commitment to "strategic autonomy"—its reluctance to appear to be signing on to an agenda crafted anywhere else (especially in Washington).

These two drivers will remain critical for the United States. The Obama administration's decision in mid-2010 to start looking at India in the context of broader issues involving both South and East Asia is likely to prove its wisdom over time. So too is the basic commitment to engage with China.

This study argues for weaving two additional features into U.S. policy. The first is to treat the Indian Ocean as a single policy space. The rise of India and China will be felt throughout that region. The problem of piracy in the Arabian Sea, the most pressing short-term security threat in South Asia, cannot be divided into chunks that correspond to the different U.S.

bureaucratic jurisdictions. Second, relationships with the smaller South Asian countries have more strategic import than they are sometimes credited with having. This is especially true of Sri Lanka, which, in the absence of more effective engagement with the United States, could be an important partner in expanding China's South Asian footprint. Although Washington should not seek to exclude China from one of the great oceans of the world, it has no interest in enhancing China's position in an environment critical for the United States.

EXECUTIVE SUMMARY

This chapter presents a comparative analysis of the impact of China's and India's rise on Southeast Asian regional autonomy and considers implications for the U.S.

MAIN ARGUMENT:
Southeast Asian states seek to advance their national interests through the Association of Southeast Asian Nations (ASEAN) in order to promote regional autonomy and ASEAN's centrality in the region's security architecture. While welcoming the rise of the region's two large neighbors, especially for the economic opportunities they offer, ASEAN states are also concerned with preserving regional autonomy. They seek an equilibrium in external relations based on engagement with China and India, the enmeshment of both rising powers in ASEAN-centric multilateral institutions, and the continuance of U.S. presence in the region. Although Southeast Asian states favor U.S. regional involvement, they do not want to be forced to choose between external powers.

POLICY IMPLICATIONS:
- Regional states are concerned that a power shift in China's favor is underway. The U.S. should continually demonstrate that it retains sufficient military power to deter Chinese assertiveness.

- As East Asia grows in economic strength, the U.S. must redouble its efforts to remain an attractive market and source of technological innovation.

- Southeast Asian states have become more proactive in promoting ASEAN's centrality in the region's security architecture. The U.S. would benefit from putting more diplomatic effort into consulting and coordinating with regional states in advance of ASEAN-related summits and ministerial meetings.

- India has ambitions to become a global power. The U.S. should support a greater, independent Indian role in Southeast Asian security affairs.

The Rise of China and India: Challenging or Reinforcing Southeast Asia's Autonomy?

Carlyle A. Thayer

This chapter presents an analysis of the rise of China and India and its implications for Southeast Asia, as well as for U.S. interests in the region. Southeast Asian states welcome China's rise because of the economic opportunities it offers, while they look to India as a source of technology and a market for goods and investment. But they are also concerned with preserving regional autonomy in their relations with the major powers and seek an equilibrium based on continuing U.S. engagement, the enmeshment of China in multilateral institutions, and an enhanced role for India in the region's security architecture. In particular, China's rise poses a challenge to the United States' long-standing primacy in Southeast Asia. Tensions in U.S.-China relations thus have a considerable impact on the region, particularly in the maritime domain. Although each Southeast Asian state has developed its own set of bilateral relations with these major powers, individual states prefer not to choose between China and the United States, instead favoring a united approach through the Association of Southeast Asian Nations (ASEAN). Member states therefore promote ASEAN's centrality in the region's security architecture to enhance regional autonomy and minimize major power interference.

The rise of China and India as major economies has resulted in the heightened salience of the maritime domain, particularly the sea lines of communication (SLOC) that traverse the northern Indian Ocean and South China Sea. Since the 1990s, India has pursued a "look east" policy designed to promote economic linkages. As a result, the boundaries between South

Carlyle A. Thayer is Emeritus Professor at the University of New South Wales at the Australian Defence Force Academy, Canberra. He can be reached at <c.thayer@adfa.edu.au>.

and Southeast Asia are becoming blurred. India can no longer be viewed as merely a subcontinental power; instead, it is an emerging power with strategic interests in the security of Southeast Asia.

This chapter is divided into six sections. The first section assesses the impact of the rise of China and India on Southeast Asia's strategic interests. These interests are defined as national resilience (promoted through policies of comprehensive security) and regional resilience (promoted through the assertion of regional autonomy and ASEAN norms). China's rise poses challenges to the contemporary regional security order as well as to Southeast Asia's economic development. In response to these challenges, ASEAN has encouraged the United States to remain engaged in the region while viewing India as adding ballast—that is, geostrategic weight—to relations with China. ASEAN seeks to moderate great-power rivalry by enmeshing the major powers in ASEAN-centric multilateral institutions such as the ASEAN Regional Forum (ARF), ASEAN Defense Ministers' Meeting-Plus (ADMM-Plus), and East Asia Summit (EAS).

Section two canvasses the key forms of China's and India's interactions with Southeast Asia across six dimensions: historical, geostrategic, economic, cultural, military, and nonproliferation. The third section considers Southeast Asia's changing perceptions of China's and India's rise. During the Cold War, China was viewed as a threat and India was viewed as a Soviet surrogate. As a result of domestic economic reforms, however, first in China and then in India, both are now viewed as major economic partners and contributors to regional security. Section four then discusses the main strategies pursued by ASEAN in its relations with both countries: economic interdependence, socialization into ASEAN norms, and soft-balancing.

Section five assesses the impact of relations among China, India, and Southeast Asia on the United States and its interests. Whereas China's military modernization challenges U.S. naval supremacy in the Western Pacific, India and the United States have developed a nascent strategic partnership that remains a work in progress. Southeast Asian states have sought reassurance that the United States will remain engaged in the region, while also encouraging India to play a greater role in the region's multilateral institutions.

Last, section six analyzes four key Southeast Asian states' bilateral relations with China and India. These states are grouped into three categories: continental (Myanmar and Thailand), littoral (Vietnam), and maritime (Indonesia). The continental states have attempted to engage both China and India as economic and security partners. Vietnam, as a littoral state, has developed a complex strategy of "cooperating and struggling" with China to protect its national interests. Indonesia has also developed a dual-track policy of engaging both China and India on economics and security matters, but it cooperates more with India on maritime security issues.

The Impact of the Rise of China and India on Southeast Asia's Strategic Interests

With a total population of nearly 600 million and a combined economy of $1.5 trillion in 2008, Southeast Asia is the United States' third-largest Asian trading partner after China and Japan (and the fifth-largest partner overall). It is also the largest destination for U.S. investment in Asia.[1]

Of all the regions in Asia, Southeast Asia has developed the strongest sense of regional identity and the most enduring multilateral institution, ASEAN. Strategic analysts often divide Southeast Asia into two subregions—the mainland or continental states and the maritime states—bisected by important shipping routes that extend from the Persian Gulf through the Straits of Malacca and Singapore to the Western Pacific. The economic rise of China and India has altered this geostrategic framework by heightening the importance of the maritime domain, particularly the South China Sea. Southeast Asian states thus may be grouped into three categories: mainland (Myanmar, Thailand, Laos, and Cambodia), littoral (Philippines, Brunei, Malaysia, and Vietnam), and maritime (Singapore and Indonesia).

During the past six and a half decades, Southeast Asia has been vitally dependent on U.S. leadership for maintaining regional stability and security. In 1967, five key Southeast Asian states joined together and founded ASEAN. All were anti-Communist in orientation and either formally allied with or inclined toward the United States.[2] ASEAN has managed relations with the major powers by promoting both the regional autonomy of Southeast Asia and the centrality of ASEAN in Southeast Asia's security architecture. In 1971, for example, ASEAN states declared that Southeast Asia was a Zone of Peace, Freedom and Neutrality (ZOPFAN), and in 1976 they adopted the Treaty of Amity and Cooperation (TAC) that enjoined member states from using force or the threat of force against each other. Likewise, in 1995 ASEAN states adopted a treaty declaring Southeast Asia a nuclear weapon–free zone. ASEAN further asserted regional autonomy by expanding its membership to include Brunei in 1984, socialist Vietnam in 1995, Laos and Myanmar in 1997, and Cambodia in 1999. In 2003, ASEAN

---

[1] See "ASEAN Matters for America," East-West Center and Institute of Southeast Asian Studies. This interactive database may be accessed at http://aseanmattersforamerica.org/.

[2] The five states that founded ASEAN are Indonesia, Malaysia, the Philippines, Singapore, and Thailand.

set the goal of creating an ASEAN community by 2015, and in 2007 the organization took on a formal legal personality by the adoption of a charter.

Although up until the end of the Cold War ASEAN avoided direct involvement in regional security, it has since then sought to promote its importance in Southeast Asia's security architecture. In 1994, it founded the ARF as a vehicle to promote regional autonomy with ASEAN "in the driver's seat." The ARF counted as founding members all of ASEAN's dialogue partners, including China and the United States. In 1997, ASEAN initiated the ASEAN +3 process with China, Japan, and South Korea. Finally, since 2003 sixteen countries outside Southeast Asia have acceded to the TAC, which was opened for accession by external powers in 1987.

U.S. strategic interests in Southeast Asia have remained relatively constant over the past 65 years. First, the United States has maintained a security order based on alliances, designed to prevent any power, regional or external, from exerting hegemony over the region. For example, the 2010 *Quadrennial Defense Review Report* states: "The foundation of our presence in Asia remains our historical treaty alliances. These alliances have helped maintain peace and stability for more than sixty years, particularly through the continued presence of capable U.S. forces in the region, and we remain steadfastly committed to the security commitments embodied in these agreements."[3] Second, Washington has promoted a liberal international economic order based on free trade and investment. Third, it has encouraged economic development through assistance programs to Southeast Asia's developing economies. Fourth, the United States has promoted democracy, human rights, and religious freedom in the region. Finally, after the terrorist attacks of September 11, Washington has pursued a global war on terrorism that has focused specifically on terrorist groups in Southeast Asia.

How does the rise of China and India affect Southeast Asia's strategic interests and relations with the United States? Regarding China, individual states have different perceptions of the challenges and opportunities posed by its rise. Several states, such as Indonesia and Malaysia, initially viewed China's economic rise as a challenge because of fears that it would lead to a diversion of trade and investment from Southeast Asia. Some states were further concerned about being pulled into China's orbit in a dependent relationship based on supplying raw materials. Gradually, ASEAN states began to collectively view China's economic rise as an opportunity and moved to enhance their unity and cohesion by forming a viable ASEAN Free Trade Area to facilitate collective bargaining with China. At the same time, China's economic rise has raised concerns among some ASEAN

---

[3] U.S. Department of Defense, *Quadrennial Defense Review Report* (Washington, D.C., February 2010), 59.

states that the United States might disengage from the region and pursue protectionist policies—anxieties that were heightened in 1994 with the signing of the North American Free Trade Agreement (NAFTA).

China's economic power has provided the foundation for the modernization and transformation of its armed forces. It is evident that Beijing is developing robust anti-access/area-denial capabilities that will affect the ability of the U.S. Navy to operate in the Western Pacific. This increased military prowess also has implications for the South China Sea, where four Southeast Asian states have conflicting territorial and maritime disputes with China. China's growing assertiveness in the form of naval exercises has raised regional security concerns about the decline in U.S. primacy and the United States' disengagement from Southeast Asia.

India's rise has provided ASEAN with the opportunity to add geostrategic weight to the region's relations with China, thus reinforcing ASEAN's centrality in Southeast Asia. ASEAN secured India's membership in the ARF and, more significantly, in the EAS process. Both India and ASEAN have come to view each other as attractive markets; New Delhi values investment in India's infrastructure, while ASEAN seeks access to India's IT sector. In addition, several ASEAN states and India now see each other as potential partners in providing maritime security in the eastern Indian Ocean and northern approaches to the Strait of Malacca.

The greatest threat to Southeast Asia's strategic interests lies in the potential for great-power rivalry to undermine regional autonomy. Military friction between China and the United States in East Asia would quickly spill over into Southeast Asia. U.S. allies and strategic partners such as the Philippines, Thailand, Singapore, and Malaysia would be pressured to side with the United States, and all member states would need to decide whether ASEAN multilateralism was a better guarantee of their national security than alignment with a major power. Security relations with the United States could be undermined if regional states felt that Washington had entrapped them in a dispute not of their own making. At the very least, military friction between the United States and China would severely test ASEAN's unity and cohesion.

Key Forms of Southeast Asian Interaction with China and India

This section reviews the key forms of Southeast Asian interaction with China and India across six dimensions: historical, geostrategic, economic, cultural, military, and nonproliferation.

Historical

Contemporary Southeast Asia has been profoundly influenced by the interaction of states in the region with the precolonial empires of India and China. Precolonial Indian influence was pervasive due to the spread of Buddhism and Hinduism. However, the most significant form of strategic interaction took place through China's tributary system. This system served three purposes: it acknowledged imperial China's primacy, it enhanced China's security by creating a buffer of friendly states on the country's southern periphery, and it regulated trade, often to the advantage of the supplicant. In contrast, India had no comparable strategic mechanism to structure its relations with Southeast Asia.

Southeast Asia's autonomous interactions with India and China were largely curtailed during the colonial era by European powers incorporating Southeast Asian states into their empires. Although Burma was ruled as part of British India, elsewhere in the region relations with India and China were truncated. The one exception to this was the migration of large numbers of Chinese and Indians to work as laborers on plantations and other infrastructural projects.

The postcolonial era gave birth to new nation-states and new forms of interaction between Southeast Asian states and India and China. India emerged as a strong proponent of decolonization and played a leading role in promoting nonalignment. In particular, New Delhi's advocacy of the five principles of peaceful coexistence resonated in Burma, Indonesia, and Cambodia. Elsewhere in the region, anti-Communism assumed greater salience following the Chinese Communist Party's ascension to power and the onset of the Cold War in Asia. China established close relations with Communist Vietnam in 1950 but found itself ostracized elsewhere. The end of the Cold War later created the conditions for both China and India to re-engage with Southeast Asia.

Geostrategic

Decolonization after World War II was a decade-long process marked by the independence of the Philippines in 1946 and Malaya (subsequently renamed Malaysia) in 1957.[4] The new states of Southeast Asia pursued three different patterns of alignment: pro-Western (Philippines, Thailand, Malaya/Malaysia, and South Vietnam), neutral or nonaligned (Burma, Indonesia, Cambodia, and Laos), and pro-Communist (North Vietnam). The United States exerted influence bilaterally with its treaty allies the Philippines and

---

[4] Thailand was never colonized. Singapore, Brunei, and East Timor became independent in 1963, 1984, and 2002, respectively.

Thailand and multilaterally through the Southeast Asia Treaty Organization (SEATO).[5] India and China both emerged as proponents of the five principles of peaceful coexistence and were prominent at the Afro-Asian Conference held in Bandung, Indonesia, in 1955. Similarly, India played a major role as chair of the International Control Commission in Cambodia, Laos, and Vietnam, which oversaw the Geneva Agreements of 1954. India and China also supported the policies of neutrality adopted by Burma and Cambodia. At the same time, India developed close political and military ties with Indonesia until the mid-1960s, while China, along with the Soviet Union, became a strong supporter of North Vietnam.

The foundations of modern Southeast Asian regionalism were developed in World War II when Britain set up the South East Asia Command as an anti-Japanese theater of operations covering Thailand, Malaya, and Indonesia. Regionalism took steps forward with the creation of SEATO in 1954, the Association of Southeast Asia in 1961, and Maphilindo in 1963.[6] By the 1960s, the idea of Southeast Asia as a distinct region had taken hold among indigenous elites, who consciously promoted the idea of a common regional identity, and in 1967 it emerged as a distinct geopolitical region with the formation of ASEAN.

Economic

Southeast Asia sits at the crossroads of historic SLOCs between the Indian and Pacific oceans that developed from the fifteenth to seventeenth centuries. During this period, Southeast Asia became the vital entrepot for trade from Europe, the eastern Mediterranean, and India to China and Japan. The "age of commerce" came to an end in the seventeenth century, and the role of India and China receded during the colonial era.

In the postcolonial era India turned inward economically, developed trade links with the Soviet Union, and remained disengaged from Southeast Asia. Similarly, the People's Republic of China (PRC) turned inward in the 1950s and 1960s and, with the exception of relations with Vietnam, remained cut off from Southeast Asia economically. China and India only re-emerged as major economic players in Southeast Asia in the 1990s after separately carrying out domestic economic reforms and seeking integration with the global economy. High growth rates made China, India, and Southeast Asia mutually attractive markets. A key

---

[5] Thailand and the Philippines were the only regional members alongside Australia, France, New Zealand, Pakistan, the United Kingdom, and the United States. SEATO provided security guarantees for the non-Communist states of Laos, Cambodia, and South Vietnam.

[6] The Association of Southeast Asia included Malaysia, the Philippines, and Thailand, while Maphilindo was a stillborn association of Malaysia, the Philippines, and Indonesia.

turning point in China's relations with the region came in 2002 with the signing of a framework agreement for the China-ASEAN Free Trade Agreement (CAFTA).[7] India followed suit seven years later by signing an agreement with ASEAN covering the free trade of goods.

Cultural

As discussed above, India's cultural influence in Southeast Asia was pervasive in the precolonial era and led to what historians call Indianization. Indianization refers to the process by which local rulers underpinned their legitimacy by grafting the values of Hinduism and Buddhism onto indigenous belief systems. With the exception of Vietnam, Theravada Buddhism became the state religion of all mainland states. Hinduism and Buddhism formed the basis of state legitimacy in the Indonesian archipelago until the arrival of Islam in the thirteenth century. Such deep cultural connections between India and Southeast Asia have not proved durable enough, however, to translate into more permanent bonds in the contemporary period. Indian influence in Southeast Asia is now mainly transmitted by the large diaspora communities in Malaysia (2 million), Myanmar (1 million), Singapore (371,000), and Thailand (150,000), as well as by overseas Indian residents who work in Southeast Asia.[8] In Singapore the Indian diaspora has played a major role in developing ties with India, whereas political and economic discrimination against the diasporas in Myanmar and Malaysia, respectively, has impeded the development of bilateral ties between India and those countries.

By way of contrast, in the precolonial, colonial, and postcolonial eras, China made a sustained cultural impact on only one state in Southeast Asia: Vietnam. However, the PRC and Vietnam became adversaries during the Cambodian conflict (1978–91), and all forms of cultural and educational interaction were terminated. In the late 1970s, up to 250,000 ethnic Chinese fled Vietnam to China. This hiatus in relations came to an end in 1991 when China and Vietnam restored normal relations, and Vietnamese now represent the third-largest group of foreign students in China.

Today, the overseas Chinese community constitutes a majority of the population in Singapore (74%) and over a quarter of the population in Malaysia (26%). There are also sizeable overseas Chinese communities in Brunei (15%), Thailand (14%), and Cambodia (7%).[9] Overseas Chinese

---

[7] This is sometimes abbreviated ACFTA for ASEAN-China Free Trade Agreement.

[8] CIA, *The World Factbook 2009* (Washington, D.C.: CIA, 2009), available at https://www.cia.gov/library/publications/the-world-factbook/index.html.

[9] Ibid.

influence is arguably strongest in Thailand, where a powerful Sino-Thai business class took root historically, but it is also strong in Malaysia, Indonesia, and the Philippines. Although many in the Chinese diaspora assimilated into local communities, others retained a separate sense of cultural identity through Chinese language schools and religious practices. At times, overseas Chinese communities have suffered from harsh racial discrimination, particularly in Indonesia, where the democratic government only recently removed discriminatory regulations against the indigenous ethnic Chinese community.

China has responded to the widespread interest its rise has provoked in Southeast Asia by developing Confucius Institutes to promote Chinese language and culture. By contrast, it is only in the last half decade that India has begun to systematically promote educational and cultural exchanges to enhance its relations in the region, particularly with mainland Southeast Asia.

Military

There have been three instances of China using military force against a Southeast Asian state in the contemporary period, and all have involved Vietnam. The PRC seized the southern Paracel Islands from South Vietnam in 1974 and clashed with Vietnamese naval forces in March 1988 at South Johnston Reef in the Spratly Islands. In addition, China conducted a punitive attack on northern Vietnam in February–March 1979 in response to Vietnam's invasion of Cambodia.

China only began to promote defense cooperation with Southeast Asia in the 1990s under the rubric of its "new concept of security," which will be discussed below. Between 1999 and 2000, China signed long-term cooperation framework agreements with all ten ASEAN members. Seven of these agreements (with Thailand, Malaysia, Vietnam, Brunei, Singapore, the Philippines, and Laos) include clauses on defense cooperation involving a range of activities such as high-level exchanges, naval port visits, strategic dialogues, small-scale exercises, military education and training, arms and equipment sales, and cooperation between national defense industries. In addition, China has pursued defense cooperation multilaterally by brokering agreements with ASEAN and advancing initiatives in the ARF, primarily focused on nontraditional security issues.

India's defense relations with Southeast Asia are mainly bilateral. Defense ties with Singapore are particularly close, with the two sides having conducted increasingly complex annual joint naval exercises since 1994. India also conducts joint exercises with Indonesia and Thailand, with a focus on the Andaman Sea and approaches to the Strait of Malacca, and hosts a major naval exercise, Milan, in the Andaman Sea. In February 2011, warships from Indonesia, Malaysia, Myanmar, Singapore, and Thailand participated in the exercise, while Brunei, the Philippines, and Vietnam sent naval observers. In terms of arms sales, India sells weapons, equipment, and spare parts to Myanmar and Vietnam.

Nonproliferation

No Southeast Asian state possesses nuclear weapons.[10] As mentioned earlier, in 1995 ASEAN members adopted the Southeast Asia Nuclear Weapon-Free Zone (SEANWFZ) Treaty, which enjoins signatories not to develop, manufacture, or control nuclear weapons and prohibits them from stationing, transporting, using, or testing nuclear weapons in Southeast Asia. ASEAN states have since encouraged the nuclear powers to accede to this treaty. But when China offered to do so first, ASEAN demurred, hoping to bring the other nuclear states on board at the same time.[11] Although ASEAN supports the international nonproliferation regime, its members do not always present a united front. In May 1998, for example, when India conducted a series of nuclear tests, only Malaysia, the Philippines, and Thailand condemned India, whereas Vietnam merely called for nuclear disarmament without singling India out.[12] Senior ASEAN officials declined to make a statement. When the issue was raised at the annual ARF meeting, the ASEAN Chair deleted all references to India in the final statement. Similarly, only four ASEAN members have supported the U.S.-led Proliferation Security Initiative (Singapore, Brunei, Cambodia, and the Philippines), while the remaining six members either actively opposed it (Indonesian and Malaysia) or declined to support its principles (Laos, Myanmar, Thailand, and Vietnam).

---

[10] Reports that North Korea is providing nuclear technology to Myanmar have not been verified.

[11] The academic literature erroneously reports that China was the first country to sign the protocol to the SEANWFZ Treaty. An official summary of ASEAN's relations with China prepared on November 29, 2010, states, "China has also expressed its intention to accede to the Protocol to the [SEANWFZ]." See "ASEAN-China Dialogue Relations," November 29, 2010, http://www.aseansec. org/5874.htm.

[12] G.V.C. Naidu, "The Manila ASEAN Meetings and India," Institute of Defence and Strategic Analysis (IDSA), November 2008, http://www.idsa-india.org/an-nov8-4.html; and "India Goes Nuclear: Political, Diplomatic and Economic Implications," India Strategy, India Focus, May 1998, http://www.indiastrategy.com/may98.htm.

Southeast Asian Perceptions of the Rise of China and India

China

Southeast Asian perceptions of the PRC, Asia's first Communist state, were heavily influenced by Cold War alignments, Chinese intervention in the Korean conflict, and PRC support for Communist Vietnam and Communist insurgencies in Southeast Asia. The region's pro-Western states viewed China as a threat and withheld diplomatic recognition for a quarter of a century. In contrast, the nonaligned states extended diplomatic recognition to China.

Perceptions of China began to alter in the 1970s as the Vietnam War wound down and the United States completed military disengagement from mainland Southeast Asia. Malaysia established diplomatic relations with China in May 1974, as did the Philippines and Thailand a year later. Nonetheless, China's past support for regional Communist parties left a residue of suspicion that lingered for over a decade and a half. It was not until 1990 that Indonesia restored diplomatic ties with China, thus opening the door for Singapore and Brunei to follow suit.

There is no one Southeast Asian perception of China; rather, perceptions vary from country to country and are shaped by differing factors, including the particular issues of concern to each state. In 1989, China's brutal suppression of the pro-democracy movement in Tiananmen Square raised concerns about the "China threat" in the region's democratic and democratically inclined states. By the early 1990s, those states with a littoral on the South China Sea had become alarmed by the manner in which China was pursuing its maritime claims. They widely viewed the PRC's adoption of the Law on the Territorial Sea and Contiguous Zone in 1992 as a claim to the entire sea. China's oil exploration activities brought it into conflict with Vietnam and led both countries to scramble to occupy island features. ASEAN responded by issuing a declaration of concern urging unnamed parties to resolve the matter peacefully. The anxieties of Southeast Asia's littoral states concerning Chinese assertiveness were aroused again in 1995 when China occupied Mischief Reef, which had been claimed by the Philippines. ASEAN issued another public declaration calling for restraint and the peaceful settlement of disputes.

By 1995, virtually all members of ASEAN perceived China as a security threat to the region. So prevalent was this view that Chinese strategists and policymakers began to re-evaluate how best to assuage Southeast Asian concerns. The end result was China's "new security concept," which was first presented to a meeting of the ARF in 1997. The new security concept signaled Beijing's intention to pursue a policy of cooperative multilateralism with ASEAN and its members, including a major emphasis on nontraditional security threats.[13] In 2002, after several years of negotiations, the PRC and ASEAN agreed to a Declaration on Conduct of Parties in the South China Sea (DOC), reducing concerns about China's territorial ambitions. As a further demonstration of reassurance, China became the first external power to accede to the protocol endorsing the TAC in 2002.

In the decade and a half after 1995, concerns shifted from the China threat to the implications of the PRC's economic rise for the region.[14] Southeast Asian states initially feared that Chinese growth would be at their expense and take the form of trade and investment diversion. These fears intensified as China began negotiations for entry into the World Trade Organization, which it eventually joined in 2001. A major turning point occurred during the Asian financial crisis of 1997–98, however, when Beijing's supportive policies contrasted with those of the International Monetary Fund (backed by the United States), which imposed conditions on its loans. China not only refrained from devaluing its currency but also contributed to regional bailout packages. As a result, Southeast Asian states came to view the PRC's economic rise more as an opportunity than a challenge. In sum, China came to be perceived as an indispensable economic partner and the main engine of regional growth.

This phenomenal economic growth, however, provided the foundation for China to modernize and transform its military forces. Although Beijing's new cooperative approach to Southeast Asian security had been well received in the region, some states began to suspect that one of China's motivations for advancing its new security concept was to undermine the U.S. alliance system that had been the mainstay of regional security for over four decades. China's approach failed to gain traction and proved counterproductive, as it stimulated Southeast Asian states, particularly Singapore, to seek reassurance from Washington that the United States would remain engaged in regional affairs.

In particular, littoral states on the South China Sea became increasingly concerned about the growth of Chinese naval power, especially after satellite imagery confirmed that China had constructed a major base on Hainan Island. After 2007, renewed Chinese assertiveness in the South China Sea further heightened regional concerns about Beijing's intentions.[15] In 2009, China not only protested against submissions by Malaysia and Vietnam to

---

[13] Carlyle A. Thayer, "China's 'New Security Concept' and Southeast Asia," in *Asia-Pacific Security: Policy Challenges*, ed. David W. Lovell (Singapore: Institute of Southeast Asian Studies, 2003), 89–107.

[14] Evelyn Goh, "Southeast Asian Perspectives on the China Challenge," *Journal of Strategic Studies* 30, nos. 4 and 5 (August–October 2007): 809–32.

[15] Carlyle A. Thayer, "Recent Developments in the South China Sea: Grounds for Cautious Optimism?" S. Rajaratnam School of International Studies (RSIS), Nanyang Technological University, RSIS Working Paper, no. 220, December 14, 2010.

the UN Commission on the Limits of the Continental Shelf but officially tabled a map of the South China Sea marked with nine dashed lines. This map implied that China was claiming 80% of the maritime area. Other incidents followed in March and May 2011, when Chinese patrol boats acted aggressively toward Philippine and Vietnamese exploration vessels, respectively, in contested waters.

In sum, Southeast Asian states have oscillated from viewing China as the main threat to regional security in the 1960s and 1970s—due to Beijing's support for Communist insurgencies—to viewing its rise in the 1990s as the main driver of regional economic growth, and then back to a middle position of viewing China's economic rise positively but its military rise with apprehension. China's recent assertiveness in the South China Sea has detracted from the positive-sum view of the country's economic rise and caused Southeast Asian states to reconsider their perceptions about the benign nature of the PRC's growing power. China's actions are seen not only as directly threatening littoral states, particularly Vietnam, but as likely undermining regional security by provoking the United States. Thus, they challenge ASEAN's assertion of autonomy and centrality in regional security affairs.

India

As described above, India's precolonial relations with Southeast Asia were largely based on trade and commerce, the diffusion of Hindu and Buddhist religious practices, and generally peaceful interstate relations. India largely squandered this legacy when it allowed the momentum of its relations with the region to slow down and stagnate in the years following World War II.[16] Prior to the 1990s, India was viewed as a country locked in South Asia with a closed, backward economy that was marginal to Southeast Asian affairs. There were regional concerns, however, about the growth of Indian naval power, particularly following India's intervention in Maldives in 1988.[17]

Southeast Asian perceptions began to change in the 1990s when India's domestic reforms led to rapid economic growth and New Delhi began to engage with selected Southeast Asian states under its look east policy. India increasingly came to be viewed as an attractive market and economic

---

[16] K.V. Kesavan, "The Role of Regional Institutions in India's Look East Policy," in *South and Southeast Asia: Responding to Changing Geo-Political and Security Challenges*, ed. K.V. Kesavan and Daljit Singh (Singapore: Institute of Southeast Asian Studies, 2010), 106.

[17] C.S. Kuppuswamy, "India's Look East Policy—A Review," South Asia Analysis Group, Paper no. 3662, February 12, 2010.

partner.[18] ASEAN responded to India's rise by granting the country sectoral partner status in 1992 and full dialogue status in 1995. Two year later, it supported India's membership in the ARF, and in 2002 the two partners began to meet annually at the summit level. Concerns about India's naval power dissipated the following year after New Delhi acceded to the TAC. Relations were further strengthened when ASEAN successfully promoted India's inclusion in the EAS process in 2005.

Thus, while Southeast Asian concerns about Chinese assertiveness grew, India increasingly became perceived as a major independent power that could provide ballast in relations with external states, particularly as a member of the EAS process. The track record of recent interaction between India and ASEAN states has served to reinforce perceptions of the country's rise in positive-sum terms. India is now viewed as a dependable economic partner, a counterweight to China's rise, and a state that will be supportive of ASEAN's assertion of regional autonomy.

Factors Shaping Southeast Asia's Relations with China and India

In the 1970s, ASEAN formalized its linkages with external powers by meeting with its dialogue partners in a post-ministerial conference immediately following the annual meeting of the group's foreign ministers. This process took the form of an ASEAN meeting with all its dialogue partners as a group (ASEAN +10) and then separate meetings between ASEAN and each dialogue partner (ASEAN +1). Although individual Southeast Asian states do pursue their own bilateral relations with China and India, all take into account the multilateral framework provided by ASEAN. China and India were accorded consultative partner status in 1991 and 1992, respectively. India was subsequently elevated to the status of full dialogue partner in December 1995, with China following in July 1996.

ASEAN pursues three strategies to manage its relations with both countries: the promotion of economic interdependence, socialization into regional norms or the "ASEAN way,"[19] and soft-balancing. Each of these strategies is discussed below.

---

[18] Rajiv Sikri, "India's Look East Policy: A Critical Assessment," Institute of Peace and Conflict Studies (IPCS), IPCS Special Report, October 2009.

[19] These norms include noninterference in each other's internal affairs, respect for national sovereignty, renunciation of the threat or use of force in interstate relations, peaceful settlement of disputes, and a decisionmaking process based on dialogue, consensus, equality, and inclusivity and at "a pace comfortable to all."

Economic Interdependence

After China became a full dialogue partner, ASEAN and Beijing quickly formalized relations by setting up a joint cooperation committee to coordinate all cooperative mechanisms at the working level. The process of enmeshing China advanced in late 2002 with the adoption of a framework agreement on comprehensive economic cooperation. This agreement laid the foundation for what became CAFTA. In 2005 an agreement on trade in goods was reached, followed in 2007 by an agreement on trade in services and in 2009 by an investment agreement. CAFTA entered into force in January 2010 for ASEAN's six developed economies and will take effect for the four least-developed members in 2015.

Efforts to enmesh India in a similar web of economic interdependence have proceeded more slowly. After ASEAN accorded India sectoral dialogue partner status, the two sides began to explore cooperation in trade, investment, science and technology, and tourism. But the scope of cooperation remained restricted due to India's foot-dragging on facilitation measures. In 2003, India and ASEAN finally signed a framework agreement on comprehensive economic cooperation as the first step toward an FTA. It took another six years, however, before a trade in goods agreement was finally concluded. Subsequently, India signed a bilateral FTA with Thailand in 2003 and less formal comprehensive economic cooperation agreements with Indonesia, Malaysia, Myanmar, Singapore, and Vietnam. Negotiations are currently underway to conclude agreements covering trade in services and investments. Although India ranks among the top-ten ASEAN trading partners, the two-way volume of trade is low. The most recent figures show that bilateral trade reached only $43.9 billion in 2009–10 (see **Table A1** in the Appendix).

Socialization: Shaping Attitudes through Interaction

The end of the Cold War changed Southeast Asia's strategic context. ASEAN became more proactive in promoting its norms of comprehensive security in external relations and created an entirely new security institution, the ASEAN Regional Forum. The first meeting of the ARF was held in Bangkok in 1994 and attended by eighteen founding members. In addition to ASEAN's six foreign ministers, participants included foreign ministers from formal dialogue partners (Australia, Canada, the European Union, Japan, New Zealand, the Republic of Korea, and the United States), ASEAN's consultative partners (China and Russia), and invited observers (Laos, Papua New Guinea, and Vietnam). India formally joined in 1996.

China's interaction with ASEAN has likely contributed to its socialization into ASEAN norms; at the very least, Beijing has revised its diplomatic rhetoric in order to "talk the talk" with Southeast Asian states. In 2003, ASEAN and China issued a joint declaration on a strategic partnership, the first formal agreement of this type for both sides. The declaration included a provision for the initiation of a new security dialogue while also promoting general cooperation in political matters. The following year, ASEAN and China agreed to a five-year plan of action (running from 2005 to 2010) to raise relations to the level of an "enhanced strategic partnership."[20] Overall, there are at least 48 joint committees that provide the mechanisms for engagement between ASEAN and China, in contrast to only eighteen ASEAN-India joint committees.

China has arguably also been socialized into ASEAN norms through membership in the ARF. Although initially dismissive of multilateral arrangements, Beijing soon came to appreciate that it could benefit from active engagement and assumed a prominent role in the ARF's intersessional work program related to confidence-building measures. In 2003, it launched a major initiative by successfully proposing the creation of a security policy conference comprised of senior military and civilian officials drawn from all ARF members. China also has been a strong proponent of cooperative measures to address nontraditional security challenges.

India shares compatible values with ASEAN and is much less in need than China of socialization into the group's norms. Indeed, the five principles of peaceful coexistence advocated by India during the Cold War form the core of the ASEAN way. Both sides strongly support the norms of national sovereignty and noninterference in internal affairs. ASEAN and India also entered into a Partnership for Peace, Progress and Shared Prosperity in 2004. Yet the current five-year plan of action (2011–15), which contains 80 points for cooperation, appears rudimentary when compared to the latest China-ASEAN plan of action (2011–15) with over 200 detailed points of cooperation for the same time period.

Soft-Balancing

ASEAN has sought to enmesh all the major powers through engagement in the ARF. It insists, however, on remaining in the driver's seat as chair and that the norms embodied in the ASEAN way guide the ARF's decisionmaking process and work programs. ASEAN seeks to use these mechanisms to moderate the impact of the major powers on Southeast

---

[20] See Carlyle A. Thayer, "Vietnam's Defence Policy and Its Impact on Foreign Relations," Asien-Afrika-Institut, Universitat Hamburg, EuroViet 6, June 2008.

Asia by drawing them into ASEAN-centric multilateral arrangements. In addition, the organization seeks to uphold regional autonomy by promoting equilibrium among the major powers and avoiding circumstances where it must choose between them.

ASEAN has therefore adopted a policy of soft-balancing as a hedge against the potentially disruptive effects of China's rise and continually encourages the United States—as well as Japan, South Korea, and India—to remain engaged in regional security affairs as a counterweight to China. The group expanded its strategic linkages beyond the China-dominated ASEAN +3 framework to include the United States, Japan, South Korea, Australia, New Zealand, India, and Russia in the ADMM-Plus process. ASEAN also included India, Australia, and New Zealand in the inaugural EAS and later enlarged the EAS to include the United States and Russia.

The Impact of Southeast Asia's Relations with China and India on the United States

This section considers the impact of Southeast Asia's growing relations with China and India on U.S. interests in the region. As described earlier in the chapter, U.S. policies toward Southeast Asia are derivative of a larger global framework that seeks to maintain a "just and sustainable international order" premised on a rules-based system of representative and responsible international organizations in order to promote free trade and the values of human rights, religious freedom, and democracy.[21] Such policies are also set within the context of a broader approach to the Asia-Pacific region. For example, the United States pursues its global objectives regionally through supporting multilateral institutions such as the Asia-Pacific Economic Cooperation (APEC), the Trans-Pacific Partnership (TPP), and the EAS. In Southeast Asia, the Obama administration has given priority to developing a stronger relationship with ASEAN, re-engaging with the ARF, and becoming a charter member of the ADMM-Plus process.

The U.S. alliance system underpins regional security in both the Asia-Pacific and Southeast Asia. As the 2010 U.S. National Security Strategy makes clear, "alliances with Japan, South Korea, Australia, the Philippines, and Thailand are the bedrock of security in Asia and a foundation of prosperity in the Asia-Pacific region."[22] The Obama administration has stressed the importance of working with emerging powers, strategic partners (Singapore), potential strategic partners (Indonesia, Malaysia, and

---

[21] "National Security Strategy," Office of the President of the United States, May 2010, 12.

[22] Ibid., 42.

Vietnam), and the region's multilateral architecture to maintain a security environment conducive to economic development. In addition, the U.S. National Security Strategy underscores the importance of bilateral relations with China, India, and Russia as "critical to building broader cooperation on areas of mutual interest,"[23] such as promoting trade and investment and countering violent extremism and nuclear proliferation.

Economic Impact

China has displaced the United States as ASEAN's largest trading partner. In 2009, two-way trade between ASEAN and China was valued at $178 billion, or 11.6% of total trade (see **Table A2** in the Appendix).[24] The United States ranked fourth, after the EU-27 and Japan, at $150 billion, or 9.7% of total two-way trade, while India ranked eighth at $39 billion, or 1.6% of two-way trade. According to the ASEAN Trade Statistics Database for 2009–10, China enjoyed a surplus of $22 billion with ASEAN, over three times India's surplus of $7 billion.

Trade figures for individual countries reveal that only four of ASEAN's ten members are major players (see **Tables A3** and **A4** in the Appendix). In terms of total two-way trade, Singapore tops the list, followed by Indonesia, Malaysia, and Thailand. In terms of bilateral trade with China and India, Singapore is likewise the leading importer and exporter. Malaysia and Thailand are the next-largest ASEAN trade partners with China, while Malaysia and Indonesia are the second- and third-largest trade partners with India. Vietnam has displaced Indonesia to become the fourth-largest ASEAN destination for Chinese goods, and Thailand ranks fourth in trade with India in terms of both imports and exports.

China not only buys primary commodities and natural resources, particularly oil and gas, from the ASEAN states but also buys electronic parts and components. The country's economic rise has also altered the region's political economy, given that Southeast Asian states manufacture parts and components that are shipped and assembled in China prior to export abroad. In other words, ASEAN states are both dependent on and subordinated in a production network that feeds China's export-orientated manufacturing industries.

The United States has promoted free trade primarily through APEC, but progress stalled as countries failed to meet commitments agreed to at

---

[23] "National Security Strategy," Office of the President of the United States, May 2010, 43.

[24] Nonetheless, U.S. investment in Southeast Asia continues to dwarf Chinese investment. Cumulative U.S. direct investment in ASEAN states for 2000–2008 totaled $34.8 billion, compared to a total of $5.1 billion in Chinese direct investment for the same period. See *ASEAN Statistical Yearbook 2008* (Jakarta: ASEAN Secretariat, 2009), 144, http://www.asean.org/publications/aseanstats08.pdf.

the 1994 Bogor summit held in Indonesia. In 2002 the Bush administration launched the Enterprise for ASEAN Initiative to facilitate bilateral trade agreements between the United States and individual member countries. Singapore quickly came on board, but FTAs with Thailand and Malaysia have foundered. The Obama administration has subsequently adopted a regional approach through the TPP, a multilateral FTA formed in 2006. According to U.S. Trade Representative Ron Kirk, the TPP is a critical element for "unlocking the Asia-Pacific region to U.S. businesses."[25] The United States has entered into negotiations with TPP members Singapore, New Zealand, Brunei, and Chile to create an expanded trade agreement providing greater market access and is strongly encouraging Malaysia and Vietnam to join these efforts. There are no prospects, however, for an ASEAN-U.S. FTA, and the TPP is unlikely to expand to include more than a handful of Southeast Asian states.

U.S. interests in Southeast Asia are more seriously challenged by the United States' lopsided economic relationship with China, especially regarding U.S. debt, and the U.S.-induced global financial crisis. As senior officials readily admit, Washington's authority to promote good governance and economic growth has been severely diminished.[26] In addition, China's no-strings-attached approach to aid has opportunistically taken advantage of situations where local states rankle over the conditions attached to U.S. assistance programs.

It is also worth noting that China's construction of dams on the upper Mekong River to provide electricity for the country's southern provinces has potentially serious consequences for the economic viability of downstream states. There are two major bodies that promote responsible development— the Mekong River Commission and the Greater Mekong Subregion (a development project funded by the Asian Development Bank)—but the central Chinese government is not represented in either organization.[27] The Obama administration has sought to address the concerns of mainland Southeast Asian states over this issue by launching the Lower Mekong Initiative to promote environmental, educational, and infrastructural development. Secretary of State Hillary Clinton has met four times with the foreign ministers of Thailand, Laos, Cambodia, and Vietnam to advance development projects.

---

[25] Mackenzie C. Babb, "U.S. Makes Progress on Trans-Pacific Trade," Bureau of International Information Programs, U.S. Department of State, April 6, 2010.

[26] Carlyle A. Thayer, "Maritime Strategic Overview of the Asia-Pacific Region," in *Realising Safe and Secure Seas for All: International Maritime Security Conference 2009*, ed. Joshua Ho (Singapore: Select Publishing in association with Republic of Singapore Navy and RSIS, 2009), 26.

[27] China is a dialogue partner of the Mekong River Commission but not a formal member. It is represented on the Greater Mekong Subregion Economic Cooperation Program by Yunnan Province and the Guangxi Zhuang Autonomous Region.

India's growing economic engagement with Southeast Asia, although still dwarfed by China's, is complimentary rather than competitive with U.S. interests and has created a new market for Southeast Asian goods and investment. Furthermore, with projections indicating that India will have the world's third-largest economy by 2025, the country's economic presence in Southeast Asia can be expected to increase vis-à-vis China.[28]

Political-Security Impact

China has attempted to offset U.S. political and security influence in Southeast Asia by promoting exclusive arrangements with East Asia, such as the ASEAN +3 summit process. China has been proactive in pushing the ASEAN +3 to institutionalize defense cooperation and military exchanges among its members, with a particular focus on nontraditional security issues.[29] These efforts to promote East Asian exclusivism resulted in disagreement among Southeast Asian states. Malaysia favored retaining the ASEAN +3 as the main vehicle for regional economic integration, whereas Singapore and Indonesia favored developing more inclusive multilateral arrangements such as the EAS. The latter countries successfully promoted India as a founding member in 2005 and added the United States and Russia as members five years later.

China also employs both multilateral and bilateral mechanisms to enmesh ASEAN states in a web of security cooperation. By depreciating arrangements that focus on conventional or traditional security issues in favor of nontraditional security issues, China plays into ASEAN's predilection to give priority to transnational security threats. In 2002, for example, China and ASEAN issued a Joint Declaration on Cooperation in the Field of Non-Traditional Security Issues, and in 2009 ASEAN upgraded its Ministerial Meeting on Transnational Crime to include China as a full participant. Likewise, China has used its membership in the ARF to promote dialogue, confidence-building measures, and multipolarity, particularly to address nontraditional security issues such as humanitarian assistance and disaster relief, in contrast to unnamed powers that Beijing alleges practice hegemonism, bullying, and gunboat diplomacy.[30] In 2002, ASEAN responded to pressure from the Bush administration to prioritize the global war on terrorism and pressure from Beijing to address

---

[28] Robert O. Blake, Jr., testimony before the House Foreign Affairs Committee, Subcommittee on the Middle East and South Asia, Washington, D.C., April 5, 2011.

[29] David Arase, "Non-Traditional Security in China-ASEAN Cooperation: The Institutionalization of Regional Security Cooperation and the Evolution of East Asian Regionalism," *Asian Survey* 50, no. 4 (July/August 2010): 808–33.

[30] Speech by Chinese president Jiang Zemin in Bangkok, as reported by Xinhua, September 3, 1999.

nontraditional security issues by bracketing both concerns and setting up the ARF Inter-Sessional Meeting on Counter-Terrorism and Transnational Crime. But China's proposal of a regional security treaty for adoption by the ARF was left on the table by ASEAN members who perceived it as an attempt to undermine U.S. engagement in Southeast Asia.[31]

In contrast, India's political and security engagement with Southeast Asian states, particularly Indonesia, Vietnam, Thailand, and Malaysia, has complimented rather than conflicted with U.S. interests and priorities. India supports the "Eyes in the Sky" program of the littoral states along the Malacca Strait, and an increasing number of regional navies have begun to participate in the Milan exercise hosted by India in the Andaman Sea. India also offers valuable capacity-building by hosting Southeast Asian officers in professional military education and training programs.

In sum, Southeast Asian states seek to enmesh all major external powers in ASEAN-centric multilateral institutions such as the ARF, ADMM-Plus, and EAS in order to moderate their rivalry and reduce their impact on regional security. To do this, ASEAN states have pursued three interrelated strategies—soft-balancing, the promotion of ASEAN norms, and economic interdependence with China and India. ASEAN has been largely successful in integrating China into the regional architecture, whereas India's integration is still at the formative stage. However, recent Chinese assertiveness in the South China Sea has led ASEAN to promote additional soft-balancing measures to moderate Beijing's behavior. Key members of the organization have also encouraged both India and the United States to play a greater role in the region to offset Chinese assertiveness.

Southeast Asian States between China and India

This section reviews the interaction of four key Southeast Asian states with China and India, considering the continental states first and then the littoral and maritime states.

Myanmar

Myanmar shares land borders with China and India and has become a cockpit of geostrategic rivalry between them. China opportunistically intervened when Myanmar was slapped with sanctions by the West after repressing the pro-democracy movements in 1988 and 1990. Having provided the State Law and Order Restoration Council (SLORC) with

---

[31] Carlyle A. Thayer, *Southeast Asia: Patterns of Security Cooperation*, ASPI Strategy Report (Canberra: Australian Strategic Policy Institute, 2010), 22.

nearly $2 billion in military assistance, Beijing gained access to signals intelligence from listening posts monitoring naval movements in the Indian Ocean. China is presently the most important source of trade, investment, and development assistance to Myanmar. In particular, the PRC has focused on building energy and transportation infrastructure—roads, rail, and gas pipelines—that link southern China with ports on the Indian Ocean. The China National Petroleum Corporation (CNPC) is exploring for oil in waters off Rakhine State as well as constructing a pipeline to link the port in Kyaukpyu to the town of Muse on the border. In addition, in April 2011, China and Myanmar signed a memorandum of understanding (MOU) to jointly construct a railway parallel to the pipeline.

India initially sided with the international community in condemning Myanmar but soon reversed policy in response to growing Chinese influence in the country.[32] India's look east policy was initially aimed at cultivating Myanmar as a land bridge to the markets of Southeast Asia. Later, however, India sought to overcome endemic insurgency in its northeast states from groups based in Myanmar by eliciting the cooperation of the SLORC and its successor, the State Peace and Development Council (SPDC). India's counterinsurgency strategy also included road-building projects to link its northeast to Myanmar and Thailand.[33]

India is one of Myanmar's largest trade partners, with the balance of trade five to one in Myanmar's favor (see Table A1 in the Appendix), and in June 2010 the two countries reached a trade agreement that slashed import duties on a large number of goods. Trade is concentrated in three main sectors: hydrocarbons, pharmaceuticals, and beans and pulses. India, which is not self-sufficient in energy, has prioritized investing in Myanmar's oil and gas sectors. ONGC Videsh Limited, for example, is exploring blocks off Sittwe in Arakan State.

China's interaction with Myanmar has led to the migration of Chinese businessmen into northern Myanmar, where they dominate cross-border trade. Beijing has an interest in maintaining a peaceful border and supported the status quo when the SPDC negotiated ceasefire agreements with ethnic minority groups and their armed forces. However, China found itself in a dilemma in 2009 when the SPDC moved to incorporate ethnic minority forces into the national army prior to the 2010 elections. When fighting broke out after the government moved against the Kokang ethnic minority, 30,000 people fled into China's Yunnan Province, temporarily straining

---

[32] Renaud Egreteau, "India's Ambitions in Burma," *Asian Survey* 48, no. 6 (November–December 2008): 936–57.

[33] Dominic J. Nardi, "Cross-Border Chaos: A Critique of India's Attempts to Secure Its Northeast Tribal Areas through Cooperation with Myanmar," *SAIS Review* 28, no. 1 (Winter-Spring 2008): 161–71.

relations between the two countries.[34] China responded by mobilizing military forces and closing the border. Visits by Jia Qinglin, chairman of the Chinese People's Political Consultative Conference, to Myanmar immediately after the 2010 elections and by newly elected president Thein Sein to Beijing in May 2011 signaled that relations had returned to normal.

Thailand

Thailand is a treaty ally of the United States and hosts the largest multilateral military exercise in the world, Cobra Gold. Thailand was also the first Southeast Asian state to sign a long-term cooperation framework agreement with China in 1999. This agreement included a defense clause that has led to the gradual development of military cooperation, including naval port visits, military officer exchanges, joint patrols, small-scale joint exercises by special forces, limited arms sales, and an annual strategic dialogue. The election of Thaksin Shinawatra as prime minister in 2001 resulted in the development of close economic and political ties between Bangkok and Beijing. Thaksin was particularly concerned with protecting Thailand's agricultural sector and repeatedly sought special access to the Chinese market.

Thailand has sometimes acted equivocally as a U.S. ally. For example, the Thaksin government did not immediately support the global war on terrorism. Although later, after a change in Thai policy, the United States designated Thailand a major non-NATO ally. Washington suspended military assistance in 2006 when the Thai military seized power. China opportunistically stepped in with its own military assistance package, and in 2010 Thailand (along with Myanmar, Laos, and Cambodia) refrained from joining other ASEAN members and the United States in raising the South China Sea issue at the seventeenth ARF meeting.

Thailand shares a maritime border with India as well as convergent views about maritime security. Both navies conduct joint exercises and coordinate patrols in the approaches to the Strait of Malacca, and India, Thailand, and Myanmar are signatories to the Tripartite Maritime Agreement. In October 2003, India and Thailand signed their first framework agreement for an FTA alongside several MOUs covering cooperation in tourism, biotechnology, agriculture, and intelligence-sharing on counterterrorism. New Delhi has offered to assist Thailand in the development of nuclear energy, along with encouraging Thai investment in India's northwest provinces and promoting the construction of a highway linking the two countries via Myanmar.

---

[34] "China's Myanmar Strategy: Elections, Ethnic Politics and Economics," International Crisis Group, Asia Briefing, no. 112, September 21, 2010, 2–3.

In 2010, Indian investments in Thailand stood at $1.5 billion, while Thai investments in India totaled $800 million. During Prime Minister Abhisit Vejjajiva's state visit to India in April 2011, the two sides agreed to step up negotiations to conclude an agreement on goods, services, and investments, as well as to initiate a ministerial-level defense dialogue and consider cooperating on antipiracy and defense technology.

Vietnam

Until the end of the Cold War, India's close political relations with Vietnam were always overshadowed by Soviet-Vietnamese relations. But the collapse of the Soviet Union reinforced the commonality of strategic interests between Hanoi and New Delhi, particularly vis-à-vis China, and provided India with the opportunity to develop relations with Vietnam as part of its look east policy. Defense cooperation has played a central role in the bilateral relationship due to India's considerable experience with producing and maintaining Soviet-manufactured equipment.[35] The first protocol on defense cooperation was signed in September 1994, and this was later upgraded into a more formal defense cooperation agreement (DCA) in March 2000 during the first visit by an Indian defense minister to Vietnam. Under the terms of the DCA, India agreed to assist Vietnam with upgrading its fleet of MiG-21 aircraft and naval warships (frigates and fast attack craft), help train the Vietnamese military, and enhance cooperation between the two states' national defense industries. In 2005, Vietnam and India initiated an annual strategic dialogue at the senior level.

The year 2007 marked a major turning point in relations between the two countries. In November, Vietnam and India raised their bilateral relationship to a strategic partnership, and in December they stepped up defense cooperation as a result of Defense Minister A.K. Antony's trip to Vietnam. India subsequently provided Vietnam with a massive amount of spare parts to keep its Soviet-era fleet operational, including modernizing the military's anti-submarine warfare capabilities. India has also expanded professional military education and training programs for Vietnamese defense personnel, and Indian Navy ships regularly call at Vietnamese ports. Defense Minister Antony returned to Vietnam in October 2010 to further consolidate defense ties.

As is clear from the level of defense cooperation, India and Vietnam have convergent security interests, not the least of which is to maximize their room for maneuver in dealing with China and other major powers.

---

[35] Pankaj K. Jha, "India-Vietnam Relations: Need for Enhanced Cooperation," *Strategic Analysis* 32, no. 6 (November 2008): 1085–99.

India's relations with Vietnam, as with other Southeast Asian states, provide a basis for a larger Indian role in East Asia. Vietnam's relations with India enhance Hanoi's drive to avoid dependency on any one external power. Both share mutual benefits in the defense relationship. India's sale of arms, equipment, and spare parts enhances Vietnam's ability to modernize its armed forces while avoiding complete dependency on Russia.

By contrast, Vietnam's framework for its hugely asymmetric relationship with China is one of "cooperation and struggle" (*doi tac va doi tuong*).[36] In this context, cooperation refers to the enhancement of bilateral relations for mutual benefit, whereas struggle refers to Vietnamese resistance when Chinese power and influence impinges on national interests. Although Vietnam and China normalized relations in 1991 after more than a decade of estrangement, it was not until 1999 and 2000 that the two ruling Communist parties and states codified their relationship in long-term cooperative framework agreements. These agreements provide for regular high-level visits by party and government officials, including party chiefs, heads of government, and defense ministers. Vietnam and China have also developed a dense network of bilateral relations that is coordinated by a joint steering committee headed by deputy prime ministers (who are also members of their respective ruling politburos). The two sides succeeded in negotiating a treaty on their land border and demarcating the Gulf of Tonkin, where they have set up a joint fishery. Additionally, the two navies regularly conduct joint patrols and search and rescue exercises. Since 2008, People's Liberation Army Navy (PLAN) warships have begun to call at Vietnamese ports, while Vietnam has made two port visits to China.

The major point of friction between Vietnam and China lies in their competing claims in the South China Sea. Since 2008, China has aggressively imposed an annual fishing ban during the height of Vietnam's traditional fishing season. Vietnamese vessels are chased, rammed, impounded (with loss of their catch, valuable navigation aids, and communications equipment), and even sunk. In 2010, elements of China's North, East, and South Sea Fleets conducted joint exercises between Okinawa and the Philippines, in one instance entering the South China Sea to come to the aid of a fisheries administration vessel besieged by Vietnamese fishing craft.

Having failed to moderate such behavior through high-level summitry and diplomacy, Vietnam has initiated a robust program of military modernization, including the acquisition of Gepard-class frigates and Su-30 multirole jets, both equipped with antiship missiles, and has also announced it will procure six conventional Kilo-class submarines from

---

[36] Carlyle A. Thayer, "Vietnam and Rising China: The Structural Dynamics of Mature Asymmetry," in *Southeast Asian Affairs 2010*, ed. Daljit Singh (Singapore: Institute of Southeast Asian Studies, 2010), 406.

Russia. Vietnam has also reached out to other states to help balance tensions in its relationship with China. In 2010, Vietnam successfully leveraged its position as Chair of ASEAN to internationalize the South China Sea issue at the seventeenth ARF meeting and at the inaugural meeting of the ADMM-Plus. The net result has been the revival of multilateral discussions between ASEAN and China in their Joint Working Group to Implement the Declaration on the Conduct of Parties in the South China Sea. Likewise, Vietnam and India reaffirmed their strategic partnership in October 2010 when President Manmohan Singh visited Hanoi. Vietnam has also signaled that it is ready to step up the pace of defense cooperation with the United States and has offered the facilities of Cam Ranh Bay to all navies.

Another irritant in bilateral relations with China is the trade imbalance between the two countries. The trade relationship is heavily skewed in China's favor, with Vietnam's deficit reaching $13 billion in 2010. This contrasts with Vietnam's surplus of nearly $9 billion with the United States. Chinese investment in the country is quite low when compared with that of other external powers. Hanoi has repeatedly raised the issue of its trade imbalance in high-level discussions with China's leaders and sought to offset this imbalance by encouraging increased Chinese investment in Vietnam. However, such investment has become a highly charged domestic political issue due to tensions arising from territorial disputes in the South China Sea.

Indonesia

Indonesia's relations with China and India have been late to develop compared with those of other regional states. For example, although Indonesia and China resumed full diplomatic relations in August 1990 and India inaugurated its look east policy in 1991, it was not until 2005 that Indonesia agreed to establish separate strategic partnerships with China and India.

The development of significant ties between Indonesia and China after 1990 was hostage to three main issues—the treatment of ethnic Chinese in Indonesia, relations with Taiwan, and the South China Sea issue—in addition to Indonesia's initial preference to deal with China through multilateral forums such as ASEAN and the ARF. The Asian financial crisis of 1997–98 and the collapse of Suharto's New Order regime, however, proved a turning point.[37] China responded to the financial crisis by selling rice and medicine to Indonesia, contributing $400 million to IMF

---

[37] Rizal Sukma, "Indonesia-China Relations: The Politics of Re-engagement," *Asian Survey* 49, no. 4 (July–August 2009): 591.

relief packages, and extending $200 million in export credits. Beijing also supported Indonesia in the UN over the East Timor issue.

In October 1999, President Abdurrahman Wahid made his first overseas visit to China and unsuccessfully promoted the idea of a trilateral partnership between China, India, and Indonesia. Wahid's successor, Megawati Sukarnoputri, responded to Chinese concerns by muting relations with Taiwan.[38] During this period, Sino-Indonesian economic relations developed steadily as China began to purchase oil and gas from Indonesia and invest in palm oil, energy, and infrastructure projects. By 2004, China had become Indonesia's fifth-largest trading partner.

China's decision to downplay the ethnic Chinese issue, engage positively with the ARF, and provide prompt assistance after the 2004 tsunami all contributed to changing Indonesian perceptions of China. Beijing was now viewed in Jakarta as a reliable political and security partner, which was reflected in April 2005 when the presidents of Indonesia and China, Susilo Bambang Yudhoyono and Hu Jintao, agreed to a strategic partnership. In July 2005, during the course of President Yudhoyono's visit to Beijing, the two countries signed MOUs covering trade, investment, and defense technology. By this time, two-way trade had topped $17 billion, China had extended Indonesia $800 million in loans, and Chinese investment had risen to $7.4 billion. In 2010, defense industry sources reported that Indonesia purchased C-802 and C-705 antiship missiles from China for mounting on frigates and fast patrol boats.

New Delhi's look east policy led Indonesia to support India's membership in the ARF in the mid-1990s. The Asian financial crisis also proved a catalyst for improved relations, as an economically depressed Indonesia began to view India as a potential economic partner. Presidents Wahid and Sukarnoputri paid visits to New Delhi in 2001 and 2002, respectively. In 2003, Indonesia and India set up a joint commission to oversee bilateral relations, and in 2006 they adopted a plan of action to develop economic ties. By 2006–7, bilateral trade had climbed to $6.2 billion and Indian investment in Indonesia had reached $2.5 billion, with much of this in the oil and gas sectors off the coast of Aceh. Nearly half India's imported coal now comes from Indonesia. By 2009–10, bilateral trade had grown to $11.7 billion. In October 2010, when India and Indonesia reached an FTA in goods, they pledged to raise two-way trade to $25 billion by 2015.

Indonesia and India share a maritime border. Aceh Province is only 162 kilometers from Indira Point in the Bay of Bengal. Due to a convergence in maritime security interests, Indonesia and India entered into a defense

---

[38] Rahul Mishra and Irfa Puspita Sari, "Indonesia-China Relations: Challenges and Opportunities," IDSA, IDSA Issue Brief, November 22, 2010, 1–8.

cooperation agreement in 2001, mainly involving Indian support for the Indonesian navy. In 2004 both countries commenced joint patrols in the approaches to the Strait of Malacca. India's major role in tsunami relief in 2004–5 further raised its profile in Indonesia as a reliable security partner and reinforced Jakarta's decision to support India's membership in the inaugural EAS. The two countries also have convergent interests in countering international terrorism and disrupting the linkages between extremist groups in Indonesia and Pakistan.

In November 2005, relations were raised to the level of a strategic partnership following the exchange of visits between Singh and Yudhoyono.[39] Indonesia and India pledged to promote broad-based development in political, security, economic, commercial, cultural, and science and technology fields based on their shared values and commitment to democracy. The two sides also agreed to an annual senior-level strategic dialogue and signed three MOUs. The first covered marine and fisheries cooperation, the second involved training programs for diplomats, and the third set up a joint study group to negotiate a Comprehensive Economic Cooperation Agreement. Two years later, Indonesia and India set up a joint defense cooperation committee to promote the procurement and co-production of weapons and equipment. Bilateral relations were raised to new heights in January 2011 when Yudhoyono was the chief guest at India's Republic Day ceremonies.

The case studies considered in this section reveal the difficulty of generalizing about Southeast Asia's relations with a rising China and a rising India. Each of the four examples reveals different patterns in relations with China and India from what a broader analysis of China-ASEAN or India-ASEAN relations would suggest.

In general, however, China's economic influence looms large but its impact is uneven and does not invariably translate into direct political influence. All four countries seek to balance China's economic influence through relations with other major powers. Thailand, Indonesia, and Vietnam look to the United States and India as counterweights, while Myanmar has few options but to look to India. China's increased military power is of greater concern to Vietnam and Indonesia than it is to Myanmar and Thailand, due to Chinese assertiveness in the South China Sea. India's economic influence, which has grown from a low base, lags behind China's mainly due to bureaucratic hurdles imposed by India itself. With the exception of the Philippines, Southeast Asia's maritime and littoral states look to the Indian navy as a potential counterweight to China. All

---

[39] Pankaj K. Jha, "India-Indonesia: Emerging Strategic Confluence in the Indian Ocean Region," *Strategic Analysis* 32, no. 3 (May 2008): 439–58.

the region's states value India for the political influence it might wield in multilateral forums on their behalf.

Conclusion

Since its founding in 1967, ASEAN has promoted Southeast Asian regionalism. For each of its ten members, the organization is central to their national strategies for coping and managing relations with major external powers. As an institution, ASEAN has developed three main strategies to manage relations with external powers: economic interdependence, socialization into ASEAN norms, and soft-balancing.

Collectively, the Southeast Asian states promote regional autonomy and ASEAN's centrality in the region's security architecture. The key markers of regional autonomy are, *inter alia*, the TAC, the ASEAN Charter, and the goal of creating an ASEAN community by 2015. The organization's centrality in the regional architecture is evidenced by its chairmanship of the ARF and leading role in the ADMM-Plus and EAS processes. ASEAN's promotion of these objectives provides a measure of protective insulation for its members—individually and collectively—in their external relations with the major powers.

For most of its existence, ASEAN has benefited from the security order shaped by U.S. engagement in Southeast Asia. Until the 1990s, many states viewed China as the main threat to regional security, while India was viewed as marginal to regional affairs. In the mid-1990s, Southeast Asian perceptions of both countries began to improve. China, to a certain extent, has been able to leverage its historical ties under the tributary system and the presence of a large number of overseas Chinese communities to advance its commercial interests. India, which had an immense religious and cultural impact on Southeast Asia in the precolonial period, has not been as successful in leveraging this legacy.

China's rise is transforming the regional order in fundamental ways. The country's sheer economic weight poses challenges to the national resilience of each individual state as trade patterns alter in China's favor. China has not only displaced the United States as the region's main trading partner, but its growing political and military power poses challenges to regional resilience by undercutting 60 years of U.S. primacy. Although each Southeast Asian state has is own unique relations with the major powers, collectively these states are in general agreement that regional autonomy is best preserved through continued U.S. engagement in Southeast Asia, enmeshment of China in ASEAN-centric multilateral institutions, and an enhanced economic, political, and security role for India.

At the same time, the economic rise of China has increased the salience of the maritime domain and the SLOCs from East Asia through the South China Sea to the Indian Ocean and Middle East. The traditional boundaries between Southeast Asia and Northeast Asia are thus being eroded as a new East Asian region takes shape. The emergence of ASEAN +3 is the most visible development of this trend. However, India's economic rise has added another dimension to the changing boundaries of Asian regionalism. New Delhi's engagement with ASEAN and the new security architecture is beginning to erode the traditional boundaries that once separated South Asia from Southeast Asia. Some strategic analysts see the emergence of an Indo-Pacific maritime region (encompassing the Bay of Bengal and the South China Sea) as capturing this new dynamic.

China's assertiveness in the South China Sea has further eroded traditional distinctions between the continental and maritime states of Southeast Asia. Vietnam, as a littoral state, has emerged as a distinct actor with both continental and maritime interests and pursues a policy of "cooperation and struggle" with China. Indonesia, as a maritime power, pursues a dual-track policy of developing relations with China while promoting enhanced cooperation with India. The continental states generally pursue economic and security relations with both China and India.

China has interacted with Southeast Asia economically by promoting CAFTA. In the security sphere, Beijing promotes its new security concept as an alternative to the U.S. alliance system. India's rise has been accompanied by a look east policy of economic integration with its nearest neighbors in Southeast Asia and a greater political-security role in regional affairs. The United States has responded to these developments by renewing its commitment to ASEAN-centric multilateralism. ASEAN has in part tried to balance China's rise by including India as a member of the inaugural EAS and also expanding membership to Russia and the United States.

ASEAN's promotion of Southeast Asia's autonomy and the institution's centrality in the regional security architecture is a continuing work in process. ASEAN's collective unity will be severely challenged now that it has engaged the major powers in two new regional bodies, the ADMM-Plus and the EAS. Continued rivalry and friction between China and the United States will be quickly transmitted to Southeast Asia. The dilemma for each ASEAN state will be how to weigh the costs and benefits of collective action against national interests. Territorial and sovereignty conflicts in the South China Sea will be a litmus test in this regard. Will all ten ASEAN states band together in defense of the claims and interests of the littoral and maritime states? If ASEAN states fail to reach a consensus, hedge, or break ranks, the idea of a formal ASEAN community in 2015 could become a paper tiger.

The United States, which already has economic problems at home, will also face a major problem in addressing China's challenge to U.S. naval supremacy in the Western Pacific. This is a matter of maintaining not only the requisite military power but the political support of allies, strategic partners, and friendly states in the region. Although Southeast Asian states want the United States to remain engaged, they will not support policies that appear designed to contain China. Nor do regional states want to be placed in the difficult position of taking sides. Traditional U.S. leadership through the hub-and-spoke model will need to give way to greater reliance on consensus-building through the already existing multilateral institutions that have ASEAN at their core.

Appendix

TABLE A1   India's trade with Southeast Asia, 2009–10 ($m)

Country	Exports	Imports	Total
Brunei	24.44	428.65	453.09
Cambodia	45.54	5.05	50.59
Indonesia	3,063.36	8,656.66	11,720.02
Laos	16.93	20.05	36.98
Malaysia	2,835.41	5,176.78	8,011.78
Myanmar	207.97	1,289.80	1,497.77
Philippines	748.77	313.07	1,061.84
Singapore	7,592.17	6,454.57	14,046.74
Thailand	1,740.16	2,931.52	4,671.68
Vietnam	1,838.95	521.81	2,360.76
Total	18,113.71	25,797.96	43,911.67

SOURCE: Export-Import Data Bank website, Government of India, Department of Commerce, May 11, 2011, http://commerce.nic.in/eidb/default.asp.

TABLE A2   Inter-ASEAN trade and ASEAN's trade with China, India, and the United States, 2009

Trade partner	Value ($m)			Share of total ASEAN trade (%)		
	Exports	Imports	Total trade	Exports	Imports	Total trade
ASEAN countries	199,587.3	176, 620.1	376,207.3	24.6	24.3	24.5
China	81,591.0	96,594.3	178,185.4	10.1	13.3	11.6
India	26,520.3	12,595.5	39,115.8	3.3	1.7	2.5
United States	82,201.8	67,370.3	149,572.1	10.1	9.3	9.7
Total trade with partners	389,900.4	353,180.2	742,080.6	48.1	48.6	48.3
Total trade with all countries	810,489.2	726,354.1	1,536,843.3	100.0	100.0	100.0

SOURCE: ASEAN Trade Statistics database, July 2010.

TABLE A3   ASEAN member states' trade with China, 2004–8 ($m)

Country	2004	2005	2006	2007	2008
Brunei	243	234	174	201	0
Cambodia	12	15	13	11	13
Indonesia	4,605	6,662	8,344	8,897	11,637
Laos	1	4	1	35	15
Malaysia	8,634	9,465	11,391	15,443	18,422
Myanmar	75	119	133	475	499
Philippines	2,653	4,077	4,628	5,750	5,467
Singapore	15,321	19,770	26,472	28,925	29,082
Thailand	7,098	9,083	10,840	14,873	15,931
Vietnam	2,711	2,828	3,015	3,336	4,491
ASEAN exports	*41,352*	*52,258*	*65,010*	*77,945*	*85,558*
Brunei	87	94	120	157	171
Cambodia	337	430	516	653	933
Indonesia	4,101	5,843	6,637	8,616	15,247
Laos	89	185	23	43	131
Malaysia	11,353	14,361	15,543	18,897	18,646
Myanmar	351	286	397	564	671
Philippines	2,659	2,973	3,647	4,001	4,250
Singapore	16,137	20,527	27,185	31,908	31,583
Thailand	8,183	11,116	13,578	16,184	19,936
Vietnam	4,416	5,322	7,306	12,148	15,545
ASEAN imports	*47,714*	*61,136*	*74,951*	*93,173*	*107,114*

SOURCE: ASEAN Trade Statistics database, July 2009.

TABLE A4   ASEAN member states' trade with India, 2004–9 ($m)

Country	2004–5	2005–6	2006–7	2007–8	2008–9
Brunei	5.06	42.94	8.31	10.43	17.64
Cambodia	18.13	24.19	52.07	53.50	46.90
Indonesia	1,332.60	1,380.20	2,032.96	2,164.17	2,559.82
Laos	2.65	5.47	2.39	3.86	9.00
Malaysia	1,984.06	1,181.86	1,305.22	2,575.26	3,419.97
Myanmar	113.19	110.70	140.44	185.82	221.64
Philippines	412.23	494.66	580.98	620.32	734.77
Singapore	4,000.61	5,425.29	6,053.84	7,379.20	8,444.93
Thailand	901.39	1,075.31	1,445.54	1,810.87	1,938.31
Vietnam	555.96	690.68	985.69	1,610.09	1,738.65
ASEAN exports	*8,425.89*	*10,441.30*	*12,607.43*	*16,413.52*	*19,140.63*
Brunei	0.54	0.88	285.38	227.24	397.52
Cambodia	0.24	0.78	1.60	2.90	2.72
Indonesia	2,617.74	3,008.11	4,181.96	4,821.25	6,666.34
Laos	0.05	0.10	0.35	0.11	0.53
Malaysia	2,299.01	2,415.61	5,290.31	6,012.90	7,184.78
Myanmar	405.91	525.96	782.65	808.63	928.97
Philippines	187.39	235.49	166.79	204.54	254.77
Singapore	2,651.40	3,353.77	5,484.32	8,122.63	7,654.86
Thailand	865.88	1,211.58	1,747.75	2,300.93	2,703.82
Vietnam	86.50	131.39	167.38	173.68	408.66
ASEAN imports	*9,114.66*	*10,883.67*	*18,108.49*	*22,674.81*	*26,202.96*

SOURCE: Export-Import Data Bank website, Government of India, Department of Commerce, May 21, 2011, http://commerce.nic.in/eidb/default.asp.

STRATEGIC ASIA 2011–12

INDICATORS

TABLE OF CONTENTS

Strategic Asia
by the Numbers

The following twelve pages contain tables and figures drawn from NBR's Strategic Asia database and its sources. This appendix consists of fourteen tables covering politics, economies, trade and investment, energy and the environment, security challenges, and nuclear arms and nonproliferation. The data sets presented here summarize the critical trends in the region and changes underway in the balance of power in Asia.

The Strategic Asia database contains additional data for all 37 countries in "Strategic Asia" across 70 indicators arranged in ten broad thematic areas: economy, finance, trade and investment, government spending, population, energy and the environment, communications and transportation, armed forces, nuclear arms, and politics. Hosted on the program's website (http://strategicasia.nbr.org), the database is a repository of authoritative data for 1990–2009. New this year, the database's public interface was upgraded and now includes a mapping feature that displays current and historical Asian military developments, including international military assets, exercises, and peacekeeping operations. The Strategic Asia database was developed with .NET, Microsoft's XML-based platform, which allows users to dynamically link to all or part of the Strategic Asia data set and facilitates easy data sharing. The database also includes additional links that allow users to access related online resources seamlessly.

The information for "Strategic Asia by the Numbers" was compiled by NBR Next Generation Fellows Ryan Zielonka and Anton Wishik.

Politics

In 2011, many Asian countries prepared for leadership transitions. North Korea's Kim Jong-il hinted at a forthcoming transfer of power to his son Kim Jong-un. In the wake of the Tohoku earthquake, Japanese prime minister Naoto Kan pledged to resign once sufficient recovery was made. In China, vice president Xi Jinping was widely expected to become president in 2012.

- With a leadership succession approaching, China faced calls for a "Jasmine Revolution" following upheaval in the Middle East. Beijing responded with increased security, censorship, and detentions.

- Thailand's July 2011 elections led to the defeat of the ruling Democrat Party by the Pheu Thai party, with Yingluck Shinawatra, sister of former prime minister Thaksin Shinawatra, slated to become the nation's first female prime minister. Pheu Thai's strong mandate increased the prospect of political stability.

- Taiwan's 2012 elections were predicted to be closer than those in 2008, with mid-2011 polls showing a slight lead for the ruling KMT. With the opposition DPP advocating greater autonomy from China, perceptions of cross-strait relations are likely to be a decisive factor in the elections.

TABLE 1   Political leadership

	Political leaders	Date assumed office	Next election
Australia	Prime Minister Julia Gillard	June 2010	2013
Canada	Prime Minister Stephen Harper	February 2006	2012
China	President Hu Jintao	March 2003	2012*
India	Prime Minister Manmohan Singh	May 2004	2014
Indonesia	President Susilo Bambang Yudhoyono	October 2004	2014
Japan	Prime Minister Naoto Kan	June 2010	2014
Kazakhstan	President Nursultan Nazarbayev	December 1991	2012
Malaysia	Prime Minister Mohamed Najib bin Abdul Razak	April 2009	2013
Pakistan	Prime Minister Syed Yousuf Raza Gilani	March 2008	2012
Philippines	President Benigno Simeon Cojuangco Aquino III	June 2010	2016
Russia	President Dmitry Medvedev	May 2008	2012
South Korea	President Lee Myung-bak	February 2008	2012
Taiwan	President Ma Ying-jeou	May 2008	2012
Thailand	Prime Minister Yingluck Shinawatra	July 2011	2015
United States	President Barack Obama	January 2009	2012

SOURCE: Central Intelligence Agency (CIA), *The World Factbook*, 2011.

NOTE: Table shows the next election year in which the given leader may lose or retain his position. In some countries, elections may be called before these years. Asterisk indicates that although China will not hold a popular vote, a leadership transition is widely expected in 2012.

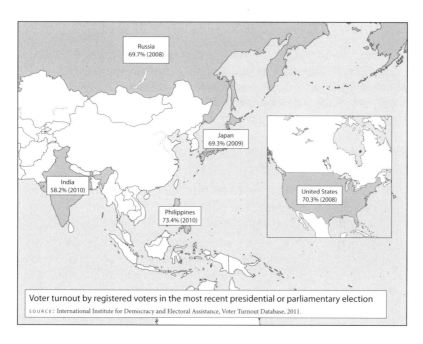

Voter turnout by registered voters in the most recent presidential or parliamentary election

SOURCE: International Institute for Democracy and Electoral Assistance, Voter Turnout Database, 2011.

TABLE 2 Political rights, corruption, and democracy

	Political rights score		Corruption index		Democracy index	
	2000	2010	2000	2010	2006	2010
Australia	1	1	8.3	8.7	9.1	9.2
Canada	1	1	9.2	8.9	9.1	9.1
China	7	7	3.1	3.5	3.0	3.1
India	2	2	2.8	3.3	7.7	7.3
Indonesia	3	2	1.7	2.8	6.4	6.5
Japan	1	1	6.4	7.8	8.2	8.1
Kazakhstan	6	6	3.0	2.9	3.6	3.3
Malaysia	5	4	4.8	4.4	6.0	6.2
Pakistan	6	4	–	2.3	3.9	4.6
Philippines	2	4	2.8	2.4	6.5	6.1
Russia	5	6	2.1	2.1	5.0	4.3
South Korea	2	1	4.0	5.4	7.9	8.1
Taiwan	1	1	5.5	5.8	7.8	7.5
Thailand	2	5	3.2	3.5	5.7	6.6
United States	1	1	7.8	7.1	8.2	8.2

SOURCE: Freedom House, "Freedom in the World," 2001 and 2010; Transparency International, "Corruption Perceptions Index," 2001 and 2010; and Economist Intelligence Unit, "Democracy Index," 2006 and 2010.

NOTE: Political rights score = ability of the people to participate freely in the political process (1 = most free/7 = least free). Corruption = degree to which public official corruption is perceived to exist (1 = most corrupt/10 = most open). The democracy index = level of democratization (0 = least democratic/10 = most democratic). Dash indicates that no data is available.

Economies

Asia's steady post-crisis economic growth continued, despite concerns over inflation, rising oil prices, and the Tohoku earthquake. The IMF projected that Asia's developing economies will grow by 8.4% in 2011, reaffirming the region's leading role in the global economic recovery.

- The IMF downgraded GDP growth forecasts for 2011 to 9.6% for China, 8.2% for India, 5.4% for the ASEAN-5 economies, and 2.5% for the United States.

- China's new five-year plan targeted an annual growth rate of 7.0%, down from 7.5% in the previous five-year plan and below the previous decade's average growth rate of 10.3%.

- Following the Tohoku earthquake, the IMF projected Japan's economy to contract by 0.7% in 2011, a turnaround from the 4% growth in 2010. Japan is the only major economy expected to experience a reduction in GDP in 2011, though it is expected to return to positive growth in 2012.

- Increased demand from Asia contributed to a rise in commodity prices, with global inflation reaching 4% in early 2011.

TABLE 3   Gross domestic product

	GDP ($b constant 2000)				Rank	
	1990	2000	2009	2009 growth (%)	1990	2009
United States	7,055.0	9,764.8	11,364.2	-1.3	1	1
Japan	4,111.3	4,667.4	4,869.9	-5.7	2	2
China*	444.6	1,198.5	2,937.5	12.9	4	3
India	269.4	460.2	885.4	8.3	8	4
Canada	535.6	724.9	846.8	-3.0	3	5
South Korea	283.6	511.7	752.8	0.3	6	6
Australia	280.5	399.6	548.1	5.1	7	7
Taiwan	–	303.2	427.0	-1.9	–	8
Russia	385.9	259.7	397.9	-7.5	5	9
Indonesia	109.2	165.0	258.5	4.6	9	10
Hong Kong	108.4	169.1	234.2	-2.9	10	11
Thailand	79.4	122.7	173.9	-2.2	11	12
Singapore	44.7	92.7	143.5	5.9	14	13
Malaysia	45.5	90.3	137.1	-1.5	13	14
Philippines	55.8	75.9	111.7	0.9	12	15
World	23,996.7	31,876.3	39,758.5	-1.2	N/A	N/A

SOURCE: World Bank, "World Development Indicators," 2011; and data for Taiwan is from the CIA, *The World Factbook*, 2011.

NOTE: These values show GDP converted from domestic currencies using 2000 exchange rates. Figures for Taiwan are calculated using current exchange rates. Dash indicates that no data is available. Asterisk indicates that in 2010 China's economy surpassed Japan's to become the second-largest in the world.

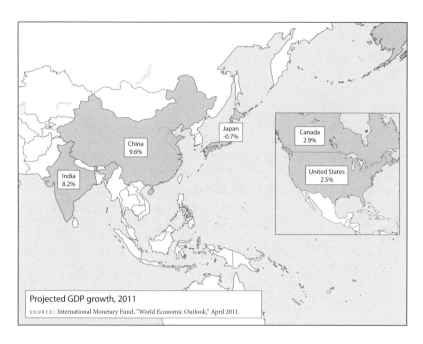

Projected GDP growth, 2011

SOURCE: International Monetary Fund, "World Economic Outlook," April 2011.

TABLE 4 GDP growth and inflation rates

	Average GDP growth (%)			Average inflation rate (%)		
	2000–4	2005–9	2010	2000–4	2005–9	2010
United States	3.0	1.4	2.7	2.5	2.6	1.4
Japan	1.3	0.3	3.0	-0.5	0.1	-0.7
China	8.4	10.7	10.3	0.8	2.7	5.0
India	5.7	8.0	8.3	5.0	7.1	11.7
Canada	3.0	1.4	3.0	2.4	1.5	1.6
South Korea	5.7	3.4	6.1	3.0	3.0	3.0
Australia	3.9	2.6	3.3	2.1	3.0	2.9
Taiwan	3.4	2.8	10.5	0.6	1.5	1.0
Russia	5.7	4.1	3.8	15.9	11.4	6.7
Indonesia	4.1	5.6	6.0	9.1	9.2	5.1
Hong Kong	4.6	4.1	6.8	0.4	1.3	4.5
Thailand	4.7	3.1	7.6	1.8	3.2	3.3
Singapore	3.8	4.3	14.7	1.0	1.6	2.8
Malaysia	5.0	4.0	7.2	1.5	3.0	1.7
Philippines	4.2	4.6	7.3	4.5	5.9	3.8

SOURCE: CIA, *The World Factbook*, 1990–2011.

Trade and Investment

Asian trade continued to perform strongly, with year-on-year imports and exports up 26% and 25%, respectively, in early 2011. FDI inflows rose more than 60% in 2010, while FDI outflows grew by more than 20%. The United States served as the 2011 APEC host country.

- In a move to reduce emphasis on capital investment and exports and to increase domestic consumption, China's leadership determined it would raise wages, de-emphasize manufacturing, and increase social security spending in its new five-year plan. In 2010 the U.S.-China trade gap hit a record $273.1 billion.

- By early 2011, Asia held nearly half the world's total of $10 trillion in reserves, enhancing the influence of Asian central banks. China held $2.8 trillion and Japan $1.0 trillion, while Taiwan, India, South Korea, Hong Kong, and Singapore together held $1.5 trillion.

- Emerging nations sought a larger role within the IMF. China will rank third in terms of voting rights by the end of 2012 and in 2011 filled the newly created fourth deputy managing director position intended for a representative from an emerging economy.

TABLE 5   Trade flow and trade partners

	Trade flow ($b constant 2000)			Trade partners	
	2000	2009	2008–9 growth (%)	Top export partner, 2009	Top import partner, 2009
United States	2,572.1	3,039.1	-10.6	Canada (19%)	China (19%)
China	530.2	2,045.5	36.5	U.S. (20%)	Japan (12%)
Japan	957.6	1,105.2	-19.9	China (19%)	China (22%)
Hong Kong*	475.3	868.2	2.6	China (51%)	China (46%)
South Korea	401.6	766.1	-3.4	China (22%)	China (18%)
Canada	617.4	607.7	-14.9	U.S. (78%)	U.S. (52%)
India	130.5	395.1	-3.5	UAE (12%)	China (11%)
Russia	176.8	367.9	-20.2	Netherlands (12%)	Germany (14%)
Australia	178.0	315.2	17.5	China (22%)	China (15%)
Malaysia	206.7	275.8	-9.8	Singapore (14%)	China (14%)
Thailand	153.3	210.2	-17.0	U.S. (11%)	Japan (19%)
Indonesia	117.9	194.8	-12.0	Japan (20%)	Singapore (17%)
Philippines	82.7	105.6	-8.8	U.S. (18%)	Japan (13%)
Vietnam	35.1	101.9	8.6	U.S. (19%)	U.S. (22%)
New Zealand	36.6	44.2	-11.2	Australia (23%)	Australia (18%)

SOURCE: World Bank, "World Development Indicators," 1990–2011; and CIA, *The World Factbook*, 2011.
NOTE: Asterisk indicates that data for Hong Kong is for 2008 rather than 2009 and 2007–8 rather than 2008–9. No comparable data from the "World Development Indicators" is available for Singapore or Taiwan.

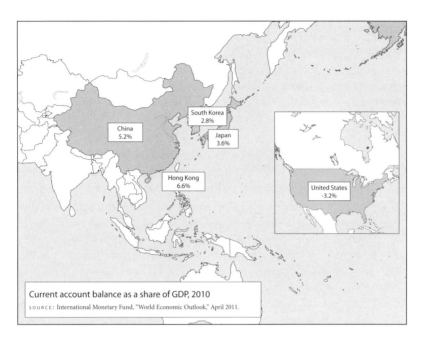

Current account balance as a share of GDP, 2010

SOURCE: International Monetary Fund, "World Economic Outlook," April 2011.

TABLE 6 Flow of foreign direct investment

	FDI inflows ($b)				FDI outflows ($b)	
	1995–2005 annual avg.	2009	2008–9 growth (%)	2009 rank	1995–2005 annual avg.	2009
United States	140.5	129.9	-59	1	132.3	248.1
China	48.8	95.0	-12	2	3.8	48.0
Hong Kong	22.2	48.5	-23	3	25.4	52.3
Russia	5.5	38.7	-45	4	4.9	46.1
India	4.1	34.6	-17	5	1.0	14.9
Australia	9.6	22.6	-52	6	4.0	18.4
Canada	20.7	18.7	-58	7	27.3	38.8
Singapore	13.2	16.8	-26	8	8.1	6.0
Kazakhstan	1.9	12.7	-12	9	0.0	10.1
Thailand	4.8	6.0	-41	10	0.4	3.8
South Korea	5.3	5.8	-24	11	4.0	10.6
Indonesia	1.4	4.9	-38	12	0.9	3.0
Pakistan	0.7	2.4	-56	13	0.0	0.0
Malaysia	4.1	1.4	-83	14	2.0	8.0
New Zealand	1.9	0.4	-80	15	0.0	0.0
World	741.1	1,114.2	-34	N/A	717.9	1,101.0

SOURCE: UN Conference on Trade and Development, *World Investment Report*, 2010.

Energy and the Environment

On March 11, 2011, Japan endured one of the most devastating natural disasters in modern history when a 9.0 magnitude earthquake and a tsunami struck Tohoku, killing over 15,000 people. As oil, gas, and coal prices climbed, energy security and clean energy innovation remained vital for the region's major energy-consuming nations.

- The Fukushima nuclear crisis resulting from the disaster in Japan led many to question the safety of nuclear power. Analysts forecasted a short-term slowdown in nuclear energy development, which may raise the importance of natural gas for meeting global energy demand.

- Energy prices were expected to remain high as demand increases and outputs from existing fields decline. According to the International Energy Agency, 75% of the world's oil-production fields will need to be replaced by other sources to meet global energy demand by 2035.

- In 2010, Asian energy consumption grew by 8.5% and accounted for 38.1% of global primary energy consumption, the largest share of any region. On a per capita basis, however, OECD nations consumed approximately 270% more energy than Asia-Pacific nations in 2010.

TABLE 7   Energy consumption

	Energy consumption (quadrillion Btu)				Rank	
	1990	2000	2010	2009–10 growth (%)	1990	2010
China	27.2	38.4	96.6	11.2	2	1
United States	78.0	91.7	90.7	3.7	1	2
Russia	–	25.2	27.4	5.5	–	3
India	7.7	12.7	20.8	9.2	5	4
Japan	17.2	20.4	19.9	5.9	3	5
Canada	9.8	11.5	12.6	1.3	4	6
South Korea	3.6	7.6	10.1	7.7	6	7
Indonesia	2.1	3.8	5.6	5.9	8	8
Australia	3.5	4.4	4.7	-5.8	7	9
Taiwan	2.0	3.8	4.4	6.0	9	10
Thailand	1.2	2.4	4.3	5.4	10	11
Kazakhstan	–	1.6	2.9	7.9	–	12
Pakistan	1.1	1.6	2.7	1.1	11	13
Malaysia	1.0	1.8	2.5	3.6	12	14
Uzbekistan	–	2.0	2.0	3.9	–	15
World	322.7	369.4	476.5	5.6	N/A	N/A

SOURCE: BP plc, "BP Statistical Review of World Energy," 2011.
NOTE: Dash indicates that no data is available.

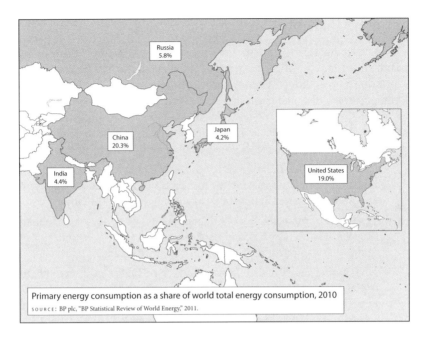

Primary energy consumption as a share of world total energy consumption, 2010

SOURCE: BP plc, "BP Statistical Review of World Energy," 2011.

TABLE 8   Energy consumption by fuel type

	2010 energy consumption by fuel type (%)					
	Oil	Gas	Coal	Nuclear	Hydro	Renewables
China	17.6	4.0	70.5	0.7	6.7	0.5
United States	37.2	27.2	23.0	8.4	2.6	1.7
Russia	21.4	54.0	13.6	5.6	5.5	0.0
India	29.7	10.6	53.0	1.0	4.8	1.0
Japan	40.2	17.0	24.7	13.2	3.9	1.0
Canada	32.3	26.7	7.4	6.4	26.2	1.0
South Korea	41.4	15.1	29.8	13.1	0.3	0.2
Indonesia	42.6	25.9	28.1	0.0	1.9	1.5
Australia	36.0	23.1	36.7	0.0	2.9	1.3
Taiwan	41.8	11.5	36.5	8.5	0.8	0.9
Thailand	46.5	37.6	13.7	0.0	1.1	1.0
Kazakhstan	17.2	31.2	49.6	0.0	2.1	0.0
Pakistan	30.3	52.5	6.8	0.9	9.5	0.0
Malaysia	40.2	51.1	5.4	0.0	3.3	0.0
Uzbekistan	10.0	82.3	2.6	0.0	5.0	0.0

SOURCE: BP plc, "BP Statistical Review of World Energy," 2011.

NOTE: Due to rounding, some totals may not add up to exactly 100%.

Security Challenges

In November 2010, North Korea shelled South Korea's Yeonpyeong Island in an attack widely regarded as related to the North's leadership succession. In addition, China clashed with Vietnam, Japan, and the Philippines over disputed maritime claims, causing the latter three countries to bolster their militaries and seek closer U.S. ties, while China insisted on bilateral, rather than multilateral, talks as the main resolution mechanism. In May 2011, U.S. Special Forces killed Osama bin Laden in Pakistan.

- China's People's Liberation Army test flew its new J-20 stealth fighter, prepared its first aircraft carrier for sea trials, and used its ships and aircraft to evacuate Chinese citizens during the crisis in Libya.

- Operation Tomodachi, the U.S.-Japanese joint response to the Tohoku disaster, was the largest combined forces operation ever undertaken under the auspices of the two nations' security alliance.

- NATO forces halted and in some cases reversed Taliban gains in southern Afghanistan and near Kabul. Washington planned to accelerate U.S. troop withdrawal and set 2014 as the target for the transition of national security responsibilities to the Afghan government.

TABLE 9   Total defense expenditure

	Expenditure ($b)				Rank	
	1990	2000	2009	2008–9 growth (%)	1990	2009
United States	293.0	300.5	661.1	-5.0	1	1
China*	11.3	42.0	166.2	10.8	3	2
Japan	28.7	45.6	51.1	11.1	2	3
Russia	–	7.3	38.3	-34.0	–	4
India	10.1	14.7	38.3	21.6	6	5
South Korea	10.6	12.8	22.4	-7.4	4	6
Canada	10.3	11.5	19.6	-1.0	5	7
Australia	7.3	7.1	19.5	-11.8	8	8
Taiwan	8.7	8.9	9.5	-9.5	7	9
Singapore	1.7	4.8	7.8	2.6	11	10
Indonesia	1.6	1.5	4.8	-5.9	12	11
Malaysia	1.7	2.8	3.9	-11.4	10	12
Pakistan	2.9	3.7	3.8	-13.6	9	13
Vietnam	–	1.0	2.1	-27.6	–	14
Myanmar	0.9	2.1	–	–	13	–
World	954.0	811.4	1,452.3	-6.2	N/A	N/A

SOURCE: International Institute of Strategic Studies, *The Military Balance*, various editions; SASI Group and Mark Newman, "Military Spending 1990," 2007; and data for China is based on various sources.

NOTE: Estimates for China vary widely. Asterisk indicates that the 2009 value for China is a PPP estimate and that the 2008–9 growth rate is based on the *Strategic Asia 2010–11* figure of $150 billion for 2008. Dash indicates that no data is available.

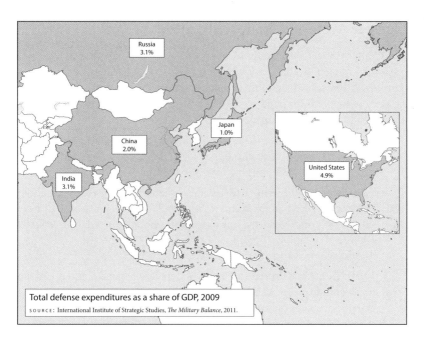

Total defense expenditures as a share of GDP, 2009

SOURCE: International Institute of Strategic Studies, *The Military Balance*, 2011.

TABLE 10 Armed forces

	Armed forces (th)				Rank	
	1990	2000	2011	2010–11 change (th)	1990	2011
China	3,030	2,470	2,285	0	2	1
United States	2,118	1,366	1,564	-16	3	2
India	1,262	1,303	1,325	0	4	3
North Korea	1,111	1,082	1,190	84	5	4
Russia	3,988	1,004	1,046	19	1	5
South Korea	750	683	655	-32	7	6
Pakistan	550	612	617	0	8	7
Vietnam	1,052	484	455	0	6	8
Myanmar	230	344	406	0	13	9
Thailand	283	301	306	0	10	10
Indonesia	283	297	302	0	10	11
Taiwan	370	370	290	0	9	12
Japan	249	237	248	18	12	13
Sri Lanka	65	–	161	0	14	14
Bangladesh	103	137	157	0	15	15
World	26,605	22,237	20,267	-467	N/A	N/A

SOURCE: International Institute of Strategic Studies, *The Military Balance*, various editions.

NOTE: Active duty and military personnel only. Data value for Russia in 1990 includes all territories of the Soviet Union. Dash indicates that no data is available.

Nuclear Arms and Nonproliferation

Controversies over nonproliferation and the Fukushima nuclear crisis heightened debate about nuclear safety and security. The Obama administration continued to make nuclear disarmament a focus of its global security policy and initiated a review of the U.S. nuclear arsenal that could extend tactical weapons cuts beyond U.S. treaty obligations.

- In late 2010, the new U.S.-Russia Strategic Arms Reduction Treaty (START II) limited the number of tactical nuclear warheads each side can deploy to 1,550, roughly one-third of that allowed by START I.

- Following Osama bin Laden's death, concerns re-emerged about Pakistan's military and nuclear weapons. Pakistan is estimated to have significantly increased its stockpile, with enough material for 40–100 additional weapons, putting it on track to become the fifth-largest nuclear weapon state after the United States, Russia, China, and France.

- North Korea is believed to have 8–12 nuclear weapons and appeared to have interpreted the NATO bombing of Libya as confirmation of the importance of a nuclear arsenal. Iran continued to approach the threshold for developing nuclear weapons.

TABLE 11   Nuclear weapons

	Nuclear weapons possession				Total inventory
	1990	1995	2000	2011	2011
Russia	√	√	√	√	~12,600
United States	√	√	√	√	~9,600
China	√	√	√	√	~240
India	√	√	√	√	80–100
Pakistan	–	–	√	√	70–90
North Korea	?	?	?	√	~12

SOURCE: "Nuclear Weapons: Who Has What at a Glance," Arms Control Association, 2011.
NOTE: Table shows confirmed (√) and unknown (?) possession of nuclear weapons. Dash indicates that no data is available. Total inventory includes both active and stockpiled arms.

TABLE 12   Intercontinental ballistic missiles

	Number of ICBMs			
	1990	1995	2000	2011
United States	1,000	580	550	450
Russia	1,398	930	776	376
China	8	17+	20+	66
India	–	–	–	In development
Pakistan	–	–	–	–
North Korea	–	–	–	?

SOURCE: International Institute of Strategic Studies, *The Military Balance*, various editions.
NOTE: Dash indicates that no data is available. Question mark indicates unconfirmed possession.

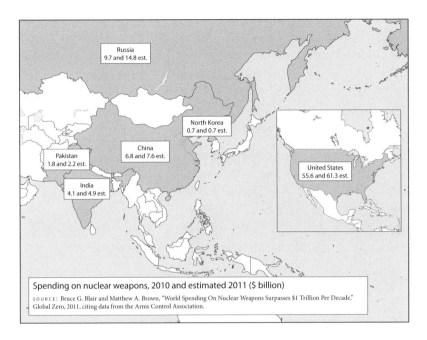

Spending on nuclear weapons, 2010 and estimated 2011 ($ billion)

SOURCE: Bruce G. Blair and Matthew A. Brown, "World Spending On Nuclear Weapons Surpasses $1 Trillion Per Decade," Global Zero, 2011, citing data from the Arms Control Association.

TABLE 13   Nonproliferation treaties

	NPT	Additional Protocol	CTBT	CWC	BTWC
Russia	Ratified	Signatory	Ratified	Ratified	Ratified
United States	Ratified	Signatory	Signatory	Ratified	Ratified
China	Ratified	Ratified	Signatory	Ratified	Ratified
India	–	–	–	Ratified	Ratified
Pakistan	–	–	–	Ratified	Ratified
North Korea	Withdrew	–	–	–	Acceded

SOURCE: Nuclear Threat Initiative; and Monterey Institute for International Studies.
NOTE: NPT = Non-proliferation Treaty. Additional Protocol = IAEA Additional Protocol. CTBT = Comprehensive Test Ban Treaty. CWC = Chemical Weapons Convention. BTWC = Biological and Toxic Weapons Convention. Dash indicates nonparticipation.

TABLE 14   WMD-export control regimes

	Nuclear Suppliers Group	Australia Group	Wassenaar Arrangement	Zangger Committee	MTCR
United States	Member	Member	Member	Member	Member
Russia	Member	–	Member	Member	Member
China	Member	–	–	Member	–
India	–	–	–	–	–
Pakistan	–	–	–	–	–
North Korea	–	–	–	–	–

SOURCE: Nuclear Threat Initiative; and Monterey Institute for International Studies.
NOTE: Dash indicates nonparticipation.

About the Contributors

Richard J. Ellings (PhD, University of Washington) is President and Co-founder of The National Bureau of Asian Research (NBR). Prior to serving with NBR, from 1986 to 1989 he was Assistant Director and on the faculty of the Jackson School of International Studies of the University of Washington, where he received the Distinguished Teaching Award. He served as Legislative Assistant in the U.S. Senate, office of Senator Slade Gorton, in 1984 and 1985. Dr. Ellings is the author of *Embargoes and World Power: Lessons from American Foreign Policy* (1985); co-author of *Private Property and National Security* (1991); co-editor (with Aaron Friedberg) of *Strategic Asia 2003–04: Fragility and Crisis* (2003), *Strategic Asia 2002–03: Asian Aftershocks* (2002), and *Strategic Asia 2001–02: Power and Purpose* (2001); co-editor of *Korea's Future and the Great Powers* (with Nicholas Eberstadt, 2001) and *Southeast Asian Security in the New Millennium* (with Sheldon Simon, 1996); founding editor of the *NBR Analysis* publication series; and co-chairman of the *Asia Policy* editorial board. He also established the Strategic Asia Program and AccessAsia, the national clearinghouse that tracks specialists and their research on Asia.

Michael J. Green (PhD, Johns Hopkins University) is Associate Professor at the Edmund A. Walsh School of Foreign Service at Georgetown University and Japan Chair and Senior Adviser at the Center for Strategic and International Studies (CSIS). He previously served as Special Assistant to the President for National Security Affairs and as Senior Director for Asian Affairs at the National Security Council (NSC) from January 2004 to December 2005 after joining the NSC in April 2001. Dr. Green spent over five years in Japan working as a staff member of the National Diet, as a journalist for Japanese and U.S. newspapers, and as a consultant for U.S. business. He also has been on the faculty of the Johns Hopkins School of Advanced International Studies (SAIS), a Fellow at the Council on Foreign Relations, a staff member at the Institute for Defense Analyses, and a Senior Adviser to the Office of Asia-Pacific Affairs in the Office of the Secretary of Defense. Dr. Green is a member of the Council on Foreign Relations, the International Institute for Strategic Studies, and the Aspen Strategy Group, as well as Vice Chair of the Japan-U.S. Friendship Commission. He serves on the advisory boards of the Center for a New American Security and the Australian American Leadership Dialogue as well as on the editorial board of the *Washington Quarterly*.

M. Taylor Fravel (PhD, Stanford University) is an Associate Professor of Political Science and a member of the Security Studies Program at the Massachusetts Institute for Technology (MIT). He has been a Postdoctoral Fellow at the Olin Institute for Strategic Studies at Harvard University, a Predoctoral Fellow at the Center for International Security and Cooperation at Stanford University, a Fellow with the Princeton-Harvard China and the World Program, and a Visiting Scholar at the American Academy of Arts and Sciences. In 2010, he was named Research Associate with the National Asia Research Program launched by The National Bureau of Asian Research and the Woodrow Wilson International Center. Dr. Fravel studies international relations, with a focus on international security, China, and East Asia. He is author of *Strong Borders, Secure Nation: Cooperation and Conflict in China's Territorial Disputes* (2008) and his research has appeared in journals such as *Foreign Affairs* and *International Security*. He is currently completing a book-length study on major change in China's military doctrine since 1949, entitled *Active Defense: Explaining the Evolution of China's Military*.

Jessica Keough is Publications Director at The National Bureau of Asian Research (NBR). In this role, she is responsible for all editorial and managerial aspects of publications at NBR, and is also Managing Editor of NBR's journal *Asia Policy*. She has been involved with the Strategic Asia Program since joining NBR in 2004, and has served as technical editor for five volumes in the *Strategic Asia* series as well as for many other NBR publications. Prior to joining NBR, Ms. Keough worked in the health care field. Ms. Keough received an MSc in International Relations from the London School of Economics and Political Science in 2003.

Chung Min Lee (PhD, Tufts University) is Dean of the Graduate School of International Studies and the Underwood International College at Yonsei University in Seoul, South Korea, a position he has held since 2008. Professor Lee joined Yonsei University in 1998 after spending a decade at leading think tanks in Korea, the United States, and Japan, including the RAND Corporation, the Sejong Institute, and the National Institute for Defense Studies (Tokyo). Professor Lee is a specialist in East Asian security, crisis management, and intelligence, and is a frequent commentator on inter-Korean and Northeast Asian security. He served as Ambassador for International Security Affairs and as a member of the President's Foreign Policy Advisory Council (2009–10).

Rory Medcalf is Director of the International Security Program at the Lowy Institute for International Policy in Sydney, Australia. He is also Senior Research Fellow in Indian Strategic Affairs at the University of New South Wales and an Honorary Fellow at the Australia-India Institute. He has worked as a diplomat, intelligence analyst, and journalist. From 2003 to 2007, Mr. Medcalf was a Senior Strategic Analyst in the Office of National Assessments, with a focus on Asia. His service in the Australian Department of Foreign Affairs and Trade included a posting to New Delhi, a secondment to the Japanese foreign ministry, truce monitoring in Bougainville, policy development on the ASEAN Regional Forum, and extensive work on nonproliferation. He has contributed to three major arms control reports: the Canberra Commission, Tokyo Forum, and International Commission on Nuclear Non-proliferation and Disarmament. His journalism has been commended by Australia's premier media awards, the Walkleys. He maintains a strong research interest in India and convenes Track 1.5 dialogues between India and Australia.

Harsh V. Pant (PhD, University of Notre Dame) is a Reader in International Relations in the Defence Studies Department at King's College London. He is also an Associate with the college's Centre for Science and Security Studies and an Affiliate with its India Institute. His current research is focused on Asian security issues. Recent books that Dr. Pant has authored or edited include *The U.S.-India Nuclear Pact: Policy, Process, and Great Power Politics* (2011), *China's Rising Global Profile: The Great Power Tradition* (2011), *The China Syndrome: Grappling with an Uneasy Relationship* (2010), *Indian Foreign Policy in a Unipolar World* (2009), and *Contemporary Debates in Indian Foreign and Security Policy: India Negotiates Its Rise in the International System* (2008).

Kenneth B. Pyle (PhD, Johns Hopkins University) is the Henry M. Jackson Professor of History and Asian Studies at the University of Washington and Founding President of The National Bureau of Asian Research. From 1978 to 1988, Professor Pyle was Director of the Henry M. Jackson School of International Studies. He was appointed by President George H.W. Bush to chair the Japan-U.S. Friendship Commission during 1992–95, and he served concurrently as Co-Chairman of the U.S.-Japan Conference on Cultural and Educational Interchange. He is the author and editor of numerous books on modern Japan and its history, including *Japan Rising: The Resurgence of Japanese Power and Purpose* (2007), *From APEC to Xanadu: Creating a Viable Community in the Post–Cold War Pacific* (1997), *The Making of Modern Japan* (1996), *The Japanese Question: Power and Purpose in a New Era* (1992), *The Trade Crisis: How Will Japan Respond?* (1987), and *The New*

Generation in Meiji Japan (1969). He was also founding editor of the *Journal of Japanese Studies* from 1974 to 1986. Professor Pyle has been a member of the Board of Governors of the Henry M. Jackson Foundation since 1983, and was a founding board member of the Maureen and Mike Mansfield Foundation, on which he served from 1981 to 1988. In 1999, the government of Japan decorated Professor Pyle with the Order of the Rising Sun for his contributions to scholarship and cultural exchange. The Japan Foundation gave its 2008 Award for Japanese Studies to Professor Pyle.

Teresita C. Schaffer writes and speaks on economic, political, security, and risk-management trends in South Asia. She is a Nonresident Senior Fellow at the Brookings Institution, and also serves as a Senior Adviser to McLarty Associates, a Washington-based international strategic advisory firm. Prior to this, Ambassador Schaffer spent 30 years as a U.S. diplomat, serving in Pakistan, India, and Bangladesh and as Ambassador to Sri Lanka. She also served as Deputy Assistant Secretary of State for the Near East and South Asia, which at that time was the senior-most position in the State Department for the region. After her career in the Foreign Service, Ambassador Schaffer created the South Asia program at the Center for Strategic and International Studies (CSIS), which she directed for twelve years. She is the author of *India and the U.S. in the 21st Century: Reinventing Partnership* (2009) and co-author with Howard Schaffer of *How Pakistan Negotiates with the United States: Riding the Roller Coaster* (2011). Their website, South Asia Hand, includes widely acclaimed analyses of South Asia.

Travis Tanner is Senior Project Director at The National Bureau of Asian Research (NBR) and Director of NBR's Kenneth B. and Anne H.H. Pyle Center for Northeast Asian Studies. In these roles, Mr. Tanner creates and pursues business opportunities for NBR, determines significant and emerging issues in the field, manages project teams, and is responsible for the success of research projects. Prior to joining NBR, he was Deputy Director and Assistant Director of the Chinese Studies Program at the Nixon Center in Washington, D.C. He also worked as a research assistant at the Peterson Institute for International Economics. Mr. Tanner's interests and expertise include Northeast Asian regional security, China's economy and foreign affairs, and Taiwanese politics. His publications include *Strategic Asia 2010–11: Asia's Rising Power and America's Continued Purpose* (co-edited with Ashley J. Tellis and Andrew Marble, 2010), *Strategic Asia 2009–10: Economic Meltdown and Geopolitical Stability* (co-edited with Ashley J. Tellis and Andrew Marble, 2009), *The People in the PLA: Recruitment, Training, and Education in China's Military* (co-edited with Roy D. Kamphausen and Andrew Scobell, 2008), and

Taiwan's Elections, Direct Flights, and China's Line in the Sand (co-authored with David M. Lampton, 2005). Mr. Tanner holds an MA in International Relations from the Paul H. Nitze School of Advanced International Studies (SAIS) at the Johns Hopkins University.

Ashley J. Tellis (PhD, University of Chicago) is Senior Associate at the Carnegie Endowment for International Peace, specializing in international security, defense, and Asian strategic issues. He is also Research Director of the Strategic Asia Program at The National Bureau of Asian Research and is co-editor of the seven most recent annual volumes in the series, including *Strategic Asia 2010–11: Asia's Rising Power and America's Continued Purpose* (with Andrew Marble and Travis Tanner, 2010). While on assignment to the U.S. Department of State as Senior Adviser to the Undersecretary of State for Political Affairs (2005–8), Dr. Tellis was intimately involved in negotiating the civil nuclear agreement with India. Previously he was commissioned into the Foreign Service and served as Senior Advisor to the Ambassador at the U.S. embassy in New Delhi. He also served on the National Security Council staff as Special Assistant to the President and Senior Director for Strategic Planning and Southwest Asia. Prior to his government service, Dr. Tellis was Senior Policy Analyst at the RAND Corporation and Professor of Policy Analysis at the RAND Graduate School. He is the author of *India's Emerging Nuclear Posture* (2001) and co-author of *Interpreting China's Grand Strategy: Past, Present, and Future* (with Michael D. Swaine, 2000). His academic publications have also appeared in many edited volumes and journals.

Carlyle A. Thayer (PhD, Australian National University) is Emeritus Professor at the University of New South Wales at the Australian Defence Force Academy, Canberra, from where he recently retired after 31 years of service. He spent his entire academic career teaching in a military environment, first at the Royal Military College–Duntroon between 1979 and 1985, and then at the Australian Defence Force Academy from 1985 to 2010. His later career involved attachments to the Asia-Pacific Center for Security Studies in Hawaii (1999–2002), the Centre for Defence and Strategic Studies (2002–4), and the Australian Command and Staff College (2006–7 and 2010). Professor Thayer has been honored by appointments as the inaugural Frances M. and Stephen H. Fuller Distinguished Visiting Professor at Ohio University in 2008 and the C.V. Starr Distinguished Visiting Professor at the School of Advanced International Studies (SAIS) at Johns Hopkins University in 2005. He is the author of over four hundred publications, including *Southeast Asia: Patterns of Security Cooperation* (2010).

Dmitri Trenin (PhD, Institute for the USA and Canada Studies, Russian Academy of Sciences) is Director of the Carnegie Moscow Center and a Senior Associate of the Carnegie Endowment for International Peace, where he chairs the Foreign and Security Policy Program. Prior to joining Carnegie in 1994, he served in the Soviet and Russian army, during which he also taught at the Military Institute. After retirement from the military, he was a Senior Fellow at NATO Defense College in 1993, a Visiting Professor at Vrije Universiteit Brussel during 1993–94, and a Senior Research Fellow at the Institute of Europe in the Russian Academy of Sciences in 1994–97. Dr. Trenin is the author of many publications in English and Russian, including *Post-Imperium: A Eurasian Story* (2011), *Solo Voyage* (2009), and *Getting Russia Right* (2007). He is a member of the Russian International Affairs Council and the International Institute for Strategic Studies in London. He serves on the board of trustees of the Moscow School of Political Studies and the international advisory board of the Finnish Institute for International Affairs, as well as on the editorial boards of the *Washington Quarterly*, *International Politics*, *Pro et Contra*, *Insight Turkey*, and *Baltic Course*.

S. Enders Wimbush is Senior Director, Foreign Policy and Civil Society, at the German Marshall Fund of the United States. Before joining the German Marshall Fund, Mr. Wimbush served as Senior Vice President of the Hudson Institute. Prior to this, he spent ten years in the private sector with Booz Allen Hamilton and Science Applications International Corporation (SAIC) directing analyses of future security environments for government and corporate clients. His work focused on nuclear proliferation, Asia's changing strategic environment, energy competition, and scenario development. From 1987 to 1993, he served as Director of Radio Liberty, and in 2010 Mr. Wimbush was confirmed by the U.S. Senate as one of eight governors of the Broadcasting Board of Governors, the oversight body for all U.S. international broadcasting. He was trained as a Central Asianist at the University of Chicago, where he worked and collaborated with the late Alexandre Bennigsen. He is the author, co-author, or editor of seven books and dozens of policy studies, as well as of numerous articles in professional, policy, and popular publications, including the *Wall Street Journal*, *Christian Science Monitor*, *Los Angeles Times*, *Washington Times*, *Journal of Commerce*, *National Interest*, *Survival*, *Global Affairs*, and *Weekly Standard*.

About Strategic Asia

The **Strategic Asia Program** at The National Bureau of Asian Research (NBR) is a major ongoing research initiative that draws together top Asia studies specialists and international relations experts to assess the changing strategic environment in the Asia-Pacific. The program transcends traditional estimates of military balance by incorporating economic, political, and demographic data and by focusing on the strategies and perceptions that drive policy in the region. The program's integrated set of products and activities includes:

- an annual edited volume written by leading specialists

- an Executive Brief tailored for public- and private-sector decisionmakers and strategic planners

- an online database that tracks key strategic indicators

- briefings and presentations for government, business, and academe that are designed to foster in-depth discussions revolving around major, relevant public-policy issues

Special briefings are held for key committees of Congress and the executive branch, other government agencies, and the intelligence community. The principal audiences for the program's research findings are the U.S. policymaking and research communities, the media, the business community, and academe.

The Strategic Asia Program's online database contains strategic indicators—economic, financial, military, technological, energy, political, and demographic—for all of the countries in the Asia-Pacific region.

To order a book or access the database, please visit the Strategic Asia website at http://www.nbr.org/strategicasia.

Previous Strategic Asia Volumes

Over the past eleven years this series has addressed how Asia is increasingly functioning as a zone of strategic interaction and contending with an uncertain balance of power. The first volume, *Strategic Asia 2001–02: Power and Purpose*, established a baseline assessment for understanding the strategies and interactions of the major states within the region. *Strategic Asia 2002–03: Asian Aftershocks* drew upon this baseline to analyze changes in these states' grand strategies and relationships in the aftermath of the September 11 terrorist attacks. *Strategic Asia 2003–04: Fragility and Crisis* examined the fragile balance of power in Asia, drawing out the key domestic political and economic trends in Asian states supporting or undermining this tenuous equilibrium. Building on established themes, *Strategic Asia 2004–05: Confronting Terrorism in the Pursuit of Power* explored the effect of the U.S.-led war on terrorism on the strategic transformations underway in Asia, and *Strategic Asia 2005–06: Military Modernization in an Era of Uncertainty* appraised the progress of Asian military modernization programs. Turning to focus on other factors that motivate states' choices, *Strategic Asia 2006–07: Trade, Interdependence, and Security* addressed how changing trade relationships affect the balance of power and security in the region, and *Strategic Asia 2007–08: Domestic Political Change and Grand Strategy* examined internal and external drivers of grand strategy on Asian foreign policymaking. Returning to the themes found in the first volume, *Strategic Asia 2008–09: Challenges and Choices* examined the impact of geopolitical developments on Asia's transformation over the previous eight years and assessed the major strategic choices on Asia facing the new U.S. president. *Strategic Asia 2009–10: Economic Meltdown and Geopolitical Stability* analyzed the impact of the global economic crisis on key Asian states and explored the strategic implications for the United States. Marking the tenth anniversary of the series, *Strategic Asia 2010–11: Asia's Rising Power and America's Continued Purpose* provided a continent-wide net assessment of the core trends and issues affecting the region by examining Asia's performance in nine key functional areas.

Research and Management Team

The Strategic Asia research team consists of leading international relations and security specialists from universities and research institutions across the United States and around the world. A new research team is selected each year. The research team for 2011 is led by Ashley J. Tellis (Carnegie Endowment for International Peace). In July, we were deeply saddened by the passing of one of the program's senior advisors and long-time champion, General John Shalikashvili. His contributions to the program were immense and he will be very much missed. Aaron Friedberg (Princeton University, and Strategic Asia's founding research director) and Richard Ellings (The National Bureau of Asian Research, and Strategic Asia's founding program director) continue to serve as senior advisors.

The Strategic Asia Program depends on a diverse base of funding from foundations, government, and corporations, supplemented by income from publication sales. Major support for the program in 2011 comes from the Lynde and Harry Bradley Foundation and the National Nuclear Security Administration at the U.S. Department of Energy.

Attribution

Readers of *Strategic Asia* and visitors to the Strategic Asia website may use data, charts, graphs, and quotes from these sources without requesting permission from NBR on the condition that they cite NBR and the appropriate primary source in any published work. No report, chapter, separate study, extensive text, or any other substantial part of the Strategic Asia Program's products may be reproduced without the written permission of NBR. To request permission, please write to:

NBR Publications
The National Bureau of Asian Research
1414 NE 42nd Street, Suite 300
Seattle, Washington 98105
publications@nbr.org

The National Bureau of Asian Research

The National Bureau of Asian Research is a nonprofit, nonpartisan research institution dedicated to informing and strengthening policy. NBR conducts advanced independent research on strategic, political, economic, globalization, health, and energy issues affecting U.S. relations with Asia. Drawing upon an extensive network of the world's leading specialists and leveraging the latest technology, NBR bridges the academic, business, and policy arenas. The institution disseminates its research through briefings, publications, conferences, Congressional testimony, and email forums, and by collaborating with leading institutions worldwide. NBR also provides exceptional fellowship and internship opportunities to graduate and undergraduate students for the purpose of attracting and training the next generation of Asia specialists. NBR was started in 1989 with a major grant from the Henry M. Jackson Foundation.

Index